Anonymous

Papers of the American School of Classical Studies at Athens

Vol. V

Anonymous

Papers of the American School of Classical Studies at Athens
Vol. V

ISBN/EAN: 9783337180164

Printed in Europe, USA, Canada, Australia, Japan

Cover: Foto ©ninafisch / pixelio.de

More available books at www.hansebooks.com

Archæological Institute of America

PAPERS

OF THE

AMERICAN SCHOOL OF CLASSICAL STUDIES AT ATHENS

VOLUME V

1886–1890

BOSTON
DAMRELL AND UPHAM
AND
LEIPZIG: HARRASSOWITZ
1892

PREFACE.

THE present volume includes the work of the American School of Classical Studies at Athens from 1886 to the summer of 1890. With reports of the work of the School at Sikyon, Ikaria, Stamata, Anthedon, Thisbe, and Plataia, a larger part of this volume is given up to the results of actual excavation than has been the case with any of its predecessors. In surveying these results, the School can fairly claim that some real gains have been made in the domains of Greek topography, architecture, and art.

The thanks of the Managing-Committee are due to Dr. Theodor Mommsen, who has placed his high authority at their service in his article commenting on the fragment of the Edict of Diocletian found by the School at Plataia, which forms one of the papers presented.

In pursuance of an agreement made in March, 1889, by the Managing-Committee with the *American Journal of Archaeology*, the papers collected in this volume have appeared already, from time to time, in the *Journal*. The object of the agreement was to secure earlier publication for the work of the School than would, in general, be possible were it necessary to await the accumulation of sufficient material for a volume of the regular series. As a consequence of this agreement, the system of spelling adopted by the *Journal* for Greek proper names has been allowed to stand in the following pages, though the system in question does not receive the sanction of the Committee on Publications, nor that of some of the writers of the papers.

The Plate numbered XVII would naturally precede in order Plate XV: the two photographs of Plataian walls united in this plate were not received, however, by the editors until too late to alter the numbering.

AUGUSTUS C. MERRIAM,
THOMAS W. LUDLOW,

February, 1892. *Committee on Publications.*

CONTENTS.

	PAGE
1. EXCAVATIONS AT THE THEATRE OF SIKYON	1
General Report of the Excavations, by W. J. McMurtry	1
Results of the Excavations at the Theatre	6
Excavations outside of the Theatre	15
Inscriptions from Sikyon	16
Supplementary Report of the Excavations, by Mortimer Lamson Earle	20
A Sikyonian Statue, by Mortimer Lamson Earle	27
A New Sikyonian Inscription, by Mortimer Lamson Earle	39
2. DISCOVERIES IN THE ATTIC DEME OF IKARIA, 1888, by Carl D. Buck	43
Chronological Report of Excavations	43
Topography of the Ikarian District	47
Architectural Remains	54
Inscriptions from Ikaria	71
The Choregia in Athens and at Ikaria	77
Inscriptions from Ikaria	93
Sculptures	109
Stele of a Warrior	126
3. GREEK SCULPTURED CROWNS AND CROWN-INSCRIPTIONS, by George B. Hussey	135
Crowns	135
Crown-Inscriptions	145
Arrangement of the Crowns	150
Tables	155
4. THE NEWLY DISCOVERED HEAD OF IRIS FROM THE FRIEZE OF THE PARTHENON, by Charles Waldstein	162
5. THE DECREES OF THE DEMOTIONIDAI: A STUDY OF THE ATTIC PHRATRY, by F. B. Tarbell	170
6. REPORT ON EXCAVATIONS NEAR STAMATA IN ATTIKA, by Charles Waldstein and F. B. Tarbell	189
Sculptures	190
Inscriptions	192

	PAGE
7. DISCOVERIES AT ANTHEDON IN 1889	194
REPORT ON EXCAVATIONS AT ANTHEDON, BY JOHN C. ROLFE	194
ARCHITECTURAL DISCOVERIES AT ANTHEDON, BY JOHN C. ROLFE	199
The Foundations by the Sea	199
The Small Temple	202
BRONZE IMPLEMENTS FOUND AT ANTHEDON, BY JOHN C. ROLFE	202
INSCRIPTIONS FROM ANTHEDON, BY C. D. BUCK AND F. B. TARBELL	206
List of Recruits	206
Dedications	208
List of Magistrates	211
Inscriptions in the Epichoric Alphabet	214
Epitaphs and Fragments in the Ionic Alphabet	216
Bilingual Inscriptions	223
8. DISCOVERIES AT THISBE IN 1889	224
REPORT ON EXCAVATIONS, BY JOHN C. ROLFE	224
INSCRIPTIONS FROM THISBE, BY F. B. TARBELL AND J. C. ROLFE	225
9. DISCOVERIES AT PLATAIA IN 1889	233
A NEW FRAGMENT OF THE PREAMBLE TO DIOCLETIAN'S EDICT, "DE PRETIIS RERUM VENALIUM," BY J. C. ROLFE AND F. B. TARBELL	233
REPORT ON EXCAVATIONS AT PLATAIA IN 1889, BY CHARLES WALDSTEIN, F. B. TARBELL, AND J. C. ROLFE	244
INSCRIPTIONS FROM PLATAIA, BY F. B. TARBELL AND J. C. ROLFE	248
10. AN INSCRIBED TOMBSTONE FROM BOIOTIA, BY JOHN C. ROLFE	252
11. DISCOVERIES AT PLATAIA IN 1890	253
GENERAL REPORT ON THE EXCAVATIONS, BY CHARLES WALDSTEIN	253
DETAILED REPORT ON THE EXCAVATIONS, BY HENRY S. WASHINGTON	256
DESCRIPTION OF THE SITE AND WALLS OF PLATAIA, BY HENRY S. WASHINGTON	260
NOTES ON THE BATTLEFIELD OF PLATAIA, BY W. IRVING HUNT	271
12. THE MANTINEIAN RELIEFS, BY CHARLES WALDSTEIN	284
13. A GREEK FRAGMENT OF THE EDICT OF DIOCLETIAN, FROM PLATAIA, BY THEODOR MOMMSEN	302
14. APPENDIX, BY A. C. MERRIAM	313

LIST OF CUTS IN THE TEXT.

	PAGE
1. Facsimile of Sikyonian Inscription.	39

IKARIA.

2. Upper Surface of Roof of Choregic Monument	55
3. Lower Surface of Roof of Choregic Monument	55
4. Choregic Monument Restored	56
5. Diagram of Masonry	62
6. Diagram of Masonry	62
7. Part of the Wall of the Peribolos	63
8. The Threshold of the Pythion	63
9. One of the Double Seats	65
10. Details of Vase-Ornament, and of Cap	66
11. Sculptured Marble Vase	67
12. Griffin-Heads	68
13. Facsimile of Inscription	87
14. Fragment of Tripod-Base	90
15. Tripod-Base found near the Ilissos	91
16. Torso of Archaic Statue	111
17. Archaic Head	111
18. Archaic Hand, with Kantharos	114
19. Feet of Archaic Statue	114
20. Fragment of Relief	116
21. Relief of Herakles and Other Figures	117
22. Torso of Satyr	122
23. Head of Child	122
24. Breast of Seilenos	122
25. Statue of Girl	123
26. Incised Bronze Anathema	123
27. Carved Marble Slab	124
28. Marble Griffin-Head	124
29. Stele of Aristion	127
30. Slab from East Frieze of the Parthenon	166
31. Sketch-Plan of Harbor and Foundations at Anthedon	196
32. Object in Poros found at Anthedon	198

PLATAIA.

	PAGE
33. Facsimiles of Letters from Inscription	234
34. Ground-Plan of Byzantine Church	246
35. Diagram of Tombstone	252
36–40. Plans of Five Byzantine Churches	257
41. Section of Aqueduct	258

LIST OF PLANS AND MAPS.

1. Plan of Excavations of the Theatre at Sikyon	Opposite page	6
2. Plan of the Excavations at Ikaria (I. and II.)	" "	44
3. Map of the Northeastern Part of Attica	" "	48
4. Plan of Excavations at Anthedon	" "	196
5. Plan of Temple at Anthedon	" "	202
6. Map of Plataia and of the Battlefield	" "	256

LIST OF PLATES.

I. Theatre of Sikyon. General View of Excavations in the Spring of 1887.
II. Theatre of Sikyon. Seats and Semicircular Conduit.
III. A Sikyon Statue.
IV. Ikaria. View of Church from the South.
V. Ikaria. View Eastward over Choregic Monument.
VI. Ikaria. View Southeastward over the Pythion toward Pentelikon.
VII. Ikaria. Marble Reliefs.
VIII. Ikaria. Fragment of Marble Relief.
IX. Ikaria. Archaic Warrior Stele.
X. Crown-Inscriptions.
XI. Crown-Inscriptions.
XII. Head of Iris from the East Frieze of the Parthenon.
XIII. Marble Torso from Palaio-Stamata.
XIV. Anthedon. Bronze Implements.
XV. Mantineian Reliefs and Monument, Restored.
XVI. Attic Sepulchral Stelai.
XVII. Walls at Plataia.
XVIII. Facsimile of the Plataian Fragment of the Edict of Diocletian.

EXCAVATIONS AT THE THEATRE OF SIKYON.

GENERAL REPORT OF THE EXCAVATIONS.

[Plates I, II, Plan.]

The excavations at Sikyon by the American School were begun March 23, 1886, during the directorship of Professor M. L. D'Ooge, and were continued, with some interruptions, until May 10. In the succeeding session of the School, under the directorship of Professor A. C. Merriam, the excavations were resumed under the supervision of Mr. M. L. Earle, who will present a final report of the work done.* The choice of the site of Sikyon as a field for archaeological investigation was recommended by the fact that, in spite of the antiquity of the city and its particular importance in the history of art, no systematic excavation had ever been made there. Whether it was due to the charm of the surrounding landscape, or to a happy blending of Ionian and Dorian elements in the population, or again to the circumstances of the political history of the city, or, what is most probable, to the united action of all these causes, few cities in Hellas were more renowned as art centres.

Sikyon first comes into view in the Homeric line, καὶ Σικυῶν', ὅθ' ἄρ' Ἄδρηστος πρῶτ' ἐμβασίλευεν (*Iliad*, II. 572). Hesiod (*Theog.*, 536) makes it the scene of a contest between gods and men. He calls the place Μηκώνη, an appellation which undoubtedly originated from the abundant growth of wild poppies, which still, at the present day, are scattered over the plateau upon which the old city was built. At the Dorian conquest, the Ionian inhabitants seem not to have been expelled or violently oppressed, as in nearly all the regions of the Peloponnesos, and they came to form a fourth tribe beside the three tribes of the Dorians. To this difference of race among the inhabitants, and to the jealousies and variances that would naturally arise from it, may be attributed the long duration in Sikyon of the rule of tyrants. In

---

* The PLAN of the theatre so far as excavated by Mr. McMurtry was made by Mr. S. B. P. Trowbridge. To this the results of Mr. Earle's work have been added by Mr. J. W. Cromwell. The PLATES are from photographs taken by Mr. W. L. Cushing.

fact, tyranny was the usual rather than, as in other Hellenic communities, the exceptional form of government. One family of despots, the Orthagoridai, held sway for a century, a circumstance without parallel among Greek states. The government of this family was very successful. They formed extensive commercial relations, carried on victorious wars, encouraged artistic enterprises, and won chariot-victories for their city in the national games. The period of Kleisthenes especially was one of the most flourishing in the history of Sikyon. Herodotos' story (VI. 126) of the marriage of the daughter of that prince gives a picture of the contemporaneous importance of the city. The Orthagoridai seem not to have belonged to the Dorian portion of the people, and to have done everything in their power to repress the citizens of that race. Kleisthenes went so far as to change the ancient and venerated names of the three Dorian tribes and to force upon them new and odious designations. But Kleisthenes was the last ruler of his line, and it is probable that after his death there came a Dorian reaction. At any rate, we find that Sikyon was a member of the Dorian league during the Persian and Peloponnesian wars. During the struggle between Sparta and Thebes the city suffered severely. It gradually lost its importance, became subject to Ptolemy, and finally fell into the hands of Demetrios Poliorketes, who played a prominent part in its later history. Previous to his time, the main portion of the city stood in the plain at the foot of the large plateau upon which the akropolis was located. Probably for the reason that the population had become so reduced in numbers as to be inadequate for the defense of so large an extent of wall, Demetrios compelled the citizens to abandon the town in the plain, and to build upon the acropolis. Upon the smaller and somewhat more elevated plateau immediately behind the earlier acropolis, he placed his own, fortifying the entire height, already by nature almost impregnable, by means of a wall, considerable portions of which are still standing.

When the Achaian league became powerful, its most efficient leader was Aratos, a Sikyonian, who freed his native city from the oppressive sway of tyrants under Macedonian protection, and induced it to join the league. After the destruction of Corinth by the Romans, Sikyon, delivered from the rivalry of that city, increased in power and secured the administration of the Isthmian games. The period of prosperity, however, was of short duration. Roman cupidity was tempted by the numerous and valuable works of art in the city, and many of the most precious treasures were removed to contribute to the splendor of the imperial metropolis. Afterward, earthquakes destroyed many of the art-treasures which the Romans had left behind. Yet, when Pausanias was at Sikyon in the second century A. D., he found it, though a place of small population, still in possession of notable works of art.

It was in the field of art rather than of politics that Sikyon won her fame. There, for a long period, was one of the chief seats of Greek artistic activity; indeed, one tradition places the invention of painting at Sikyon; and, as Pliny says (*H.N.*, xxx. 11), *Diu illa fuit patria picturae*. One of the great schools of painting has its name from Sikyon, a school founded by Eupompos, and of which Pamphilos and Apelles were pupils.[1] In sculpture, too, the fame of Sikyon was no less great. While tradition assigns to a native of Sikyon the invention of painting, Pliny (*H.N.*, xxxv. 43) tells us that Butades, a Sikyonian, was the first to make images of clay. Dipoinos and Skyllis, the early sculptors, though Kretans by birth, were connected with Sikyon in their work.[2] The first native sculptor of importance was Kanachos: the most famous was Lysippos. The city was also famed throughout Hellas for the taste displayed by the inhabitants in the manufacture of various articles of dress, especially a certain kind of shoe.[3]

No Greek city had a more advantageous site, or more beautiful natural surroundings than Sikyon. The extensive plateau which formed the original acropolis, and was made by Demetrios the site of the new town, is situated about two miles back from the gulf of Corinth. Its level, fertile surface would have been adequate for the support of a large populace in case of a protracted siege. Water was conveyed to it by rock-cut aqueducts, which are still to be seen. In the rear of this plateau, to the southward, a smaller one rises above it, having about one-third the area of the lower, from which it is separated by a rocky slope. This was made by Demetrios the new acropolis. On either side of the entire height a small river flows toward the gulf. The larger of these, that on the east side, is the ancient Asopos: the smaller stream, that toward the west, was probably the ancient Helisson. At the foot of the large plateau, a fertile plain stretches northward in several descending terraces to the brilliant blue waters of the

---

[1] PLIN., *H.N.*, xxxv. 10. [2] PLIN., *H.N.*, xxxvi. 4. [3] STEPH. BYZANT., s. v. Σικυών.

gulf. It is now covered, as undoubtedly it was of old, by vineyards. On the opposite side of the gulf rise the peaks of Parnassos, Helikon, and Kithairon. To the eastward stretches the rich plain, the fertility of which gave rise to the proverbial wish, Εἴη μοι τὰ μεταξὺ Κορίνθου καὶ Σικυῶνος. On this side, the landscape is shut in by the Isthmian mountains and Akrokorinthos. At sunrise and sunset especially, the view is of surpassing loveliness.

Pausanias' description of the city (II. 7) is so indefinite in its topographical allusions that very little can be made of it in an attempt to fix the actual location of the temples and other monuments. The theatre is the only object, in his description, of which the site is now certain. He tells us that upon the stage was the statue of a man with a shield, said to represent Aratos. Beyond the theatre (μετὰ τὸ θέατρον), he says, is a temple of Dionysos. He speaks of about fifteen temples, some of them already at that time in ruin. In the agora, he saw bronze statues of Zeus and Herakles, by Lysippos. He speaks of two gymnasia, in one of which was shown a marble statue of Herakles by Skopas.

On the site of Sikyon, as seen to-day, there are, scattered here and there over the lower and the upper plateau, numerous foundations of buildings, some of them cut out of the living rock. These remains are most numerous in the vicinity of the theatre, which is partly hollowed out from the rocky declivity separating the two plateaus. A short distance northeast from the theatre are considerable remains of a Roman building, consisting of brick walls eight or nine feet high, with numerous small compartments in the interior. This was probably a bath. A short distance to the west of the theatre are the conspicuous remains of the stadion, not mentioned by Pausanias. It was constructed in the usual manner, the northeast extremity of the course being built up with a wall of polygonal stones. On the upper plateau only a few foundations appear. It is hardly probable that there were ever any great number of buildings here: Pausanias mentions only two temples. Underneath this plateau, aqueducts are cut in the rock at a considerable depth; indeed, both natural and artificial underground cavities are very numerous about Sikyon. On the lower plateau at various points the location of the old streets is indicated by long lines of stones, extending from N. E. to S. W., and from S. E. to N. W. Of the numerous foundations upon this plateau some have evidently belonged to large structures. At the present time, the northeastern side is occupied by the Albanian village of Basilikó, the name of which doubtless originated from the extensive ruins near by. Some architectural fragments are to be seen about the village church, within which there is a large Corinthian capital.

The ruins at Sikyon, and particularly the theatre, have been described by various scholars and travellers, of whom the most prominent are Leake,[4] Curtius[5] and Bursian.[6] A very brief account of the theatre, accompanied by a plan, is given by Blouet in the *Expédition scientifique de Morée*. The most peculiar feature of the theatre, the two arches affording an entrance to the κοῖλον on either side, is noticed by all these writers. Both Curtius (*op. cit.*, II. 490) and Bursian (*op. cit.*, p. 28) seem to have thought, as they had no other means of judging than the scanty traces of the stage-foundations that were visible previous to our excavations, that these foundations were cut from the natural rock, while we now know that they were largely constructed of masonry.[7]

The Theatre previous to the Excavations.—The declivity from which the κοῖλον of the theatre is excavated, consists of a soft poros-stone, and this same stone was used in the construction of the masonry. The structure faces toward the northeast, and commands the beautiful view which has been described. The diameter of the κοῖλον is about four hundred feet. These dimensions were not secured entirely by excavation of the side-hill; the sides of the κοῖλον were extended by masonry covered with earth. Before we began our work, at each end of the space that was evidently occupied by the stage-structure, a mass of rock projected above the surface. Between these rock-masses appeared slight traces of the foundation-walls of the stage. The orchestra was covered by a deposit of earth that had been washed down from above; this earth was found to have a depth increasing from one meter

---

[4] *Travels in the Morea*, vol. III, p. 364 ff.   [5] *Peloponnesos*, II. 482 ff.
[6] *Geographie von Griechenland*, II, 23 ff.
[7] The space occupied by the stage-structure, as a whole, was originally formed of an irregular mass of rock, some two meters or so in height toward the orchestra at each side, but cut asunder by a depression through the middle. The rock was cut down to the level of the orchestra for the reception of the ends of the walls of the scene-structure *a–bb*, leaving considerable masses on either side, which were smoothed or left rough as exigencies required. The projections of these rock-masses were seen by Curtius, and others.

in front to three in the rear. The seats were visible here and there in the upper portion of the κοῖλον, those in the lower part being covered with earth. So great a mass of material overlaid the orchestra that it was out of the question, with the means at our command, to undertake to uncover the theatre completely. Our aim was therefore restricted to such excavation as would fully bring to light the plan of stage-structure and orchestra. Moreover, we were not without hopes that some works of art might have been covered up and hence preserved in the theatre.

RESULTS OF THE EXCAVATIONS AT THE THEATRE.

THE STAGE-STRUCTURE.—The PLAN of the excavated portion of the Theatre (see also PLATE I) shows that there are five main foundation-walls belonging to the stage-buildings, marked A, B, C, DD, E. Of these, A and E, the front and rear walls, are of about the same length, projecting on the west side a little more than six meters beyond the others. The rock has been cut away, in both front and rear, in order to admit of this projection.

The Wall A.—The total length of this wall is 23.60 meters. A piece of it at the east end is formed of two upright slabs of stone, 0.70 m. high. The remainder of the wall is composed of small blocks of poros intermingled with bricks and mortar. The average height is about 0.55 m., the thickness, 0.65 m. There are three doorways in this wall. The first is 2.56 m. from the east end, and its width is 1.05 m. Upon either side of this doorway, as well as of the others in this wall, there is a cavity for the door-post. At a distance of 7.32 m. from this doorway there appears to have been a double door. The openings are each 1.05 m. wide, and are separated by a pier formed of two blocks of stone. On the west side of the western doorway the end of the wall is plastered over, and preserves some traces of ornament in color. The third doorway is 2.65 m. distant from the western end of the wall: like the others, it is 1.05 m. wide. The portion of wall beyond this door is higher than the rest, having a height of 0.80 m.

In front of the base of the wall A, a marble step or plinth extends almost the entire length: it begins at the east side of the eastern door, and continues to the western end of the wall. The width of the blocks is 0.57 m., and they project 0.40 m. These blocks were

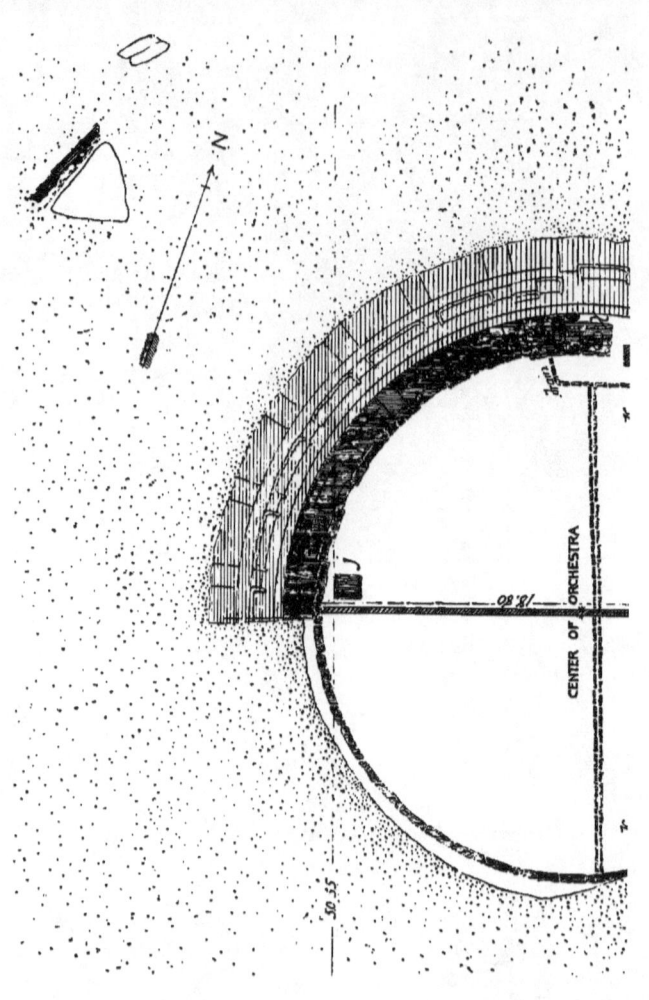

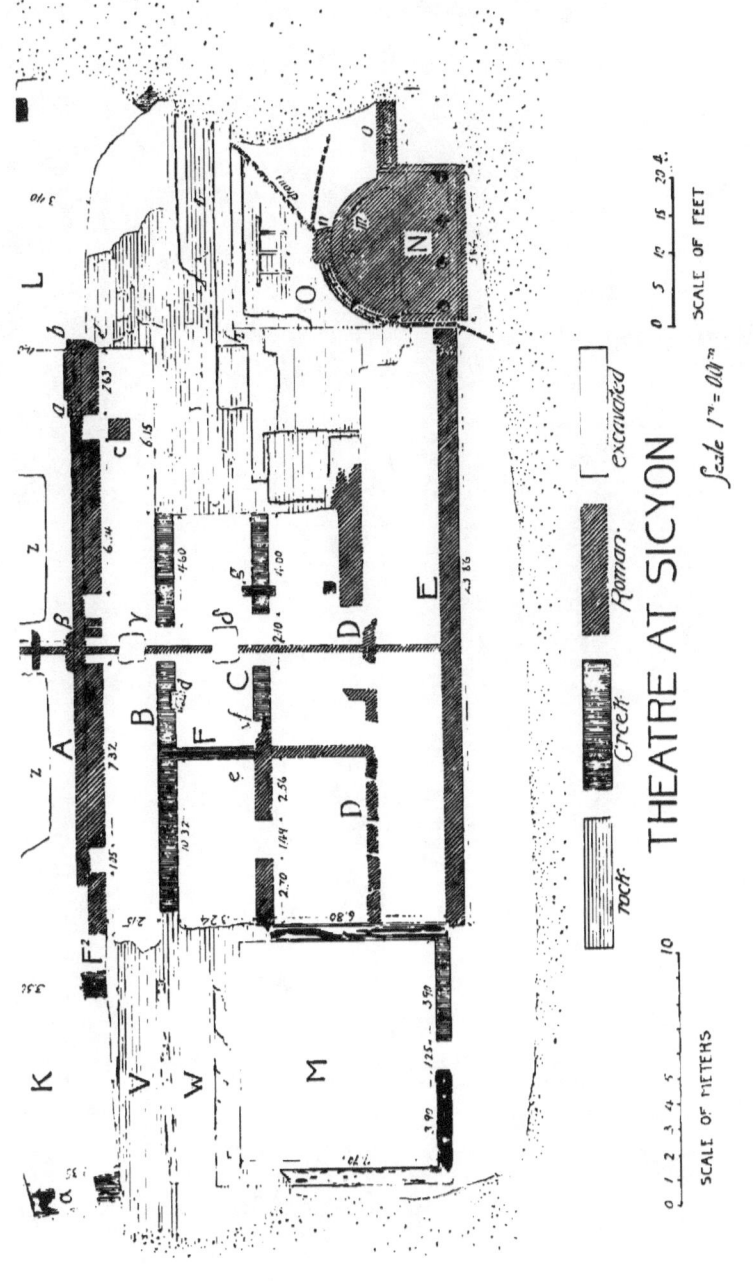

undoubtedly taken from another structure. In proof of this, I observed a shallow circular cavity cut in one of the blocks and extending partly under the wall, evidently having no connection with the present position and use of the block. Moreover, upon another of these blocks, at the west end of the wall, there is an inscription which, in the present position of the block, is inverted. Upon the ends of a number of these marble blocks we found the masons' marks in the form of Greek letters. These are as follows, proceeding from east to west: (1) none; (2) K —; (3) — Λ; (4) Λ — M; (5) Ɵ — ㄱ; (6) ㄱ —; (7) ≤ —; (8) none; (9) Δ — Ǝ; (10) H — Ɵ; (11) Ɵ — I; (12) A — Ɵ; (13) I —. It will be observed that the first and eighth blocks are unmarked, and that some of the others are marked only at one end. The irregular order of the letters seems to indicate that they were not cut with reference to the existing arrangement. A remarkable peculiarity is the archaism in some of the letters, especially the angular *beta*. The *alpha* is of the type of the Macedonian period.

In front of that part of the wall lying to the west of the western door stand two marble bases (marked *a* and *b* in the PLAN). The length of *a* is 0.66 m.; height, 0.37 m.; width, 0.56 m. Both *a* and *b* rest upon a stone foundation. Upon the upper surface of *a* is cut a rectangular cavity, 0.33 m. by 0.26 m., and 0.04 m. deep. The dimensions of *b* are similar to those of *a*, except that it is not quite so long; it also has, upon its upper surface, a cavity similar to that of *a*. These bases probably supported statues, or columns or pilasters, most likely the latter. In the space of 1.85 m. between them, there is a continuation of the marble foundation-step, consisting of two slabs; and beneath these slabs and projecting in front of them there appears a foundation of stone. Upon the face of the second slab (the western one) is an inscription of the Macedonian period, which records the victories gained in various games by a certain Kallistratos, son of Philothales. This inscription, the second one found, is given below: it is inverted, as already observed.

Directly opposite the western door, on the north side of the wall *A*, there is a stone block, marked *c* on the PLAN, 0.75 m. long, 0.85 m. wide, and 0.38 m. thick. It has a circular hole cut through it, lying a little back of the centre, the diameter of this hole at the top being 0.45 m., and decreasing gradually downward. On either side of this hole is cut a deep groove in a slanting direction to the edges of the block. This stone has every appearance of being *in situ*. It may have served as a support for some revolving stage-machine.

Both the material and the method of construction of the wall *A* mark it as of Roman origin. The position of the doors displays a lack of symmetry. We should naturally expect the double doorway to be midway between the other two: we find, however, that on the east side the interval is 7.32 m., while on the west side it is but 6.14 m. The position of the double door was probably determined with reference to the doors in the walls *B* and *C*.

The Wall B.—This wall is at a distance of 2.15 m. from *A*, with which it is parallel. Its total length is 16.07 m., average height, 1.10 m., and thickness, 0.65 m. It has one doorway, 1.15 m. wide, 4.60 m. distant from the west end. The construction of this wall is entirely different from that of *A*, and it is undoubtedly one of the original Hellenic walls. It consists of two courses of large blocks of stone in isodomic masonry, resting upon a low stone foundation: the blocks have a uniform length of 1.30 m. At a distance of about 1.50 m. east of the door, on the north side of the wall, is a buttress-like projection, marked *d* on the PLAN, having in the top a deep rectangular cavity. Immediately opposite this, there remains a small fragment of what may have been a similar projection from the wall *C*.

The Wall C.—This wall is 3.24 m. distant from *B*. Its length is 16.29 m., average height, one meter, thickness, like *B*, 0.65 m. It has two doorways, the first of which is 2.70 m. from the east end, and is 1.49 m. wide. At the west side of this doorway there is an upright block of stone projecting 0.55 m. above the wall. The second doorway is four meters from the west end of the wall, and is 2.10 m. wide. At a distance of about three meters from the west end of the wall there is a projection from it on each side, formed by the transverse position of two blocks, 1.30 m. long, laid one above the other. The wall *C* is of mixed construction, part being of the same nature as *B*, and of Hellenic origin; while the remainder is like *A*, and Roman.

The Cross-wall F.—This wall extends between *B* and *C*, at a distance of 6.95 m. from the east end. Its length is 3.24 m., height the same as that of *B* and *C*, its thickness 0.31 m. The construction is Hellenic, of the same nature as that of *B*. Near its northern end there are singular projections (marked *e* and *f*), one on either side of the wall, each formed of two blocks of stone, the second block on each side having the upper lateral edges cut out squarely. These blocks seem to be in position; yet they have no foundation, resting merely on the earth filling the space between B and C.

The Wall DD.—This wall is about 3.75 m. distant from C, with which it is parallel and of equal length. It is of very irregular and rough construction, composed of a single course of stones, and evidently of Roman date.

The Wall E.—This wall, the fifth and last main foundation-wall of the stage-structure, is of much better construction than DD; although it, too, is undoubtedly Roman. Its length is 23.86 m., and its thickness, 0.70 m. At about seven meters from the west end, we found, standing upright upon the wall, a piece of a column of poros, apparently *in situ*. Its diameter is 0.43 m., and it is fluted only on the northern side. This column suggests that the wall E served as the front foundation of a stoa decorating the side of the theatre facing the city. The wall terminated at the west end in a corner built of brick. Immediately opposite, a short pilaster of brick-work is built out from the rock, leaving sufficient space for a door leading into the structure on the west side, an account of which will be given below.

THEORY AS TO THE CONSTRUCTION OF THE STAGE-STRUCTURE.— The similarity in the dimensions and mode of construction of A and E makes it probable that both were built at the same time, when the stage of the theatre was altered and probably enlarged to conform with the Roman standard. In the Hellenic form of the theatre, the wall C, as I believe, formed the foundation of the rear wall of the stage, or the front wall to a person approaching the theatre from the city. Possibly a portico extended along the north side of C. But this wall did not constitute the entire foundation; the structure continued northwestward, with the natural rock as a foundation, as far as the point marked h on the PLAN. If the κοῖλον and orchestra had practically the same width in both the Hellenic and the Roman form of the theatre, and it is evident that they had, it is impossible to suppose that the stage originally extended only so far as the outcrop of rock. As the walls now stand, the cross-wall F, one of the original walls, seems to be unsymmetrical. But, if there was another compartment extending from the edge of the rock-mass to h, it would correspond in length with the compartment east of F, the middle compartment being somewhat longer than those at each end. Hence, the hypothesis of an extension to *h* gives a natural explanation of the position of *F*. At *i*, in the PLAN, there is an approach to the stage consisting of an ascending passage or ramp cut in the rock, and there must have been a door giving communication from this passage to the western compartment. There may have been a similar arrangement at the eastern end; but we did not dig at that point.[8] The Hellenic stage proper would project in front of the wall *B*. When the Roman stage was built, the Greek one was removed, in any case, so that no traces of it remain. The wall *A* seems to have been the front foundation-wall of the Roman stage. The rooms in the rear would serve for dressing-rooms, *etc*.

THE ORCHESTRA.—The orchestra was buried in earth to such a depth that the removal of the entire mass was too great an undertaking. Our aim was necessarily limited to the laying bare of the boundary, so as to show the form of the orchestra. First, we dug a trench from the middle point of the wall *A* to the opposite point at the rear of the orchestra. The PLAN shows that the orchestra, within the line of seats, comprises somewhat more than half the circumference of a not entirely perfect circle, the diameter of which is about twenty meters. If carried up to the wall *A*, the orchestra would still fall considerably short of the complete circle. The floor of the orchestra, at least as we found it, is of earth (κονίστρα).

The theatre had an elaborate drainage-system. On the west side of the orchestra, where we laid bare not only the boundary of the orchestra, as on the east side, but also a portion of the κοῖλον, we found a carefully constructed drain extending around the orchestra (PLATE II). This drain is about 1.25 m. wide, and about a meter deep. Opposite each stairway of the κοῖλον, a stone slab, with an average width of about 0.75 m., is laid across the drain to serve as a bridge. The average distance between these bridges is about 2.15 m. This drain closely resembles that in the Dionysiac theatre at Athens. Another drain extends from the centre of the orchestra, and passes, at right angles, underneath the wall *A* and the other walls of the stage-structure parallel to *A*. Within the orchestra, this drain is covered over with blocks of stone laid transversely, some of which were found displaced. On each side of *A*, this covering is formed of pieces of columns of poros-stone. A third drain extends from the west side of the orchestra, at a point opposite the termination of the κοῖλον, to the central drain.

[8] See *Supplementary Report of the Excavations*, below.

This now consists of two parallel lines of stones.[9] At its west end, on the south side, a drain of earthen pipe, near the level of the orchestra, connects with it. The stone slabs near by (marked k^2) may have served as steps. A similar slab was found at the middle point in the rear of the orchestra. The earth was removed from one πάροδος, that on the west side. It has a width at the entrance of 4.08 m. The side forming the end of the κοῖλον is composed of a strong retaining-wall of large rectangular blocks, which shares in the upward slope of the κοῖλον. The coping-stones of this wall have something of an ornamental finish. The opposite side of the πάροδος is inclosed by the natural rock.

THE Κοῖλον.—The lower part of the κοῖλον, like the orchestra, had a thick covering of earth. We were able to excavate only a small portion of the western half, including three complete tiers of seats and the front of another. The κοῖλον was found to be divided into fifteen sections (κερκίδες) by fourteen stairways. Accordingly, a line drawn from the middle point of the stage through the centre of the orchestra passes through the middle of the eighth section of seats, and does not coincide, as in some theatres, with one of the stairways. This, at least, is the method of division beneath the διάζωμα. One διάζωμα is easily recognized by portions of a wall composed of upright slabs, about a meter in height, that formed one side of the passageway. At the base of this wall, we uncovered a portion of an open drain that undoubtedly extended along the entire length of the wall. We dug a little, in the hope of discovering whether there was a second διάζωμα above; but the upper portions of the κοῖλον, here, had been so far destroyed that our search was not successful. The general configuration of the surface, as well as the great distance from the διάζωμα found to the summit of the κοῖλον, give ground for the belief that a second διάζωμα did exist at the point where it might naturally be looked for. The entire number of rows of seats seems to have been about forty; the uppermost tiers, though cut out of the natural rock, are very incomplete.

The seats of the first tier that we laid bare are superior in character to the others; they correspond to the marble chairs in the Dionysiac

[9] [As these project above the level of the orchestra, it may be questioned whether they did not rather form the front wall of a still later Roman stage, like the Phaidros wall in the theatre at Athens. The drain of earthern pipe is close to the surface, not at the bottom of the conduit surrounding the orchestra.—A. C. M.]

theatre at Athens, and were plainly intended for the accommodation of priests or other officials. But, unlike the Athenian chairs, they are made of the same poros stone as the ordinary seats. Each seat extends across the front of a κερκίς, the first one at the west end of the κοῖλον being placed a step higher than the others. These seats have backs, and arms at the ends; each seat is cut from two blocks, which are joined at the middle. The average length is about 2.45 m. The seat proper has a width of 0.45 m. and a height of 0.43 m. The side elevation of the back is 0.54 m., rear elevation 0.35 m. Some of the arms show remains of ornamental scroll-work on the outer side. The back and arms of the first seat are destroyed; one block of the second is overturned; the others are in a good state of preservation. The average length of the ordinary seats in the first tier is about 2.70 m., in the second, about 2.90 m. They are divided into two parts by a longitudinal depression. The front part, or seat proper, is 0.35 m. wide; while the back part, upon which the persons sitting behind placed their feet, is 0.20 m. wide. The entire width of the seat is 0.85 m., the height 0.35 m. The front edge has a projection of 0.06 m. The rock-cut seats still remaining in the upper portion of the κοῖλον differ in form from the lower ones. The feet of the row of persons behind were not on the same level as the surface on which the persons in front sat, but rested on an elevation which was 0.35 m. above the seat and the same in width. The seats of this type have a total width of 0.75 m.

THE VAULTED PASSAGES (*P* and *Q*).—The arched passages, one on the east and the other on the west side of the κοῖλον, served as entrances by which the people could pass directly from without, and issue upon the first διάζωμα. The arches or vaults are still in good preservation, and are important as instances of true Greek arches. That the vaults belong to the purely Hellenic portion of the theatre seems clear from their structure. The eastern passage is now about fourteen meters long, but a portion has fallen at the outer entrance. The original length may have been about sixteen meters; the width is 2.55 m. The vault is formed of six courses of poros blocks on either side, exclusive of the keystone course. It is noteworthy that the blocks have the same dimensions and are laid in the same manner as those in the Hellenic stage foundation-wall *B*. The length of the stones is 1.30 m., and their thickness 0.65 m. As in the wall *B*, the joints between the blocks are placed beneath the middle of the blocks above. The similar character of the masonry seems an indication that the vaults and the wall

B were built at the same time. The absence of any mortar or brick in the arches distinguishes them very clearly from the Roman wall *A*. At the interior entrance of the vault, a wall projects, on each side, to a length of 3.40 m. and a height of about one meter. The distance between the two walls of the passage is 3.95 m. The western passage is similar to the eastern.

THE STRUCTURES ON THE EAST AND WEST SIDES OF THE STAGE.— In front of the mass of rock on the east side of the stage are the foundation-walls of a structure (marked *M* in the PLAN) 10.35 m. long and 8.55 m. wide. The walls are 0.65 m. thick, and appear to be of Hellenic construction. In the middle of the front wall there is a doorway 1.25 m. wide. The front of the structure falls nearly in line with the Roman stoa. Immediately beyond the western extremity of the wall *E*, we came upon some foundations (marked *N* in the PLAN), built on the north side of the westerly portion of the rock-mass, measuring in length 5.84 m., and in width, at the widest part, about 5 m. The structure is double, the front being rectangular, the rear part semicircular. Two low steps extend along the entire front of the structure: in the lower step is cut a deep groove along the base of the upper one. Along their front stand, at regular intervals, the lower parts of four columns (PL. I), having a diameter of 0.52 m. The fragments are about a meter in height, and show the same peculiarity instanced in the piece of column found on the wall *E*, only a part of the flutes having been cut. The column on the corner toward the east has fourteen flutes cut; the other three, eleven. The corner one has a larger number of flutes, evidently because of its more exposed position. The floor of the front part of the structure is a coarse mosaic of pebbles. At a distance of 1.58 m. from the columns is a wall separating the two portions of the structure. This wall is 0.50 m. high. At each end, a stone block stands upright in front of it, one of these being one meter, the other 1.30 m. high, and both being 0.50 m. broad and 0.27 m. thick. The wall is pierced in the middle by a circular hole. The height of the rear wall of this semicircular part, on the inner side, is 1.60 m. At its base, on the same side, is a semicircular mass (marked *m* in the PLAN), projecting 0.54 m., 0.85 m. wide at the base, and 0.65 m. high. Both the semicircular wall and the straight front wall are coated with a coarse stucco. Upon removing the earth within, we found numerous fragments of earthen tiles, which must have belonged to the roof; and in front we found also ashes and pieces of burnt lime. It is, thus, possible that the building was destroyed by fire.[10] In the rear of the semicircular wall the rock has been cut away, making a triangular space with a floor of natural rock. On the south and east sides of this space there is a low projection of stone, like a seat. The rear wall of the semicircular structure has an exterior elevation of 0.40 m. At its middle point, a hole is cut through, similar to the one in the front wall. Below this hole there is a trough-like hollow surrounded by a wall, within which is a semicircular projection with a hole in the top and a niche cut in the outer edge. From this cavity a narrow channel, 0.60 m. deep, is cut around the eastern half of the semicircular wall. Measured within this channel, the wall is 0.23 m. thicker than above it. At the bottom of it we found fragments of earthen tile, showing that it served as a water-course or drain. Two other water-courses were found, leading to the southwest corner of the trough or reservoir n. Another earthen water-pipe was found extending along the east side of the front part of N, and passing between it and the extremity of the wall E. On the west side of N we found a structure, O, presenting the appearance of a seat. Its length is 2.52 m., height 0.50 m., width 0.65 m. At the rear is a back with an elevation of 0.56 m. Upon the upper surface are two trough-like depressions, 0.42 m. wide and 0.15 m. deep. It is manifest that the structure N was an ornamental fountain.[11] The numerous drains, the reservoir n at the back, and the perforations in both the rear walls, together make this attribution certain. O may have been a drinking-trough for the use of horses. The entire structure is of Roman date.

OBJECTS FOUND.—We had less good fortune than had been hoped for in finding remains of art. Most of the objects found were uncovered while removing the earth from between the stage-walls, particularly along the front wall A. The remains of sculpture comprise the following fragments, now preserved in the school-house at Basilikó:—
(1) A piece, 0.28 m. long, of the leg of a marble statue, apparently of good style.—(2) The lower part of a female figure in marble, wearing the long χιτών, found resting on the marble plinth in front of wall A, about 5.80 m. from the east end of the wall. Its height, including the base, is 0.25 m. The right foot, of which the toes are visible, rests full upon the base; while the left foot, of which the greater part is exposed,

---

[10] [The original Greek building here probably balanced the rectangular structure on the E. side.—T. W. L.]

[11] [A similar structure has been found by Professor E. Petersen, in connection with the theatre at Side in Pamphylia.—M. L. D'O.]

rests upon the toes.—(3) The arm of a marble statue of above life-size, in two pieces ; the fingers are lost.—(4) A lion's claw of marble, belonging to a lion-skin that served as a robe.

The following architectural members, fragments, and other objects may be mentioned :—(1) Doric epistyle-block of marble, 1.53 m. in length. Upon one face is an incomplete inscription, given below in No. 1.—(2) Ionic epistyle-block of poros, 1.35 m. long.—(3) Piece of an Ionic marble column, 0.83 m. long ; diameter 0.25 m. × 0.27 m.—(4) Two large fragments of an Ionic base, of marble, 0.21 m. thick ; one, 0.90 m., the other, one meter long.—(5) A Doric semi-capital of poros.—(6) Fragment of a peculiar Ionic capital of poros.—(7) Fragment of a triglyph of poros, upon which are traces of blue coloring. Other fragments were found having upon them traces of blue, and some of red.—(8) Large fragment of an earthen water-spout or gargoyle, of a usual lion-head design.—(9) Terracotta fragment having upon it a volute and flower-bud.—(10) Terracotta antefix of graceful design.—(11) Antefix of poros-stone.—(12) Ten earthen lamps of usual form.—(13) A number of copper coins, most of them bearing the dove, the symbol of Sikyon. Upon one the letters ΔH appear, showing it to be a coin of Demetrios.

EXCAVATIONS OUTSIDE OF THE THEATRE.

While the design of our work at Sikyon was limited, in the main, to investigation of the plan of the theatre, we thought it advisable to make excavations about some of the numerous foundations in the vicinity of the theatre, hoping that, by discovery of inscriptions, we might determine the location of some of the buildings mentioned by Pausanias, or that we might happen upon some art-remains. Neither of these hopes was fulfilled. I spent a little time in digging on the smaller plateau, above the theatre, hoping to identify some remains there as belonging to one of the two temples said by Pausanias to have been located upon this height; but we found nothing that threw any light upon the nature of the structure. We also excavated a little at two points in the plain below the theatre. At one of these places we found the floor, paved with slabs of black and white marble, of what must have been a building of elaborate construction. We also found here a small piece of marble upon which are the toes of one foot of a statue, but nothing else of importance. A little to the west of this site there are extensive foundations, where we dug with no further result than the finding of a large Ionic capital of poros.

INSCRIPTIONS FROM SIKYON.

No. 1.

On the Doric epistyle mentioned above.

```
N             ΡΟΥΤΙΜΑΣΑΙΩΣΜΕΝΤΟΝ
Ι             ΚΑΤΑΓΡΑΓΜΑΤΑΤΑΓΕΡΙΑΥΤΟΝ
ΝΙΣ           ΟΝΤΑΕΙΣΑΓΟΚΑΤΑΣΤΑΣΙΝΕΛ
ΒΟΝ           ΘΗΙΟΤΙΜΝΑΣΘΗΣΕΙΤΑΙΚΑΤΑΞΙ
ΝΩ            ΩΣΑΥΤΟΥΤΙΜΑΣΑΙΟ¹²        ΔΑΜΟΣ
ΦΑ            ΓΡΕΣΒΕΙΣ    ΕΡΑΤΟΚΛΗΣ
ΟΝ            ΚΤΗΣΙΓΓΟΣ
ΙΣ
Ν         Ι                                     Κ
ΑΙ
Ν
Σ (?)
ΕΑ
ΕΝ
ΑΥΤΟΝ
ΚΟΤΑΣ
ΛΝΕΑ (?)
ΛΦΟ
```

Νικα]φόρου τιμᾶσαι ὡς μὲν τὸν κατὰ πράγματα τὰ περὶ αὐτὸν ὄντα εἰς ἀποκατάστασιν ἔλθῃ ὅτι μνασθησεῖται καταξίως αὐτοῦ τιμᾶσαι ὁ δᾶμος. Πρέσβεις Ἐρατοκλῆς Κτήσιππος.

This inscription is incomplete; and the letters on the left-hand edge of the face of the block indicate that a part of this column of the inscription was inscribed upon an adjoining block. The letters Ι and Κ are undoubtedly masons' marks made at about the same time and for the same purpose as those on the marble blocks of the plinth of the theatre-wall *A*.[13]

---

[12] Break in surface of stone.

[13] [The letters of the inscription itself belong to the later Macedonian period, probably the first half of the second century B. C. The lines of the letters run largely in curves. Α has the curved bar, Ε the middle bar formed by a dot only, placed at some distance from the perpendicular limb; Μ and Ν are quite wide; Ο, Θ, Ω are smaller than the other letters; Γ has the upper bar extending beyond the right limb which is curved and does not come down to the line; in the Σ, the upper and lower bars are not horizontal, but curve out above and below; Ρ is long, and Β has

No. 2.

On the marble slab between the two marble bases mentioned above.

```
ΚΑΛΛΙΣΤΡΑΤΟΣ ΦΙΛΟΘΑΛΕΟΣ
ΓΑΙΔΑΣΒΑΣΙΛΕΙΑΓΑΛΑΝ          ΙΣΟΜΙΑΑΓΕΝΕΙΟΥΣΚΑΙΑΝΔΡΑΣΓΥΓΜΑΝ
ΛΥΚΑΙΑΓΑΓΚΡΑΤΙΟΝ             ΤΑΙΑΥΤΑΙΙΣΟΜΙΑΔΙ
ΙΣΟΜΙΑΓΑΓΚΡΑΤΙΟΝ             ΝΕΜΕΑΓΑΓΚΡΑΤΙΟΝ
ΓΑΝΑΘΗΝΑΙΑΓΥΓΜΑΝ             ΝΕΜΕΑΓΑΓΚΡΑΤΙΟΝ
ΝΕΜΕΑΓΥΓΜΑΝ                  ΝΕΜΕΑΓΥΓΜΑΝΚΑΙΓΑΓΚΡΑΤΙΟΝ
ΑΣΚΛΑΓΙΕΙΑΓΑΓΚΡΑΤΙΟΝ         ΤΑΙΑΥΤΑΙΝΕΜΕΑΔΙ
ΝΑΑΓΑΛΑΝΚΑΙΓΥΓΜΑΝ            ΙΣΟΜΙΑΓΥΓΜΑΝ
ΚΑΙΓΑΓΚΡΑΤΙΟΝ                ΓΥΘΟΙΓΥΓΜΑΝ
```

the lower loop larger than the upper. In a word, the chief characteristics (notably of M and N) are those to be seen on the Pugioli vases from Alexandria published in *Am. Journ. Arch.* (vol. 1, pp. 21–22), which seemed to belong to the first half of the third century B. C. The flourishes of the pencil or the reed pen found their way into monumental writing, and a good example of a stage still more elaborate than that of the present inscription is the award of the Milesian arbitrators on the basis of the Nike statue of Olympia (DITTENBERGER, *S.I.G.*, No. 240; HICKS, *Hist. Inscr.*, No. 200), of which I have a squeeze. The date of this falls about 140 B. C., and ours would naturally come somewhat earlier (*cf.* Löwy, *Inschrift. gr. Bildhauer*, No. 272).

The inscription is a decree of the people in honor of some person or persons now impossible to determine. The existing fragment resembles a clause in numerous decrees whereby some honor is conferred on the deserving, and its inscription is commanded, in order that it way be generally known that the State rewards services fittingly, and that others may be incited to similar service or benefaction. The following from Priene may be cited by way of example: *ἵνα δὲ αἵ τε τιμαὶ αἱ δεδομέναι Λαρίχῳ ἐπιφανέστεραι ὦσιν, καὶ τῶν ἄλλων οἱ προαιρούμενοι τῇ πόλει παρέχεσθαι τὰς χρείας θεωρῶσιν ὅτι ὁ δῆμος τοῖς καλοῖς καὶ ἀγαθοῖς ἀνδράσιν ἐπίσταται χάριτας ἀποδιδόναι καταξίας, ἀναγράψαι τόδε τὸ ψήφισμα εἰς στήλην λιθίνην καὶ στῆσαι παρὰ τὴν εἰκόνα. Anc. Grk. Inscr. Brit. Mus.*, 416.

It is a noticeable fact that in Athens, where our records are most complete, this formula does not occur till about the middle of the fourth century B. C.; but when the fashion is once set it prevails almost immediately and has a long existence, together with the other flourishes of the Hellenistic period. Its phraseology is quite varied, but nowhere have I found anything so extraordinary as in this Sikyonian inscription. It runs somewhat in this way : " Decreed by the people] to honor so and so, son of Nikaphoros, in order that he who does a service to the State may rest assured that the people will remember to honor him in a manner worthy of itself. Ambassadors, Eratokles, Ktesippos."

Noticeable are, (1) *μέν, solitarium :* (2) *τὸν* . . *ὄντα*, acc. where a nom. is to be expected—we may compare XEN., *Kyrop.*, II. 1. 5; *τοὺς Ἕλληνας οὐδέν πω σαφὲς λέγεται εἰ ἔπονται:* (3) *εἰς ἀποκατάστασιν ἔλθῃ*, in POLYBIOS, IV. 28. 1 (*ἕως ἂν ἐκ τοῦ γεγονότος κινήματος εἰς τὴν ἀποκατάστασιν ἔλθῃ τὰ κατὰ τὴν πόλιν*), means to come to a settled condition.—A. C. M.]

ΡΙΕΙΑΓΑΛΑΝΚΑΙΓΥΓΜΑΝ   ΛΥΚΑΙΑ..Γ. ΑΝΔΙΣ
ΚΑΙΓΑΓΚΡΑΤΙΟΝ   ΛΙΓΥΓΜΑΝΚΑΙΓΑΓΚΡΑΤΙΟΝ
    ᴖᴖΙΝΙΑΣΤΓΙΣ¹¹

          Καλλίστρατος Φιλοθάλεος
Παῖδας Βασίλεια πάλαν,   Ἴσθμια ἀγενείους καὶ ἄνδρας πυγμὰν
Λύκαια παγκράτιον,   Τᾷ αὐτᾷ Ἰσθμιάδι,
Ἴσθμια παγκράτιον,   Νέμεα παγκράτιον,
Παναθήναια πυγμάν,   Νέμεα παγκράτιον,
5 Νέμεα πυγμάν,   15 Νέμεα πυγμὰν καὶ παγκράτιον
Ἀσκλαπίεια παγκράτιον,   Τᾷ αὐτᾷ Νεμεάδι,
Νᾶα πάλαν καὶ πυγμὰν   Ἴσθμια πυγμάν,
καὶ παγκράτιον,   Πυθοῖ πυγμάν,
Ῥίεια πάλαν καὶ πυγμὰν   Λύκαια [πυ]γ[μ]ὰν δίς,
10 καὶ παγκράτιον.   .... κα]ὶ πυγμὰν καὶ παγκράτιον.

[11] [This is to be read (Θοινίας Τεισ)[ικράτου ἐποίησε. Teisikrates is, no doubt, the pupil of Euthykrates the son of Lysippos, who was said by PLINY (*Hist. Nat.*, XXXIV. 8. 19. 67) to have approached closer to the art of Lysippos than did Euthykrates himself. His name has been found as artist in an inscription in Thebes and at Oropos (Löwy, *Inschrift. gr. Bildhauer*, 120, 121). The period of his activity lies between 320 and 284 B. C. (Löwy, 120). His name is always written *Teisikrates*, even on a base found at Albano (Löwy, 478). His son Thoinias appears also on monuments, one from Tanagra, one from Oropos, and a third from Delos (Löwy, 121, 122, 122a). On that from Oropos he is denominated a Sikyonian, as his father is named by Pliny. His career as artist would fall about the middle of the third century, probably for some years both before and after. Xenokrates, a pupil of Euthykrates or of Teisikrates, was engaged at Pergamon on the battle-monuments of Attalos I (B. C. 241–197), and the characters of our inscription resemble very closely those there employed, especially i² in Löwy, p. 116. The bar of A and the horizontal lines of Σ are slightly curved; M has its sides nearly or quite perpendicular; Θ and O are somewhat below the average size; Γ has the upper bar passing beyond the uprights, left and right. On the whole, the letters are quite regular and handsome without affectation. The identification of the artist's name among these broken letters is of interest in many ways. It gives a fixed date for the inscription; and, as an artist would not have signed a memorial bearing an inscription merely, we may conclude, that a statue of the athlete formed part of the monument; furthermore, that a monument of this kind would not have been torn down and used to construct the wall in the theatre, unless some disaster had befallen it. We know of no occasion for this in the history of Sikyon from this time on, unless the statue was carried off by the Romans among the numerous art-treasures which they conveyed to Rome, or the monument was destroyed in the great earthquake which visited the city, probably in the reign of Tiberius. Hence it may be said, again, that the wall *A* was not constructed till many years after Greece was reduced to a Roman province, and perhaps not till after the beginning of our era.—A. C. M.]

Translation.—" Kallistratos, son of Philothales, in the contests of boys was victorious at the Basileia in wrestling; at the Lykaia in the pankration; at the Isthmian games in the pankration; at the Panathenaia in boxing; at the Nemean games in boxing; at the Asklepieia in the pankration; at the Naïa in wrestling, boxing, and the pankration; at the Rhieia in wrestling, boxing, and the pankration. At the Isthmian games he was victorious in boxing over both youths and men, at the same Isthmian festival; at the Nemean games in the pankration; at the Nemean games in the pankration; at the Nemean games in boxing and the pankration, at the same Nemean festival; at the Isthmian games in boxing; at the Pythian games in boxing; at the Lykaia twice in wrestling; .... in boxing and the pankration."

Comment.—Nothing is known of Kallistratos, of whose athletic victories the above inscription is a record. An inscription of similar character is found in *C.I.G.*, I, 1515. The games mentioned in both inscriptions are much the same.

1. Βασίλεια. These games are mentioned in *C.I.G.*, I, 1515. Böckh remarks: *Basilia sunt Lebadeae acta, eadem quae Trophonia; sed etiam in Euboea celebrata Basilia esse monui ad Pindar.* The inscription at Sikyon probably refers to the festival at Lebadeia.

6. Ἀσκλαπίεια probably refers to the games at Epidauros.

7. Νᾶα. These games are mentioned in *C.I.G.*, II, 2908. The following note is given: Νᾶα sunt Νάϊα s. Νᾶα, Jovi Naio acta. *Demosth. Cont. Meid. p. 531, ed. Reiske.* According to Strabo, Zeus was called Νάϊος owing to the moisture about Dodona, *Schol. Il.*, XVI. 233. WELCKER, *Griech. Götterlehre*, I. 203. *Cf. C.I.A.*, II, 1318, 1319.

9. ʽΡίεια were games celebrated at ʽΡίον. *Cf.* PLUT., *Sept. sapp. conv.*, c. 19: ἐτύγχανε δὲ Λοκροῖς ἡ τῶν ʽΡίων καθεστῶσα θυσία καὶ πανήγυρις, ἣν ἄγουσιν ἔτι νῦν περιφανῶς περὶ τὸν τόπον ἐκεῖνον.

12 and 16. Ἰσθμιάδι and Νεμεάδι are nominal adjectives with ἑορτῇ understood. Pindar uses both Ἰσθμιάς (I. 8. 5) and Νεμεάς (N. 3. 4). We find the former in Thoukydides also (VIII. 9).[15]

[15] [Kallistratos has gained a victory among the beardless youths, the class intermediate between boys and men, and among the men at the same festival. The mind naturally reverts first to that disputed passage of PINDAR, *Ol.* IX. 89, relating to Epharmostos at Marathon (συλαθεὶς ἀγενείων, μένεν ἀγῶνα πρεσβυτέρων). BÖCKH, in his note on the passage, says that Epharmostos must have just arrived at manhood, and could not have contended as a youth among the men; for, if he had been a youth in fact, it is not probable that he would have been permitted to enter the contest with the men. But Böckh was wrong. The Scholiast did not have Böckh's objection in mind,

18. Πυθοῖ, not Πύθια, because the Sikyonians celebrated a Πύθια at home.

19. Λύκαια are the games in honor of the Lykaian Zeus.

W. J. McMURTRY.

SUPPLEMENTARY REPORT OF THE EXCAVATIONS.

On December 5, 1887, I went down from Athens to Basilikó to continue the work on the theatre of Sikyon, to which duty I had been detailed by Professor Merriam. The next day, a small beginning was made, trouble being experienced both in securing workmen and from a heavy rain. From December 7, however, the work was pushed vigorously, through the generous assistance of the demarch of Sikyon. Our efforts were directed chiefly toward clearing away the very heavy deposit of earth in the πάροδοι and the orchestra. A trench cut toward the N. E. from the wall E revealed nothing more than a sort of floor of cement, the terracotta pipes of a drain, and a few copper coins of no value.

On December 9, the first object of art was found, about 1 m. S. E. of the middle of kk. This was a marble right hand, somewhat above life-size, grasping what might be the hilt of a sword. It evidently belonged to an excellent piece of sculpture, the veining on the back of the hand in particular being executed with much skill. On the next day, at a point 3.30 metres from the outer angle of the S. E. doorway in the wall A in the direction and at about the original level of the orchestra, a fine marble head was discovered.

From this date till December 23, the digging continued rather monotonously. The deep strata of earth were gradually removed from the orchestra and the πάροδοι, while the clearing out of the large square

and PAUSANIAS tells us distinctly of an Artemidoros of Tralleis who, at the same games in Smyrna, won the victory among the boys, the beardless youths and the men (κρατῆσαι παγκρατιάζοντα ἐπὶ ἡμέρας τῆς αὐτῆς τούς τε ἐξ Ὀλυμπίας ἀνταγωνιστάς, καὶ ἐπὶ τοῖς παισὶν οὓς ἀγενείους καλοῦσι, καὶ τρίτα δὴ ὅτι ἄριστον ἦν τῶν ἀνδρῶν: VI. 14, 3). EUSEBIOS, too, mentions the case of Stratonikos the Alexandrian, who won four crowns at Nemea on the same day among the boys and beardless youths (ὃs Νεμέᾳ τῇ αὐτῇ ἡμέρᾳ παίδων καὶ ἀγενείων τέσσαρας στεφάνους ἔσχεν: Chron. Hist., I. p. 238, Migne); and that of Pythagoras the Samian, who was rejected from the youths and laughed at as too effeminate, but who entered the lists with the men and vanquished all in succession (ἐκκριθεὶς παίδων πυγμήν, καὶ ὡς θῆλυς χλευαζόμενος, προβὰς εἰς τοὺς ἄνδρας, ἅπαντας ἐξῆς ἐνίκησε: Chron. Hist., I. p. 227, Migne).—A. C. M.]

chamber *M*, which had not been completed before, was begun. On the afternoon of December 23, appeared a most welcome supplement to the head found on the 9th, which had meanwhile been removed to Athens by Mr. Kabbadias: this was a fine male torso of white marble, discovered about 0.60 m. below what was apparently the original level of the Greek orchestra, 3.50 m. out from a point 2.27 m. south of the middle of the marble surbase of *A*. The fragment was removed to Kiáto, whence it was subsequently transported to Athens. After it had been deposited in the Central Museum, Mr. Kabbadias, in the presence of Professor Merriam and myself, placed the previously discovered head upon the broken neck; and, although a considerable fragment on the left side of the throat was lost, the remaining portions of the two surfaces, on the back and on the right side of the neck, coincided with perfect exactness, proving that the connection of head and torso as portions of the same statue did not admit of question.

The remainder of our work in the theatre did not result in the discovery of other artistic treasures. A trench run s. E. from the chamber *M* disclosed nothing but a drain, apparently of Roman construction; and our work was brought to an end on December 30. An intended resumption of work in the spring was found impracticable, desirable as it would have been for the solution of some interesting problems in regard to the original structure and arrangement of the theatre.

To this brief chronicle belongs some account of certain minor excavations. On December 14–17, I made several attempts to uncover ancient tombs at various points in the immediate vicinity of Basilikó. The remains of such tombs certainly exist on the slope of the plateau toward the Asopos, south of Basilikó, and at the foot of an odd-looking conical hill[1] s. E. of the last-mentioned point and close to the bank of the river. Tombs are also present on the slope of the plateau above the village of Moúlki, which lies on the edge of the plain, N. of Basilikó and near the Ποτάμι τῆς Λέχοβας ('Ελισσών), as well as on the declivity toward this river, N. of the theatre and N. W. of Basilikó. The most interesting of the tombs on the ancient site are those above and below the fountain called Μικρὴ Βρύσις (probably the ancient

---

[1] The opinion has been, I believe, entertained, that this hill is artificial: an examination of the entire circuit of the old site has convinced me that this is not the case. Other similar hills are observable toward the s. w. near the Asopos, the hard clay soil naturally assuming shapes which appear as if artificial.

Στάζουσα[2]), the northernmost fountain of Basilikó, situated north of the village in the gorge through which passes the ordinary road from Moúlki. Our attempts, however, which could not be pushed so vigorously as to interfere with our main work at the theatre, resulted in nothing beyond confirming the opinion of my workmen: 'Υπάρχουν τάφοι, ἀλλ' εἶναι ὅλοι ἀνοιγμένοι! "There are graves, but all have been opened." I made other attempts on January 4, 1888, at a point north of and below the Μικρὴ Βρύσις, and on the following day on the plain toward Kiáto, where some Christian tombs, containing terra-cotta bowls, etc., of small interest, were the only reward of some hours of work in a bleak and piercing north wind.

Returning now to the theatre, I will endeavor to state, as exactly as possible, what additions were made to our knowledge of its construction and arrangement by the excavations of this second season.

In the orchestra, as already stated, we removed the heavy deposit of earth, down to what seemed to be the original κονίστρα, which, like that in the theatre of Epidauros, consisted simply of stamped earth. The hard, whitish clay soil of Sikyon lent itself readily to this use. This was probably the original condition of the entire orchestra; but at some subsequent period, most likely during the Roman domination, an alteration was made in the space between kk and A. Here the soil, differing from that on the other side of kk in being of a mixed character and not the whitish clay, was removed, in the spaces indicated on the plan as ZZ, to a depth of some 0.60 m. below the apparent original orchestra-level. It was in this space on the east side that the head and torso of the marble statue were found. Between these spaces and the marble surbase before A, was found what seemed to be a pavement of rough mosaic-work. The conjecture may be hazarded, that the so-called drain kk is to be dated with the ancient hollowing out of this part of the orchestra. Between the double line of stones forming kk, were found fragments of poros columns, and an irregularly-shaped block of marble 0.75 m. in length.

---

[2] This fountain is at present concealed by a Turkish wall, but the dropping can be heard through a small square aperture in the wall. Lapse of time may easily have wrought changes in the conspicuousness of this fountain, aside from its artificial concealment. Rangabé, cited by Melinrákes (Γεωγραφία 'Αργολίδος καὶ Κορινθίας, p. 117), seems wrong in identifying Στάζουσα with the Τρανὴ Βρύσις, if that is taken as the name of the southern fountain.

A small rough drain (?), to the west of and nearly parallel with kk, runs at a distance of 2 m. to 2.60 m. from it. It is 0.35 m. wide, formed, like kk, of a double line of stones, and runs across the orchestra from the large square stone (indicated at X on the PLAN) to a similar stone on the other side. Its greatest distance from kk is at the extremities. A marble basis, F^2, was discovered on the second day of our excavations. Its dimensions are: length, 0.82 m.; breadth, 0.75 m.; thickness, 0.21 m. In the upper surface is a hollow, 0.63 m. by 0.135 m., with a depth of 0.07 m. This block, which is apparently *in situ*, probably served as the base for a statue, but whether for the statue discovered by us cannot be determined.

We now come to the πάροδοι (K and L), of which that toward the s. E. (K) is the better preserved. This is at its entrance rock-cut, the native rock outside it being graded down, and the point where the πάροδος proper begins being marked by a sharp downward cut. The sill thus formed, which is indicated on the PLAN, is about 0.25 m. high. Within this there are remains of door-posts, that at the right hand upon entering being almost destroyed, but that on the left, against the ἀνάλημμα,[4] rising to a height of 1.35 m. with a thickness of 0.42 m. The distance from its inner angle at the base to the point at which the ἀνάλημμα meets the orchestra is, as accurately as the measurement could be made, 10.77 m. This door-post (a on the PLAN), above which the artificial portion of the ἀνάλημμα now rises only 0.65 m., seems to have been altered, presumably in Roman times; for its original thickness is increased by the adjunction to it, on the outer side with a mortar-joint, of a piece, which, to judge from the moulding on the face toward the orchestra, might have formed part of a cornice. The ἀνάλημμα is here very handsome, being built of large blocks of the native stone, most carefully set and with beveled joints. This πάροδος, of which the floor, after passing the rock-cut entrance, seems to have been of cement or concrete, slopes downward toward the orchestra, the fall from the sill to the point where the ἀνάλημμα meets the orchestra being about 0.50 m.—the height of one course of stone in the ἀνάλημμα. The width of the πάροδος, taken at a point just within the line of the door-posts, is about 3.35 m., and from the basis F before mentioned to the ἀνάλημμα 3.50 m. Traces of stucco appear on the rock-cut wall

---

[4] Cf. MÜLLER, *Lehrbuch der griechischen Bühnenalterthümer*, p. 64, and Notes 6, 8, ad loc.

on the side opposite the ἀνάλημμα, both in this πάροδος and in that opposite.

At the entrance of the N. W. πάροδος (L) also, we find a door-post about 1.50 m. in height, cut out of the solid rock which here forms the ἀνάλημμα, though the latter is constructed of masonry near the orchestra. From the door-post to the point where the ἀνάλημμα of that side meets the orchestra the distance is, roughly, 10.85 m., or approximately the same as at the S. E. πάροδος. The very ruinous state of this πάροδος prevented the taking of further dimensions, except the breadth near the entrance, 3.40 m. It may be said, however, that it seems doubtful whether the ἀνάλημμα here was ever of so handsome workmanship as in the other parodos, which seems to have been the principal entrance for the townspeople.

Between the S. E. πάροδος and the square chamber (M), there are two rock-cut ramps[5] (V and W) leading up from the rock-cut entranceway outside the πάροδος, one to the scene-structure of the Greek period, the other to the Roman. The wall which separates them was stuccoed on the side toward the πάροδος. The inner ramp (V) is somewhat lower than the other (perhaps as much as 0.20 m.), and, in its present condition at least, appears to have been more carefully finished. It ends at the top of the rock in which it is cut, which here seems much weatherworn. Its width is 1.80 m. at a point about 0.90 m. up from the line of the sill of the πάροδος; and 2.14 m. at a point some 5.50 m. up toward the σκηνή from the same line, at which point the cutting of the ramp, as now existing, ends. The highest part of this ramp is at least 2 m. above the corresponding point of the πάροδος.

The outer ramp (W) was apparently separated from the large S. E. chamber (M) by a wall, whether entirely of the native rock subsequently destroyed, or constructed in part of masonry, cannot now be determined. It is certain that the native rock rises at least a little higher than the ramp at this part, the width of the ridge of demarcation being about 0.88 m. The width of the ramp itself is 1.30 m., and that of the rock-cut wall separating it from the inner ramp, about 0.80 m.

On the other side of the σκηνή the shattered condition of the rock precludes study. The outer ramp (i) is well preserved, being deeply cut in the solid rock. Its width is 1.55 m. at the entrance, and 1.45 m.

---

[5] Perhaps to be designated as ἄνω πάροδοι? Cf. MÜLLER, op. cit., p. 58. The theatre at Epidauros had a ramp on each side.

near the point where it ends above (as indicated on the PLAN). It thus does not coincide exactly in dimensions with *W*. The width of the wall dividing this from the inner ramp is from 0.50 m. to 0.60 m.

In regard to the large S. E. chamber (*M*), which is now fully excavated, a few details may be added to the results obtained by the former investigations. Around the interior walls of this chamber, there is a continuous rock-cutting in the form of a bench or seat, broken only by the doorway of the chamber. The width of this bench is about 0.45 m., and its height from the floor about 0.40 m. It was coated with stucco. At the doorway of the chamber there is a low step ; and in the centre of the chamber we found what appeared to be the base of a pillar or roof-support of poros. A considerable quantity of broken roofing-tiles was found within the chamber. The largest of these measures 0.415 m. by 0.16 m., the length having been originally greater. With these tiles were found a small figurine of a cock, in terracotta, one or two common terracotta lamps, and some other insignificant objects.

In the course of the work on the theatre, some thirty-five copper coins were found, most of them in exceedingly bad preservation. Of these, several are unmistakably Sikyonian. They were found chiefly in the πάροδοι.

A few remarks must be added with respect to the so-called ὑπόνομος, assumed above to be a portion of the central drain of the orchestra extending transversely under the entire Graeco-Roman σκηνή from *A* to *E*.[6] In the course of the work, I had one of the massive coverstones of this cavity removed (at δ in the plan), and found a deep channel, 0.65 m. wide, partly cut in the solid rock and partly built up. It was unobstructed for a considerable distance, so that a man could easily make his way in it about as far as the wall *E*, where it was closed by the solid rock. Its depth was somewhat over a meter. There was a deposit of earth in the bottom which has been but in part removed. The depth of the cutting is certainly over 2 m. Two fragments of poros columns, which lay in front of *A* (at β in the PLAN), were rolled away, and some earth removed from beneath them. Here, as was noted at the time, the ὑπόνομος appeared clogged with earth, and the exact manner of its connection with the orchestra-drain did not appear. At γ (between *A* and *B*), some digging revealed

---

[6] [This has been designated, on the PLAN, as Roman, but it must belong to the same period as the conduit surrounding the orchestra.—A. C. M.]

a block of stone, shaped like a double step, and apparently having some connection with the ὑπόνομος.

The exact extent and depth of this interesting cutting, and its use—whether it served as reservoir, drain, or for some other purpose—have not been definitely determined. Indeed, this must be left, for the present, among several other unexplained problems of the theatre, which we had intended to solve but were, to our regret, prevented from taking up.

MORTIMER LAMSON EARLE.

A SIKYONIAN STATUE.

[PLATE III.]

Of the mutilated marble statue found at Sikyon, as stated in the preceding article,[1] some mention has already been made in archæological publications;[2] but no exhaustive discussion has appeared of the qualities of the work and the interesting questions which it suggests.[3]

The statue[4] represents a nude youth resting upon the left leg and with the back of the left hand upon the hip. A considerable portion of the bent left arm is missing. It was carved from a separate piece of marble, and was attached by metal pins, as is evident from the seven holes, with the trace of an eighth, which appear in the vertically cut surface to which it was secured. About this arm a himation is draped, and it falls, from a point just below the shoulder, in straight folds, with a gradual increase of fullness as it descends. Doubtless it originally reached the base of the statue and served as a support. As such, it is well motived; for the sharpness of the folds shows that the fabric is of comparatively light texture, as can be gathered also from the manner in which it is held, the hand upon the hip supporting easily the bulk of the weight without the appearance, between wrist and arm-pit, of a brooch or clasp to help

---

[1] *Supplementary Report of the Excavations* (pp. 20–21).

[2] *Seventh Annual Report Am. School*, p. 46 (MERRIAM), with a cut from *Scribner's Magazine*, 1888; *Journ. Hell. Studies*, 1888, p. 130 (HARRISON).

[3] The plate which accompanies this article is made from an indifferent photograph by Panagopoulos of Athens, to which, with another similar one from a different point of view and a third photograph of the head, I have been limited in the preparation of this paper. The lack of a cast has necessarily left much to be desired.

[4] The dimensions of the statue in its present condition are as follows: length of face, from roots of hair to end of chin, 0.16 m.; breadth of face, 0.11 m.; measure over face from ear to ear, 0.21 m.; height of forehead, 0.06 m.; length of nose, about 0.055 m.; length of eye, 0.03 m.; of mouth, 0.035 m.; distance of nose from ear, 0.08 m.; tip of lobe of ear below plane of outer angle of eye, 0.03 m.; measure around chin and crown of head, 0.67 m.; around head above curls, 0.56 m.; over breast from arm-pit to arm-pit, 0.34 m.; from throat to navel, 0.33 m.; from navel to pubes, 0.12 m.; between hips, 0.26 m.; around waist, 0.71 m.; from shoulder to shoulder, 0.35 m.; from back of neck to small of back, 0.40 m.; across back from arm-pit to arm-pit, 0.34 m.

hold it, such as we find elsewhere in a somewhat similar conception.[5] Thus, the garment was practically a support, artistically a graceful relief to the nude figure. The statue is still further mutilated by the loss of the right arm from a little below the shoulder, the greater portion of the right leg, and somewhat less of the left, with the contiguous drapery. The *membrum virile*, which was not, as very commonly,[6] carved separately and set in, is broken off; a considerable portion of the left side of the throat is missing, rendering restoration here necessary; and the nose is somewhat mutilated, as well as the curls. The head was broken into three large pieces,[7] which were still in contact. The greatest break comes just above the forehead, on the right side of the head, and may be distinguished in the photograph. The right arm was extended, as is shown by the direction of the remaining portion; the motive of this will be considered later in connection with the identification of the statue. The pupils of the eyes were not plastically indicated, but were painted red, and traces of the yellow coloring of the hair were plainly visible just after the unearthing of the head.

The surface of the marble—the provenience of which I am unable to state—is somewhat corroded; but the fine Greek workmanship remains plainly evident, and the finish was most careful in all parts of the statue except the hair, of which more below.

The following questions naturally suggest themselves with reference to our statue: *first*, whether it represents a god or a man; *second*, if the former, what god is represented; *third*, what motives known to the history of Greek sculpture does the work embody; *fourth*, to what age of Greek sculpture is it to be referred, to what school, and, perchance, to what artist.

As regards the first question, there can scarcely be a doubt that we

---

[5] *Cf.* Hermes in Berlin (*Verzeichniss der ant. Skulpturen*, No. 196); brooch on left shoulder, left hand extended, garment (chlamys) falling around and below left arm; Hermes on Ephesian *columna caelata* (FR.-WOLT., 1242-3, OVERBECK, *Plastik* (3) II, p. 97); sequel to preceding motive, chlamys has slipped from shoulder bringing brooch in bend of left arm (left hand on hip). In connection with this last figure, it may be mentioned that, in attitude, it corresponds very closely with the figure of an athlete in an Attic relief of the fourth cent. B. C. figured in the *Annali*, 1862, *tav. d'agg. M* (text by MICHAELIS, *ib.* pp. 208–16).

[6] *Cf.* Berlin originals, *Verzeichn.*, Nos. 258, 259 (Satyrs of "Periboëtos" type), FR.-WOLT., No. 1578 (Eros of Centocelle), *etc.*

[7] Two small fragments filling fractures in the curls were also found: now probably lost.

have before us the statue of a god. A consideration of the whole form and character of the work precludes the supposition that the artist was elaborating portraiture of any sort. There are no features of actual human personality; on the contrary, the whole is pervaded with the spirit of ideality. Nor can it be considered an idealized athlete or ephebe portrait; for neither is the muscular development such as to warrant this opinion, nor is the pose that of an athlete; one of the most characteristic features—though not adequately rendered in the photograph—is a plump fullness and a heavy sensuous droop about the region of the loins that show a far different character. The body is languid, and far more suggestive of soft, seductive ease than of the *palma nobilis;* in fact, I can find no better expression of the whole spirit and character of the body than the admirable words in which Overbeck[8] describes the Praxitelean satyr-type: *Zu ringen und zu kämpfen oder selbst zu einem eilenden Botengange würde dieser Satyrkörper nicht taugen, für ihn passt nur das freie Umherstreifen, ein Tanz mit den Nymphen oder diese behäbige Ruhe, die wir vor uns sehn und welche ihn von oben bis unten durchdringt und selbst für den Arm auf die Hüfte einen Stützpunkt suchen lässt.* Attention should also here be called to the fullness of the breasts and the distinctly feminine form of the shoulders, to which further reference will be made. It is not, however, to be assumed, from the implied comparison with the Praxitelean satyr, that we have before us a type intermediate between god and man. The expression of the features, though sensuous, is yet lofty and ideal. It is plain, then, that it is the statue of a god; and let us attempt to answer the question, What god is represented?

The opinion that we have here a Dionysos was broached in the first instance by M. Kabbadias; indeed, he made his assumption before it had been demonstrated that head and torso were parts of the same statue. To this he appears to have been led by a certain likeness to the so-called Ariadne head.[9] It seems proper to refer here to this designation, inasmuch as it was made public at the time in the daily Ἐφημερίς of Athens, and was followed in a brief report on the excavations at Sikyon, published in the New York Evening Post in 1888. It is also accepted as probable by Miss Harrison,[10] while Professor Merriam[11] left the question an open one by describing the statue simply as "a naked

---

[8] *Plastik*[(3)], II, p. 42.   [9] See FR.-WÖLT., No. 1490, for data in regard to this head.
[10] *Journ. Hell. Stud., ut supra.*   [11] *Seventh Ann. Report Am. School, ut supra.*

male figure of pronounced feminine type." Allowing this assumption to rest for the present, let us seek to gain firmer ground by a process of elimination. Considerable stress should be laid upon the feminine forms of our statue, particularly the breasts and the shoulders. Such shoulders appear in statues of Apollo, Dionysos, Eros, and (rarely) Hermes.[12] An identification with Hermes is to be excluded, inasmuch as there is not a hint of the swift messenger of the gods, nothing of the lightness and lithe ephebic or mellephebic vigor which characterizes the youthful Hermes type. Eros also must be stricken from the list; for there is in our statue no trace of wings, which are required in an Eros,[13] to say nothing of the greater boyishness of most of the types of Eros.

We have then to decide between Apollo and Dionysos—a task by no means easy. The statues of the youthful Apollo exhibit a boy of graceful and agile form, with an inherent capacity for action, as in the Sauroktonos.[14] On the contrary, we find in our statue an inertia, a fleshiness about the body, not marked enough to be in any wise gross, and yet plainly and skilfully suggested. We have this much, then, to urge in favor of the identification with Dionysos; and we can find still further support for it. The statue was found in the theatre, which was consecrated to Dionysos, who had moreover at Sikyon a temple in

[12] *Cf.* the Florence statue (FR.-WOLT., No. 1534). I am unable at present to give another instance. Even in this figure there is a plump firmness about the shoulders distinctly at variance with our statue.

[13] On this question, see FURTWÄNGLER (ap. ROSCHER, art. *Eros*, p. 1350): *Von Anfang an erscheint Eros als Knabe oder Mellephebe gebildet und mit Flügeln ausgerüstet.* Particularly also the following: *Ungeflügelte Bildung des Eros ist nirgends als beabsichtigt, sondern nur aus Nachlässigkeit erstanden und zwar namentlich in spätrömischer Zeit zu konstatieren, wo man die Flügel bei bekannten Typen zuweilen auch an Statuen aus Bequemlichkeit wegliess* (*l. c.*, p. 1369). We have, of course, in the present instance nothing either *nachlässig* or *spätrömisch;* as wingless, may be mentioned the St. Petersburg torso (FR.-W., 217), a replica of the same original as the Sparta torso (FR.-W., No. 218), which latter shows evident traces of wings. *Cf.* also the wingless group in Berlin (*Verz.* 150) to which the designation *Eros und Psyche* (?) is given and favored, *obwohl das übrigens nicht gerade unerlässliche Abzeichen der Flügel den Figuren fehlt.*

[14] *Cf.* BAUMEISTER, *Denkmäl., s. v., Apollon*, p. 95 *sqq.*; especially p. 98, where we read: *Die grosse Menge der sonst erhaltenen Apollonstatuen geben den Charakter wieder, welchen Praxiteles seinem Sauroktonos aufgeprägt hatte: eines Epheben von schlanker Bildung, Kraft und Zartheit der Glieder vereinigend, zwischen Hermes und Dionysos die Mitte haltend. Cf.* the remark of FURTWÄNGLER (ap. ROSCHER, p. 467): *Die Körperformen* [*des Apoll*] *sind regelmässig sehr jugendlich und weich, oft denen des Dionysos sich nähernd.* I am well aware that it is frequently difficult to distinguish mutilated statues of Dionysos from those of Apollo, and the attempted restorations are frequently dubious: *cf.* BRUNN, *Beschreib. der Glyptothek*, Nos. 97, 103. Examples might be multiplied.

the immediate vicinity—μετὰ τὸ θέατρον, in the words of Pausanias. This argument, while of some value as corroborative testimony, is worth but little *per se*, for we find a statue of Apollo in the great theatre of Dionysos at Athens.[15]

But it may here be urged, in favor of the identification as Apollo, that the face of our statue has an expression too lofty and intellectual for the youthful Dionysos. This objection may be satisfactorily answered, if we consider on what it chiefly rests, namely, the high forehead. For the mouth, though not broad as in Satyr-faces, will be found full and sensuous, while the cheeks and chin sink so softly into the unusually full throat that the uncommon heaviness here strikes one immediately when the statue is viewed in profile. Furthermore, a high forehead is precisely what we find in Seilenoi and Satyrs;[16] and the apparent lowness of the brow in many statues of Dionysos is due to the arrangement of the hair or to the head-band across the upper part of the forehead, while the height of forehead is noticeable only in those statues of Apollo which exhibit some such arrangement of hair about the face as in our figure.[17] We have, also, a noteworthy instance of a sweet femininity and quite as much intellectuality in a head in the Berlin Museum,[18] which was at first, like the Sikyonian, assumed to be that of a female, but has been unhesitatingly declared to be a Dionysos by an authority so competent as Furtwängler.

We have next to consider what Greek sculptural motives the statue embodies : (1) the general pose of the body and legs ; (2) the evident

[15] *Cf.* on this subject SCHREIBER (*Mittheilungen Athen.*, IX, p. 248), whose arguments against Waldstein's athlete hypothesis seem convincing. He would make the familiar Athenian figure an original by Kallimachos the κατατηξίτεχνος. The statue, according to him, is that of Apollo Daphnephoros, the chair of whose priest we find in the theatre: *cf. ut supra.*

[16] *Cf.* the ἀποσκοπεύων (FR.-W., No. 1429). The comparison of Sokrates with his high forehead to a Seilenos is well known.

[17] *Cf.* the so-called Ariadne head (FR.-W., No. 1490). Many statues of Dionysos have low brows, but the same is true of heads of Apollo: *cf.* the Belvedere and Apollino, with the high forehead (fourth-century type), with FR.-WOLT., Nos. 222-4.

[18] *Verz.*, No. 118; FURTWÄNGLER, *Sammlung Sabouroff*, *Tafel* XXIII. *Gefunden zu Athen beim Lykabettos. Höhe* 0,24. *Gesichtslänge* 0,12.—*Pentelischer Marmor* (FURTWÄNGLER, *l. c.*, Note 1 under text). The marked femininity of the face, the sweetness of expression and the high forehead are points of comparison with our statue which at once struck me. *Wir haben hier*, says Furtwängler, *einen ganz unverschrten, etwas unterlebensgrossen Dionysoskopf vor uns, der aus einem attischen Atelier der Zeit des Praxiteles selbst stammt.*

motive of the left arm; (3) the probable motive of the lost right arm; (4) the head and arrangement of hair.

As regards the pose, we observe that the weight of the body rests on the left leg, and that there is a corresponding graceful sway in the hips and loins. As is admitted, on the testimony of Pliny[19] and the evidence of replicas of the Doryphoros and other statues, Polykleitos was the first to introduce into Greek sculpture the distinction which is well described by the German terms *Standbein* and *Spielbein*—the leg on which the weight of the body rests and that which is free to pose in any one of several graceful attitudes. Praxiteles added a graceful sweep and curve of the body, giving to it, as a whole, a sort of S-shape. This is admirably exemplified in the Olympian Hermes. The Praxitelean type is at once evident in our Sikyonian statue, and that, too, not as a novelty but as part of the common stock of artistic tradition.

Concerning the left arm there are several points to consider. The left hand supported on the hip is noted as a favorite motive with Praxiteles, though it may have had an earlier origin. It is easily demonstrable that the resting of the left hand on the hip may be so motived as to express more than one artistic idea. Let us take, for example, a satyr-statue of the Periboëtos type (*e. g.*, Berlin originals Nos. 258, 259; Overbeck, *Plastik*[(3)], II, p. 41). Here we see the back of the left hand resting softly against the side, rather below the hip: this, together with the graceful and delicate pose of the whole figure, may fairly be considered as the fully developed Praxitelean motive. This is essentially the position of the hand in our Sikyonian statue, though here there is a fuller and firmer resting of the back of the hand against the side, which, in a draped statue of an elderly man, would give an air of dignified composure. If the motive were that in which the back of the hand is turned outward and the knuckles rest firmly against the side, there would be a greater sturdiness, a certain holding of force in reserve, particularly when accompanied by a firmer pose of the whole body.[20] The same may be said of the position of the

---

[19] *H.N.*, XXXIV. 56; *cf.* OVERBECK, *Schriftquellen*, No. 967.

[20] It is instructive to observe the effect of the supporting of the right hand upon the side (in the instance about to be cited, fingers outward in plain view, thumb behind) in the figure of Pelops from the east pediment of the temple of Zeus at Olympia. *Cf.* FR.-W., p. 125: *Nicht ohne Absicht scheint für ihn der Künstler die selbstbewusste, fast trotzige Haltung gewählt zu haben: den Kopf etwas zurückgeworfen, die Hand in die Seite gestemmt, steht er seines Sieges bewusst da.* A somewhat similar attitude in a nude Poseidon statuette is described (FR.-W., No. 1763) as *mehr energisch als stolz.*

hand with the fingers extended forward, the thumb behind, to us perhaps the most common and natural of these attitudes.

It is essential here to give in historical sequence a brief list of instances of the left hand supported against the side more or less in the manner of the Sikyonian statue. From the Parthenon we have the following: (1) Standing semi-draped male figure on W. frieze (Michaelis, 9. I. 1); in which the left hand rests rather below and somewhat behind hip: cf. Carrey's drawing ap. Michaelis. (2) Standing male figure on E. frieze (Michaelis, 14. III, 19), back of left hand on hip, staff under right arm, also draped. Together with these may be grouped a number of Attic reliefs in which the traces of Pheidian art are evident. I give the numbering of the casts ap. Friederichs-Wolters. (3) Standing figure of Asklepios (Fr.-W., No. 1070), the familiar draped type resting on staff with left hand concealed in garment and supported on hip. Such figures have a close likeness to that cited above from the E. frieze of the Parthenon.[21] As Overbeck (*Plastik*[(3)], I, pp. 274, 279) has no hesitation in deriving the seated statues of Asklepios (cult-statues), whether through Alkamenes or Kolotes, from the Zeus of Pheidias; so we may claim the standing figures of Asklepios on the reliefs as Attic and Pheidian, in view particularly of the Parthenon figure alluded to above. Similar figures are Fr-Wolt., Nos. 1085, 1196. It is not always possible to determine whether the back of the hand rests on the hip or whether the doubled hand holding a portion of the robe rests the knuckles upon the hip. This latter posture in connection with a more erect position of body, necessitating the firmer holding of the robe, is expressive of sturdier dignity. This position of the hand we have clearly in the Berlin statue *Verzeich.*, No. 71, and apparently in the fine statue of Sophokles in the Lateran (Fr.-Wolt., No. 1307). For left hand on hip, cf., also, Fr.-Wolt., Nos. 1085, 1147, 1150, 1151, 1161, 1195, 1196, 1445. To these should be added, as Praxitelean, the Periboëtos satyrs (e. g., Berlin *Verz.*, Nos. 258, 259); the Hermes of the *columna caelata* (Overbeck, *Plastik*,[(3)] II, 97; Fr.-Wolt., No. 1242–3); an athlete in an Athenian relief previously cited (*Annali*, 1862, *tav*, *M*). An archaistic Hermes on the "Altar of the Twelve Gods" in the Louvre (Fr.-Wolt., No. 422) stands stiffly with left hand on hip. A standing figure of Ammon from Pergamon may

---

[21] *Cf.* Fr.-Wolt., pp. 327, 328, for some remarks on the connection between such reliefs from Parthenon and other sculptures.

be added—a draped figure with left hand on hip, reminding one strongly of Attic work.

In the preceding list we have either Attic works or at least Attic types. Since it appears already in Pheidian art, it is plain that the motive in question in its more general aspect cannot be called Praxitelean; but there seems no just ground for refusing it this title, when it appears as developed in the more restricted type of the fourth century, and as applied to nude or nearly nude youthful male statues.

As regards the right arm, it is evident from the remaining portion that it was at least somewhat extended; and, in consonance with the rest of the figure, it may most readily be assumed that it was supported upon an object of some height. If the figure is Dionysos, this object may with great probability have been the familiar thyrsus. An interesting comparison may here be made between our statue and a relief on one side of a white marble disk in Berlin (*Verz.*, No. 1042), found at Gabii, thus described: *in flacherem Relief und flüchtiger ausgeführt die stehende Figur des jungen Dionysos in Chiton [?] und Umwurf [Himation], auf einen Stab (Thyrsos) gelehnt; auf Felsen neben ihm brennt eine Flamme. Römische Arbeit.* The figure looks toward the spectator's right and somewhat downward; the left hand is supported on the hip, the hair seems to be gathered in a knot on the back of the neck, the right arm is bent sharply at the elbow and the hand, held high, grasps the thyrsus; the weight of the body rests on the left leg, the right is bent in the same manner as the left leg of the Ephesian Hermes. The points in common with the Sikyonian statue are the following: (1) left hand on hip; (2) weight on left leg; (3) right arm raised; (4) garment (himation) over left arm—although in the disk figure it is draped over the left shoulder, and, leaving the left elbow bare, falls in front of the left arm as far as the knee, being then brought around behind the figure and looped from before over the bent right arm. It seems not improbable that the Roman disk figure goes back to a much earlier Greek original; and one is reminded of the Dionysos by Eutychides in the house of Asinius Pollio.[22] The comparison affords us, at all events, an interesting parallel; and, aside from this, the thyrsus seems the most natural explanation for the position of the right arm in our statue.

As regards the position of the head, I fancied I could detect, in

---

[22] Overbeck, *Plastik*[(3)], II, 135.

the inclination toward the right with the gaze turned toward the left, something borrowed from the Alexander type, which is undoubtedly due to Lysippos.[23] But if there is just reason for this conjecture, the motive is here merely hinted at; it is already an artistic commonplace of the post-Lysippian epoch. But we have particularly to notice the free handling of the hair, reminding in a measure of the heads of Alexander, in which we have, as in the Sikyonian statue, a simple arrangement of the locks, which are drawn down from the crown of the head and curl freely upward over the forehead and temples, falling somewhat lower on the neck behind.[24] This, so far as I am aware, we do not observe in the Praxitelean types and can hardly date earlier than Lysippos, to whom, indeed, it seems attributable. It is the germ of the treatment in later types, such as the Pergamene figures, where we see the hair, as in the Laocoön and the busts of Zeus, rising in a sort of halo about the head and face. The conception of this arrangement may, of course, be sought earlier. We have, in a diskobolos of Attic type[25] and in the Eubuleus of Praxiteles, ephebic figures in which the short hair is secured simply by a band or fillet, in strong contrast with the Attic *krobylos*[26] in vogue till the middle of the fifth century B. C., though scarcely appearing on the Parthenon.[27] In our statue, the hair behind and above the line of curls exhibits very rough and superficial workmanship, and was evidently not intended to be seen. We observe, also, the great fullness of this portion of the head, more noticeable in profile. Taking this in connection with the presence of a number of holes in the marble above the line of the curls, we may conclude that the head had some sort of decoration, which concealed the unfinished upper portion. We observe the same workmanship in other statues with a similar arrangement of hair about the face and with indubitable traces of wreaths.[28] What more natural, then, than

[23] On this subject, cf. BAUMEISTER, *Denkm.*, s. v., *Alexandros*, and particularly EMERSON in *Am. Journ. Arch.*, vol. II, pp. 408-13; vol. III, pp. 243-60. Cf. OVERBECK, *Plastik*(3), II, p. 110 sqq., in regard to portraits of Alexander by Lysippos.

[24] We see this, also, in the Monte Cavallo colossi, which exhibit traces of Lysippian influence.

[25] FR.-WOLT., No. 465; OVERBECK, *Plastik*(3), I, p. 276.

[26] SCHREIBER, *Mitth. Inst. Athen.*, VIII, p. 246 f.

[27] Cf. *Mitth. Inst. Athen.*, VIII, p. 262, a figure *in der Gruppe der schönen Greise, der Thallophoren*.

[28] Cf. FR.-WOLT., No. 1283 (Asklepios?) for arrangement of hair, for high forehead, and for a certain community of expression (e. g., similarity of mouth) with our statue,

to suppose, about the head of our statue, an ivy-wreath of bronze, with broad, full leaves? The height of the forehead, as already shown, though not necessarily conflicting, yet seems unusual in a Dionysos. Furtwängler, in his excellent notice of the Berlin head, already referred to,[29] says that it can be none other than that of Dionysos on account of the fillet in the hair which touches the middle of the forehead and there conceals the roots of the hair—a characteristic of Dionysos. *Die gewöhnliche Binde,* he continues, *wurde bekanntlich viel weiter hinten im Haare getragen. In älterer Zeit trägt Dionysos ganz regelmässig den Epheukranz um das Haupt und dieser scheint auch unserem Kopfe nicht gefehlt zu haben; eine schräge Reihe kleiner Löcher hinter dem Vorderhaar (darin z. Th. noch Reste eiserner Stifte) zeugen davon, dass ein solcher aus Metallblättern angesetzt war.* Here we have something parallel to our statue. From the end of the fifth century there appears in figures of Dionysos, besides the wreath or instead of it, a broad fillet, like that previously described, above the middle of the forehead. This arrangement, derived from the symposial habits of the time and explained by Diodorus Siculus (IV. 4.4), was adopted as a peculiar attribute of Dionysos, and from it he derived the epithet μιτρηφόρος. This fillet, originally separate from the wreath, as we see it in the Berlin head, was later for the most part adorned with ivy-leaves and ivy-berries, and came to form an integral part of the wreath (*mit dem Kranze zu einem Ganzen verbunden*). Such an arrangement is common in terracottas of Asia Minor and marbles of the Roman period. Can we now assume any such arrangement in the case of our statue? That the fillet was not indicated in the marble is at once evident; and without a cast it is impossible to state whether it might have been formed in metal and connected with the wreath. It is worthy of note, and plain in the photograph, that the hair immediately over the forehead is, near its roots, in noticeably lower relief than the waving locks which rise above it, and that, in the depressions of the curls at either side, a metal fillet might have rested with the wreath. This point, however, cannot at present be fully settled.

Before leaving this subject, I must again call attention to the paper of Furtwängler which has been previously quoted. He has summed

though No. 1283 is bearded. It may be added that the fullness of the back of the head is far more Praxitelean than Lysippian.

[29] *Sammlung Sabouroff*, text to *Taf.* XXIII.

up and characterized the features of the Berlin head in words which apply in great part to our statue, as well, although the eye is here not so deeply set. The breadth of the root of the nose is certainly noticeable; and we have also the same peculiar fullness of the chin and throat, which in our statue is even more marked than in the Berlin head.

The epoch and school to which our statue belongs will now be considered. As we have seen, it has in it no elements earlier than Praxiteles, while the treatment of the hair and perhaps the position of the head are rather Lysippian. We must, indeed, admit that a distinctively Sikyonian element in the work cannot be proved to any marked extent, and it is certainly not in any way strongly Lysippian. It partakes rather of the character of a generalized post-Alexandrine or Hellenistic art. At the same time, we see in it no trace of the overwrought pathos of the Pergamene and Rhodian schools, or of the archaistic tendencies of Pasiteles. These considerations will weigh in approximating the date of the work, particularly if we bear in mind that all its characteristics appear as fixed artistic elements and in no wise as inventions. That the work is Sikyonian is unquestionable.

The later history of Sikyonian sculpture is known to us through scattered references, especially in Pliny. Inscriptions also have of late come most serviceably to our aid. According to Pliny, Greek sculpture fell into decay after the time of Lysippos and his immediate successors, to revive again in Ol. CLVI. As has already been said, we have in our statue nothing of this *ars renata*, as it is known to us in the later schools. It must then be attributed to one of the successors of Lysippos; and, as we can trace no strong Lysippian elements in it, to some artist not under the immediate sway of the master—to one who displayed a spirit rather pan-Hellenic than Sikyonian.

So far as we can estimate on the data of Pliny, the activity of the artists named as followers of Lysippos must have continued into the latter portion of the third century B. C. Our knowledge on this subject may be resumed as follows :—The pupils of Lysippos, who according to Pliny flourished Ol. CXIII,[30] were Daippos, Boedas, Euthykrates son of Lysippos, Phanis, Eutychides, Chares of Lindos ;[31] of whom Eutychides and Daippos, on the same authority,[32] flourished Ol. CXXI, i. e., about a generation later than their master. Euthykrates had a disciple Teisikrates,[31] while Xenokrates is mentioned as disciple of

[30] *H. N.*, XXXIV. 51; OVERBECK, *Schriftquellen*, No. 1443.
[31] *Cf.* OVERBECK, *Schriftquellen*, No. 1516. [32] *H. N., l. c.* [33] *H. N.*, XXXIV. 67.

either Euthykrates or Teisikrates.[34] From Pausanias, we learn that Eutychides had a disciple Kantharos, a Sikyonian.[35] Furthermore, the inscriptions collected by Löwy (see above p. 18) show that the Sikyonian Thoinias son of Teisikrates was the son and disciple of Teisikrates son of Thoinias. The name of this Thoinias son of Teisikrates, moreover, occurs in the Sikyonian inscription No. 2, published above, and assigned to the second half of the third century B. C.

Starting from Lysippos,[36] we may draw up the following artistic genealogy:

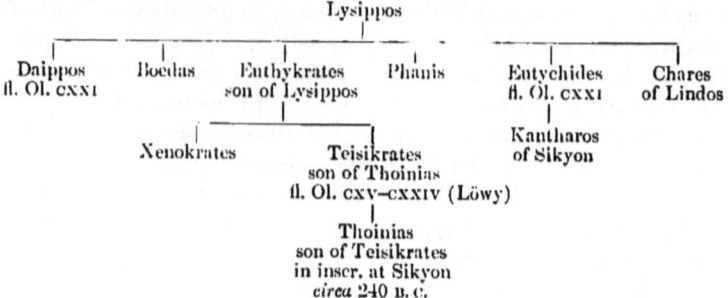

Combining the approximate date of the above-mentioned Sikyonian inscription with Pliny's chronology, we may place Teisikrates son of Thoinias at about Ol. CXXVIII–IX, and Thoinias his son at about Ol. CXXXVI. But, according to Pliny (*H. N.*, XXXIV. 52), between the time of Eutychides and Ol. CLVI *cessavit ars;* so that Thoinias may be reckoned among the last of Lysippos' successors.

Hence, we may say so much:—*First;* we have a statue of the youthful Dionysos, of good workmanship, a product of Sikyonian art. *Second;* we may assign this work, on grounds of Greek art-history, presumably, to the third century B. C. and to one of the more distant followers of Lysippos. *Third;* we know that Thoinias son of Teisikrates was active at Sikyon and elsewhere in the Greek world in the middle and latter half of the third century B. C. *Fourth;* we have in our work a certain pan-Hellenistic spirit, such as we may apprehend could have been exhibited by Thoinias.

Berlin, MORTIMER LAMSON EARLE.
August 6, 1889.

[34] *H. N.*, XXXIV. 83.   [35] PAUS., VI. 3. 6.
[36] Who was αὐτοδίδακτος, according to PLINY, *H. N.*, XXXIV. 61.

A NEW SIKYONIAN INSCRIPTION.

Δ ί ω ν
Κ α λ λ ί [ω ν
Μ ο ῦ σ ο ς
Ἀ ρ μ ό δ ι [ο ς
Ἐ ρ ά σ ι π π [ο ς
Α ἰ σ χ ί ν α [ς
Ἀ ρ ι σ τ ο κ [λ ῆ ς¹

In December 1887, while I was residing at Kiáto, the chief town (πρωτεύουσα) of the modern deme of Sikyon, during the progress of the excavations at the old theatre of Sikyon, an Albanian peasant named Geórgios Agrapedákes told me that some blocks of stone containing παλαιὰ γράμματα had been found in a field belonging to him in the village of Moúlki.² On December 18, I went up to Moúlki in company with my friend Dr. Eustáthios Tournákes of Kiáto, and there we found two blocks of stone, said to have been dug up some three years previously. On one of these the inscription, of which a facsimile is given above, was quite plainly legible. The length of this block is 0.70 m.,³ the same as that of the other, on which there seemed to be traces of letters obliterated beyond the possibility of decipherment. The height of the letters themselves is from 0.02 m. to 0.025 m., the former being that of the O, except in the first line. The stone is of a

¹ These names are all to be found in Pape. Only two are cited as borne by Sikyonians, Aischines (PLUT., *De Her. mal.*, 21) and Aristokles (PAUS., VI. 9. 1; VI. 3. 11). A Mousos is mentioned (PAUS., V. xxiv. 1; OVERBECK, *Schriftq.*, 2080) as the unknown artist of a statue of Zeus set up at Olympia by "the *demos* of the Corinthians."

² Moúlki (Μούλκι) is situated N. W. of Basilikó (the modern representative of the upper town of Sikyon), near the Ποτάμι τῆς Λέχοβας, the ancient Ἑλισσών. It undoubtedly formed part of the old city before its capture by Demetrios Poliorketes. *Cf.* DIODOR., XX. 102, 2–4.

³ The thickness of the block is 0.26 m: the original width cannot be determined.

brownish color, fairly hard and of coarse grain. It is broken on the right-hand side, whence the loss of one or more letters in every word except the first and third. The characters, as will be noticed in the facsimile, are neatly formed and arranged nearly στοιχηδόν. I made a copy of the inscription at the time, as did also Dr. Merriam, to whom I exhibited the new find before my return to Kiáto; and, on December 22, I took a squeeze, on which the facsimile is chiefly based.

I will now consider the inscription from an epigraphical standpoint. The reading, as given in the facsimile, is quite certain; but the first and sixth letters in the second name, the seventh letter in the fourth, and the seventh letter in the sixth are somewhat defaced. The inscription, when complete, was apparently as transcribed above.

As regards the characters, we observe: first, the angular form and small size of the O, except in the first line (*cf*. Roehl, *I. G. A.*, *27a Add.*); secondly, the four-barred *sigma*; thirdly, the angular form of the *rho;* fourthly, the form of the *chi*, as contrasted with that (+) of the Caere inscription (*I. G. A.*, *22*; Roberts, *G. E.*, No. 95); fifthly, the forms of *mu* and *nu*; sixthly, the form Ӿ = ε. On this last, special stress is to be laid, as being a point of the greatest importance.

That Ӿ = ε was a form peculiar to Sikyon, is not recognized by Roehl, nor does Roberts lay it down as a fixed principle, while Kirchhoff (*Stud.*,[4] 104–5) still retains under the head of Corinth the inscription of the Caere vase (*I. G. A.*, *22*; Roberts, No. 95), in which this sign occurs four times. I shall endeavor to show that not only have we no proof that the sign Ӿ was employed in the Corinthian alphabet, but that, in view particularly of the present inscription, the first one found *ipso loco* containing this sign, we seem warranted in assuming that it was peculiar to the Sikyonian alphabet, which appears to have been pretty sharply defined, and to have developed with considerable regularity as well as conservatism.

The fact that no inscription has been found at Corinth, or to be with certainty traced to Corinth, containing this form of *epsilon*, when viewed in connection with the fact that ε in the early alphabet of Corinth, as well as in that of her colonies, appears as Ᏸ or B (this form being also employed for the η, and ει being usually written as E [5]), goes a long way toward a demonstration of the non-existence of the form Ӿ = ε in the Corinthian alphabet. The proximity of Corinth and Sikyon is nothing in favor of influence one way or the

---

[4] *Cf. I.G. A.*, *21, 22* (ROBERTS, Nos. 94, 95) with *I.G.A.*, *26a Add*. (ROBERTS, No. 93).
[5] *Cf.* ROBERTS, p. 134.

other; for Sikyon at least seems to have been conservative in a very high degree.

In this connection, we must, however, admit that too much stress has been laid on the peculiar local form of the name, Σεκυών. Roehl (*I. G. A.*, *17*) claims that the inscription scratched on a spear-head found at Olympia cannot be the work of a Sikyonian, because the early local form of the name was Σεκυών, and not Σικυών, as found in this case: but one is startled to find in the *Addenda* (*27a*) a spear-head inscription attributed to a Sikyonian, but apparently from the same hand as the last, in which the form Σ = ε occurs in the same word. The similarity of the two inscriptions is most striking, notwithstanding this variation, the same unusual pentagonal *o* occurring in each, and the forms of the other letters, carelessly made it is true, being essentially the same as those of *I. G. A.*, *17*. One is also surprised to notice that Roehl reads *17*, Σικυών, rightly considering the three parallel scratches at the end as a mark of punctuation,[6] while he reads *27a Add.*, Σεκυωνί(ων), taking the perpendicular mark after the N — which is taller than any of the undoubted letters—as I, although such a form of *iota* is here, to say the least, in the highest degree improbable. It seems to me quite certain that we should read, here, simply Σεκυών. The testimony of the coins cannot be adduced in support of any theory of a consistent local employment of the form Σεκυών in the fifth century at least;[7] and, indeed, if the two spear-heads were engraved by the same hand, we find here a confirmation of what we may gather from the coins, namely, that the local usage was not at all stable, both forms being used indifferently.[8] We are then, in my judgment, quite safe in numbering *I. G. A.*, *17*, among Sikyonian monuments.

We must, therefore, guard against an assumption of over-conservatism on the part of the Sikyonians, but at the same time must not be led to assume that their alphabet developed with the same rapidity as that of Corinth, a point to be emphasized in estimating the probable date of the inscription now under consideration.

Roberts, who groups together the inscriptions of Corinth and its colonies and those of Sikyon (*G. E.*, pp. 119–37), distinguishes three periods, as follows (pp. 134–5): first, that comprising the most primitive inscriptions, in which *san*, the older form of μ (M), the crooked

---

[6] *Lineola quae ad dextram exarata est, non est litterae vestigium, sed finem tituli indicat.*
[7] *Cf.* HEAD, *Historia Numorum*, p. 345.
[8] Σικυώνιοι is the reading of Fabricius on the serpent-column at Constantinople (*cf.* ROBERTS, p. 259.)

iota, the closed *spiritus asper*, the older *theta*, certain peculiar forms of *gamma* (C, ⟨, I), and remarkable forms to express β and the E-sounds (ᛇ, B, or Ͳ⁹) appear; secondly, that comprising inscriptions "which exhibit the straight *iota* but retain the *san*" (p. 135); thirdly, that comprising inscriptions marked by, (1) "the adoption of the four-stroke *sigma*," (2) "the gradual substitution of the open H for the closed form," (3) "the introduction of the normal form for β" (p. 135). The first of these periods is to be placed as early as the sixth century B. C., the second would correspond to the earlier half of the fifth century, and the third to the latter half of the same century.[10]

In view of the arguments adduced in the course of the previous discussion, we seem justified in attributing to Sikyon both the spear-head inscriptions already alluded to (*I. G. A.*, *17*, and *27a Add.*). In one of these the form ϟ = ι appears, and in both we have *san*. These, then, are plainly older than *I. G. A. 21* and *22*, which must be classed together and are to be assigned to the earlier half of the fifth century. Certainly later than these, again, is our new inscription, between which and those just mentioned I am in favor of dating *I. G. A. 27c Add.*, which is, then, probably to be restored: ϟΤΚΥΟΝΙΟ[Ν or ϟΤΚΥΟΝΙΟ[Ι.[11] In both these last we find Τ retained, though in the former we have *alpha* and *kappa* of later form than in any other early Sikyonian inscription, and even later than in *I. G. A., 26a Add.*, a Corinthian inscription commemorating the battle of Tanagra (457 B. C.). In the last-mentioned, however, we have the normal ε, and *a*, *v*, and *χ* of the same form as in our new inscription. In view of the latter coincidence, as well as of the conservatism of the Sikyonians, we need have no hesitation in placing our inscription at least as late as 457 B. C., and probably somewhat later. In fact, I would propose the following chronological classification of early Sikyonian inscriptions:

I period, latter part of sixth century B. C. (*I. G. A. 17* and *27a Add.*);
II period, first half of fifth century B. C. (*I. G. A. 21, 22*);
III period, middle and latter half of fifth century B. C. (*I. G. A. 27c Add.* and the new inscription).

MORTIMER LAMSON EARLE.

Columbia College, New York.
   December, 1888.

---

[9] "Τ at Sicyon, at least in the 2d period."

[10] For the grounds of this chronology, which seems very satisfactory, see ROBERTS, p. 136.

[11] *Cf.* ROEHL's remarks *ad loc.*

DISCOVERIES IN THE ATTIC DEME OF IKARIA, 1888.*

CHRONOLOGICAL REPORT OF EXCAVATIONS.

[PLATES IV, V, VI, PLAN I, II, MAP.]

For an account of the manner in which our attention was directed to Dionysos, the reader is referred to the *Seventh Annual Report of the American School at Athens*, containing Professor Merriam's report as Director of the School for 1887-8. I was appointed by him to superintend excavations at Dionysos, in case it should seem advisable to undertake such work, and toward the last of October 1887 we made a trip to examine the district; as a result of this, Professor Merriam decided to take down the walls of the ruined church and see if the identity of the spot could not be fixed beyond doubt by inscriptions and other data. Permission to excavate was applied for at once, but was not obtained till the month of January; and on Monday, Jan. 30, work was begun with six workmen, the plan being to clear the ground in the immediate vicinity of the church and to remove the walls. PLATE IV gives the appearance of the church before work was begun, and shows the ancient monument which had been transformed into the apse of the church. The most important find made during the first three days was that of the wall-blocks and flat roof-pieces of this monument. These were found directly behind the apse, where the architrave had been lying ever since the time of Chandler.[1] On Thursday I took two workmen to show me a stone which had "flowers and letters" on it. They led me nearly to the western extremity of the valley, and on a ridge called Κόκκινο Χοράφι, a short distance to the north of the road to Kephisia, they pointed out a grave partially uncovered, and close to it the torso of a seated woman in very high relief, the head of which had been broken off and sent to Germany.

---

* I desire to make acknowledgment of my great obligation to Professor Merriam for his direction, advice and constant assistance in all my work, and also to Dr. Waldstein and Dr. Tarbell for assistance and suggestions in the arrangement of this report.
[1] *Travels in Asia Minor and Greece*, vol. II, p. 200.

The grave was of a late period, though possessing an earlier boundary-wall of good construction. For one of the sides had been used a sepulchral stele which bore two rosettes and an inscription of the 4th century recording the names of the two deceased, one a Plotheian and the other an Ikarian. This inscription, as I believed, had never been published, and it seemed a discovery of importance in relation to the sites of the demes of Ikaria and Plotheia, the proximity of which had already been surmised. Not till some months later was it found that our inscription had already been seen and copied by Milchhöfer.[2] On the same day there was found to the west of the church a massive marble seat (PLATE V and *Fig. 8*) which had been brought here from its original position, as was determined afterward by the discovery of other seats of similar form remaining *in situ* (at *K* on PLAN I).

On Friday, Feb. 3, work was carried on north of the church, and resulted in the most important discoveries of the first week, including a nude male torso of archaic style; a draped statue of a young woman, wanting the arms and head; a female head (afterward stolen) found directly above the draped statue but perhaps too small to belong to it; a fragment of a relief of the best period, representing a seated woman with a vessel in her right hand while with the left she holds the mantle away from her breast; three inscriptions, one a boundary-stone, the other two, decrees of the Ikarians. The one which came to light first was on a stele in perfect preservation and supplied absolute proof that here was actually the site of the deme of Ikaria (see below, p. 71)—more than this, that the official seat or centre of the deme could not be far distant. Gravestones with mention of the deme to which the deceased belonged establish nothing more than a possibility that the place of finding may have been the actual deme-site, but it is hardly conceivable that a public decree of a deme concerning only its internal affairs should be set up anywhere but within the limits of the deme. Thus, by the discovery of this inscription alone, the first object of our excavations was accomplished. During the remainder of this week the finds were of no special importance, and on the first of the following week a violent snowstorm obliged us to return to Athens.

Wednesday, Feb. 15, work was resumed, and the remainder of the week was devoted mainly to taking down the walls of the church and to digging beneath it. These walls were formed chiefly of large blocks

[2] *Mitth. Inst. Athen.*, 1887, p. 312.

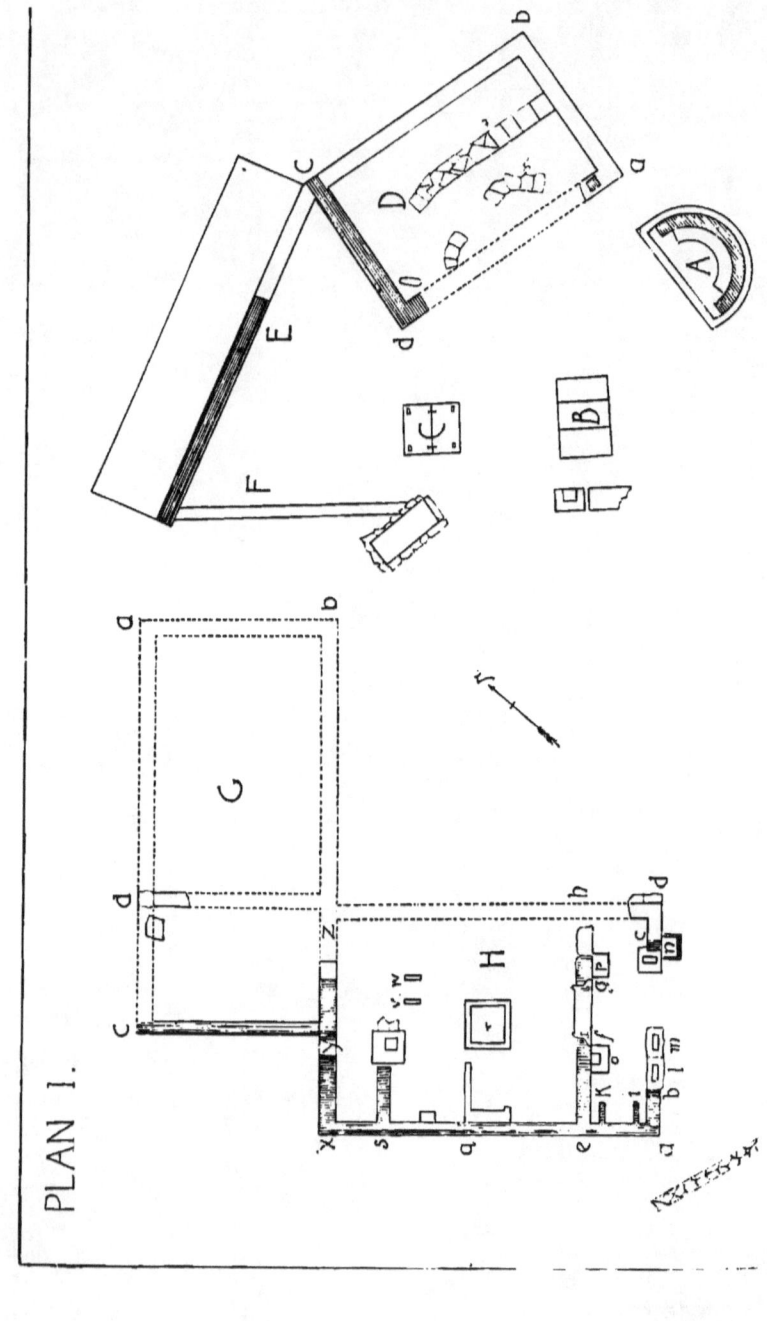

PLAN 1.

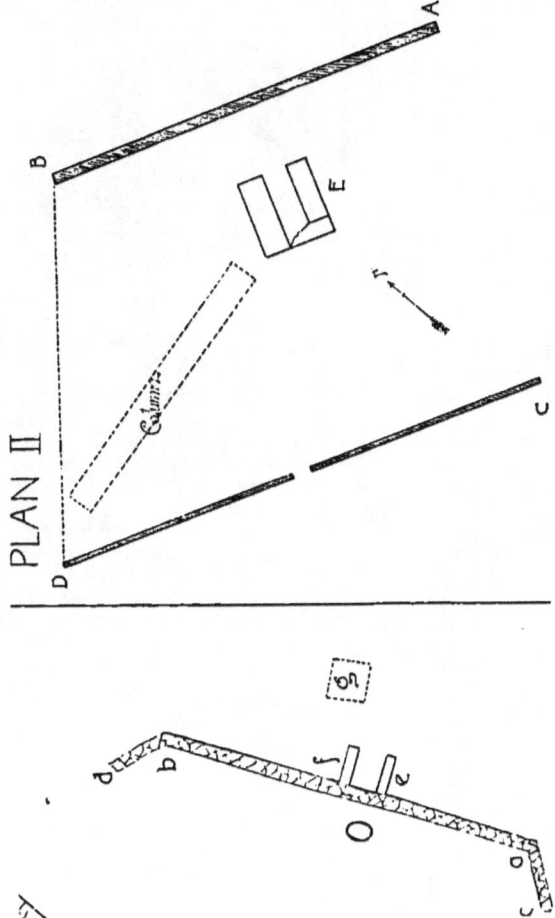

of marble taken from other structures, such as architraves, pieces of flooring, blocks from peribolos-walls, slabs ornamented in the Byzantine style and belonging to an earlier church; but with these were found also a large number of fragments of reliefs, statues, and inscriptions. Beneath the flooring in the centre of the nave we came upon the torso of an archaic draped statue; between the narthex and the nave was found, doing service as a sill, the archaic stele of a hoplite closely resembling the stele of Aristion (see below, "Sculpture"); and from the substructure of the front wall there was taken a colossal head in the archaic style, and a stone having inscribed on one side a long pre-Eukleidean decree, and, upon the other, various accounts of moneys transferred from demarch to demarch. These are of different periods, the oldest showing the three-barred *sigma*. The two bases indicated on PLAN I of the excavations as *B* and *C* were below the level of the church, of which the front wall passed over *C*, and one of the side walls over *B*.

The work of the following week, beginning with Monday, Feb. 20, was devoted to laying bare the walls *ac* and *cd* of the structure *D*, and resulted in the finding of the upper portion of the torso of a Seilenos, a child's head, a bronze *anathema* incised with the figure of some divinity, and a tragic masked head. During the week beginning Monday, Feb. 27, the few days on which the weather was clear were employed in sinking trenches on the slight eminence immediately to the south of the site of the church. While some of these trenches yielded no result, one of them struck the large base or platform indicated on the plan as *I*, and another led to what proved to be the pronaos of the Pythion, where we found a small relief representing Apollo sitting on the omphalos with an adorant before an altar in front, and the inscribed threshold of the naos (*Fig. 7*). Work was continued at the same time on the lower level. The wall *ab* of *D* was laid bare, and just outside of it were found two hands, one of colossal and the other of less than life size—both of fine workmanship. A portion of the next week was employed in digging to a considerable depth within the walls of *D* and inside the peribolos-wall *E*, where there was a large mass of rubbish which had evidently been thrown in designedly as filling. This labor was well rewarded by the discovery, within the structure *D* about a meter below the bottom of the wall, of a portion of the beard of the archaic colossal head, every fragment of which is of value for deciding the important questions suggested by it. A trench 3 m. deep and 10 long was run west from the end of the peribolos-wall without finding anything. On the upper level were disclosed the walls L, M, N, O, and the seats at K. Two days were devoted to work on a second site, about half a mile N. W. from the principal excavations, near the road, where a column with its drums strewn on the ground, and a portion of a wall seemed to invite investigation (see PLAN II). At the end of the column were found fragments of a large marble vase (*Fig. 10*), and near these the heads and necks of three griffins (*Fig. 11*).

On the week beginning Monday, March 12, one day was given up to the thorough clearing out of the little enclosure in the locality just referred to, but the remainder of the time was spent on the principal site, in laying bare the whole of the Pythion and the structure G; so that all the outlines can be made out (PLATE VI). This completed our work for the spring of 1888.

On November 13, work was resumed with the object of clearing away the large mass of soil between the Pythion and the two bases on the lower level. Last spring, a trench was cut here down to virgin soil, without revealing anything, but it seemed advisable to clear out the whole mass, in order to leave no possibility untested. The results were of less importance than those previously attained, but were still of value, especially when we remember that every stone *in situ* is of the greatest moment in making out any general plan. South of the base B were found two smaller bases for votive offerings. The wall O, which seemed last spring to belong to some building, was found to extend both ways for a short distance, then to diverge at each end for about two meters, and there stop. This wall is thus shown to be of entirely different character from what had been supposed. The sculptural finds in this part of the excavations consisted of a haunch of a lion or griffin and a male portrait-head of the Roman period. An overhauling of the *débris* to the southeast of the apse yielded a few fragments which had been overlooked last year, one of these of great importance, namely, the left thigh of the archaic draped torso, proving that it was a seated statue. To the north of wall E there was found last year a platform of rather rough stones laid close together. It was our intention to follow out this platform this year, and discover, if possible, what it was. For this purpose a passage was cut along the wall *bc* of D in order that the workmen might have an easy exit. About half-way between the two ends of *bc* was found a large marble slab cut pyramidally on one side and hollowed out on the other. On the side, along the three edges which are intact, five strange objects are sculptured. A corner piece having on it a similar object was found last year. The platform was found to continue to the west, but the great depth of the soil deposited over it made the work so slow that it seemed best to abandon it, at least temporarily, and to devote all our resources to clearing up the whole space within the precinct.

Some excavations on a small scale were made in various parts of the region where it seemed that there might be graves. Upon the ridge which runs down from Pentelikon close to the site of the chief excavations, we found a sarcophagus of Hellenic workmanship, absolutely without ornament but very beautifully finished. It contained a skeleton, but no remains of vases. In another place, to the west of the principal site, we discovered a wall 14.85 m. long, constructed of two courses of blocks averaging 1.20 m. long, and 0.80 m. high. A space about 6.00 m. wide was cleared away behind this, and at a depth of 1.60 m. a marble urn was found, filled with ashes and the bones of a child, together with a few fragments of vases. There was a precisely similar urn in the nave of the old church before our excavations were begun, this having probably served as a font: the bottom of still another one was found in the course of the excavations: we have thus abundant evidence that at Ikaria, as perhaps in all parts of Greece, cremation was practised contemporaneously with the burial of the body.[3]

In the valley along the course of the old road, northwestward, are several short walls forming the fronts of separate grave-enclosures, perhaps family μνήματα.[4]

In the second week in January, 1889, the excavations were continued during a few days. The platform outside wall E was entirely cleared, and a trench was sunk in the terrace N. W. of the excavation. The virgin soil was reached at a depth of over two meters, but nothing was found. We must therefore be content with a negative result, which, indeed, is not without value.

TOPOGRAPHY OF THE IKARIAN DISTRICT.

A word may first be said upon the name of the district where the excavations were made. In a note which the Ephor-General of Anti-

---

[3] Cf. BECKER-GÖLL, *Charikles*, III, p. 132 ff.; HERMANN, *Privataltertümer*, § 40.
[4] DEMOSTHENES, vs. *Eubulid.* § 28; vs. *Makart.* § 79.

quities, Mr. Kabbadias, furnished to Professor Merriam in the autumn of 1887, giving directions for finding the site, the name was written στὸ Διόννσο. Afterwards, I was careful to note how the workmen, who were peasants from the surrounding region, spoke of the place, and I never once heard στὸ Διόννσο except where the preposition εἰς would naturally be used (e. g., Πᾶμεν στὸ Διόννσο = Πηγαίνομεν εἰς τὸ Διόννσο). However, this would not determine whether the name were masculine or neuter, since the vernacular, with certain exceptions, drops the final ν of the masculine accusative singular. Mr. G. Heliopoulos, the brother of the owner of the property, informs me that Διόννσος is the correct form, and that it is so written on the old Turkish map which came into the owner's hands at the time the property was purchased. Dionysos is, moreover, the form given on Leake's map in some of the later copies of his *Demi of Attica*, and also by Rangabé.[1] Curtius and Kaupert[2] write *Dionyson*, which is undoubtedly incorrect.

In the speech of the people it is habitually Dionyso. It seems extremely probable that the name is a reminiscence of the cult of Dionysos applied to the whole region, and has remained in the mouths of the people for more than two thousand years. According to Chandler,[3] who visited the place in 1766, the church was sacred to St. Dionysios, and so it is given on Finlay's map[4] of the region; but Rangabé " would not venture to say that the church was dedicated to this saint." While we were taking down the walls of the church, some of the workmen spoke of St. Dionysios being present ; but this may have entered their heads merely from the similarity of the name. Mr. Heliopoulos says that it is not known to what saint the church was dedicated, and there seems to be now no solid tradition that it was sacred to St. Dionysios. But nearly all of the peasant families in Stamata are newcomers of the present century, and perhaps among the inhabitants whom Chandler found in Old Stamata there may have been a genuine tradition. If the older church structure was actually sacred to St. Dionysios the Areopagite, not the Zakynthian saint, this would be an instance of the frequent transfers from the ancient religion to hagiology. But that in any case the name of the region owes its origin directly to the ancient cult of the wine-god and not to the saint succeeding him is evidenced by the fact

[1] *Antiquités Helléniques*, No. 985. [2] *Karten von Attika*, XII (Pentelikon).
[3] *Travels in Asia Minor and Greece*, vol. II, p. 200.
[4] *Remarks on the Topography of Oropia and Diacria*. This map, somewhat reduced, was used for the *Seventh Annual Report* of the School, and is again utilized here.

that the name is *Dionysos* not *Dionysios*. Here, then, at Dionysos we have the site of the deme of Ikaria. The spot at which the principal excavations were made appears on the upper edge of Curtius and Kaupert's map of Pentelikon. Here was the ἕδρα, the political and religious centre of the deme. Let us attempt to determine its boundaries. To the north, close to the deme-centre, looms up the height which on Leake's map is called *Aforismó* and on that of Curtius and Kaupert, *Stamatavuni*. The name Aphorismó is sometimes applied more distinctively to the height at the end of the range, close to Vraná.[5]

The name Stamatavuni (Stamata Mountain) is unknown among the peasants here who call it, rather, in Albanian Mäl'[6] Dionyso (Mountain of Dionysos). This height is the turning-point of a whole range reaching to the Marathonian plain on the north and the Kephisian plain on the west, but towers far above the rest of the range with the exception of Aphorismó, which seems to be of about the same elevation. Here we certainly have the ancient Mons Icarius, the name being, perhaps, extended to the whole range.

To the east of the excavations are three terraces, on one of which are remains of a fine marble wall of a good period, which must have belonged to a building included in the limits of the deme. Beyond these terraces is a deep ravine, through which a path leads to Marathon, and here may be placed the eastern boundary of the deme. Crossing several ridges beyond this ravine, we arrive at the ruined village of Rapedosa,[7] where Leake placed Ikaria; and Hanriot,[8] Tithras. This locality would naturally be a site for a deme, but there are no remains in the village to show that there actually was here a deme-centre of importance. There is hardly a piece of marble to be found, all the walls being composed of rough blocks of mica-schist. Still further to the east is the range called Argaliki, which skirts the coast, leaving room for the present carriage-road from Athens to Marathon. This is the mountain which Leake thought to be Mons Icarius. The southern

---

[5] LEAKE fixes the name here in his text (*Demi of Attica*, p. 78), though he gives it a wider range on his map.

[6] Pronounced nearly *málya*.

[7] Rapentosa, Rapendosa, or Rapendosia are the usual spellings, but Rapedosa as given in Curtius is correct, as it is an Albanian word (*Rape-dosa*), and has no n-sound. Rapentosa must be a mere transliteration of the modern Greek pronunciation. But neither in English nor in German is there any excuse for inserting n. Rapatosa and Rapotosa are given on Finlay's two maps of this region.

[8] *Recherches sur la topographie des dèmes*, p. 168.

boundary of Ikaria is formed by the steep and rugged side of Pentelikon, from which a low ridge runs down to the seat of the excavations. Upon the eastern side of this ridge was found the unornamented Greek sarcophagus described above. It is not unlikely that there were buildings belonging to the deme along the ridge; several terrace-walls are still visible on the slopes. To the east of this elevation the plain extends for a considerable distance before meeting the main range of Pentelikon, and there was room here for a considerable population. But habitable land in greater extent is afforded by the valley which stretches northwestward from the deme-centre, between Pentelikon on the southwest and the range which begins in the Kephisian plain on the north, and rises gradually until it culminates in the height Māl' Dionyso. The ancient road leading through the valley can be traced in several places by its border-lines of graves. The enclosure with the fallen column (see PLAN II) was close to the road directly opposite a grave-enclosure. About a quarter of a mile west of Κόκκινο Χοράφι are several huge marble blocks which must have belonged to a structure of large dimensions. One of these blocks is 1.68 m. long, 1.20 m. wide, 0.60 m. thick. The inscription on the stele found at Κόκκινο Χοράφι established a certain probability that the site of the ancient deme of Plotheia was near; but the recent excavations conducted for the American School by Mr. Washington at Old Stamata have resulted in the finding of three dedicatory inscriptions of Plotheians, one of them upon a large stone not easily to be moved any great distance; so that the Plotheian deme-seat, with its various temples, mentioned in an inscription published many years ago,[9] may be placed almost with certainty at Old Stamata, which is situated just beyond the ridge that bounds the Ikarian valley on the northeast. A road leads from Old Stamata across the ridge to the road which passes through the valley to Dionysos, the journey from Plotheia to Ikaria requiring about an hour. Another road leads up from Κόκκινο Χοράφι to the present village of Stamata, passing quite near Old Stamata. It is not impossible that the territory of Plotheia extended down to Κόκκινο Χοράφι and touched the territory of Ikaria in the valley; but the range of hills seems a natural boundary, and I am more inclined to think that the whole valley, including the locality where our stele was found, was within the limits of Ikaria.

[9] C. I. A., II, 570.

Now that the sites of both Ikaria and Plotheia have been determined, we ought to be able to make a reasonable conjecture as to the position of another deme which is usually grouped with these two, namely Semachidai. The similarity of the myths of Ikaria and Semachidai has been noted by Leake[10] as evidence of the contiguity of these two demes; and that Semachidai was near Plotheia is proved by the fact that they were both members of a community called Epakria,[11] of which more below. Now, in which of the neighboring localities where ancient remains are visible can we with the greatest probability place the site of Semachidai? About a quarter of a mile west of Old Stamata is a small hill, called Bāla by the Albanians, upon the sides of which are a few unimportant remains, mentioned by Milchhöfer.[12] Still further to the west, beside the road leading from Kephisia to Stamata, are some ancient remains, including some large bases for votive offerings. The locality is called Old Spata. The place called Bāla was undoubtedly a portion of Plotheia, and the remains at Old Spata are not of a nature to encourage the hypothesis that there was a distinct deme-centre there. North of the present village of Stamata, at a distance of perhaps a mile and a half from Old Stamata, is a place called Amygdalésa. Here excavations were made by Mr. Washington, but no inscriptions identifying the place were found. Although the remains show that there were ancient buildings on this site, I do not feel satisfied that it indicates the position of a deme-centre. But the site, being only a few rods away from the present road to Marathon, would be entirely suitable for the deme of Hekale.[13] Hanriot[14] maintains that the present village of Stamata is on the site of Hekale, and Lolling[15] thinks this possible. But at Stamata itself there are, so far as I know, no ancient remains whatever. Leake[16] placed Hekale at the village of Grammatiko, Kastromenos[17] prefers Kalentzi.

Following the road to Marathon over several ridges, after a walk of about three-quarters of an hour from Stamata, a vale called Κουκου-

[10] *The Demi of Attica*, p. 104.
[11] STEPHAN. BYZ.: Σημαχίδαι, δῆμος 'Αττικὸς, ἀπὸ Σημάχου, ᾧ καὶ ταῖς θυγατράσιν ἐπεξενώθη Διόνυσος, ἀφ' ὧν αἱ ἱερεῖαι αὐτοῦ. "Εστι δὲ τῆς 'Αντιοχίδος φυλῆς. Φιλόχορος δὲ τῆς 'Επακρίας φησὶ τὸν δῆμον. *C. I. A.* II, 570: ὅποι ἂν δέ[ῃ Πλ]ωθέας ἅπαντας τελεῖν ἀργύριο[ν ἐς ἱ]ερά, ἢ ἐς Πλωθέας ἢ ἐς 'Επακρέα[ς ἢ ἐς 'Α]θηναίους, κ.τ.λ., where the arrangement of the words seems to indicate a progress in each case from a smaller to a larger body.
[12] *Mitth. Inst. Athen.*, 1887, p. 312, where the name is wrongly spelled *Pala*.
[13] PLUT. *Theseus*, § 14. [14] *Recherches sur la topographie des dèmes*, p. 167.
[15] BAEDEKER, *Griechenland* (1888), p. 127. [16] *The Demi of Attica*, p. 122.
[17] *Die Demen von Attika*, p. 80.

νάρι is reached, lying at the foot of Mt. Aphorismó, and shut in on all sides except the south. At about the centre of the opening there are ruins of a church and a monastery, in the walls of which are utilized many large blocks that must have belonged to ancient structures. Two reliefs mentioned by Milchhöfer [18] are lying on the ground close by. This spot has not, so far as I know, been mentioned as a deme-site by any of the numerous writers on Attic topography, but there are few places of which such an assertion can be made with greater plausibility. The circumstance that the plain is shut in on nearly all sides practically excludes the possibility that the remains which are here visible have been brought from a distance. If the ancient road to Marathon followed the same course as the present one, which crosses the northern extremity of this open space, and then divides, one branch leading to Vraná, the other to Marathona, then Koukounári would be as likely a site for Hekale as Amygdalésa. But the ancient road to Marathon may have been more direct than that of to-day, which turns rather abruptly to the right just after passing Amygdalésa. The demolition of the walls of the structures here would probably lead to the discovery of some inscription which would settle the identity of the site; but the owner, Mr. Heliopoulos, is not at present willing that this should be done. I am disposed to think, however, that we have here the site of the deme of Semachidai. We have literary evidence that the Epakrian community was situated near the Marathonian Tetrapolis,[19] and it is interesting to note that, on Finlay's map [20] of this district, Epakria is so placed as exactly to cover this vale of Koukounári, and to include Old Stamata, also running down to the south into the region of Rapedosa and Ikaria. In his text, Finlay says: "Epakria bordered on the Tetrapolis and apparently embraced the northern and eastern slopes of Pentelicus, but neither its extent nor the situation of its capital can be determined." Hanriot and others have attempted to locate it in the region north of Marathon. Now that we can form a more accurate idea of its position, having definitely located one village included in it, we have new reason to look with interest upon the history and development of the community.

Philochoros, as quoted by Strabo,[21] states that Kekrops first brought

---

[18] *Mitth. Inst. Athen.*, 1887, p. 313, where the place is wrongly called *Kukunarti*.
[19] BEKKER, *Anecdota Graeca*, 1, p. 259: Ἐπακρία· ὄνομα χώρας πλησίον τετραπόλεως κειμένης. [20] See MAP.
[21] STRABO, IX. 1.20: Κέκροπα πρῶτον εἰς δώδεκα πόλεις συνοικίσαι τὸ πλῆθος, ὧν ὀνόματα Κεκροπία Τετράπολις Ἐπακρία Δεκέλεια Ἐλευσὶς Ἀφιδνα (λέγουσι δὲ καὶ πληθυντικῶς Ἀφίδνας) Θόρικος Βραυρὼν Κύθηρος Σφηττὸς Κηφισιά . . . .

the population of Attika together into twelve πόλεις (which must mean communities rather than cities), and he gives the names of these with one omission. One of these was Tetrapolis, which we know was made up of the four villages, Marathon, Oinöe, Probalinthos, and Trikorythos; another was Epakria. The statement of Philochoros is undoubtedly founded on a genuine tradition, although we cannot put confidence in the number twelve, which may have been chosen by the historian as corresponding to the number of the original phratries. As Wilamowitz suggests,[22] topographical researches are the most trustworthy means of determining how many of these old communities there were. It is useless to attempt, with Leake,[23] to reconcile with the statement of Philochoros a certain passage which occurs in nearly the same form in both the *Etymologicum Magnum* and Suidas: Ἐπακρία χώρα· Ἀθηναίους πάλαι κωμηδὸν οἰκοῦντας πρῶτος Κέκρωψ συναγαγὼν κατῴκισεν εἰς πόλεις δυοκαίδεκα· καὶ τὴν τῶν πολιτῶν ἐπωνυμίαν ἀφ' ἑαυτοῦ Κεκροπίαν προσηγόρευσε· δύο δὲ τετραπόλεις ἐκάλεσεν, ἐκ τεσσάρων πόλεων ἑκατέραν μοῖραν καταστήσας· τρεῖς δὲ τὰς λοιπὰς ἐπακρίδας ὠνόμασε· καὶ ἡ προσεχὴς χώρα ταύταις ταῖς τρισὶν αὐταῖς Ἐπακρία ἐκαλεῖτο. This must be looked upon as merely a forced attempt to make up the number of twelve communities from the few which survived as such in the historical period. The only value of the passage lies in its record of the tradition that Epakria was composed of three villages, and this is generally accepted as a fact by modern writers on Greek Constitutional History. Thus Busolt[24] speaks of *der Semachidai, Plotheia und eine dritte Gemeinde umfassende Verein der Epakrier*.

What was this third village? Hanriot[25] conjectured that it was Ikaria, but he had nothing on which to support his conjecture, as he did not know the site of even one of the three demes, nor was he able to prove that Ikaria was in the vicinity of Plotheia. But, now that we know that Ikaria and Plotheia were adjacent demes, I think that his conjecture may be renewed with much greater probability. Let us continue with the history of Epakria, which gains a new interest for us if, as I believe, Ikaria was actually the third member of the union. Now, although these old unions had already lost all political significance previous to the historical period, some of them survived all the reforms,

[22] *Philologische Untersuchungen*, I, p. 123. [23] *The Demi of Attica*, p. 30.
[24] *Staats- und Rechtsalterthümer*, § 115, in *Handbuch d. kl. Alter.*
[25] *Recherches sur la topographie des dèmes*, p. 152.

even that of Kleisthenes, under the guise of religious communities. Thus, an inscription[26] found between the present village of Marathona and the sea shows that in the fourth century the four demes of the Tetrapolis maintained a religious community of which there was an archon, perhaps chosen in turn by the different demes, and also four ἱεροποιοί, one from each deme. The decree of the deme of Plotheia, already referred to more than once, shows that Epakria also survived as a religious community after it had lost all political significance.

The name of Epakria is met with in certain inscriptions in a quite different sense, namely, as a τριττύς.[27] A τριττύς was a third part of a tribe, a division adopted for convenience in naval assessments.[28] Late historians and lexicographers speak of the τριττύς as a division of the old tribes prior to Kleisthenes; but this may be nothing more than an attempt to trace a historical institution back to the mythical period. But Epakria as a τριττύς cannot be identical with Epakria as a community, for one deme, Semachidai, belonged to the tribe Antiochis, while Plotheia and Ikaria were of the tribe Aigeis. Dittenberger[29] suggests, however, that, while these religious communities were usually composed of demes of different tribes, it would be natural that, because of the membership of one or more demes of a tribe in such a community, one τριττύς of this tribe should be named from it. Applied to the particular case in point, this would imply that the most important demes in one τριττύς of the tribe Aigeis were Ikaria and Plotheia; and that, since these were two of the three demes constituting the religious community of Epakria, the name of this community was transferred to the τριττύς.

ARCHITECTURAL REMAINS.*

Our architectural work at Ikaria centres about the remains of a monument of semicircular form (*A;* PLAN I; see PLATES IV and V), used in

---

[26] *Mitth. Inst. Athen.*, 1878, p. 261 = DITT., *Syll.*, 304.
[27] Ross, *Demen von Attika*, p. 8; DITT., *Syll.*, 300.
[28] DEMOSTH. XIV. 23.   [29] *Hermes*, XVI, p. 187.

* The original plan of the excavations was made by Mr. S. B. P. Trowbridge. We are indebted to Messrs. H. S. Washington and R. W. Schultz for additions and elevations, and to Professor W. R. Ware for preparing these for reproduction, and for the restoration of the semicircular monument showing the object of the vertical band on the front stones, viz., to produce the effect of pilasters. The Plates are from photographs by Professor Louis Dyer.

later times to form the apse of a Christian church. The front portion of the substructure, the pavement, and the first course of blocks have the appearance of being *in situ;* but the rear of the substructure has been repaired at a late time, as is evidenced by the presence in it of bricks and mortar, and of a block which was originally one of the end pieces of the uppermost course, holding the architrave. The floor

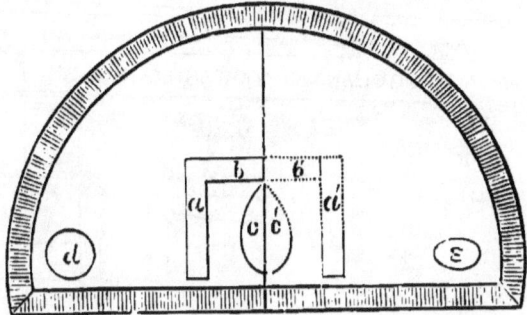

FIG. 1.—*Upper surface of roof of Choregic Monument.*

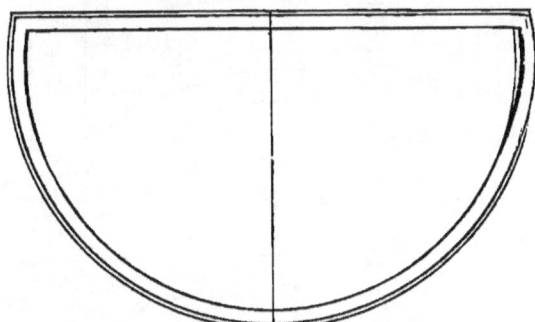

FIG. 2.—*Lower surface of roof of Choregic Monument.*

has spread somewhat, and one of the blocks in the lowest course has been broken, allowing its fellows to slide in toward the centre. A groove in the upper stones of the substructure shows the original position of the lowest course. In the second course, as now existing, all the blocks are of different heights. One block, now in the interior, appears to have been originally an end piece, as is shown by the projecting vertical band at the end, so that not more than one block of this course can be *in situ*. Behind the apse, an architrave with an inscription had long been exposed to view, and, during the first few days of our excavations, there were found two large slabs fitting together and forming a semicircular roof, and also seven blocks similar to those in the apse. As the roof-pieces afford the surest basis for a reconstruction of the monument, both lower and upper sides are shown in *Figures 1, 2*. The

FIG. 3.—*Choregic Monument restored.*

under side, which is worked smooth, is surrounded by a shallow channel, 0.10 m. wide and 0.015 m. deep, the edges of which are carefully beveled. This channel undoubtedly overlapped the walls at the sides and the architrave in front, the overlapping portion forming a simple cornice. Taking the measurements inside the channel as representing accurately the dimensions of the original walls, we will compare them with those taken from the other pieces. The length of the interior arc is 4.83 m. The present interior length of the first course, the height of which is 0.82 m., is 4.74 m., leaving 0.09 m., which is accounted for by the end blocks on both sides being broken. The height of the two blocks which supported the architrave is 0.635 m., and, taking the other two stones that have the same height as also belonging to the upper course, we obtain a length of 4.82 m. The blocks are roughly cut, so that a difference of one centimeter in the measurements may be passed by. For the two original intervening courses, there are eight blocks, four having a height of 0.65 m., and four of 0.625 m. Of the four of the latter height every stone is intact, and these give a length of arc of exactly 4.83 m. One block of the remaining course is broken on one edge; and the length of the stones of this course comes to 4.81 m. The front width of the roof-pieces inside the channel is 2.83 m., which agrees perfectly with the length of the architrave. The extremities of the architrave are not square, but are cut with a curve corresponding to that of the walls. Comparing the measurements of the architrave with those of the end pieces of the upper course, the widths of the cutting and of the architrave are found to be exactly the same, being 0.36 m., but the depth of the cutting is 0.40 m., while that of the architrave is only 0.315 m., leaving a space of 0.085 m., which must have been filled by small capitals. *Fig. 3* gives the front elevation of the monument, as restored from the existing remains. There may also have been columns, one on each side, as in a temple *in antis;* but no remains of such columns were found, nor does the architrave show any trace of such supports. The roof undoubtedly held adornment of some sort, as is shown by the cuttings on the upper side of the stones. The presence of such adornment and the inscription on the architrave, besides the general form of the structure, constitute the data from which we must form our conclusion as to the character of the monument. That it was a memorial of victory is set forth by the inscription; but are we justified in holding that the victory had connection with the choregia, and thus in calling it a choregic monument?

The choregic monuments of which we know the exact form are three, all at Athens: the well-known monument of Lysikrates in the Street of the Tripods; the monument of Thrasyllos, which, up to the time of the Greek Revolution, stood above the Dionysiac Theatre on the south side of the Akropolis, drawings of it being given by Stuart and Revett;[1]

[1] *Antiquities of Athens,* vol. II, chap. IV, pls. I, II, III, ff.

and the monument of Nikias, which Dr. Dörpfeld has reconstructed from the fragments found in the Beulé gate.[2] The monument of Lysikrates is an elaborately ornamented circular building, counted among the earliest surviving examples of Corinthian architecture. Upon the roof is a large three-branched acroterium disposed as a base for holding the tripod, and the architrave bears the inscription,[3] which has the regular form of an official choregic memorial. The monument of Thrasyllos was in the form of a portico, having upon the roof a statue of Dionysos, which is now in the British Museum. Whether the tripod rested on the knees of the seated statue, as some maintain, or was displayed in the interior of the structure, is still an unsettled question. For the inscription, see below, p. 78. The monument of Nikias had the façade of a small hexastyle Doric temple. There is nothing to show where the tripod was placed. For the inscription on the architrave, see below, p. 81.

We will now compare the Ikarian monument with these three chief examples. The Nikias and Thrasyllos monuments are both of such form that they admit of being called ναοί, the word which Pausanias uses in describing the structures on the Street of the Tripods. The foundation of a fourth choregic monument, now exposed in the cellar of a house near the Lysikrates monument, is of quadrangular shape. A semicircular exedra-like form, such as that of the Ikarian monument, has been unexampled among choregic monuments; but the number which we know is so small, and the variety exhibited by even these few so great, that this does not make positively against identification of the monument at Ikaria as choregic.

The surface of the upper side of the roof-stones (*Fig. 1*) is rough, and the top is surrounded by a bevel 0.11 m. wide on the curved side and 0.13 m. across the front. The socket at *d* is circular with a diameter of 0.22 m., that at *e* is about 0.32 by 0.24 m., but very roughly made. The right-hand side of the central socket has been split away, as is indicated by dotted lines in the sketch, but a fragment found in the débris shows that the original cutting was the same as on the other side; *a* and *b* form one continuous cutting, but *b* is cut two centimeters deeper than *a*; the cutting *c* is only 0.03 m. deep. I have no opinion to advance as to the nature of the object which these cuttings were made to receive. I hold that they could not have been intended for the direct support of a tripod, and that so complicated an arrangement

[2] *Mitth. Inst. Athen.*, 1885, p. 217 ff.   [3] Ditt. *Syll.*, 415.

would not be necessary for a tripod-base. If the top of the monument was adorned with a group of figures, a tripod might have been displayed in connection with the figures, or within the monument. As I take it, the roof-pieces furnish no data which make decisively either for or against the choregic character of the monument.

The inscription on the architrave (*Fig. 3*) reads:

ΑΓΝΙΑΣΞΑΝΘΙΠΠΟΣΞΑΝΘΙΔΗΣΝΙΚΗΣΑΝΤΕΣΑΝΕΘΕΣΑΝ
'Αγνίας, Ξάνθιππος, Ξανθίδης, νικήσαντες ἀνέθεσαν:

"Hagnias, Xanthippos, and Xanthides, having won, dedicated (this monument)."

The height of the letters varies from 0.05 to 0.06 m. This inscription was first seen, in 1766, by Chandler, who gave the first word as Αἰνίας.[4] Αἰνίας is given also by Böckh,[5] by Rangabé,[6] and again by Milchhöfer in his letter to the *Philologische Wochenschrift*.[7] But the second letter of the first name is certainly a *gamma*, and thus we have, in place of a name of which there is no absolutely certain occurrence,[8] a name by no means uncommon and used in Ikaria, as we know from two inscriptions[9] in which one 'Αγνίας 'Ικαριεύς[10] is mentioned as a trierach. The use of ἀνέθεσαν and the circumstance that the victors are three in number would show that the inscription, if choregic at all, belonged to the class of private monuments. But, even under this supposition, there would be difficulties, inasmuch as the two known choregic inscriptions in which three victors are mentioned[11] seem best explained by the fact that the three are of one family, while in the present case there is nothing to indicate any relationship.[12] But, aside from the preceding, the fact

[4] *Travels in Asia Minor and Greece*, vol. II, p. 200.
[5] *C.I.G.*, 237. [6] *Antiquités Helléniques*, vol. II, 985.
[7] The inscription is repeated in the volume of the *C.I.A.*, II, which has just appeared, No. 1317, and ΔΙΝΙΑΣ is given on the authority of Lolling. KÖHLER remarks that, if confidence can be placed in Lolling's copy, the inscription cannot be earlier than the beginning of the second century b. c.; but I see nothing in it which would preclude the idea that it is as early even as the fourth century.
[8] *C.I.G.*, 4668: 5377, 7789 are fragments, and the exact form of the name is not certain.
[9] *C.I.A.*, II, 794, 811.
[10] See *Seventh Annual Report of Am. School at Athens*, pp. 87–8.
[11] DITT., *Syll.*, 422, and *Inser. No. 7 from Ikaria*, below, p. 87.
[12] REISCH, *De Musicis Graecorum Certaminibus*, takes this as a choregic inscription of a nature similar to that in Dittenberger referred to in last note, which he believes to relate to several different contests.

remains, that there is no mention whatever of the choregia in the inscription. What justification is there for holding that χορηγοῦντες or χορηγήσαντες was tacitly understood, as one is compelled to hold if he maintains that the monument is choregic? To be sure, from the size of the monument, it is not easy to believe that it was commemorative of any less important victory than that of the choregia, and if the presence of a tripod could be proved, as it can be in the case of another base the inscription upon which omits the χορηγῶν (*Ikarian Inser. No. 6*, below, p. 87), we should be justified in supplying χορηγοῦντες in the inscription. But the remains preserve nothing to show decisively that the monument was choregic; so, while not absolutely denying that the monument may have been choregic, it seems to me that this attribution should still be held in suspense.[13]

The base *B* (PLAN 1), measuring 2.615 by 1.66 m., is constructed of three marble blocks fitted closely together but not held by clamps. The surface is well finished, but the edge toward the base *C* is smoother, showing that another course of slabs covered the whole surface except at this edge. Close to this base, and at the same depth, was found the torso of an archaic seated statue; and it seems probable that this was the object which the base supported. The three blocks rest directly on the earth, without any substructure. The base *C* consists of a substructure of large roughly-hewn stones, and, above these, two marble blocks,

[13] [I cannot agree with Mr. Buck here. A careful review of all the evidence before us has led me to the belief that this monument could be choregic only, and I have so called it (*Report*, p. 54, etc.). The monument itself and the form of the inscription had already led RANGABÉ (*Antiq. Hellén.*, No. 985), MILCHHÖFER (*Berlin. philol. Wochenschrift*, June 18, 1887), REISCH (*Mus. Gr. Cert.*, p. 46) to this conclusion, though they did not have before them the results of our excavations, by which the decisive proof has been furnished. BÖCKH (*C. I. G.*, 237) and KÖHLER (*C. I. A.*, II, 1317) classed the inscription among those of agonistic or uncertain type. But its form is most closely allied to that of the Ikarian choregic Ergasos monument (see below, p. 87, *Inscription No. 7*), and that of Timosthenes (below, p. 80, DITTENBERGER, *Sylloge*, 422), which has recently been found by Milchhöfer to have been rural likewise, from the Mesogaia near Kalyvia (*Mittheilungen Inst. Athen.*, 1887, p. 281). The omission of χορηγοῦντες and of the designation of kinship are due, I think, to one and the same cause, the thought that these were immaterial in consideration of the position of the monument, and a desire not to cumber the architrave with too much detail, conspicuousness being preferred to exactness. The omission of χορηγῶν occurs in four inscriptions of *C. I. A.*, II (1248, 1283, 1285, 1286), where the employment of χορῷ renders the reference certain. More important is the Ikarian Archippos inscription (below, p. 87, *Inser. No. 6*) mentioned above, in which the omission is quite as striking as in the monument under consideration. (To this may

smooth on the top and sides and bolted together by two clamps shaped thus ⊢——⊣, the surface measuring 1.88 by 1.61 m. Two upright bolts indicate that another course rested upon the two blocks *in situ*, and a border, of which the surface is slightly smoother, enables us to give the dimensions of the second course as 1.54 by 1.27 m. The remains would be well adapted for an altar-base. A large marble altar was found in the front wall of the church, its dimensions being: height, 1.115 m.; sides, 0.87 and 0.665 m. Around the upper margin runs a moulding, and in the top there is a cutting 0.06 m. deep and 0.10 m. wide. Around the bottom edge, also, a moulding was carried, this being now entirely broken away. Estimating its thickness at 0.02, and adding twice this, 0.04, to the measurements of the altar, we get for the bearing surface 0.91 by 0.705 m. If we suppose this to have rested on the second course of the base last considered, we shall have left a margin of 0.32 by 0.28 m.; but, if this seems too wide, we may insert a third step having the dimensions of 1.22 by 0.985 m., thus giving two steps about 0.15 by 0.14 m. In the structure *D*, *ab* and *bc* are foundation-walls formed of large oblong blocks roughly hewn on the outer side, and lined on the inner side with small uncut stones. The average length of the blocks is a trifle over one meter; the thickness of the wall is 0.65 m. The width of the facing-blocks varies from 0.35 to 0.50 m. Of the wall *ad* only a portion of the substructure is left and one stone of the upper course, distant 1.77 m. from the corner *a*. In *cd*, there

be added as a parallel the omission to name the kind of chorus in three out of 22 inscriptions collected by Reisch; see below, p. 82.) This only reiterates a not uncommonly recurring fact, that the precinct itself was often regarded as sufficient indication of the purpose of a monument. The importance of the site of our excavations as a centre for dedications may be seen from the fact that 27 bases for this purpose were found. Of these, 8 were *in situ* and 5 were inscribed. All the latter related either to the drama or to its patron divinity. The only contest here of which our materials give any trace is that of the drama, and as the Hagnias monument is a local one, set in the midst of Dionysiac dedications, surely it would be dedicated to no god except to him before whose statue it probably stood. The question of a tripod is immaterial; indeed, according to Mr. Buck's argument, below, p. 88, the monument, if choregic, should have no tripod. The question whether one victory is intended, or more, and whether these victories were gained by father and sons or by each separately, is also immaterial. Certain it is, that there is victory, and there is dedication—undoubtedly to Dionysos. The monument is therefore choregic, and matches fitly with the record of Hagnias' two liturgies as trierarch of the State. And Hagnias is the only Ikarian of whom we have mention as displaying such liberality toward the State and toward his native deme.—A. C. M.]

is, besides the substructure, a course of the wall itself. This is of the peculiar double construction seen in all the walls here which are in any way finished. They are, as shown in *Fig. 4*, made up of stones cut evenly on the outside, but irregular on the inside, and, as an inner facing for these, of smaller stones cut evenly on the exposed side. The walls *g c*, which are of irregular polygonal stones, have no apparent connection with the building, and are probably older. Their upper surface is below that of the substructure-walls of the building. About 0.50 m. from the corner *d* and 1.25 m. below the wall *cd*, lies a sort of trough of schistous stone, the outside measurements of which are 1.32 by 0.80 m., the inside, 0.84 by 0.50 m. The depth of the hollow is 0.18 m. This trough or basin, evidently *in situ*, at such a depth must point to some very early occupation of the site. Exactly what was the

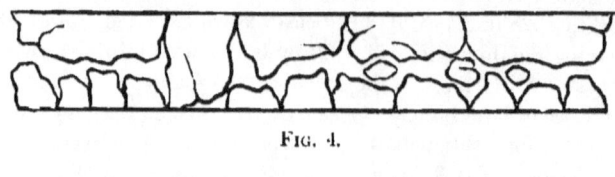

FIG. 4.

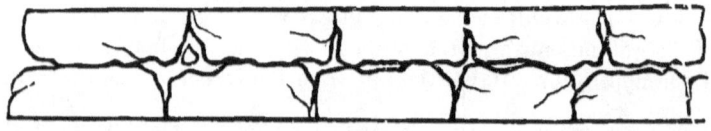

FIG. 5.

purpose of the structure *D*, I am unable to suggest. The wall *E*, 12.10 m. long, forms part of the peribolos-wall, which was in part made up by the walls of some of the buildings enclosed within the sacred precinct. This wall also is double, but the blocks are of large dimensions on both sides, as is shown in *Fig. 5*. *Fig. 6* gives a side view of the substructure and of the upper course, which now begins 4.03 m. from the corner *e*. The *Figure* shows the peculiar cutting upon the face of these stones, namely, in long nicks arranged alternately. The length of these nicks varies from 0.02 to 0.05 m. Along the whole length of this wall there extends on the outside, upon a level with the lower part of the substructure, a platform formed of irregularly shaped slabs. The greatest width of this platform is 2.28 m., but the average width is about 2 m.

ARCHITECTURAL REMAINS IN IKARIA.

The wall F, which terminates in a Byzantine grave, belongs to a late period, and is built of small stones. Upon it rested the column with the Ergasos inscription (No. 7). We turn now to the building H, which, as we know from an inscription on the door-sill, was the Pythion, or temple of the Delphian Apollo (PLATE VI). This building is on a much higher level than the remains heretofore mentioned, the difference in level between the base B and the threshold of the Pythion being 2.074 m. Though much of the north side[14] of the temple has disappeared, not even the substructure of the wall on this side being left,[15] the material for a restoration is ample. The anta b, in the front, is 1.35 m. from the corner

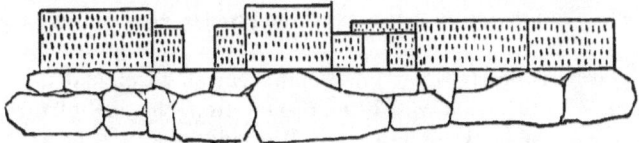

FIG. 6.—*Part of the wall of the Peribolos.*

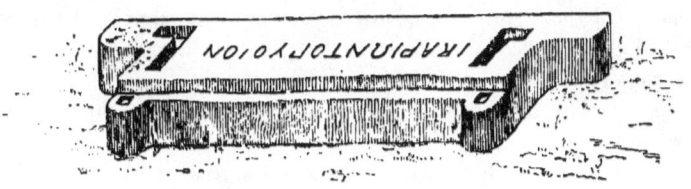

FIG. 7.—*The threshold of the Pythion.*

a. At the point e, the lower part of the opposite anta remains, broken off short; and, measuring 1.35 m. from this, we have the position of the corner d, of which the substructure is still extant. From the point h, on the line drawn at right angles to the corner as found, to g, the end of the threshold, is 2.95 m., while from the other end to the exterior face of the wall e is 3.73 m. This threshold, shown in *Fig. 7*, is of very careful workmanship, and compares favorably, for instance, with the threshold

---

[14] More properly northeast side, as the front does not face the east, but the south-east.

[15] This may be due in part to the fact that the water from the higher ground found an outlet by the north side, and had cut a channel several feet deep beside it, passing over the foundations of the building G.

which was unearthed by the excavations of the Athenian Archæological Society in the Peiraieus.[16] Upon the surface is the inscription ΙΚΑΡΙΩΝΤΟΓVΘΙΟΝ—'Ικαριῶν τὸ Πύθιον, the Pythion of the Ikarians.[17] The height of the letters varies from 0.06 to 0.07 m. They are of the fourth century; and, though the O and Θ of the last word are much worn, their outlines are still visible. It is very unusual for a Greek temple to be "labeled" in this way. At *i* and *k* are two upright slabs, 0.82 m. apart, probably holding up another slab, making a kind of table or altar; in front of these was found the relief with Apollo, Artemis, and an adorant. *l, m, n, o* and *p* are all bases for votive offerings, as in the pronaos of the Heraion at Olympia, and are apparently *in situ*. The internal dimensions of the pronaos are: width, 6.63 m.; depth, 1.83 m.

The cella is nearly square, its depth being 6.40 m. and its width 6.63 m. At the point *q*, 3.72 m. distant from the wall of the pronaos (measured in the interior), an insignificant wall, 2.55 m. long, projects toward the altar *r*, which is formed of four slabs of mica-schist overlapping each other at the ends, and filled in with small stones.[18] From the north side of the altar to the line of the north wall of the temple the distance is 2.78 m.; the altar, like the door, was thus not in the axis of the building, but was somewhat nearer to the south wall, while the door was considerably nearer to the north wall.

At *s* is a wall which separates the cella from a small chamber (ἄδυτον) in the rear, which had no entrance from the outside. At 2.00 m. from *s* a base (*t*) is inserted for some votive offering; *v* and *w* are two marble slabs similar in purpose to those (*i* and *k*) in the pronaos. The depth of the rear chamber is 1.36 m. The interior wall of the Pythion is double, and is built with small stones on each face.[19]

[16] *Cf.* Πρακτικά of 1886, p. 83 and πίναξ 2.
[17] *Cf.* MEISTERHANS, *Grammatik d. att. Inschriften*(2), § 55, 9, and Note 1019.
[18] [These were packed so firmly within the upright slabs that they have seemed to me to indicate a foundation especially prepared for a very heavy object, such as a large statue.—A. C. M.]
[19] [Dr. DÖRPFELD, who kindly visited the site with me, called my attention to a terracotta fragment among many, mainly roof-tiles, which I had saved from the earth-heap. This fragment showed that it was originally about a foot in diameter, formed like a pipe with a rim around the bottom. This was used, Dr. Dörpfeld said, for the purpose of admitting light through the roof into the garret above the ceiling, and was similar to contrivances found at Pompeii.—A. C. M.]

Abutting on the Pythion in the rear is the structure G, possibly intended for the priests. Of its wall ab the substructure is complete; of ac only scattered blocks of the substructure remain; of cy we have both substructure and some of the upper wall: cy was not built into xz, but terminated against it, yz forming a common party-wall for the two buildings.

I is a large base or platform made up of at least twenty marble slabs, of which fifteen are still in place. Here may have been the great altar of the deme-centre.[20]

At K there are two massive marble seats, one a double seat (arms broken) finished smooth on the right-hand side, and on the other side finished smooth only on the edges, evidently intended to fit to another seat. The other seat is single, and is so worked as to show that it was

FIG. 8.—*One of the double seats.*

fitted to others on both sides. The back of this seat is quite gone. The heavy slabs upon which the seats rest are *in situ*, although they have been much canted, and they show that the seats are in their original position. Another double seat, which was found near the church during the first week of the excavations, and is the best preserved, is shown in *Fig. 8* (see PLATE V). It has precisely the same measurements as the double seat at K, and is worked smooth on the left-hand side only. It is thus plain that this seat was carried from K, where it originally belonged, so that the series of five seats was

[20] [The axis of the threshold of the Pythion and of its altar or statue-base appears to intersect the centre of this platform. If we take the platform as the site of the chief altar, the unusual and unsymmetrical placing of the doorway of the Pythion may find a possible explanation in the desire to leave the line of vision unobstructed from the statue of Apollo to the great altar of the deme.—T. W. L.]

originally placed as shown on the plan.[21] The length of the base is 3.55 m., the combined length of the two double seats and one single one, 3.48 m. *L*, *M*, and *N* are rude walls of uncut stones. *O* is of the same construction, but, on account of its shape, is more interesting. The length of the straight portion *ab* is 10.60 m. At both ends, the walls *ac* and *bd* are carried out at approximately the same angle, each about two meters long. *e* and *f* are short foundation-walls intended to support the slab *g* of corresponding dimensions, which was found near them. I do not see how this wall could have formed part of any temple-building, nor does it appear to have anything to do with a peribolos. Can it be part of a rude structure for theatrical representations?[22] The slight eminence behind the marble seats would be an excellent sitting-place for an audience, commanding a view of the plain of Marathon and water beyond between Aphorismó and Argaliki on the left, and of the sea between the coast of Attika and Euboia directly in front. The wall *M* cannot be part of an original *choros*, or dancing-place, for various reasons. It is not a continuous curve; and, if it were, it would meet the hill behind the marble seats before becoming a circle. If it is taken as a wall of the orchestra, the seats for the priests come in a straight line across the centre of the orchestra. Such an arrangement is unheard of in any known Greek theatre. Still, the theatres in the rural demes must have been

DETAIL OF ORNAMENTS ON VASE

DETAIL OF CAP.

FIG. 9.

[21] [In a line with these seats toward *I* was another with a rounded back: total height, 0.95 m.; height of seat above ground, 0.38; width, 0.71; horizontal depth of chair outside, 0.57; depth of seat inside, 0.34; width of seat, 0.48. With these seats one may compare the four *in situ* at Rhamnous, described by Lolling, *Mittheilungen Inst. Athen.*, 1879, pp. 284–6. Others existed originally beside them. By their inscription, they were consecrated to Dionysos, and this has led Lolling to conjecture that they stood before a sanctuary of that deity. At Ikaria, I would suggest that their site was that of the deme agora, of which mention is made by inscriptions in other demes (*C. I. A.*, II, 571, 573). We sank a trench in front of these seats toward the wall *O* to a depth of 3 meters: only ordinary soil was found.—A. C. M.]

[22] [Or the λέσχη, as in the deme of Αἰξώνη, *C. I. G.*, 93?—A. C. M.]

rude affairs at best, and may often have differed very widely from generally received principles of construction.[23]

Besides the remains *in situ*, there are on the ground many architectural fragments, both structural and ornamental, including some good akroteria. Two drums of fluted poros columns were found. One was broken at one end; diameter of the other end 0.42 m. The second drum measured 0.41 m. in diameter at one end, 0.42 m. at the other. There are also some fine examples of Byzantine decorative ornament, which would be of interest to students of that art.

PLAN II shows the remains of importance found upon the second site where excavations were carried on. *AB* is a well-built wall, 13.65 m. in length. The lowest course, made up of well-finished blocks 0.40 m. high and averaging about 1.36 m. long, is still *in situ*, though some of the blocks have slipped toward the decline and are somewhat out of line. There are blocks forming a substructure under the east end, but the west end rests directly on the ground. Upon this foundation rested two courses of blocks set upright. One of these, 1.85 m. long and 0.38 m. high, is still in position. *CD* is a poor wall of unfinished slab-like stones, 17 m. long. In about the middle there is an opening, perhaps the entrance to the enclosure. *E* is a base of mica-schist blocks upon which stood the column that now lies stretched out on the ground over a space of ten meters.[24] This column consisted of seven unfluted drums secured together by iron bolts. The holes for these bolts are of peculiar and ingenious shape for securing firmly the lead by which they were fastened, when once run in and set. In the top of each lower drum there is a socket about 0.15 m. deep, 0.05 m. broad, and about 0.15 m. long at the top but narrowing down at one end for about half the depth and then widening again. A small channel for running in the lead communicated with the socket

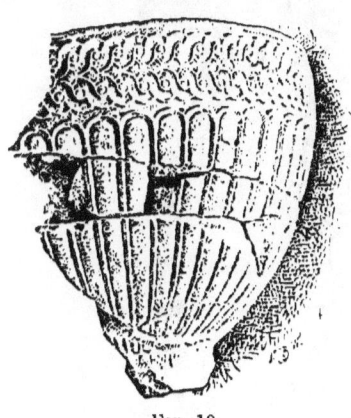

FIG. 10.

[23] Some of the walls mentioned may have been terrace walls.

[24] [*Cf*. PLUT., *Vit. Isocr.*: αὐτῷ δ᾿ Ἰσοκράτει ἐπὶ τοῦ μνήματος ἐπῆν κίων τριάκοντα πηχῶν, ἐφ᾿ οὗ Σειρὴν πηχῶν ἑπτά. This was near Kynosarges.—A. C. M.]

from the outer edge of the drum. The corresponding socket in the bottom of the upper drum is not so long, and is a plain cutting of the same section throughout. The uppermost drum is ornamented with a narrow moulding (*Fig. 9*) and has on the top a circular socket 0.55 m. in diameter and 0.03 deep. Lying exactly at the head of the column, as it lay on the ground, were found fragments of marble which make up a large vase-shaped object with a beautiful guilloche and fluted ornament

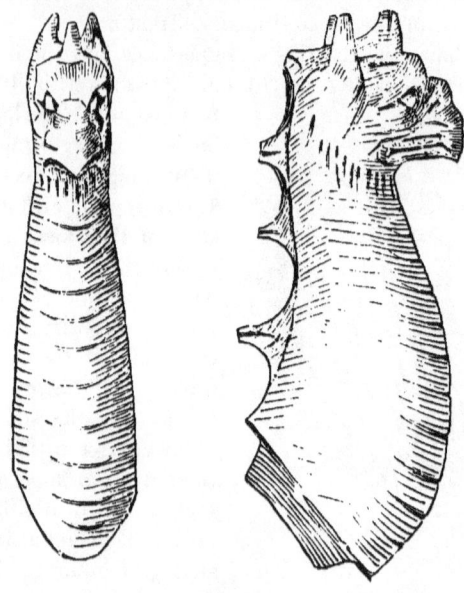

FIG. 11.

(*Fig. 10*). Close to this spot were also found two griffin-heads with a portion of the neck (*Fig. 11*); and a third head was found below the wall *AB*. The whole of the ground between the two walls *AB* and *CD* was thoroughly cleared, but nothing else was discovered. The few objects mentioned are accordingly the only materials from which to form a conjecture as to the occupation of the site. The enclosure lies exactly on the line of the ancient road leading through the valley to Ikaria. Two vases similar to ours are shown on a Panathenaic vase set up, apparently as votive offerings, on slender columns.[25] For the

---

[25] SALZMAN, *Camiros*, pl. 57: cf. *Jahrbuch Arch. Inst.*, II, p. 151.

decoration of such vessels with griffins' heads, we have not merely literary evidence, such as the krater dedicated by the Samians and described by Herodotos (IV. 152) as having heads of griffins ranged about it at intervals, but extant examples, as, for instance, two bronze kraters in the Vatican Museum, one with six griffins' heads turned inward, and another with five heads facing outward. Our griffins' heads are of a later type than those found at Olympia and the few specimens found in Athens on the Akropolis. Furtwängler[26] has made a careful classification of griffin types, which do not concern us now except in their relation to Greek art in general. The griffins found by Schliemann at Mykenai are closely akin to some Egyptian types of XVIII–XX dynasties, which again are borrowed from Syrian, probably Hittite, art. The first purely Greek type presents the eagle's head with wide-open mouth (in earlier types the mouth is always closed or only half-open), locks hanging down the neck, and large ears between which is a horn-like projection. In the later examples of this type, the projection becomes a mere conventional knob. This is the only type found at Olympia, and is also found in many other places, and shown on the oldest coinage. In the fifth century this type disappears. Its successor keeps the ears but removes the middle projection and the side locks, substituting a mane or comb running over the top of the head and the back of the neck. To this last class our griffin-heads belong, though they have the mouth closed, a still later variation.[27]

Athens,   CARL D. BUCK.
January, 1889.

[26] ROSCHER, *Lex. Myth.*, "*Gryps.*"

[27] [The enclosure was situated upon a small ridge running back toward Pentelikon from the ancient roadway, elevated some four or five meters above it, and sloping in all directions except behind. Graves existed on the opposite side of the road; but we found that these had already been opened. Many pieces of marble, some finely cut, lay about. The despoilers had also torn up the foundation of the column in search of treasure, and had dug underneath it. Two large blocks of schist were still in place, and part of a third extending between them. Upon these blocks there had undoubtedly been slabs of marble upon which the column immediately rested. One of these lay close by, a fragment only, and in it was the dowel hole for a clamp of this shape ⌐⌐. The vase which stood on the column was composed of several pieces, and within was roughly hollowed out somewhat. We succeeded in piecing together two sections only in height, and only one side of these, less than a half, though there were many other fragments. The two sections were of nearly equal height,

amounting together to 0.98 m. measured on a perpendicular; largest diameter, 1.33 m.; length of fluting, 0.72; width of flutes at bottom, 0.03 m., at top, 0.09 m.; width of guilloche, 0.21 m. Upon the top of the upper section something else rested. At intervals of 0.61 m. on the upper surface, just within the edge, were sockets about 0.08 m. wide, sloping inward about 0.05 m. to the depth of a centimeter. There were three of these on the portion built up, and no doubt the series was continued at equal intervals about the entire circumference. These sockets could not have been for the griffins' necks, as the tenon of one of the latter still exists, and is considerably longer than the sockets, and of a totally different shape. That the griffin-heads ornamented the upper part of the vase as a whole seems necessary, but, to admit of this, the vase must have had a third section, which, being lighter than the lower portions, was secured by means of the notches just described. This section, narrowing above, as is usual with sepulchral vases, would finally give a proper support for the three griffin *protomai*, serving a decorative purpose. The use of such heads in this way is said by Furtwängler to have ceased in the fifth and fourth centuries (*op. cit.*, p. 1771). It is at this period that I place the monument, for many reasons. Not only is this the epoch of the ⊢—⊣ bolt, but it does not seem to me possible that so exquisite an example of the double guilloche ornament (*Fig. 10*) could belong to a later time. Both in this ornament and in the flutings, the simplicity, purity and perfection of touch exhibit the highest art. The peculiar form of this guilloche is found in a severe type upon the gable ornamentation of the treasury of the Geloans at Olympia (*cf.* BAUMEISTER, *Denkmäler*, p. 1075), on terracottas of Sicily (W. ZAHN, *Ornamente klass. Kunst-Epoch.*, IV Heft, Taf. 16), and is employed by HITTORFF in his restoration of the interior decoration of Temple T at Selinous. The griffin with closed mouth appears on coins of Abdera in the first part of the fourth century, and especially on the gold medallion from Koul Oba representing the head of the Parthenon statue of Pheidias. This medallion cannot be later than 350 B. C. and is probably much earlier, and it is claimed by KIESERITZKY (*Mittheilung. Inst. Athen.*, 1883, p. 315) to represent the original most faithfully. Furthermore, all the buildings that we know in Ikaria show a uniformity in their mode of construction, even in slight details, which brings them closely within a restricted period. Earlier temples existed there during the fifth century, as appears from an inscription; and the necessity for rebuilding within the fourth century may be divined as one stands near the entrance of the valley and, casting his eyes across upon Dekeleia, observes how completely defenceless was Ikaria against the raids of the merciless Spartans and still more merciless Athenian exiles, in the Dekeleian war. And if I were to hazard one guess among many that might be made, as to the purpose of this unusual monument, it would be that it was erected as a cenotaph, after the return, in honor of the dead of that long reign of terror—Οὐs δὲ μὴ εὕρισκον κενοτάφιον αὐτοῖs ἐποίησαν μέγα. XEN., *Anab.*, VI. 4. 9.—A. C. M.]

DISCOVERIES IN THE ATTIC DEME OF IKARIA.
1888.

INSCRIPTIONS FROM IKARIA.

No. 1.

Public decree of the deme of Ikaria inscribed across the middle of a gable-top marble stele: total height, 0.765 met.; width at bottom, 0.32; width at top, 0.29; height of letters, 0.005.

```
ΚΑΛΛΙΠΠΟΣΕΙΠΕΝΕΨΗΦΙΣΟΑΙΙΚΑΡΙΕΥΣ
ΙΝΕΠΑΙΝΕΣΑΙΝΙΚ⌒ΝΑΤΟΝΔΗΜΑΡΧΟΝΚΑΙ
ΣΤΕΦΑΝ⌒ΣΑΙΚΙΤΤΟΣΤΕΓΑΝ⌒ΙΚΑΙΑΝΕΙΓ
ΕΙΝΤΟΝΚΗΡΥΚΑΟΤΙΣΤΕΦΑΝΟΥΣΙΝΙΚΑΡΙ
ΕΙΣΝΙΚ⌒ΝΑΚΑΙΟΔΗΜΟΣΟΙΚΑΡΙΕ⌒ΝΤΟΝΔ
ΗΜΑΡΧΟΝΟΤΙΚΑΛ⌒ΣΚΑΙΔΙΚΑΙ⌒ΣΤ⌒ΙΔΙΟ
ΝΥΣ⌒ΙΤΗΝΕΟΡΤΗΝΕΠΟΙΗΣΕΝΚΑΙΤΟΝΑΓ⌒
ΝΑΕΠΑΙΝΕΣΑΙΔΕΚΑΙΤΟΥΣΧΟΡΗΓΟΣΕΠΙΚ
ΡΑΤΗΝΚΑΙΠΡΑΞΙΑΝΚΑΙΣΤΕΦΑΝ⌒ΣΑΙΚΙΤ
ΤΟΣΤΕΦΑΝ⌒ΙΚΑΙΑΝΕΙΠΕΙΝΚΑΘΑΠΕΡΤΟΝ
ΔΗΜΑΡΧΟΝ
```

Κάλλιππος εἶπεν· ἐψηφίσθαι Ἰκαριεῦσ|ιν· ἐπαινέσαι Νίκωνα τὸν δήμαρχον καὶ | στεφανῶσαι κιττῷ στεφάνῳ καὶ ἀνειπ|εῖν τὸν κήρυκα ὅτι στεφανοῦσιν Ἰκαρι|εῖς Νίκωνα καὶ ὁ δῆμος ὁ Ἰκαριέων τὸν δ|ήμαρχον ὅτι καλῶς καὶ δικαίως τῷ Διο|νύσῳ τὴν ἑορτὴν ἐποίησεν καὶ τὸν ἀγῶ|να, ἐπαινέσαι δὲ καὶ τοὺς χορηγοὺς Ἐπικ|ράτην καὶ Πραξίαν καὶ στεφανῶσαι κιτ|τῷ στεφάνῳ καὶ ἀνειπεῖν καθάπερ τὸν | δήμαρχον.

Translation.—"On motion of Kallippos, it was voted by the Ikarians to praise Nikon the demarch and crown him with an ivy wreath, and that the herald proclaim that the Ikarians and the Deme of the Ikarians crown Nikon the demarch because he has conducted the festival and contest in honor of Dionysos in a good and proper manner; to praise also the choregoi Epikrates and Praxias and crown them with wreaths of ivy, and that the herald make proclamation as in the case of the demarch."

Comment.—Like all Attic deme-decrees, with two exceptions (*C. I. A.*, II, 579, 580), this lacks the date by the archon's name, and there is no

71

internal evidence whatever upon which to fix the date. The letters, which are very roughly cut, but with στοιχηδόν arrangement, may be attributed to the fourth century; and, if we take as a criterion the uncertainty in the use of o or ov to express the spurious diphthong, the date of the inscription is not far from 360 B. C.* (*Cf. C. I. A.*, II, 54, where, out of twenty cases of spurious diphthong, eleven are expressed by simple o, against nine denoted by ov, as, for example, τός and τούς, προέδρος and προέδρους. The content of the inscription is very simple, being a decree in honor of the demarch of Ikaria and the choregoi for the proper fulfilment of their duties at the festival to Dionysos, which undoubtedly refers to the Rural Dionysia celebrated in the month Poseideon. The chief importance of this inscription when found was that it fixed, beyond all possible doubt, the site of the deme of Ikaria; and, though proofs have multiplied since then, it remains the most perfect and complete of all, for this purpose. It is worth noting, that this is the first Attic deme-decree found in which the demarch is expressly honored, though such can have been by no means unusual (*cf.* Dem. 1318. 64). Another of the Ikarian inscriptions, which will be found below, is also in honor of the demarch.

A point of special interest and importance is the mention, in lines 4 and 5, of the *Ikarians* and the *Deme of the Ikarians* as distinct bodies, though, in the first line, Ἰκαριεῦσιν is used in the general sense of demesmen of Ikaria. It seems highly probable that the *Ikarians* were a gens or noble family, within the deme, which claimed descent from Ikarios, and consequently was treated with special honor and possessed peculiar privileges. A more detailed discussion of this point will be deferred until we come to treat of two pre-Eukleidean inscriptions which contain many points bearing on the question.

Boundary-Stones.—One of the most numerous classes of short inscriptions found on Greek soil is that by which boundaries are denoted. Such inscriptions are occasionally cut in the solid rock, as ὅρος Διός on the *Observatory Hill* at Athens, but generally upon a movable stone which can be set up in the soil. These stones, sometimes of cylindrical form but more often roughly cut slabs or blocks, are set up on sacred precincts, as ὅρος τεμένο(υ)ς (*C. I. A.*, I, 508); on burial-lots, as ὅρος σήματος Ὀνησίμου (*C. I. G.*, 535); on roads, as ὅρος ὁδοῦ (*C. I. A.*, I, 527); and on private property, as ὅρος χωρίου Πρωτάρχου (*C. I. A.*, II, 1068); *etc.* These boundary-stones were probably in many cases the only records of the ownership of real estate, and, if

---

* See below, pp. 107-8.

such property were transferred, the "bill of sale" would be a new boundary-stone replacing the old one and inscribed with the names of vendor and purchaser and the conditions of the sale. The great importance of the boundary-stones in any legal transaction is brought out by the Attic Orators, as in *Demosth. vs. Phainippos*, 1040. 5:

καὶ πρῶτον μὲν περιαγαγὼν τὴν ἐσχατιὰν, πλέον ἢ σταδίων οὖσαν τετταράκοντα, κύκλῳ ἔδειξα καὶ διεμαρτυράμην ἐναντίον Φαινίππου, ὅτι οὐδεὶς ὅρος ἔπεστιν ἐπὶ τῇ ἐσχατιᾷ. εἰ δέ φησιν, εἰπεῖν ἐκέλευον αὐτὸν ἤδη καὶ δεῖξαι, ὅπως μὴ ὕστερον ἐνταῦθα χρέος γενόμενον ἀναφανήσοιτο ἐπὶ τῷ χωρίῳ.

To proceed, then, to the inscriptions of this class found at Ikaria.

No. 2.

Slab of greyish stone: height, 0.52 met.; width, 0.23; height of letters, 0.017.

O POΣXΩ P IΩNEN ὅρος χωρίων ἐν
A NOPE I ΩI K A IKH Ἀνθρείῳ καὶ κή-
ΠΩNKA I O I K I AΣΠE πων καὶ οἰκίας πε-
Π PAMENΩN E Π I ΛY πραμένων ἐπὶ λύ-
ΣE I Λ / Σ I Σ T PATΩI σει Λ[υ]σ[ι]στράτῳ
KEΦΑΛHΘEN Κεφαλῆθεν.

Translation.—" Boundary of lands in Anthreion and gardens and house sold, upon condition of equity of redemption, to Lysistratos of Kephale."

Comment.—The form of the letters indicates that the inscription should be referred to the fourth century B. C.

Ἀνθρείῳ: This is a name hitherto unknown, and it probably belongs to some locality included within the limits of the deme of Ikaria. It seems quite natural that the rural demes, like our own townships, should contain, besides the principal village or deme seat, a number of small hamlets, the names of which, while familiar to the members of the deme, would be little heard beyond the limits of its territory. Our excavations took place on the site which was undoubtedly the centre of population and the seat of the municipal government. This particular stone, however, was not found *in situ*, but had been brought from elsewhere.

The position of the deme of Kephale, mentioned in the last line, has never been exactly determined, but it lay somewhere in the Mesogaia, probably between Markopoulo and Keratea (*Mittheilungen*, 1887, p. 288).

πεπραμένων ἐπὶ λύσει: This technical legal phrase means that the vendor retains the increase of the property, and has the right to repurchase at the same price at which he sold it. On the other hand, he pays a rent (μίσθωμα or μίσθωσις) equal in amount to the interest on the money which he received for the property. Thus the whole transaction is practically equivalent to a mortgage loan, with this difference, that in the latter case the party who receives the loan remains (so long as he pays the interest and no foreclosure takes place), both practically and legally, the proprietor, while under the Greek law ἐπὶ λύσει the proprietorship was legally vested in the party who gave the loan (as in early English law), although possession remained with the original owner. There was a legal transfer of property, and technically, instead of interest being paid on the loan, rent was paid on the land.[1] To illustrate from our inscription: X. (name of vendor not given) desires to borrow money from Lysistratos, and, instead of giving him security in the shape of a mortgage on his lands and gardens and house and paying interest on the loan, he actually sells this property to Lysistratos, and then rents it of him at a rate equivalent to the interest on the amount which Lysistratos has paid him for it. If he should be sufficiently prosperous, he would be able by the terms of the sale to buy back the property at the same price which he received for it.

Compared to the mortgage system, this process seems complicated, and the difficulties which might arise from it are shown in the oration of Demosthenes referred to in the last note. Pantainetos borrows money from Mnesikles to buy certain mining works, but by way of security Mnesikles is considered the legal purchaser, and holds the records of the sale (τὰς ὠνὰς), whatever may have been their form. But Mnesikles afterwards demands his money, and, to pay him, Pantainetos is obliged to find new loaners, who purchase the property from Mnesikles and then rent it to Pantainetos at a rate equivalent to the 12 % interest on the amount they had paid for it: καὶ τούτοις ὑποθήκην δίδωσι τὸ ἐργαστήριον, καὶ τὰ ἀνδράποδα. γραμματεῖον δὲ, οὐχ ὑποθήκης, ἀλλὰ πράσεως γράφεται. The last sentence is rendered by Paley and Sandys:[2] "And thus the indenture is not a mortgage, but an actual conveyance." One of the several difficulties in the understanding of this oration arises from the fact that, while Pantainetos is practically owner and manager of the mining property, the ownership

[1] Dem., *Pantain.*: ὑπόθεσις: καὶ ἦν τοῦτο τῷ μὲν ἔργῳ τόκος, τῷ δὲ ὀνόματι μίσθωσις.
[2] *Select Private Orations of Demosthenes*, part I, p. 85.

has never been legally vested in him, but has been continually transferred from one party to another. The process of genuine mortgaging, however, existed alongside the one just described, and we even have boundary-stones inscribed in this fashion, as ὅρος χωρίου τιμῆς ἐνοφειλομένης Φανοστράτῳ Παιαν(ιεῖ)ΧΧ (*C. I. A.*, II, 2, 1134).

No. 3.

Fragment of thin marble slab: height, 0.21 m.; width, 0.22; height of letters varies from 0.02 to 0.035.

```
OΣXΛPIO           ὅρ]ος χωρίο
OIKIAΣ            καὶ] οἰκίας
ᐵAMENΛN           πεπ]ραμένων
/ΣEI:XΡ           ἐπὶ λ]ύσει · ΧΡ
ΞIAI              Πραξ(?)]ίᾳ
```

Translation.—"Boundary of land and house sold upon condition of equity of redemption for 1500 drachmas."

Comment.—The letters of the inscription may be assigned to the fourth century, and I feel confident that the O at the end of the first line stands alone for the spurious diphthong, though, owing to the fact that the stone is broken at this point, it is impossible to be certain that a Υ was not inscribed. The content of this inscription is identical with that of No. 2, except that in this case the amount involved is expressly stated. In the last line the marks before the *iota* may well belong to Σ, and we may conjecture that the person to whom the property was sold was the Praxias mentioned in No. 1 as one of the choregoi. This, however, must not be considered as more than a mere possibility, as the traces before the *iota* might equally well belong to E.

No. 4.

Block of roughly-cut greyish stone, broken on both sides and at the bottom: height, 0.175 m.; width, 0.31; height of letters, 0.02. It has been published by Milchhöfer,[3] who saw it in the wall of the Byzantine church the demolition of which was an important part of the work at Ikaria. By its removal from the wall a few additional letters have become visible, although, by reason of the roughness of the stone and

[3] *Mittheilungen, Athen.*, XII, p. 311.

carelessness of cutting, the reading of any part whatever is exceedingly difficult.

```
    ΟΣΧ⌒ ⏋              ὅρ]ος χωρ[ίου
  ΑΙΟΙΚ ΙΑΣΑΓΟΤ......    κ]αὶ οἰκίας ἀποτ[ίμη-
  ΓΡΟΙΚΟΣ   Ρ⌒          μα] προικός
  ΚΕΙΚ ΛΕΙΣ
  ⊃∧Ι'⌒  Ο
   Ο
```

Translation.—" Boundary of the land and house, security for the dowry," etc.

Comment.—Divorce seems to have been, among the Greeks, an all-too-common occurrence; and it was partially with the idea of giving greater stability to the union, by bringing financial interests to bear upon the question, that a dowry was bestowed upon the bride. The husband had the interest of this dowry to use as he pleased, but, if for any reason separation took place, he was obliged to restore the principal; and on this account it was customary, when the dowry was handed over to him, to require security for it on his own property.[4] To the numerous class of inscriptions recording such a mortgage belongs the one just given, which is of the fourth century B. C.

That ἀποτίμημα is not necessarily restricted to the security given by the husband, but may also be used for the security given by the bride's father for dowry not yet paid over, has been shown by Dareste,[5] whose interpretation of the inscription in relation to the dowry of Xenariste seems plainer than that of Köhler. Instead of the simple gen. προικός, we find ἐν προικί,[6] προικί,[7] εἰς τὴν προῖκα.[8]

Cambridge, England,　　　　　　　　　　　　CARL D. BUCK.
　　Oct. 23, 1888.

---

[4] *Cf.* HERMANN, *Lehrbuch der griech. Antiq.*, vol. IV, p. 264 ff.
[5] *Bulletin de Correspondance Hellénique*, II, p. 485: *cf.* XII, p. 304.
[6] DITT., *Syll.*, 434.　　　[7] *Ephemeris*, Nov., 1876.　　　[8] DITT., *Syll.*, 437.

DISCOVERIES IN THE ATTIC DEME OF IKARIA, 1888.

THE CHOREGIA IN ATHENS AND AT IKARIA.*

It is hoped that the following inscriptions will throw new light on the choregia of Attic rural demes, a subject upon which we have very little accurate information. In order to call to mind the various questions which must be proposed in examining the choregia in a country deme, it will be useful to make a summary survey of the various stages through which the choregic management passed in Athens.[1]

It is usually stated, that for all the great festivals, such as the Greater Dionysia, the Thargelia, and the Panathenaia, each tribe, by the medium of its ἐπιμεληταί, appointed one of its wealthier members to act as its representative choregos. The duties of a choregos were to supply and suitably equip a chorus at his own expense and to provide for its instruction by appointing a χοροδιδάσκαλος, whose title was commonly shortened to διδάσκαλος, who should have charge of the training of the chorus. This trainer was originally the poet himself, and for this reason Aristophanes (*Acharnians*, 628), referring to himself, uses the word διδάσκαλος in precisely this sense. The time of the festival was the occasion for judging the comparative merits of the choruses and for awarding a prize to the choregos who presented the best-trained chorus. The prize was not the same for all festivals, but, for the Great Dionysia and the Thargelia, consisted of a bronze tripod which the victor was expected to dedicate in a conspicuous position, frequently building for it an elaborate structure such as the monument of Lysikrates.

In the course of this paper, it is proposed to submit some of the

---

* Professor Tarbell, the Annual Director of the School, has been kind enough to look over this article, and I am indebted to him for several suggestions.

[1] See article *Choregia* in the standard Dictionaries of Antiquities; BOECKH, *Die Staatshaushaltung der Athener*,(3) p. 539 ff.; MÜLLER, *Lehrbuch der griechischen Bühnenalterthümer*, p. 330 ff.; and, especially for the distinction between the various classes of inscriptions, KOEHLER, *Mittheilungen d. d. archäol. Institutes*, 1878; REISCH, *De musicis Graecorum certaminibus;* BRINCK, *Inscriptiones Graecae ad choregiam pertinentes.*

foregoing statements to a more exact examination, in the light of the evidence now at hand.

The circumstances of the victory gained by the chorus are habitually recorded in an inscription, and the change which takes place, at different periods, in the phraseology of these inscriptions is very important as indicating corresponding changes in the management of the choregia itself. Koehler, who has made a careful study of choregic inscriptions, held that, while in the fifth century the tribe was accounted victor,[2] in the fourth century the choregos had become more eager for personal credit and was himself named as victor for the tribe.[3] But such a distinction cannot be maintained; since, in the fourth century, the tribe is accounted victor in two-thirds of the inscriptions in which both tribe and choregos are mentioned.

The inscription given in Note 3 is one of several which show that in the fourth century it was not uncommon to allow two tribes to combine and appoint the same man as choregos. Dittenberger, in a note to this inscription, observes that, whenever separate tribes furnish choruses, the tribe is named as victor, but, when two tribes combine, it is the choregos who is accounted victor; and he interprets this as an indication that the attribution of the choregos as victor arose from the dislike of the Greeks to name several victors in the same contest.

Reisch, noting the fact that, in nearly every case in which two tribes unite in one choregia, the chorus is of boys, deduces a general rule, and, in the single inscription in which the nature of the chorus is not stated (*De Mus.*, p. 31, III), claims that παίδων is to be understood. These generalizations of Dittenberger and Reisch, however, rest on what may be mere coincidences. In fact, the inscription on the Thrasyllos monument,[4] in which a choregos for a single tribe is named as victor, is against Dittenberger's theory, though he seeks to evade the force of it, because this inscription has in general the phraseology of a private dedication. The same holds true of the inscription on the Nikias monument.[5] Another inscription, ... ο Περιθοίδης χορηγῶν ἐνίκα | . . . . . ἰδι

---

[2] *Cf.* C. I. A., I, 336: Οἰνεὶς | ἐνίκα | παίδον | Εὐρυμένε[s] | Μελετεῶνος | ἐχορέγε | Νικόστρατος | ἐδίδασκε |.

[3] *Cf.* DITTENBERGER, *Sylloge Inscriptionum Graecarum*, 411: Αἴσιος Μνησιβούλο Σφήττιος | χορηγῶν ἐνίκα 'Ακαμαντίδι | Πανδιονίδι παίδων, Εὐκλῆς | ἐδίδασκε, Εὐδαμίσκος ηὔλε, | Χίων ἦρχεν.

[4] C. I. G., 224 = DITT., 423.

[5] KOEHLER, *Mitth.*, 1885, p. 231.

ἀνδρῶν, Φιλόφρων Φιλοκράτος [ἐδίδασκεν, | Οἰ]νιάδης Προνόμο ηὔλε, Διετρέφης ἦρχεν⁶—affords absolute proof that either one or the other of the generalizations is unsound. If at the beginning of the second line the name of only one tribe is supplied, we have an instance of a choregos for a single tribe being named as victor, and Dittenberger's theory falls to the ground. If, on the other hand, the names of two tribes are supplied, we have a case where two tribes unite to supply a chorus of men, not of boys, and Reisch's generalization no longer holds good.

Brinck maintains that, whenever there is a union of two tribes, it is for the festival of the Thargelia, and quotes, in support of this, the statement of Ulpian : ἐν τοῖς Θαργηλίοις δυοῖν φυλαῖν εἶς μόνος καθίστατο χορηγός, τοῖς δὲ μεγάλοις Διονυσίοις εἶς χορηγὸς ἑκάστης φυλῆς.⁷ This theory is thought by some to be disproved by the fact that one of the inscriptions making mention of two tribes was found on the southern slope of the Akropolis; but it is not impossible to hold that it was moved thither from elsewhere. Indeed, three bases, each with a choregic inscription referring to two tribes, have actually been found on the site of the Pythion, where Thargelian dedications were made.

A general classification of choregic inscriptions is attempted by Reisch, founded on the mention or non-mention of the flute-player, and, in case of such a mention, on the position of his name with reference to that of the *didaskalos*. Reisch states that in the fifth century the didaskalos alone appears; the reason for this being that at that period the poet and musician were one and the same person, that is, that the poet, like Pindar, composed his own music. In the fourth century, the flute-player is always mentioned—in the first half of the century after the didaskalos, in the second half, before the didaskalos, as the art of music gradually developed, and emancipated itself from its subjection to poetry.

It was Koehler who first clearly pointed out the radical change in the management of the choregia which was brought about in the last part of the fourth century. The system under which each tribe appointed a choregos was abolished, and the people collectively became the nominal choregos, but appointed, probably from the wealthier citizens, an officer called *agonothetes*, who superintended the preparation of all the

---

⁶ Reisch, p. 32, v: Rangabé, *Antiquités Helléniques*, 972.
⁷ Ulpian ad *Demosthenem, Lept.,* 28.

choruses.⁸ Even in this period a tribe was mentioned as victor, but it is not clear what was now the exact relation of the separate tribes to the choregia.

There remain a few choregic inscriptions differing from those which have been mentioned both in their phraseology and in their purpose. Perhaps the best example of these is the following: Τιμο]σθένης Μειξωνίδο|ΜειξωνίδηςΤιμοσθένος Κλεόστρατος Τιμοσθένος |[χ]ορηγοῦντες νικήσαντες ἀνέθεσα[ν] | [τ]ῶι Διονύσωι τἄγαλμα καὶ τὸμ [βωμόν].⁹ Here we observe that the word ἀνέθεσαν is used, whereas in the inscriptions referred to above the fact of the dedication is never expressly stated, the principal verb being always a form of νικῶ or χορηγῶ. The inscription also tells us that the objects dedicated were a statue and an altar, not a tripod. There are a few other inscriptions in which ἀνέθηκε is used, one belonging to the epoch before Eukleides, cut in the channels of a column. Owing to these facts, a classification has been adopted by scholars (Kirchhoff, Koehler, Dittenberger, Reisch) into *official* and *private* monuments. That is, a victor would, in his official capacity as a representative of his tribe, dedicate the tripod which he had obtained as a prize, with an inscription in the usual set phraseology; but as a private person he might also dedicate a thank-offering for his victory, the nature of which would be entirely a matter of his personal choice, and the inscription upon which would not follow a fixed phraseology, but would be a statement of dedication (ἀνέθηκε), with the optional mention of some of the circumstances connected with the choregia. The characteristics upon which this classification is founded are, then, an inscription of fixed phraseology in which ἀνέθηκε is not used, cut upon a monument intended to support a tripod; as opposed to an inscription in which ἀνέθηκε is expressed, cut upon a monument intended for the support of something other than a tripod; though it is not inconceivable that a choregos might, in his private capacity, choose to dedicate a tripod, which, however, could not be the one given him as the official prize. For this classification to be an absolute one, it must be capable of including in one class or the other every choregic inscription. An inscription with ἀνέθηκε upon a monument holding a tripod and plainly intended as a public and official dedication, or an inscription without ἀνέθηκε upon a monument intended for something other than a tripod, would be an anomaly.

⁸ *Cf.* Ditt., 418: ὁ δῆμος ἐχορήγει, Σωσίστρατος ἦρχε, |[ἀγω]νοθέτης Θεοφάνης Διοσκουρίδου Εὐωνυμεύς, |Ἐρεχθεῖς ἀνδρῶν ἐνίκα, |Σωκράτης Ῥόδιος ηὔλει, Ἐράτων Ἀρκὰς ἐδίδασκεν.
⁹ Koehler, *Mitth.*, 1878, p. 229; Ditt., 422.

Of the stones upon which inscriptions occur that do not have ἀνέθηκε, some have cuttings which show that they surely held tripods; some were found in such positions as make it extremely probable that they held tripods; some are upon architraves which may very well have belonged to large choregic monuments; but, as to many, especially those found at the beginning of this century, it is impossible to find any evidence upon which to base a conclusion as to what they may have supported. The important fact is, however, that there is no monument bearing an inscription of this class, of which there is any evidence that it held anything else than a tripod. On the other hand, we do find an anomaly in the inscriptions on the architraves of two choregic monuments, those of Thrasyllos and Nikias (*cf.* Notes 4 and 5). Both these inscriptions have the phraseology which should belong to monuments of the private class, but it is plain from their form and position that they are in fact monuments publicly and officially dedicated, as much as the famous one of Lysikrates. In publishing the Thrasyllos inscription, Dittenberger notes this fact, and accounts for it on the ground that at this date, just before the institution of the choregia of the people and the *agonothesia*, the distinction between the two classes of monuments was less strictly observed than before. Koehler,[10] in treating of the Nikias monument, which was erected in the same year as that of Thrasyllos (one being for a chorus of boys, the other for a chorus of men), claims that the pretentious character of the monuments and the unusual form of the inscriptions are alike to be accounted for by the unusual circumstances attending the celebration of the festival of this year (319 B. C.).

In the usual statement of the appointment of the choregos given above, it will be observed that no account is taken of any difference in the management of the choregia dependent on variations in the form of chorus furnished. We know that there were purely lyric choruses of men and of boys, and dramatic choruses for tragedy and for comedy; but, as the mention of choregia in literature, especially in connection with *antidosis*, naturally gives the notion of a fixed and invariable institution, it is usual to group the various classes of choregoi under one general statement, considering that all were appointed in the same manner, received the same prizes, and were, in short, identical in every way, except that their duties in preparing the chorus would of course differ according to the particular nature of the chorus. This is

[10] *Mittheilungen*, 1885, p. 234.

the view taken in the various dictionaries of antiquities, and accepted by all the authorities which are referred to at the beginning of this paper, with the exception of the last two, who depart more or less from it. It is observed by Reisch, that none of the inscriptions having the usual phraseology of monuments of the official class contains any reference to a dramatic chorus. Out of twenty-six such inscriptions or fragments collected by him, nineteen distinctly mention the kind of chorus, and it is always lyric, of either men or boys; of the remaining seven, three are complete and do not state the nature of the chorus, and four are broken, so that, if the chorus was mentioned, it is no longer possible to know its nature. There are, however, a few choregic inscriptions plainly referring to a dramatic chorus, one being of the private class and referring to a comic chorus ($\kappa\omega\mu\wp\delta o\hat{\iota}s$ being used), and two, published by Koehler,[11] which are important enough to be given in full.

Μνησίστρατος Μίσγωνος   Μνησίμαχος Μνησιστράτο
Διοπείθης Διοδώρο ἐχορήγον   Θεότιμος Διοτίμο ἐχορήγον
Δικαιογένης ἐδίδασκεν.   Ἀρίφρων ἐδίδασκε,
                                       Πολυχάρης Κώμωνος ἐ[δί]δασκεν.

The Dikaiogenes mentioned in the last line of the first is held to be identical with the tragic poet who flourished in the beginning of the fourth century. The *first* peculiarity to be observed in these two inscriptions is the fact that two persons are named together as choregoi. A passage in the Scholia to Aristophanes' *Frogs*, 406,[12] informs us that, in the archonship of Kallias (406 B. C.), it became customary for two persons to act together as choregoi for the tragic and comic choruses at the Dionysia. This passage is the authority for the statement, frequently made (as in Boeckh, *Staatsh.*,[(3)] I, p. 538), that synchoregia was one of the stages of the general system of choregia; but the words of Aristotle quoted by the Scholiast, which limit it to the dramatic chorus, are supported by the fact that it is not mentioned in any of the inscriptions relating to the lyric chorus, while in the two inscriptions just given, referring to the drama, it is found in use. However, the law under Kallias embodied only a permission for two choregoi to bear the expense of the chorus in common, not a command, as is proved by Lysias, XXI. 4, Demosthenes, *Meid.* 59 and 156 (*cf. C. I. A.*, II, 1275), where the choregos serves alone, though all three cases fall later than the

---

[11] *Hermes*, II, p. 23; *cf.* Reisch, p. 44.
[12] ἐπὶ γοῦν τοῦ Καλλίου τούτου φησὶν Ἀριστοτέλης ὅτι σύνδυο ἔδοξε χορηγεῖν τὰ Διονύσια τοῖς τραγῳδοῖς καὶ κωμῳδοῖς.

archonship of Kallias. In this respect, a precedent had already been established as early as 411–10 B. C., when two trierarchs are found serving together (Lysias, XXXII. 24); but instances occur later of the individual trierarchy (Boeckh, *Staatsh.*,[3] I, p. 638).

The *second* point to be observed in connection with the two inscriptions given above is the fact that there is no evidence that the stone upon which they are inscribed ever bore a tripod. On the other hand, there is, so far as I know, no positive evidence that it did not; and as this is an inscription with the official phraseology, if we feel compelled to believe that all choregoi received the same prize, we must believe also that this stone held a tripod. Now Plutarch (*Them.*, 5) states that Themistokles gained a victory as choregos for a *tragic* chorus, and set up a πίναξ of victory with the inscription, Θεμιστοκλῆς Φρεάρριος ἐχορήγει, Φρύνιχος ἐδίδασκε, Ἀδείμαντος ἦρχεν. But πίναξ is an extraordinary word to use, if it was literally a tripod which Themistokles set up.[13] The inscription given in the text is probably a copy of a genuine inscription (the manuscripts, of course, retain no sign of the pre-Eukleidean alphabet), since an inscription on a choregic monument dedicated by a certain Aristeides and quoted by Plutarch (*Aristeid.* 1) has actually been found, and it agrees word for word with the text. We learn also, from Plutarch's remarks on this inscription, that it was customary even in his time to pay very careful attention to both the phraseology and the palaeography of an inscription, using these as criteria for dating them, just as is the practice now. Accepting it, then, as a genuine inscription, we observe that it presents the same phraseology as the two given above, except that here the archon's name is added for the purpose of dating it. As it belongs to the period before the archonship of Kallias, one choregos only is mentioned. Here, then, are three inscriptions set up by dramatic choregoi, as to two of which there is no evidence that they were on a monument supporting a tripod, while, as to the third, it seems certain that the object dedicated was not a tripod. Is there anything in literature to show that dramatic choregoi received tripods as prizes? Theophrastos characterizes a mean man as one who, when he had gained a victory with a tragic chorus, would dedicate a wooden taenia to Dionysos and put his name upon it.[14] This seems to imply that it was optional with a tragic

---

[13] [It may have been a relief representing a tripod, in marble or in bronze. *Cf. C. I. A.*, II, 766, 835, 680, 688 c; LOEWY, *Inschriften gr. Bildhauer*, No. 533; ARISTOT., *Pol.*, viii. 6 (1341 a).—T. W. L.]

[14] [οἷος νικήσας τραγῳδοῖς ταινίαν ξυλίνην ἀναθεῖναι τῷ Διονύσῳ. *Character.* 22. This

choregos what kind of a thank-offering he should make. But those choregoi who received a tripod as a prize were certainly expected to dedicate this, though there is no record that such dedication was required by an actual law. The speaker in Lysias, *Orat.* XXI. 4,[15] after a victory with a comic chorus, dedicates apparently the costumes and other properties used in the play, though the exact sense in which he uses σκευῆς may be doubtful. Among all the references to choregic tripods which I have been able to find (the twelve given by Brinck, p. 12, and three additional ones), there is not one as to which it can be affirmed that the chorus was dramatic. In nine instances the chorus is expressly described as lyric, and in the other six cases there is nothing to define the kind of chorus referred to. The force of these facts has been admitted by Bergk,[16] and is strongly put by Brinck in the dissertation referred to above. Lolling also, in speaking of the Street of the Tripods, says[17] that it is named from the small temple-like structures, *welche zum Andenken an die mit lyrischen Chören davongetragenen Siege errichtet worden.*

To return to the two inscriptions under discussion; we observe a *third* peculiarity, namely, that no mention is made of the tribe, the same thing holding true of the inscription quoted by Plutarch. Also in two fragments[18] belonging to a list of the choregic victors, both musical and dramatic, it is to be noted that in the case of lyric choruses the name of the choregos is preceded by the name of the tribe, while, in the case of tragic and comic choruses, there is no mention of the tribe. This seems very peculiar if the dramatic choregos was appointed by his tribe in the same manner as the others. But does the common statement, that the choregos was appointed by his tribe, necessarily imply that *every* choregos was so appointed? Let us briefly review the authorities for the tribal appointment of the choregos. Two of these[19] are mere casual statements, and give no evidence as to the kind of chorus referred to. The passage of Ulpian (quoted above, Note 7) seems, to be sure, to speak in a general way of the tribal appointment of the choregos.

---

is probably the victor's taenia (ARISTOPH., *Ran.*, 393), represented in relief or otherwise, and would form part of the σκευή mentioned by LYSIAS, xxi. 4.—A. C. M.]

[15] ἐπὶ δὲ Εὐκλείδου ἄρχοντος κωμῳδοῖς χορηγῶν Κηφισοδώρῳ ἐνίκων, καὶ ἀνήλωσα σὺν τῇ τῆς σκευῆς ἀναθέσει ἐκκαίδεκα μνᾶς.

[16] *Griechische Literaturgeschichte*, III, p. 60, note.

[17] *Hellenische Landeskunde und Topographie*, in MÜLLER, *Handbuch d. klass. Alterthumswissenschaft*, III, p. 326.

[18] *C. I. A.*, II, 971 *a*, 971 *b* = DITT., 405, 406.

[19] DEM., *Philip.* I. 36; PLUT., *Quaest. conviv.* I. x. 1.

The speaker in Antiphon's speech on the chorus-boy[20] was choregos for two tribes at the Thargelia; but the chorus was lyric, not dramatic. The chief authority, however, is the oration of Demosthenes against Meidias, where he graphically describes his offer of himself as choregos to his own tribe, that it might not be for a third time without a representative; but he expressly states that he was choregos for a lyric as contrasted with a dramatic chorus.[21] Of the two arguments to this oration, written by Libanios, the first speaks of both lyric and dramatic choruses contesting at the Dionysia, and immediately upon this states that the tribes furnish the choruses and that the choregos is the one who pays the expenses in connection with the choregia. This, it must be acknowledged, would seem to indicate that the dramatic were appointed in the same manner as the lyric choregoi. But the second argument, which is longer and more specific, states that a choregos was appointed from each tribe, πρὸς τὸ τρέφειν χοροὺς παίδων τε καὶ ἀνδρῶν, and adds, ἐλάμβανε δὲ χρήματα εἰς τροφὴν τῶν τοῦ χοροῦ. ἐπιστάσης δὲ τῆς ἑορτῆς ἠγωνίζοντο πρὸς ἀλλήλους οἱ χορηγοὶ καὶ ἤριζον, ὕμνους εἰς τὸν Διόνυσον ᾄδοντες, καὶ τῷ νικῶντι τρίπους τὸ ἆθλον ἦν, κτλ. Now, we have seen that the choregia in the case of dramatic differs in some respects from the choregia in case of lyric choruses. The prize was not the same in both cases, and an important change in the dramatic choregia was introduced without affecting the system of the lyric choregia. It is true that the appointment of the choregoi is a more important feature, but, if we can rid our minds of the presumption that the choregia was a consistently invariable institution, the same for choregoi of both kinds, we see how little evidence there is to show that dramatic choregoi were appointed in any way by the tribe.

Having thus stated the most important features of the choregia for the city festivals, we may ask, What do we know of the choregia for the rural festivals?—especially for the Rural Dionysia, the most ancient of all the festivals of Dionysos, celebrated during the month of Poseideon (Dec.–Jan.) in the various country demes, and perhaps nowhere, except at Peiraieus, with so much brilliancy as at Ikaria, so intimately connected with the myth of Dionysos, the birthplace of Thespis and the primitive home of both tragedy and comedy.

The meagre information which we possess on this point has been collected by Haussoullier.[22] Two decrees of the deme of Aixone, in praise

---

[20] περὶ τοῦ χορευτοῦ, 11.
[21] § 156, τραγῳδοῖς κεχορήγηκέ ποθ' οὗτος, ἐγὼ δὲ αὐληταῖς ἀνδράσιν.
[22] La Vie Municipale en Attique, p. 169.

of their two choregoi for having performed their duties, constitute the sum total of the epigraphic material which·M. Haussoullier found at his disposal; and from this he concludes that two choregoi were regularly appointed each year, in exactly what manner he does not attempt to say, but probably from the few wealthy citizens, and without any special formalities. He then raises the question, whether there was a contest between the choregoi, and answers this in the negative,[23] stating, as his reason for this belief, that the choregoi at the city festivals contested as representatives of their respective tribes, while in the country festivals all the choregoi were members of the same deme, and, being comparatively few in number, would be likely to make common cause in giving as brilliant a spectacle as possible. This view of Haussoullier simplifies matters considerably; but, if we should find that there actually was a contest, many questions would spring up. Was there any distinction between official and private dedications? Was there any distinction between monuments dedicated by dramatic choregoi and those dedicated by lyric choruses? Indeed, were there in the rural demes both dramatic and lyric choruses? What was the object dedicated?

In one of the inscriptions of Ikaria published above, the deme praises its two choregoi, as is done in the two Aixonean decrees, and thus adds nothing to our information. The following three inscriptions are, however, the first of their kind, and constitute an important addition to our material.

INSCRIPTIONS FROM IKARIA.

No. 5.

Upon the edge of a marble slab (that illustrated in *Figure 1*), found in the wall of the church: height of letters, 0.012. They are roughly cut, and the Γ has an apex giving it somewhat the appearance of Γ. This is seen also in the inscription of the Lysikrates monument.

ΜΝΗΣΙΛΟΧΟ ΜΝΗΣΙ ΦΙΛΟΥ   Μνησίλοχο[ς] Μνησιφίλου
ΤΡΑΓ ΙΔΟΙΣΧΟΡΗΓ ΝΕΝΙΚΑ   τραγωιδοῖς χορηγῶν ἐνίκα.

"Mnesilochos son of Mnesiphilos won the victory as choregos for the tragic chorus."

No. 6.

Marble base found in the church wall: height, 0.53 m.; width, 0.43 m.; thickness, 0.225. The front is finished perfectly smooth except

---

[23] So also MÜLLER, *Lehrbuch der gr. Bühnenalterthümer*, p. 327.

about 0.09 m. at the bottom, which has been left rough, as when in position this would be concealed by earth. In the top are three holes for securing the object dedicated, the middle one being 0.065 m. × 0.05 m., and 0.05 m. deep; the smaller holes at the two sides, 0.045 m. deep. Height of letters, 0.029 m.

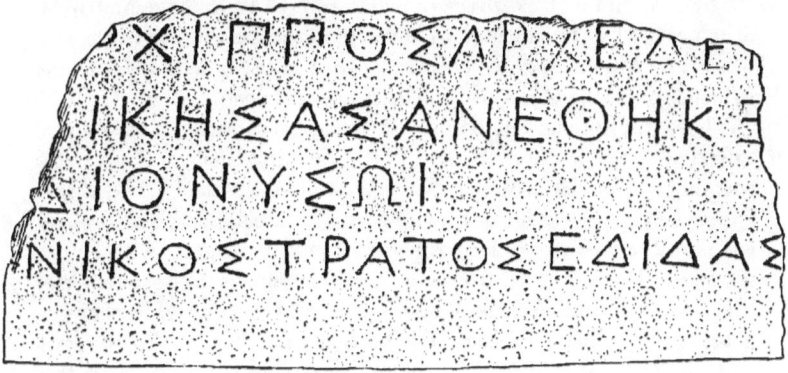

["Ἀρ]χιππος Ἀρχεδέ[κτο] [ν]ικήσας ἀνέθηκε[τῶι] | Διονύσωι, Νικόστρατος ἐδίδασ[κε.

"Archippos son of Archedektes dedicated [this] to Dionysos. Nikostratos was didaskalos."

No. 7.

Marble stele found lying upon the wall F, running in a southeasterly direction from the N. W. corner of the peribolos wall of the precinct. Height, 1.70 m.; width, 0.40 m.; thickness, 0.33 m. A moulding runs around the top, of which the surface is perfectly smooth, and thus affords no evidence of what object was dedicated upon it. Height of letters, 0.02 m. in first three lines, 0.015 in the others.

```
ΕΡΓΑΣΟΣΦΑΝΟΜΑΧΟ         Ἔργασος Φανομάχο
ΦΑΝΟΜΑΧΟΣΕΡΓΑΣΟ         Φανόμαχος Ἐργάσο
ΔΙΟΓΝΗΤΟΣΕΡΓΑΣΟ         Διόγνητος Ἐργάσο
ΤΡΑΓΩΙΔΟΙΣΧΟΡΗΓΗΣΑΝΤΕΣ  τραγωιδοῖς χορηγήσαντες
ΝΙΚΩΝΤΕΣΑΝΕΘΕΣΑΝ        νικῶντες ἀνέθεσαν.
```

" Ergasos son of Phanomachos, Phanomachos son of Ergasos, Diognetos son of Ergasos, having won the victory as choregoi for the tragic chorus, dedicated [this]."

Now, all these inscriptions show conclusively that, contrary to the view of Haussoullier and Müller, there was actually a contest between the choregoi, and that the victors were accustomed to dedicate some object to commemorate their victory. There appears to be the same distinction as at Athens between official and private dedications; for the first inscription lacks ἀνέθηκε, and the object dedicated was a tripod, as is proved by the cuttings in the top of the slab, while in the two other inscriptions ἀνέθηκε and ἀνέθεσαν are used, and, so far as the evidence goes, the object dedicated was not a tripod.

These inscriptions tell us only of dramatic choruses, Nos. 5 and 7 referring to tragic choruses, and, if the identification of Nikostratos suggested below be accepted, No. 6 to a comic chorus.[24] The phrase τραγωιδοῖς χορηγῶν is found elsewhere in inscriptions, and we may compare the passage of Demosthenes quoted in Note 21 with Lysias XXIV. 9. We also learn from No. 5, which belongs in the fourth century, but is later than Nos. 6 and 7, that at Ikaria a tragic choregos made in his official capacity a dedication of a tripod. So it seems that a tripod was the prize for the dramatic chorus here, though this was not the case in Athens.[25] In No. 6, it is remarkable that χορηγῶν is not expressed,[26] but the ἐδίδασκε of the last line is sufficient to show that the inscription is choregic. In the first line, Ἀρχεδε is a part of no name to be found in Pape-Benseler[27] or in Fick,[28] but Ἀρχε-δέκτης would be a correctly formed name (after the analogy of Θεοδέκτης, Πολυδέκτης, Fick, p. 110), and the perpendicular stroke after the E may well belong to a *kappa*. As there would be room on the stone for only three letters, we must read genitive in *omicron*. This, together with the forms of the other letters, places the inscription in the early part of the fourth century.[29]

[24] It is possible that theatrical and musical performances were so intimately connected at Ikaria that there were no choruses distinctively and solely musical; but it would be rash to assert this merely on the negative evidence of three inscriptions.

[25] [It is hardly probable that the practice in Athens and Ikaria would differ so essentially; and Koehler's explanation of *C. I. A.*, II, 1298 (KAIBEL, *Epigram. Gr.*, 924; LOEWY, *Inschr. Bild.*, 533) seems reasonable enough to justify the assumption that tripods might, at times, be dedicated for dramatic victories, in Athens as well as in the country. More than this can hardly be affirmed in the present dearth of positive evidence either way.—A. C. M.]

[26] [*C. I. A.*, II, 1248, 1283, 1285, 1286 have the same omission.—A. C. M.]

[27] *Wörterbuch der griechischen Eigennamen.*

[28] *Die griechischen Personennamen.*

[29] The form of the *omega* with its side lines nearly parallel is precisely that found

Can the Nikostratos of the last line be identified with any person known to us in literature? Among the numerous Athenians of this name connected with the stage, we find a tragic actor who lived about 420 B. C. (Xen., *Sympos.*, 6. 3; Plutarch, *Glor. Athen.*, 6), and the youngest son of Aristophanes, referred to by Athenaios (XIII. 587) as a poet of the middle comedy. The date of the actor is too early to admit of identifying him with the Nikostratos of our inscription. With regard to the son of Aristophanes little is definitely known, and we must resort to comparisons to arrive at an approximation to his date. Aristophanes' death is usually placed at 380 or 376 B.C., but there is nothing to show how long he lived after his last extant work, the second edition of the *Plutus*, which was brought out in 388 B. C., except that he seems to have done a portion at least of the work on two plays which appeared in the name of his son, Araros. Araros first exhibited under his own name in 375 B. C., but must have been active under his father's guidance for some time previous to this. It is reasonable to believe that Nikostratos made his first essays during the last years of his father's life, and a rural deme would afford a young poet an excellent field for the bringing out of his youthful productions, before he had acquired reputation enough to secure admission to the great contests in the city. So it seems plausible, and even probable, that the Nikostratos of our inscription was the son of Aristophanes.[30]

In No. 6, the dedicators are Ergasos and his two sons, one of whom is named after his grandfather Phanomachos. With this we should compare the inscription quoted above (Note 9) belonging to about the same date, and in which the dedication is also by a father and his two sons. Koehler, in publishing this inscription (*Mitth.*, 1878, p. 229), does not express an opinion as to how three persons can be named as victorious choregoi, but perhaps holds the same opinion as Reisch (*De Musicis*, p. 46), who believes that the inscription does not refer to a single victory, but was dedicated in commemoration of several different victories.[31] But a more plausible explanation, in my opinion, is that the three

in Ionic inscriptions of the middle of the fifth century and later, but this is, I think, a coincidence rather than a survival. However, this form in Attika is characteristic of the early part of the fourth century. The sporadic examples of *omega* in Attic inscriptions of the fifth cent. already show a tendency to become rounde , though the legs are very flaring, even throughout most of the fourth century.

[30] [*Cf.* Seventh Annual Report, p. 77.—ED.]
[31] [*Cf.* LYSIAS, xix. 42: 'Αριστοφάνης τοίνυν γῆν μὲν καὶ οἰκίαν ἐκτήσατο πλέον ἢ πέντε ταλάντων, κατεχορήγησε δὲ ὑπὲρ αὑτοῦ καὶ τοῦ πατρὸς πεντακισχιλίας δραχμάς.—A. C. M.]

persons from one family joined in the expense of furnishing a chorus, and so in a private dedication called themselves victors in common although one of their number must have been the official choregos, and his name alone would appear on a monument of the official class. Ergasos is a name found twice in an Eleusinian inscription of 329/8 B. C., and is probably the short form of 'Εργασίων, the name of a countryman mentioned by Aristophanes (*Vesp.*, 1201). The inscription belongs to the early decades of the fourth century.

A cut of the tripod-base of inscription No. 5 is given (*Figure 1*) inasmuch as bases for choregic tripods which show clearly the holes for setting in the tripod are not common, and as this base presents a few variations from those known already. Of the tripods set up by victorious choregoi at Athens no fragment of any value is known, and, to form an idea of the shape of such tripods, we are dependent on the innumerable instances in vase-paintings and reliefs, on the fragments of bronze tripods found in other parts of Greece, and on the bases for tripods which are known. In vase-paintings and reliefs, the tripod is usually represented without any central support, though there are instances in which this feature appears. The legs are commonly represented as plain upright pieces ending in animals' feet. The fragments of the large tripods discovered at Olympia show no trace of a central support, and the legs are simple uprights, not ending in animals' feet. The miniature tripods, however, which have been found there, and must serve as the standard for completing the fragments of the large ones, have, in some instances, a small central support of intertwining wires. The diameter of the bowl is about equal to the height of the legs; but all these Olympian examples belong to a very early period, and we know, from the representations on vases and reliefs, that the ratio of proportion was ordinarily nothing like this; the diameter of the bowls so represented would be less than half the height of the legs.

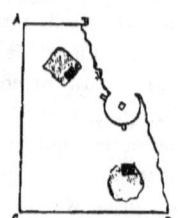

FIG. 1.—*Tripod-base found at Ikaria, on the edge of which is Inscription No. 5.*

Of bases of actual tripods, two are represented in cuts by Fabricius.[32] One of these is *in situ* on the Akropolis behind the Propylaia, near the fragment of wall belonging to the old Propylaia, and dates at least from the beginning of the fifth century B. C. The three holes for the feet of the tripod are perfectly round, but cut deeper near the edge, leaving a kind of knob in the middle. Between the three

---

[32] *Das platäische Weihgeschenk*, in *Jahrbuch d. deutsch. archäol. Instituts*, 1886, p. 187.

holes, a circular area is left rough, showing that a cylindrical central support was here present. The second base given by Fabricius has also a circular space in the middle left rough, but the cuttings for the legs are in this example not round but ⊔ shaped. The tripod on the Lysikrates monument also had a central support, as is shown by the deep central hole in the top of the acroterium.[33] The famous serpent-column in the Atmeidan at Constantinople was, according to Fabricius, the central support between the three legs of the Plataian tripod, as is set forth in the article referred to above. But the most interesting base for comparison with our own is a circular slab[34] found in 1878 near the bank of the Ilissos; and a cut of it is here given (*Figure 2*). In the same place as the slab, were found three cylindrical bases with choregic inscriptions[35] of the first half of the fourth century; and this slab must have formed the cap of a similar base, it being too large to belong to any of those actually found. In this slab the central circle is not merely a place left rough, but an actual depression 0.02 m. deep.

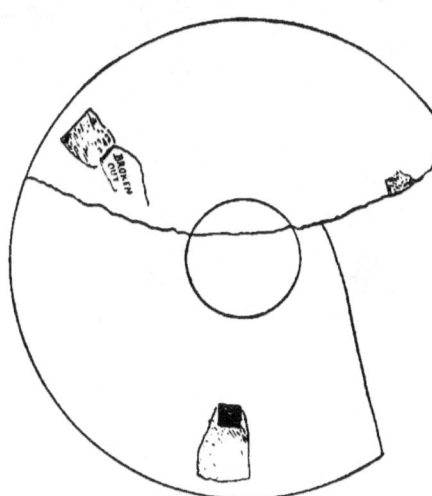

FIG. 2.—*Tripod base found near the Ilissos.*

For the support of the legs there are holes, about 0.05 m. square, cut to the depth of 0.07 m.; and an irregularly shaped area extending from these holes nearly to the outer circumference of the slab is slightly cut away (greatest depth, 0.015). This irregular cutting is held by Koumanoudes to indicate that the legs of the tripod ended in the feet of animals. In the base found at Ikaria, precisely the same arrangement appears for the support of the legs. There are square holes cut to the depth of 0.055 m., and, inclosing these, irregular areas cut out to a slight

---

[33] STUART and REVETT, *Antiquities of Athens*, vol. I, chap. IV, pl. 9.
[34] KOUMANOUDES, 'Αθήναιον, I, p. 170.
[35] 'Αθήναιον, I, p. 169 = DITT., 411, 412, 413.

depth; so that the tripod-legs must here, too, have ended in feet. The central hollow is 0.05 m. deep, and radiating from it are three narrow cuttings of the same depth. Exactly in the middle is a small square hole running through the whole thickness of the slab, and apparently intended for the passage of a rod to secure the central member more firmly. The inscription is on the side CD (*Figure 1*), close to the upper edge.

Athens,
December 12, 1888.

CARL D. BUCK.

DISCOVERIES IN THE ATTIC DEME OF IKARIA, 1888.

INSCRIPTIONS FROM IKARIA.

No. 8.

Stele with inscriptions on both sides; one (No. 8), of 24 lines, comprising six transfer accounts, the other (No. 9), a decree of which portions of 49 lines remain. Length of stone 0.93 m.; greatest width 0.38 m. Found under the front wall of church. One edge is broken off clean, the other is complete on the side of the transfer account, but broken off obliquely on the other.

No. 1.   ΗΜΑΡΧΟΝΓΑΡΕΔΩΚΕΝ
         ΑΡΓΥΡΙΟΔΙΟΝΥΣΟΧΧ ΙΙΙ
         Ο:ΧΧΗΓΗΗϹ
         ΧΧΙΙΗΗΗΗΔΔΔΗΗΗ ΙΙΙΙ

No. 2.   ΓΑΡΕΔΩΚΕΚΕΦΑΛΑΙΟΝΑΡΓΥΡΙΟ
         ΙϷΗΙΚΑΡΙΟΚΕΦΑΛΑΙΟΝΧΧΗ::
         ΤΙΙΙΗΙΙ

No. 3.   ΣΝΓΑΡΕΔΩΚΕΚΕΦΑΛΑΙΟΝΑΡΓΥΡΙΟ
         ΙΚΑΡΙΟΑΡΓΥΡΙΟΚΕΦΑΛΑΙΟΝΧΧΗΗϷΔΔ
         ΓΥΡΙΟΤΤΤΤΧΗΔΔΗΗ

No. 4.   ΔΕΜΑΡΧΟΝΓΑΡΕΔΟΚΕΝ
         ΦΑΛΑΙΟΝΤΟΔΙΟΝΥϟΟ
         ΔΓΗΙΙΙ:ΑΡΛΥΡΙΟΗΟϟΙΟ
         ϽΝ:ΤΤΤΤΧΧΗΗϷΔΔΔΓΗΗΗ Ι

No. 5.   ΕΜΑΡΧΟΝΓΑΡΕΔΟΚΕΝ
         ΚΕΦΑΛΑΙΟΝΤΟΔΙΟΝΥϟΟ
         ΔΔΓΗΙΙΙΙ:ΑΡΛΥΡΙΟΗΟϟΙΟ
         ϽΝ:ΤΤΤΤΧΧΙϷΗϷΔΔΔΗΗΗ
         ΚΑΡΛΥΡΙΟΚΕΦΑ   ΟΝ
         ///

No. 6.   ΔΗΜΑΡΧΟΝΓΑΡΕΔΟΚ Ϸ
         Ο:ΚΕΦΑΛΑΙΟΝ:ΤΤΤΤΧΧ
         ΥΡΙΟ:ΚΕΦΑΛΑΙΟΝ:ΧΧΧΙϷ
         ϽΙΟ:ΑΡΛΥΡΙΟ:ΚΕΦΑΛΑΙΟ

No. 1. ὁ δεῖνα δ]ημαρχῶν παρέδωκεν
κεφάλαιον] ἀργυρίου Διονύσου XX[XX]HH
· · · ·Ἰκαρί]ου XXHΓⱵⱵC · [ὁσίου ἀργυρίου ΤΤΤΤ]XXⱲHHHHΔΔⱵⱵⱵIIII. [ὁ δεῖνα

No. 2. δημαρχῶν] παρέδωκε κεφάλαιον ἀργυρίου [Διο-
νύσου XXXX]ⱲH · Ἰκαρίου κεφάλαιον XXHH(?)[· ὁσίου
ἀργυρίου] ΤΤΤΤHH [. . . ὁ δεῖνα

No. 3. δημαρχ]ῶν παρέδωκε κεφάλαιον ἀργυρίου [Διο-
νύσου XXXX ·]Ἰκαρίου ἀργυρίου κεφ[ά]λαιον XXHHⱣΔΔ
· ὁσίου ἀρ]γυρίου ΤΤΤΤXHΔΔⱵⱵ.

No. 4. ὁ δεῖνα] δημαρχῶν παρέδωκεν
ἀργυρίου κε]φάλαιον τοῦ Διονύσου
XXXX . . . .]ΔΓⱵIII · ἀργυρίου ὁσίου
κεφαλαι]ον ΤΤΤΤXXHHⱣΔΔΔΓⱵⱵⱵI.

No. 5. ὁ δεῖνα δ]ημαρχῶν παρέδωκεν
ἀργυρίου] κεφάλαιον τοῦ Διονύσου
. . . .]ΔΔΓⱵIIII · ἀργυρίου ὁσίου
κεφάλαι]ον ΤΤΤΤXXⱲHⱣΔΔΔⱵⱵⱵ
παρέδω?]κ' ἀργυρίου κεφά[λαι]ον.

No. 6. ὁ δεῖνα]δημαρχῶν παρέδωκ'[α]ρ?[γ-
υρίου ὁσί]ου κεφάλαιον ΤΤΤΤXX
Διονύσου ἀργ]υρίου κεφάλαιον XXXⱲ
. . . . .Ἰκα]ρίου ἀργυρίου κεφάλαιο[ν XX.

Comment.—Height of letters: in No. 1, 0.014 m.; in Nos. 2 and 3, 0.010; in Nos. 4 and 5, 0.017; in No. 6, 0.016. The inscription is not στοιχηδόν, and even in the same line the letters vary considerably in size. The various accounts are not of the same date. The oldest are Nos. 4 and 5, which belong to the period 460–447, as is determined by the three-barred *sigma*, the form of the slanting *nu*, and other indications, such as the form of the *phi* with somewhat flattened circle and crossbar passing beyond but slightly, and a strong tendency to slanting in the crossbar of *alpha*. Next in point of time was inscribed No. 6, in which there is an example of the Ionic use of H. But sporadic instances of this occur in Attic inscriptions earlier even than 445 B. C., so that we need not ascribe No. 6 to a very much later date than Nos. 4 and 5, especially as the forms of the letters differ but slightly. Nos. 1, 2, and 3 were cut, as seems to me probable, at the same time. The forms of the letters are the same in all, and the different accounts are not so distinctly separated one from another as would probably be the case if they had been cut at different times. Thus, in Nos. 2 and 3 there is not space enough for the demarch's name to appear before δημαρχῶν on the same line, and it must be supplied in the previous line immediately following the conclusion of the preceding account. In these three accounts the Ionic element in the form of the letters strongly predominates. The *gamma* and *lambda* are Ionic, and the *omega* always appears in its proper place except in the first word. If this inscription were from Athens, we should unhesitatingly place the three accounts in the years immediately succeeding the archonship of Eukleides, but there is no certainty that the change of alphabet for public records was effected in the rural districts at precisely the same time as in the city. The very end of the fifth century is the most probable date that can be given.

In the last line of No. 5, the K is, I think, certain, and involves an instance of a harsh elision, very rare in prose inscriptions.[1] The word παρέδωκε[1a] seems the most reasonable restoration in this place and is favored by the ending of the first line of No. 6, where a similar elision seems to occur, although the P is not certain.

In the earliest accounts, Nos. 4 and 5, only two classes of funds are expressly mentioned, that devoted to the cult of Dionysos, and the ὅσιον ἀργύριον, where ὅσιον has the not unusual sense of "secular" as opposed to "sacred."[2] The last line of No. 5 must be a general recapitulation of the funds. In No. 6 a new fund is introduced— Ἰκάριον ἀργύριον, "Ikarian money," and has its place beside the Dionysiac and secular funds in Nos. 1, 2, and 3, as well. Possibly, "Ikarian money" was a fund set aside for the worship of the eponymous hero of the deme; but, however this may be, the expression must be connected with the phrase which occurs in two of the other inscriptions, and it shows that there existed a body of "Ikarians" in a restricted sense distinguished from the Ikarians as a body comprising the members of the deme as a whole. The explanation maintained in the one case must hold good in the other. For further

---

[1] *Cf.* MEISTERHANS, *Grammatik der attischen Inschriften*(2), § 23.

[1a] [Προσόδου] κἀργυρίον κεφά[λαι]ον '['Ικαρίου...? My squeeze shows some traces of letters at the beginning of line 20.—A. C. M.]

[2] *Cf.* DEM. vs. *Timokrat.*, § 9: τῶν ἱερῶν μὲν χρημάτων τοὺς θεούς, τῶν ὁσίων δὲ τὴν πόλιν ἀποστερεῖ.

discussion of the question, see below. The amount of the ὅσιον ἀργύριον (26,683 drachmas in No. 5) shows that the deme of Ikaria was far from poor. It is interesting to compare its religious funds with those of the neighboring deme of Plotheia, as we find them given in an inscription (*C.I.A.*, II, 570).

No. 9.

```
         HE Σ T E V L
       N I K A P I E Y Σ I : M E N E Σ T
       T O N Δ E M O T O N K A I T O N I K A
       T O N A X O P E Λ E T O N H O T I N A N
 5.    A N T I Δ O Σ I N Δ E E N A I T O N X P
       O Δ E M A P X O E I K O Σ I E M E P O N
       N A I A N T I Δ O Σ I N E T O N Δ E M
       X O P E Λ O A Γ O Φ A I N E N T P I Σ
       A Λ O I Δ O Σ K A T A V E Λ E N T O N
10.    O Σ K A I T O X O P E Λ O E X Σ O M O
        O Σ I N Δ E K A E M E P O N E M
        Δ E T O A Λ A V M A T O Σ H A Γ
        V T O Δ E M A P X O K A I T O N
        A I A Y T O I Σ ! E X Σ O M O Σ
15.     Ͻ T O X O P O I Σ M E Γ  O H E
        Σ O Δ E Λ O N A Γ E N T E K A I
        O N . T O I Σ Γ P O T O X O P
        Γ E I Δ A N E N I A Y T O N H
        Γ O Γ E M Γ E N E A M M E Δ
20.     N E A Γ O ⁻ I N E N Γ E N
        Ͻ A Λ O I Δ O I . I O X O
        E K A N Δ P A Σ I H E K
        K A Θ E K A Σ T O N T O
        N Y Σ O Γ P A T T E N Δ E
25.     O P T E N T O X O P E Λ O
        O N O Σ E A Γ O T I N E N
        Σ I T E N E O P T E N Θ
        N O Σ T E N H E B Δ O M
        T T E N E M E P A N A
30.     Ͻ P O E N T O I Γ Y Θ
        X P O N E A Γ O T I N
        Ͻ N X O P E Λ O N
        I K O N A I Δ E N
        O N T P A Λ O I Δ
```

```
35.         ΕΣΤΟΝΧΟΡΣ
            ΓΟΤΙΝΕΤΟ
            ΑΤΤΕΤΟΗΟΖ
            ΛΕΣΜΕΔΕΝ
            ΜΕΝΟΣΧΡΕ
40.         ΠΑΧΜΑΣΚΑ
            ΑΙΓΡΑΤΤΕ
            Ο ΤΟ  ΧΟ
            ΝΕΝΑΧΕΗ
            ΟΜΜΕΔΙΔ/
45.         ΕΣ ΤΟΔ
            ΙΤΑΣΤΟ
            ΝΤΕΝΕΟΙ
            ΣΑΙΕΣ
            ΕΝΤ
```

    ]ἡ στήλη[
  ἔδοχσε]ν Ἰκαριεῦσι, Μενέστ[ρατος εἶπε.
φσήφισμα] τῶν δημοτῶν καὶ τῶν Ἰκα[ριῶν εἶναι· τραγ-
ωιδῶν ὄν]των ἀχορηγήτων ὅτιν' ἂν [

5. χορηγεῖν·] ἀντίδοσιν δὲ εἶναι τῶν χρ[ημάτων αὐτοῦ ἐναντίον τ]οῦ δημάρχου εἴκοσι ἡμερῶν [
  εἶ]ναι ἀντίδοσιν, ἢ τὸν δήμ[αρχον
  ]χορηγοῦ ἀποφαίνειν τρισ[ὶ μάρτυσι
  τρ]αγωιδοὺς καταλέγειν τὸν [

10.   ]ος καὶ τοῦ χορηγοῦ ἐξομο[σαμένου
  ]οσιν δέκα ἡμερῶν ἐμ [Πυθίωι Ἰκαριῶν
  ]δὲ τοῦ ἀγάλματος ἅπ[τεσθαι
ἐναντίο]ν τοῦ δημάρχου καὶ τῶν[δημοτῶν
  ]αι αὐτοῖσ(ι:) ἐξομόσ[ασθαι

15. πρ]ωτοχόροις μὴ π[ρ]ὸ ἡ[
  ] . . . εγωνα πέντε καὶ[
  ]ον . τοῖς πρωτοχόρ[οις
  ἐ]πειδὰν ἐνιαυτὸν '[
  ἀ]ποπέμπειν, ἐὰμ μὴ δ[

20.   ]ν, ἢ ἀποτίνειν πέν[τε
τ]ραγωιδοῖ[ς] τοῦ χο[ρ
  δ]έκ' ἀνδράσι ἐκ [
  ]καθ' ἕκαστον τὸ[ν ἐνιαυτὸν
Διο]νύσου πράττειν δε[

25. ἑ]ορτὴν τοῦ χορηγοῦ[
     ]ωνος ἢ ἀποτίνειν[
     ]σι τὴν ἑορτήν θ[εοῦ
     ]νος τὴν ἑβδόμ[ην
     ]ττειν ἡμέραν ἀ[
30. |(ο?)ρο ἐν τῶι Πυθ[ίωι
     χ?)ρον ἢ ἀποτίν[
     τ]ὸν χορηγὸν[
     ἐ]ικόνα ἰδεῖν[
     τ]ῶν τραγωιδ[ῶν
35.]εἰς τὸν χορὸ[ν
     ἀ]ποτινέτω [
     πρα]ττέτω ὁ δ[ήμαρχος
     ]γης μὴ δὲ λ[
     ]μενος χρη[μάτων
40. δ]ραχμὰς κα[
     κ]αὶ πραττέ[τω
     ]ο το χο[
     ]ν ἔλαχε '[
     ]ομ μὴ διδ[
45.]εσ τοδ[
     ]ιτας τοῦ[
     ]υτελεω[
     ]σαι ες[
     ]ἐν τ[

Comment.—The letters of the first line are larger than those of the second, and those of the second line are larger than those of the body of the inscription. Height of letters in first line, 0.013 m.; in second line, 0.011 m.; in the remaining lines, 0.009 m. The arrangement is στοιχηδόν, except in the first two lines. The surface is broken off on the left, but the extent of the stone is known, and, calculating from this, I estimate that there are seven letters missing in line 5, and from this we can easily determine the number to be supplied in other lines. The right of the inscription is entirely gone, but, judging the width of the stone from the restorations made in the inscription on the other side, I conclude that the number of letters to be supplied is about twelve.

The form of the letters is that common in the last stage of development of the Attic alphabet, a period which in Athens falls between

447 B. C. and the archonship of Eukleides, when the Ionic alphabet was officially introduced. The lower bar of the *sigma* is often nearly horizontal, but this is an individual peculiarity of the stone-cutter. There is not a single instance of encroachment of the Ionic alphabet such as we meet with in No. 8, though there are four cases of omission of the rough breathing, namely, in lines 6, 11, 27, 29. But such omissions are very common in this period;[3] and the two words in which the breathing is omitted in this inscription, ἡμέρα and ἑορτή, are especially liable to this.[4] In line 14, we have an almost certain instance of a dative in -οισι, which may serve to date the inscription more accurately within the period above suggested. Even in the earliest inscriptions there is a fluctuation in the use of -οισι and -οις, and they continue to be used with about equal frequency until 444 B. C., after which date there are only two occurrences of -οισι, one in an Athenian decree of 434, and the other in a decree of the Plotheian deme inscribed in the Ionic alphabet, a remarkable instance of rural conservatism.[5] All points considered, I am disposed to place the date of our inscription between 447 and the beginning of the Peloponnesian war. A few orthographical questions remain to be noted before we consider the subject-matter of the inscription.[6] In l. 4, are we to regard the νυ of ὄντινα as omitted owing to a blunder of the stone-cutter? This is not the kind of mistake most frequently made;

[3] *Cf.* ROBERTS, *An Introduction to Greek Epigraphy*, p. 105.
[4] Particularly, ἡμέρα, which in pre-Eukleidean inscriptions is more often written without the aspirate than with it. In looking hastily through *C.I.A.*, I and IV, I have found 16 cases of the word without the rough breathing, against 9 cases with it and 6 cases in which a preceding surd mute is made aspirate, as καθ' ἡμέραν. *Cf.* KATHMEPAN on a fourth-century inscription found at the Peiraieus and published in *Bull. Corr. Hellén.*, 1887, p. 131. These facts show that the rough breathing was very weak in this word, a circumstance which should not be overlooked by those who discuss its etymology.
[Since writing this, I note that BAUNACK (*Studien auf dem Gebiete des griech. und der arischen Sprachen*, I. 2, p. 240) cites, from the dialects, examples of this word without aspirate, and explains the processes by which this and other words may have acquired a secondary aspirate.]
[5] *Cf.* MEISTERHANS[(2)], § 47, b; CAUER, *De dialecto Attica*, p. 410.
[6] [The following is suggested as an alternative for lines 3–6, the first letter of line 4 not being certain:

Κατὰ ἔτος] τῶν δημοτῶν καὶ τῶν Ἰκα[ρίων δύο τὸν Δ-
ιονύσου ἀγ]ῶνα χορηγείτων ὥτιν' ἂν [κατασταθῆτο-
ν χορηγώ·] ἀντίδοσιν δὲ εἶναι τῶν χρ[ημάτων, ἐὰν πο-
νῆι, ἐπὶ τ]οῦ δημάρχου εἴκοσι ἡμερῶν. . . .—A. C. M.]

moreover, this document seems to be very carefully inscribed. I am
loath, therefore, to consider it a blunder, and prefer to take ὅτινα as a
genuine form of the Attic vernacular. In the genitive and dative, the
short forms ὅτου and ὅτῳ alone occur in Attic inscriptions. May not
the popular speech have in like manner preferred an accusative form
with the first element indeclinable, though for the second element
there is no short form, as Homeric ὅτινα? The solitary instance of
ὄντινα is certainly not an insuperable obstacle to this opinion.[7] In
the matter of elision, there is here the same inconsistency that characterizes Athenian inscriptions generally.[8]

The subject of our inscription seems to be a decree relating to the
choregia, with special reference to *antidosis*. In the text of the transliteration, I have given scarcely any restorations, because, even in
places where I have found some that are plausible, they are too uncertain to be of value. The bare fact that there are only three lines
in the inscription in which the number of letters extant is equal to the
number to be supplied would not in itself necessarily be discouraging,
if the subject were one upon which our information were more complete. But this decree is considerably older than our earliest literary
sources on *antidosis*, which are found in the Attic orators of the fourth
century, Demosthenes, Isokrates and Lysias; and this is, moreover,
a rural decree. Even with all the literary evidence, including the
detailed account given in the *Phaenippea*, by Demosthenes, no one
has yet been able to advance an entirely satisfactory explanation of
the working of the system of *antidosis*; and one has only to read the
various contributions to the subject by German scholars,[9] especially
the rather warm discussion between Fränkel and Thalheim in *Hermes*,
to appreciate what radically different views may be taken.

If this inscription were complete, it would undoubtedly shed a
flood of light upon the question, and enable us to arrive at its true
explanation. But even the fragments preserved are of no little importance, and they settle conclusively at least one matter of dispute.

[7] *Cf.* MEISTERHANS(2), § 59, d; G. MEYER, *Griechische Grammatik*, p. 401.
[8] *Cf.* MEISTERHANS(2), § 23.
[9] *Cf.* BÖCKH, *Staatshaushaltung der Athener*(3), I, p. 673 ff.; DITTENBERGER, *Ueber den Vermögenstausch und die Trierarchie des Demosthenes;* BLASCHKE, *De antidosi apud Athenienses;* THALHEIM, *N. Jahrbuch f. Philol.*, CXV, p. 613 ff.; FRÄNKEL, *Hermes*, XVIII, p. 442 ff.; THALHEIM, *Hermes*, XIX, p. 80 ff.; LOLLING, *De antidosi;* MEIER and SCHÖMANN, *Der attische Process*(2), p. 737 ff. Fränkel has the last word on the subject in his edition of Böckh's *Sth. d. Athener*, Note 883.

We have first to ask whether we have to deal with an original decree inaugurating the system or with a copy of an earlier regulation. Demosthenes[10] states that *antidosis* was established by Solon. Fränkel[11] thinks that this statement is to be credited only to the tendency of the Attic orators to ascribe all ancient public regulations to Solon; but most scholars accept Demosthenes as a trustworthy witness. In any case, there can be no doubt that *antidosis* was regulated at Athens at a much earlier time than the date of our inscription; there is, however, nothing to prevent us from supposing that the system may at this time first have been introduced from Athens into the deme of Ikaria, and that the purpose of our decree was to furnish the necessary regulations for its adaptation to the choregic system in force in the demes.

The first line of the inscription is evidently the heading, and symmetry would seem to require something to be supplied on the right side (τῆς χορηγίας?). The heading στήλη ... is, I think, unique; but we may compare a passage of Demosthenes where he uses στήλη in the sense of ψήφισμα.[12] Line 2 gives the name of the mover, while the decree proper begins in l. 3, where we have the phrase τῶν δημοτῶν καὶ τῶν 'Ικα[ριῶν,[13] with which we must compare the similar phrase 'Ικαριεῖς ... καὶ ὁ δῆμος ὁ 'Ικαριέων, which occurs in the deme-decree published above.[14] In both cases, "Ikarians" is used in the introduction in a general sense (ἐψηφίσθαι 'Ικαριεῦσιν and [ἔδοχσε]ν 'Ικαριεῦσι), while it is afterward used in a special sense, as of a body distinct from the demesmen. Of the same nature is the 'Ικαρίου ἀργυρίου of Inscr. No. 8. 3. I know of no better explanation than that suggested by Professor Merriam, and given in the article on the deme-decree; namely, that the "Ikarians" in the restricted sense are members of a gens claiming descent from the eponymous hero of the deme. While it is true that most names of this class are of the patronymic form in –δης, -ιδης such as Εὐμολπίδαι, Βρυτίδαι, etc., we have also in inscriptions[15] Κήρυκες and Σαλαμίνιοι.

---

[10] *Phaenippea*, § 1.   [11] *Hermes*, XVIII, p. 444, Note 1.
[12] *Vs. Leptin.*, § 159: καὶ τῆς Δημοφάντου στήλης περὶ ἧς εἶπε Φορμίων, ἐν ᾗ γέγραπται, κ.τ.λ.
[13] I supply -ριῶν, not -ριέων, since in fifth-century inscriptions the contracted form is the rule, and even in one of our later inscriptions we have 'Ικαριῶν.
[14] No. 1, p. 71.
[15] *Cf.* τοῦ γένους τοῦ Κηρύκων, DITT., *Syll.*, 385; 'Αθήναιον, VI, p. 274, καὶ εἰς τὸ γένος τὸ Σαλαμινίων.

The most important and interesting parallel is to be found in the phratry-decree, the continuation of which on the back of the stone has only recently been discovered.[16] In this inscription we have mention of the "House of the Dekeleians," τὸν Δεκελειῶν οἶκον, ὁ ἱερεὺς τοῦ Δεκελειῶν οἴκου, etc., which is understood by Köhler to mean a gens. But in the portion recently discovered we find the phrase ὅπου ἂν Δεκελειεῖς προσφοιτῶσιν ἐν ἄστει, with which Lolling compares the passage in Lysias (XXIII. 3) where the speaker tells of going to the barber-shop near the Hermai, "where the Dekeleians resort" (ἵνα οἱ Δεκελεῖς προσφοιτῶσιν), and asking all the Dekeleians whom he found there "whether they knew of a certain Pankleon, a demesman of Dekeleia." In this passage, Δεκελεῖς obviously is used of the members of the deme of Dekeleia, and must have the same force in the corresponding phrase in the inscription: so that, in the same decree, we find "Dekeleians" used in the general sense of members of the deme of Dekeleia and in the more restricted sense of members of a gens of the same name tracing their ancestry back to the hero Dekelos.[17] This gens of the Dekeleians, as Köhler remarks, seems to have held some especially important position among the other gentes of the same phratry. In the same way, our Ikarians, owing, no doubt, to their reputed descent from the eponymous deme-hero, occupied a preëminent position, so that it was a traditional custom that in deme-decrees they should be mentioned as a distinct body. We know very little about the precise relations of a gens to a phratry or to a deme, but the gens was more a religious than a political body. So the "Ikarian money" was probably a religious fund belonging to the gens. Perhaps there existed a cult of the eponymous hero Ikarios, in which case we have a double explanation for the use of the word.

In l. 4 we have a form of the adjective ἀχορήγητος, the only occurrences of which in literature are in Aristotle, where it has the meaning of "without supplies," based on the late use of the word χορηγία. At this period, however, when χορηγία had its regular technical sense, it can only mean "without a choregos" or "not having served as choregos," according to the context. This line must contain some regulation concerning the appointment of the choregos.

[16] *C.I.A.*, II. 841 b; Δελτ ον 'Αρχαιολογικόν, 1888, p. 161 ff.; see below p. 174.

[17] [Since this was written, TÖPFFER'S *Attische Genealogie* has appeared, in which the same view of the Dekeleians is advanced (p. 289) and supported by the citation of HEROD., IX. 73 : Σωφάνης . . . δῆμου Δεκελειῆθεν, Δεκελέων δὲ τῶν κοτὲ ἐργασαμένων ἔργον χρήσιμον, κ. τ. λ.—A. C. M.]

In l. 5, *antidosis* is first introduced, and one of the most important points in the whole inscription is furnished by the last two letters. For these letters can belong only to χρημάτων; and we thus have the only known instance of either ἀντίδοσις or ἀντιδίδωμι, when used in the technical sense, governing a word meaning property. In the Attic orators it is always an exchange of the *liturgy*, not of *property* which is spoken of. Dittenberger, Blaschke, and Fränkel believe that no exchange of property was ever involved in the system, and give interpretations of the word in accordance with their theory. Dittenberger maintains that ἀντίδοσις is used of the temporary confiscation which each party makes upon the property of his opponent. Blaschke, supported by Fränkel, claims that the word refers to *Zuschiebung und Zurückschiebung* of the liturgy by the two parties.[18] There are passages in literature which seem to point clearly to an actual exchange of property; but it is the object of Fränkel's paper, referred to above, to discredit the evidence of these passages. In an inscription like the one under consideration, however, which furnishes the regulations of the system, there can be no talk of jests, or private proposals for settlement.[19] On the contrary, the phrase is absolute proof that the original use of the word was that usually attributed to it, namely, an actual exchange of property; however much its use in the fourth century may vary from this. In the Orators it is either employed in several distinct senses, or else there is a common meaning which has escaped the scholars who have considered it. For example, how are we to explain the phrase in the *Phaenippea* (§ 10) μετὰ τὰς ἀντιδόσεις, when no exchange of property had taken place?

In l. 8, ἀποφαίνειν is the word used by Demosthenes for the giving in of an inventory of property by each of the two parties.[20]

In l. 12, τοῦ ἀγάλματος must refer to some well-known temple statue, perhaps the *Kultbild* of Apollo, as Πυθίωι is a possible restoration in the preceding line, and in l. 30 the Pythion is plainly mentioned. The oath was to be taken with the hand on the sacred statue.

In lines 15 and 17, the form πρωτοχόροις occurs. Athenaios[21] mentions two plays having the title of πρωτόχορος. The lexicons

---

[18] *Cf.* DITTENBERGER, *Ueber den Vermögenstausch, etc.*, p. 3 ff.; BLASCHKE, *De antidosi apud Athenienses*, p. 8 ff.; FRÄNKEL, *Hermes*, XVIII, p. 464, from whom the phrase *Zuschiebung und Zurückschiebung* is taken, as being a more compact translation of Blaschke's Latin than is possible in English.   [19] FRÄNKEL, *l. c.*, pp. 446-8.
[20] *Cf.*, for example, § 9 of the *Phaenippea*.   [21] VI, 240; VII, 287.

translate this as "the first chorus," but there is nothing in the passages to indicate that it had not rather a possessive compound meaning, "having his first chorus." The play would then be about some one who was choregos for the first time. This is certainly the more likely sense of the word in our inscription. In l. 16 we must suppose some blunder of the stone-cutter, notwithstanding the usual care with which the inscription is cut.

No. 10.

Marble stele with acroterium, found north of the church. Total height, 0.375 m.; width, 0.30 m. The lower portion of the slab is gone, and of the part remaining the left-hand side of the surface is split off obliquely.

```
ϜΥΗΦΙΣΘΑΙΙΚΑ         ........ εἶπεν·] ἐψηφίσθαι Ἰκα-
  ΙΤΟΝΔΗΜΑΡΧ         ριεῦσιν ἐπαινέσα]ι τὸν δήμαρχ-
   ΕΓΙΜΕΛΕΙΤΑ        ον ..........²¹ª ὅτι] ἐπιμελεῖτα-
    ΑΙΣΔΙΚΑΙΣΕ       ι τῶν Ἰκαριέων ἐν τ]αῖς δίκαις ε
    ΚΟΙΝΑΙΣΚΑΙ       5 ὑγνωμόνως, ἐν ταῖς] κοιναῖς καὶ
    ΓΑΤΩΝΔΗΜΟΤ                                  ]τα τῶν δημοτ-
       Λ ΙΙΙ                              ῶν
```

Comment.—Height of letters, 0.008; arrangement, στοιχηδόν. The date is probably the latter part of the fourth century. Estimating the portion of the stone which is gone and the average space taken by each letter, and allowing the same margin at the beginning of the line as at the end, I calculate that thirteen letters are missing in the first line and fifteen in the others. The restoration of the first three lines is obvious enough, except that in l. 3 it is questionable whether to give only five letters to the demarch's name and insert καλῶς between the ὅτι and ἐπιμελεῖται, or to supply a name of ten letters as I have preferred to do, in the belief that it is necessary to insert an adverb below. But of the remaining lines just enough is left to show that the decree has to do with certain functions of the demarch connected with lawsuits—a circumstance which adds to our disappointment that it is not intact. In l. 4 we must supply a genitive as object of the verb ἐπιμελεῖται. A personal object of this verb is not unknown in inscriptions, and so τῶν Ἰκαριέων, which gives the right number of

---

²¹ª [καθότι] ἐπιμελεῖτα[ι ὅπως ἂν ἐπιστῆι τ]αῖς δίκαις ε[ὖ καὶ δικαίως ταῖς] κοιναῖς, καὶ [ἔστιν ἀγαθὸς περὶ] τὰ τῶν δημοτ[ῶν ....?—A. C. M.]

letters, is a possible restoration. One naturally connects the κοιναῖς of l. 5 with the δίκαις of the preceding line, and thinks of a distinction between the law cases tried in the city, in which the demarch would be the representative of the deme as a whole (therefore called κοιναῖς), and the more unimportant cases within the deme, in which the demarch administered the oath and put the vote, without, however, having any power of decision. The deme-assemblies sometimes acted as arbitrators in a suit, and then the demarch held a position not unlike that of the chairman or moderator of an American town-meeting.[22] The E at the end of l. 4 cannot be the beginning of an adjective to contrast with κοιναῖς, as it would have the predicate position, for which there would be no reason. This E must therefore belong to an adverb modifying ἐπιμελεῖται. The contrasting adjective to κοιναῖς would then come at the beginning of l. 6.

No. 11.

Base for a votive offering, with a socket cut in the upper surface. Length, 0.55 m.; width, 0.50 m.; height, 0.17 m. Height of letters, 0.018 m. Seen by Milchhöfer in the church, built into the wall separating the narthex from the nave.

KHΦIΣIOΣTIMAPı   Κηφίσιος Τιμάρ[χου
IKAPIEYΣ   Ἰκαριεὺς
EYΞAMENOΣANEΘHKEN   εὐξάμενος ἀνέθηκεν
TΩIΔIONYΣΩI   τῶι Διονύσωι.

Comment.—Published by Milchhöfer in the *Berlin. philologische Wochenschrift* for June, 1887, and *Mitth. Inst. Athen.*, 1887, p. 311.

No. 12.

Marble stele with a square hole in the top for holding a small figure or statue. Height, 1.07 m.; width, 0.43 m.; thickness, 0.33 m. The socket in the top is 0.185 m. square and 0.15 m. deep. Upon the front side is represented in relief a beautiful crown of ivy. The right-hand upper corner of the top is broken, and a trifle is also broken away from the left-hand upper corner.

ΠIMEΛHTAITHΣEP   ἐ]πιμεληταὶ τῆς ἐρ[γασία-
ΣTOYAΓAΛMATC   ς τοῦ ἀγάλματο[ς ἀνέ-
ΘEΣANTΩIΔION   θεσαν τῶι Διον[ύσωι

[22] *Cf. C.I.A.*, ıı, 578; *Mitth. Inst. Athen.*, 1879, p. 200 ff.

Comment.—The ἐπιμεληταί, appointed to oversee the making of some important statue, were crowned by the deme and dedicated a small figure to Dionysos in honor of the completion of their task. *Cf.* Rangabé, *Antiquités Helléniques*, 1068; *C.I.A.*, II, 1208:

οἱ αἱ]ρεθέ[ν]τ[ες ὑπ]ὸ ['Α]λα[ιῶν
τὸ ἄγ]αλμα ποιήσασθαι τεῖ 'Αφ[ροδί-
τει στεφα]νωθέντες ὑπὸ τῶν δη[μοτ-
ῶν ἀνέ]θεσαν τεῖ 'Αφρο[δίτει

Then follow twenty-four names of the ἐπιμεληταί appointed. The statue dedicated cannot be the one which they were to oversee, for the measurements of the base show that it could have held only a very small figure. The honor of crowning in our Ikarian case is indicated, not in the inscription, but by the relief of the ivy wreath. The two cases are, however, essentially parallel. The statue, τοῦ ἀγάλματος, cannot be the same statue which is mentioned in Inscr. No. 9, for that is of much earlier date, and ἐργασία can, I think, refer only to the execution of a new statue, not to the restoration of an old one.

No. 13.

Massive block used as the lintel for the door leading from the narthex into the nave of the church. Length, 1.68 m.; height, 0.34 m.; thickness, 0.22 m. At the ends are Byzantine ornaments.

```
ΑΡΙΣΤΟΜΕ                    Α Ε ΤΟ
   ΕΥΤ                      ΧΧΗϹ
   ΚΑΙΤ                      ΛΗϹ
```

Comment.—The large letters on the left were seen by Milchhöfer and published in *Mitth. Inst. Athen.*, 1887, p. 310. The larger letters are of Roman imperial date, the smaller from the third or fourth century B. C. The name in small letters on the left-hand end is 'Αριστομέ[δων or 'Αριστομέ[νης, while, of the large letters, Εὐτ may be the beginning of any one of many names. On the right, I cannot make out the name in small letters.[23] The large letters of the first line seem to be a patronymic ending–άδης.

No. 14.

Tombstone with relief representing a parting-scene of the usual type.

[23] [Perhaps ['Εξά]κεστος.—A. C. M.]

Below, a few letters of the inscription can be made out with difficulty. Height of letters, 0.022 m.

```
· · · · MHMON ?   · · · · · · · · · ANΔPOKAI ?
```

No. 15.

Fragment of tombstone. Length, 0.565 m.; width, 0.27 m.

```
TIMOK        Τιμόκ[ριτος
TIMOKPA      Τιμοκρά[τους
```

Comment.—Seen by Milchhöfer in the left niche of the apse.[24] *Cf.* the Τιμόκριτος Τιμοκράτους in the list of the prytanes of the tribe of Aigeis.[25]

No. 16.

Fragment of marble block. Length, 0.72 m.; width, 0.33 m. Inscription upon the end. Height of letters, 0.014 m.

```
    IL
POΣΔHι
```

No. 17.

Fragment of rough stone, 0.35 m. by 0.27 m.

```
KOI
```

NOTE.—Inscription No. 1 (above p. 71) was dated about the middle of the fourth century, upon the usual criterion of the variation in the form of the spurious diphthong ου. As this diphthong has been found in the form o as late as the Chremonidean War, 266/63 B. C. (Droysen),[26] our inscription may be much later than was assumed above; and, when the form of the Π is taken into consideration, this becomes most likely. Dittenberger has traced the development in the forms of this letter as Ρ, Γ— rarely Γ— Π, π, and states that the form Ρ is the only one which occurs earlier than the third century. This is accepted by Reinach (*Traité d'Épigraphie Grecque*, p. 205), and is, in fact, concurred in by epigraphists in general. Hence, I think that

---

[24] *Mitth. Inst. Athen.*, 1887, p. 311.
[25] *C.I.A.*, II, 872; see *Seventh Annual Report of Am. School*, pp. 85, 88.
[26] MEISTERHANS[(2)], p. 6, Note 21.

our inscription, notwithstanding the carelessness with which it is cut, should be assigned to the third century, especially as it is from a rural district; and it is not likely that the change to Π would take place outside of Athens before it had been adopted in the city itself.[27]

Athens,   CARL D. BUCK.
February 4, 1889.

[27] [Whether the date of this inscription falls in the last quarter of the fourth century, or in the third, is of no great moment; but it is time to protest against the above dictum of Dittenberger, especially as it appears to have become so far fixed that some inscriptions of the fourth century in which undoubted instances of Π occur have been published as if Γ alone was there found, notably *C.I.A.*, II, 834 b (of 329/8 B. C.), 834 c (of 317/307 B. C.), in the former of which a few cases of Π are found in the fac-similes published by Philios, *Ephem. Arch.*, 1883; in the latter, about half the entire number (some 75) have the right limb quite down to the line, or nearly so, but not one in the *Corpus*.

The fac-similes of Philios are substantially correct, as shown by a squeeze of a part of *C.I.A.*, II, 834 c, for which I have to thank the discoverer of the inscription. These are from Eleusis, as is also another belonging to the fifth century, *Ephem. Arch.*, 1888, p. 48, with fac-simile lithographed from a squeeze. Here, in one or two cases, the right limb reaches the line, and in several it lacks little of it. The same may be said of *Bull. Corr. Hellén.*, 1888, p. 138, No. 6, found under the temple of Roma on the Akropolis, an Athenian decree of the year 378/7. The Π, however, does not appear in the published text. Still, several instances of Π assigned to the fourth century will be found in *C.I.A.*, II, after excluding all those which have not passed under Köhler's eye, or been copied by the most careful hands.

In the inscription of the Hagnias monument at Ikaria, the Γ has the right limb about three-fourths down to the line. This may also be found in inscription No. 8, above, and many times in that of Plotheia (about 400 B. C.) mentioned already in Note 5, as I have ascertained through the kindness of Mr. Louis Dyer who has examined the stone for me in the Louvre.—A. C. M.]

DISCOVERIES IN THE ATTIC DEME OF IKARIA, 1888.

SCULPTURES.*

[PLATES VII, VIII.]

The following sculptures, found at Ikaria by the American School, and described under numbers I–XXV, are, perhaps without exception, of Pentelic marble.

I.—Colossal head of the archaic period (*Fig. 1*), found beneath the front wall of the church. Length from crown of head to bottom of fracture, 0.41 m.; greatest width, 0.35 m.; average thickness from front to back, 0.21 m.; distance from hair to base of nose, 0.065 m.; width of nose at base, 0.027 m.; perpendicular depth from bridge of nose to interior angle of eye, 0.03 m.; diameter of largest curl, 0.055 m.

The back of the head has been entirely chiseled away, and the suggestion has therefore been made (Wolters, *Mitth. Inst. Athen*, 1887, p. 390), that the head could not have belonged to a statue, but was to be classed among masks which were built into walls.[1] But, if not the head of a statue, it is more likely to have been fixed on the top of a pillar, instances of which have come down to us.[2] But the present form is not necessarily original. The back may very well have been cut away later, to secure a flat surface for some purpose. The dowel-hole is evidence against immuring; moreover, the surface at the back differs from the surface under the point of the beard, where the chiseling is not so rough as on the back of the head, though worked less smoothly than it would have been if intended to be seen.

The head is of a very archaic type, and can be counted among the most ancient bearded heads which have been found on Greek soil. A

---

* Dr. Waldstein has given me the benefit of his opinion on the most important objects in our collection of sculptures. The following notes are based upon his remarks; and I owe him an additional acknowledgment for his kindness in going over this paper with me and making some valuable suggestions. I have made some additions since his departure from Athens, and it would not be just to hold him absolutely responsible for every view expressed here.

The plates and figures are from photographs taken by Mr. S. B. P. Trowbridge and Mr. Louis Dyer.

[1] *Cf.* PAUSANIAS, I. 2. 5.   [2] *Cf.* BÖTTICHER, *Baumkultus der Hellenen*, fig. 43.

109

series of bearded heads which, from their type, naturally offer themselves for comparison are those from Cyprus, now in the Metropolitan Museum at New York; and also two statue-heads now in Rome, generally considered to represent Dionysos. One of these, in the villa Albani, is reproduced in Roscher's *Lexikon der gr. und rom. Mythologie* in the article *Dionysos*. The other, in the Palazzo Doria, has never been reproduced, but while in Rome I made careful notes on it.[3] The most valuable data for comparison, however, are found in the series of archaic female statues discovered on the Akropolis within the last few years.

Looking at the head more in detail, we note that the crown was left smooth. Perhaps it was never intended to be seen,[4] since it was probably raised at some height above the eye-line. The hair in front is cut in a series of oblique, parallel waved ridges—the conventional pattern of numerous examples—all converging toward the median line of the forehead. Encircling the forehead, there is a series of large spiral curls of the usual conventional form, in comparatively high relief, but not undercut. There were originally ten of these curls. The curl on the extreme left, and Nos. 3, 4, and 5 from the right were inserted. One of these was found. As no regular order was followed in insertion, it is probable that the inserted curls were made separately merely on account of some defect in the marble at these points. Two holes, one on the right and the other on the left, in the wavy hair near the posterior line behind the temples, were undoubtedly used to affix a bronze wreath; while two smaller holes on the upper edge of the empty curl-hole nearest the median line probably served for some additional decoration. The general treatment of the hair differs little from that of many archaic male heads. One of the best examples is a Cypriote head,[5] where there is a double row of curls, and, above them, waved hair extending up to a rather flat crown, and in part covered by a wreath of flowers. The Cypriote heads of this style usually have the double row of curls; so also the Albani statue. In the Hermes Moschophoros of the Akropolis Museum, the curls are not of the spiral pattern, which can be traced to bronze work,

---

[3] Both are noted by MATZ-DUHN.

[4] [The ivy-wreath would cover most of the crown. A bronze leaf of such a wreath was found, about 0.05 m. in diameter.—A. C. M.]

[5] CESNOLA, *Atlas*, I, pl. LXXII, No. 470 (Museum No. 506); *cf.* No. 469 (Museum No. 515).

but seem rather blocked out in the technic of wood-carving. A head and mask of Dionysos found at Delos[6] show a triple range of curls.[7] In the remains of the mustache there appears the same wavy treatment as in the hair; but the ridges are here narrower and more elaborate. The circumstance that the mustache runs over and projects above the beard suggests that there may have been a tuft of hair represented in similar projection on the under lip, as in the heads of Dionysos on some Naxian coins.[8] The beard (of which the right side was found separately at a distance of some feet from the head) shows a series of symmetrical parallel ridges, but closer together than in the hair above the forehead and the mustache. One of the Cesnola Cypriote heads

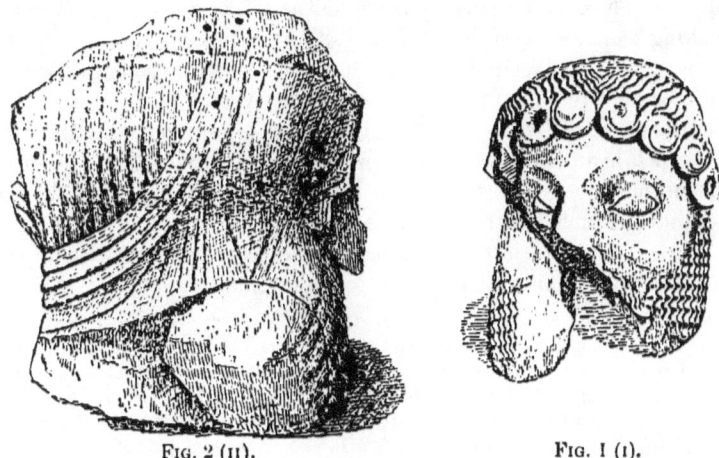

FIG. 2 (II).   FIG. 1 (I).

shows very nearly the same treatment in the beard, but its lines are more wavy in character, and present less of the notched zigzag appear-

[6] *Bull. de corr. hellén.*, 1881, pl. x, p. 507.
[7] A head from the Asklepieion, now in the Central Museum at Athens, which in many particulars resembles our head, has a single row of curls of essentially the same character but much flatter. The two curls nearest the ear on each side are on a lower line than the others. The hair on the crown of the head is cut in wavy lines converging toward the centre of the crown. The beard is marked with parallel and nearly straight ridges. The under side is left smooth. [The single row of rather flat curls is common in the helmeted Cypriote heads, noticeably in the inscribed statue holding the dove and cup: CESNOLA, *Cyprus*, p. 132. *Cf.*, also, the archaic Dionysos on the Marathonian vase, *Mitth. Inst. Athen*, 1882, pl. III.—A. C. M.]
[8] GARDNER, *Types of Greek Coins*, pl. II, No. 22.

ance.⁹ The beard of the archaic Dionysos in the Palazzo Doria shows almost precisely the same treatment as that of our statue. The forehead, brow, and cheeks are hard and smooth in modelling, but the cheek is markedly raised from the nose to the side, as is the case in one of the Akropolis female statues,¹⁰ in the Doria statue, and in several of the Cypriote heads. The eye protrudes as a whole, but inclines inward from the top downward, as in most of the Akropolis statues. The upper lid is carried in a continuous bold curve, and the two lids join at the outer angle on one plane; while at the inner angle there is a loop-like ending which has been worn away in the fragmentary portion of the right eye.¹¹ The lower lid is not so much curved as the upper. The existing portion of the left nostril is strongly distended, making the nose seem stunted in its general proportions. Stunted proportions characterize the head as a whole, and may also be observed in some Cypriote heads.¹² As Dionysos and Apollo were the only divinities, so far as we know, whose cults were of importance in Ikaria, a bearded head such as ours can represent only Dionysos, and it is consistent, moreover, with the regular type of archaic heads which have been identified as belonging to this divinity.

II.—We now turn to some fragments of a colossal seated statue (*Fig. 2*) to which this head, as we suppose, originally belonged.¹³ First,

⁹ CESNOLA, *Atlas*, I, pl. LXXXI, No. 529 (Museum No. 402); *cf.*, also, LXXII, No. 470 (Museum No. 506), where the beard is divided into six parallel ridges by horizontal grooves. [An examination of the original of No. 529 shows that the beard, in reality, does not exhibit the peculiar technic of the Ikarian head, but is wavy only, and does not belong to a very early period. The true parallel for this rare crimping in flat, sharply marked bands is to be seen in the back hair of some of the archaic female statues of the Akropolis, such as the one figured in *Ephem. Arch.*, 1886, pl. 5; 1884, pl. 8, No. 6a. I have observed another close parallel in the beard of a small bronze figure in the Bibliothèque Nationale, No. 254, and less pronounced in No. 162, a centaur with human fore-legs. *Cf.*, also, the "Zeus" head, *Mitth. Inst. Athen*, XIV, pl. III.—A. C. M.]

¹⁰ *Les Musées d'Athènes*, pl. III.

¹¹ [The last remark does not coincide with my observation. Repeated examinations of the marble convinced me that no "loop" ever existed here, but that the upper and lower lids meet in this corner at the usual sharp angle. The differences between the right and left sides of the head are many.—A. C. M.]

¹² Especially, CESNOLA, *Atlas*, I, pl. LXXII, Nos. 468, 479.

¹³ [While at first inclined to favor this view, a careful review of all the evidence has convinced me that it is not tenable. Putting aside any question of difference of style and age between head and torso, in respect to which there may easily be difference of opinion, it is difficult to reconcile the disagreement between the forms of the dowel-holes in the two. In the head enough remains of the dowel-hole to show

a male torso, preserved from neck to thighs. Height of fragment, 0.80 m.; width of breast, 0.50 m. It was found close to the base *B* (see PLAN), and it is not unlikely that this was the original site of the statue. The head must have been carved from a separate block, as is shown by the dowel-hole in the neck. The arms probably extended at right angles from the elbow. The drapery is of the customary archaic style, the chiton showing at the neck and along the right breast. The himation was folded obliquely across the chest and fell in conventional folds. A fragment which was found separately fits on the left thigh and supplies the curve which proves that the figure was seated. Still another fragment recently found belongs to the right leg just above the knee. On the left breast there are four holes, on the right, two, for the affixing of some bronze ornament.[14] Although the back of the shoulders is gone, the lower portion of the hair is preserved, and it shows the treatment usual in the Akropolis statues, namely, a wide mass divided into seven flat wavy ridges or curls. To the same statue undoubtedly belonged a hand (*Fig. 3*), found close to the wall *a b* of structure *D*, on the outside. Width of back, 0.15 m.; length from extremity of wrist-bone to end of the joint of third finger, 0.215 m.; length of second finger, 0.17 m. The long fingers and the conventional form of the thumb are highly archaic, but the execution is excellent. The hand is clasping some object. A marble kantharos

that a horizontal section was probably quadrangular, while that of the torso is pentagonal with different angles differently placed. A dowel to fit both would have been of a form so strangely contorted that it seems altogether unreasonable. Furthermore, there is a slight projection at the lower corner of the dowel-hole in the head which renders it far more likely that the dowel was inserted from the back than from below, as would be natural in affixing the piece to a wall or other vertical surface where such support would be necessary. Again, it is not probable that the back of the head would have been cut away in antiquity while the statue remained intact. This, it would seem, must be attributed to the builders of the church, if to any one, and yet the large fragment of the beard was found within the building *D*, about a metre below the lowest course of the wall of the structure, and even the main piece had not been used in the wall of the church which we demolished. We know nothing of the relation of the head to the earlier Byzantine church on the site, and, in any event, it appears that, if entire, it would have been more serviceable for building-purposes than in its present state with the dowel-hole breaking the desired surface. Finally, the fine preservation of the surface of the head is hardly consistent with the theory that it belonged to the seated statue resting on the base *B* in the open air. For a head similarly flattened at the back, see that of the Gorgon recently found on the Akropolis at Athens (*Journ. Hellen. Stud.*, 1889, pp. 265-6).—A. C. M.]

[14] [Certainly curls.—A. C. M.]

was found, corresponding in dimensions and workmanship to the hand, and it fits exactly in the hole between thumb and fore-finger, so that here we undoubtedly have the object held by the hand.[15] Width of the kantharos, inclusive of the handles, 0.21 m.; height, 0.17 m. It is shown with the hand in *Figure 3*. Finally, we have the two feet with their base in two fragments represented in *Fig. 4*. The larger fragment includes the left foot and the toes of the right; the smaller one supplies the instep of the right foot. The feet were sandaled, and the strap appears on the left foot,[16] which is in advance of the right. The right foot is somewhat raised at the heel, as in many archaic seated statues and vase-paintings, and on it appears the lower edge of the drapery, which agrees in its archaic character with that of the torso. All the toes of the left foot are cut off. These fragments are all of the same colossal proportions, and they unquestionably belong

FIG. 3 (II).

FIG. 4 (II).

to the same statue. The kantharos points to Dionysos, and strengthens our attribution of the statue to that divinity. The type seems to be much the same as that afterward followed by Alkamenes in his celebrated temple-statue of Dionysos, of which several coins[17] are supposed

[15] [The palm of the hand between thumb and fingers is left rough and thick. Near the outside of the palm, opposite the root of the thumb, is a break which shows that the hand was here attached to something, probably the knee or chair, by a marble support about 0.06 m. square. Its position is such that the kantharos must have been tipped considerably from the perpendicular. *Cf.* the Attic coin representing the statue of Dionysos by Alkamenes, and many vase-paintings.—A. C. M.]

[16] [The remains of a bronze pin or strap are still visible in the sole of the sandals on the inside of each foot near the base of the great toe, and a hole for a similar piece exists on the outside of the left foot near the nail of the small toe, but there is no trace of a corresponding one outside the right foot.—A. C. M.]

[17] BEULÉ, *Les Monnaies d'Athènes*, p. 261; HEAD, *Catalogue of Greek Coins in the British Museum, Attica*, etc., pl. XVIII.

to give a rough reproduction. Compare also the archaic relief of Zeus in Ince Blundell Hall, England.[18]

III.—There are also portions of another colossal statue of somewhat smaller proportions than that just described, namely, two fragments of arms and an unfinished hand,[19] besides two fingers of another hand belonging probably to a third colossal statue.

IV.—We come next to an archaic nude torso similar to those of the so-called Apollo series, the "Apollos" from Thera, Orchomenos, Tenea, the Apollo Ptoos, the Strangford Apollo, *etc*. This torso was found to the north of the church-wall, about half a meter below the surface. A fragment of the left leg and one of the right shoulder were found separately. Height of torso, 0.85 m.; width of shoulders, 0.36 m. The circumstance that the arms and hands were entirely free from the body indicates for this statue a date later than the type of the Thera, Orchomenos, Tenea, or Ptoos Apollos, later also than that of the similar statue from Boiotia,[20] in which the arms are separated by several inches from the body, but the hands are united to the body by cylindrical supports. The rendering of the muscles of the chest and the modelling of the back, however, show comparatively little advance from the oldest types.

V.—Belonging to this archaic period, also, is the front portion of a right foot with the long, finger-like toes characteristic of the well-known archaic Apollos just referred to.

VI.—For the basrelief very closely resembling the stele of Aristion, see below, pp. 126-134.

VII.—To the fifth century may be attributed a fragment of a sepulchral stele representing an old man holding a staff in his left hand (PLATE VII-2). Above there remain two letters of the epitaph, EY— undoubtedly 'Ικαρι]εύ[ς. Height of fragment, 0.53 m.; width, 0.23 m. Found in front of the church, close to the surface. For the type, compare certain reliefs crowning stelai, some of which have been discussed by Dr. Waldstein,[21] who has also pointed out the intimate rela-

---

[18] *Cf.* MICHAELIS, *Arch. Zeit.*, VII, p. 31; pl. 5.

[19] [One of these fragments extends from the elbow to the wrist, the other to the fingers, though broken off at the wrist (a recent break, I think). They are but roughly chiseled into shape throughout, never smoothed to a finished surface. At the elbow they are cut off squarely, and present there the same chipped or pitted appearance as the back of the colossal head described above.—A. C. M.]

[20] KABBADIAS, Κατάλογος τοῦ Κεντρικοῦ Μουσείου, No. 20.

[21] *Essays on the Art of Pheidias*, IX, pp. 303-7.

tion between many Attic sepulchral reliefs and the relief-work of Pheidias as exemplified in the Parthenon frieze.

VIII.—One of the finest pieces of sculpture found by us is a fragment of a relief, probably sepulchral, representing a female figure seated in a chair. Height, 0.26 m.; width, 0.20 m. Found north of the church, about half a meter below the surface (PLATE VIII). The left hand holds the himation up from the breast; the right hand extends a vessel, apparently a phiale.[22] About the crown of the head is

FIG. 5 (IX).

a ridge which is cut down slantingly toward the head, calling to mind, at first glance, the halo about the heads of Byzantine saints. This seems to be merely a device of the nature of that adopted in the Parthenon frieze, to make the relief appear higher than it really is.[23] The attitude of the figure and the delicacy in the treatment of the drapery remind one of some of the seated female figures in the Parthenon

[22] [If it is a phiale that is held in the right hand (as seems to me most likely) and the monument is sepulchral, it would be a new phase, indeed, in Attika at this early period; so much so that, in my judgment, it is not sepulchral, but represents a divinity. The size of the figure within the limitations of space, the shape, so far as preserved, and the comparative thinness of the slab, suggest a votive offering with adorants, rather than a sepulchral stele. This leads me to conjecture that we may possibly have here a representation of the female divinity whom, in accordance with the traditions of the spot, we ought to expect to find, namely, Erigone. If the cast of features calls to mind the Demeter (or Kore?) of the famous Eleusinian relief (FRIEDERICHS–WOLTERS, Bausteine, No. 1182) with its "eminently religious character," we may remember that Erigone and the Ikarian story are closely allied to the Eleusinian divinities and legends (Seventh Annual Report of School at Athens, pp. 66, 97).—A. C. M.]

[23] [If Constantinos's photographs do not deceive, something similar but less pronounced exists about the back of the head of the middle figure on a sepulchral stele of the Central Museum (KABBADIAS, Κατάλογος τοῦ Κεντρικοῦ Μουσείου, No. 132; Mrs. MITCHELL, Hist. Anc. Sculpt., p. 382) and above the head of the female to the left in the stele with the inscription 'Αριστέας 'Ιφιστιάδης, mentioned by KÖHLER, Mitth. Inst. Athen, 1885, p. 372. These are both assigned to the fifth century. Such concurrent circumstances may give some clue to the date of our relief. The hair was not represented plastically at all on the head, the surface being left quite rough. This is also the case with the hair of the rider on the Dexileos monument in the Kerameikos, where traces of paint show how the hair was treated, and it is probable that the same device was resorted to here.—A. C. M.]

frieze.[24] In regard to the gesture of holding the drapery up from the breast, we may compare the Myrtia Kephisia[25] relief of the Louvre. In the Hera of the east frieze, the motive seems to me to be quite different. Something similar appears in still earlier art, namely on the altar sometimes attributed to Kalamis.[26] Compare also an archaic relief from Lakonike.[27]

IX.—*Figure 5* reproduces the lower left-hand portion of a relief, representing three figures, one of which is of much greater stature than the others and is thus, probably, distinguished as a divinity. Height of fragment, 0.34 m.; width, 0.32 m. Upon the *anta* at the left of the relief are traces of a fourth figure similar to the two small figures within. The style of work seems closely akin to that of the

Fig. 6 (x).

reliefs[28] representing Asklepios and Hygieia receiving homage, the worshippers being of much smaller size than the divinities. The small figures in our relief, however, are not turned in adoration toward the large figure, but seem to be walking away. It is to be observed that they are standing upon a higher level than the large figure, as if walking over a slight eminence. The hand of the large figure seems to

[24] MICHAELIS, *Der Parthenon*, p. 204; WALDSTEIN, *Essays*, VI, p. 203.
[25] FRÖHNER, *Inscriptions grecques du Louvre*, p. 290.
[26] OVERBECK, *Gesch. d. gr. Plastik*(3), I, p. 219; KABBADIAS, Κατάλογος τοῦ Κεντρικοῦ Μουσείου, No. 54.
[27] *Mitth. Inst. Athen*, 1883, pl. XVI.
[28] *Cf. Mitth. Inst. Athen*, 1877, p. 215 ff, plates XIV–XVII; GIRARD, *Bull. de corr. hellén.*, 1878, p. 65, plates VII–IX.

rest on the shoulder of the figure directly in front, but the stone is too much damaged to show the action with certainty.[29]

X.—Two marble slabs with reliefs on both sides (*Fig. 6*): height, 0.63 m.; width at base of slab *A*, 0.63 m., of *B*, 0.58 m. In the top of each slab is a dowel-hole, placed at about an equal distance from each end. The two slabs must have formed part of a balustrade or railing, visible from both sides. *A* is an end slab, as is shown by the tree which appears on each side, in one case being the beginning of the the series of reliefs, in the other, the end. Looking at the side upon which the relief of *A* forms the beginning, we see a representation of Herakles and the Muses; Herakles, with club and himation or chlamys (lion-skin?), standing in the centre of slab *B* with a female figure on each side; before slab *A* are three female figures,[30] the central one holding a musical instrument resembling a mandolin. Upon the other side of the slabs is represented a sacrificial procession of nine figures, four on slab *A*, five on slab *B*: the foremost figure is leading a goat beneath the tree. This relief is so much damaged that only the lower portion of the figures is preserved. The work has great historic and mythologic interest, as being the only extant representation in sculp-

[29] [The explanation of this scene is to be sought in the class of reliefs treated by Löwy, *Jahrbuch arch. Inst.*, 11, pp. 109-11. They are characterized by a low altar (ἐσχάρα · χθονίοις δὲ καὶ ἤρωσι ἐσχάρας, ὑποχθονίοις δὲ βόθρους καὶ μέγαρα, PORPHYR., *De antro nymph.*) usually rounded above, by adorants, and at times by a female much larger than these, with pitcher and patera ready to pour a libation, as in the relief of the Villa Albani figured by Löwy; *cf. Mitth. Inst. Athen*, IV, pl. XVI; ROSCHER, *Lex. Myth.*, p. 406; etc. These habitually stand before the altar, behind which is a hero or god to whom the libation is to be made. Sometimes the female is omitted, as in the Theseus relief of the Louvre, and in that from the Mesogaia described by Milchhöfer, *Mitth. Inst. Athen*, 1887, p. 293. In ours, we see the ἐσχάρα, the adorants, and the colossal female, but, in the mutilated state of the relief, there may be question whether the adorants have their hands in the usual attitude, or the female is provided with a libation-vessel. Yet her right arm is certainly raised, and that of the figure before her is bent upward from the elbow. (Our artist, by the use of a magnifier, has seemed to see more than I can feel wholly certain of.) A peculiar feature is that two adorants are in front of the female and are walking past the altar and beyond it (not over it, as appears clearly, since the feet and a portion of the legs are concealed by the altar). The theory that the colossal female sometimes represents a priestess (ZOEGA, as cited by Löwy) receives some support here by the position of her left hand seemingly resting on the shoulder of the adorant before her.— A. C. M.]

[30] [The conspicuous absence of the chiton poderes in the third figure on the right, in *A*, seems to me to preclude, for this period, the idea that this figure was intended for a Muse. I think it a male.—A. C. M.]

ture of Herakles and the Muses; though these are connected on a vase recently published,[31] and on a few Roman coins,[32] all which examples are to be traced to the Muses which the Roman consul Fulvius Nobilior carried off from Ambrakia and set up in a temple dedicated to Hercules Musarum.[33] In a Chian inscription (*C. I. G.*, 2214), the victors in gymnastic contests made libations ταῖς τε Μούσαις καὶ τῷ Ἡρακλεῖ (*cf.* Ἑρμοῦ καὶ Ἡρακλέους καὶ Μουσῶν, Teos; Dittenberger, *Syll.*, No. 349). But these reliefs have especial interest and importance on the art side, belonging, as they do, to the best period of the fourth century, and showing much analogy with the reliefs of Apollo, Marsyas, and the Muses, from the pedestal of a group by Praxiteles at Mantineia.[34]

XI.—In PLATE VII-3 is represented a well-preserved ex-voto slab of a not uncommon type, representing a small temple with pilasters. On the lower edge there is a projection intended to fit into a socket. The cornice is ornamented with a range of antefixes placed at equal intervals.[35] Height of slab, 0.27 m.; width, 0.31 m.; projection at bottom, 0.05 m. deep and 0.08 m. wide. It was found in front of the two upright slabs in the pronaos of the Pythion (see PLAN, *II, i* and *k*). In the middle, Apollo is seated upon the omphalos, enveloped in a voluminous himation, which is draped in such a way as to leave his breast and right shoulder and arm bare. With his left hand he raises a lustration-branch, while in his right he holds a phiale. The representation of divinities holding vessels for the libation is not rare in the fifth century and later, and, according to Furtwängler,[36] is the result of a strong tendency, seen in vases of the period of Pheidias, to represent the gods in human relations. A certain degree of archaism is evident in the head and in the treatment of the curls. In front of Apollo stands the altar before which the worshipper is stationed, with his himation loosely thrown about him, and his right arm raised in the usual gesture of adoration. This figure displays a very close resemblance to some of the worshippers in the Asklepios reliefs,[37] also to the worshipper on the ex-voto relief to Zeus Meilichios, found at the

[31] *Notizie degli Scari*, 1884, pl. VIII, p. 377.   [32] *Cf.* BIE, *Die Musen*, p. 25.
[33] PLINY, *H.N.*, XXXV. 66; EUMENIUS, *Pro restaur. schol.*, VII.
[34] *Bull. de corr. hellén.*, 1888, plates I, II, III; pp. 104-28.
[35] [The spectator is conceived to be standing by the side of the temple and looking in upon the scene enacted there, as if no wall existed to interrupt the view.—A. C. M.]
[36] *Mitth. Inst. Athen*, 1881, p. 117.
[37] *Cf. Bull. de corr. hellén.*, 1878, pl. VII; *Mitth. Inst. Athen*, 1877, pl. XVII.

Peiraieus.[38] In the last-named work, the divinity, Zeus Meilichios, holds a phiale in the same manner as the Apollo on our relief. Behind Apollo stands Artemis, clad in the long tunic and diploïs. The top of her quiver appears above the right shoulder. The drapery recalls the various reproductions of the Athena Parthenos,[39] while the treatment of the hair is precisely the same as that of a fourth-century head in the Central Museum, which was thought to represent Hygieia by Köpp, who published it for the first time.[40] The left hand of Artemis is held upon her hip, while the right hand rests upon the outer wall of the temple.[41] The workmanship of the relief is rather careless. On the omphalos plentiful remains of red color are still distinguishable, and there are also slight traces of the same on the borders which enclose the relief.

Upon the upper and lower edges of the relief is the following inscription: ΠΥΘΑΙΣΤΗΣ ΓΕΙΣΙΚΡΑΤΗΣ | ΑΚΡΟΤΙΜΟΥ ΑΝΕΘΗΚΕΝ, Πυθαιστὴς Πεισικράτης Ἀκροτίμου ἀνέθηκεν. This is the only example of the word Πυθαιστής in an inscription,[42] though, in a long Amphictyonic decree, Böckh supplies Π[υθαιστάς. Töpffer, in an article upon *Die attischen Pythaisten und Deliasten*,[43] has shown that the Pythaistai of Strabo and the lexicographers were neither members of a certain gens of this name, nor even of any particular gens; but rather that the title was a general one given to envoys sent to consult the Pythian oracle. The inscription possesses additional interest from the fact that Ikaria lies so near the Marathonian Tetrapolis, where the worship of Apollo gained its first foothold in Attika and where, at an early day, the Delian and Pythian cults were fused.[44]

[38] *Bull. de corr. hellén.*, 1883, p. 507, pl. XVIII.
[39] *Cf.* SCHREIBER, *Die Nachbildungen der Athene Parthenos.* [For a similar habit in statues of Artemis, see ROSCHER, *Lexikon*, p. 605.—A. C. M.]
[40] *Mitth. Inst. Athen*, 1885, pl. IX. [This arrangement of the hair is a form of the double bow-knot of the later Apollo Belvedere and of many female statues, especially of Artemis and Aphrodite.—A. C. M.]
[41] [The similarity of this attitude in general to that of Hygieia in the Asklepian reliefs, and the further likeness of the full-face position, otherwise rather rare in the best period (FRIEDERICHS-WOLTERS, *Bausteine*, No. 1803), may be noticed.—A. C. M.]
[42] [This is the statement of TÖPFFER, *Hermes*, 1888, p. 322; but he has overlooked the Delian inscription (LEBÈGUE, *Delos*, p. 150) reading Ζήνωνα Ζήνωνος, κλειδουχήσαντα καὶ [πυ]θαιστὴν ἐν [Ἀθήν]αις [καὶ ἱερέα Διὸς Σώτηρος καὶ τῆς] Ἀθη[νᾶς] τῆς Σωτείρ[ας γενόμενον ..., which tends to invalidate some of T.'s conclusions.—A. C. M.]
[43] *Hermes*, 1888, pp. 321–32.
[44] *Cf.* MILCHHÖFER, *Ueber den attischen Apollon;* CURTIUS, *Griechische Geschichte*, I, p. 107.

It is an interesting coincidence that, just as the type of our relief may be considered as influenced by the Asklepian reliefs, so the Akrotimos of the inscription is probably the man who showed so warm an interest in the Asklepian cult in Athens (see *Seventh Annual Report of American School at Athens*, pp. 85–6).

XII.—Upon another slab, broken at the right, Apollo is represented, again seated on the omphalos, and playing on the lyre (PLATE VII-1). Behind him stand two female figures, probably Muses.[45] Along the top runs a cornice. Height of slab, 0.48 m.; width as far as fracture on the right, 0.43 m. Found immured in the church.

XIII.—Lower left-hand corner of relief representing a draped figure standing with legs crossed, leaning on a pillar. Height of fragment, 0.32 m.; width, 0.21 m. Found in the wall of the church. This may be one of the several types of Muses leaning upon a pillar,[46] but not enough of the relief is preserved to show what the attribute was. The drapery is of good style. Behind the figure is a tree.

XIV.—Small fragment of relief showing the legs of a young man, nude; also a hand grasping some object, perhaps the branch of a tree. Height, 0.26 m.; width, 0.125 m. Found in the south wall of the church. Beside the left leg is seen the lower corner of the chlamys.

XV.—Lower portion of a relief showing the feet and the lower edge of the drapery of a female figure. Height, 0.26 m.; width, 0.24 m. Found in the south wall of the church. The workmanship is poor.

XVI.—Sepulchral stele representing a parting-scene of the usual type. A female figure, seated in a chair, grasps the hand of a man.

---

[45] [In this once beautiful relief the omphalos exhibits plastic traces of the network of fillets (ἀγρηνόν) which is so frequently represented as covering its surface. I have already expressed the opinion (*Seventh Report*, p. 78) that the females are Artemis and Leto. There are no attributes to characterize them, but they are distinguished plainly as maiden and matron by their dress, that of Artemis being the same as in the preceding relief. A similar distinction may be noted in *Élite Céramographique*, II, pl. XXXVI; and in *Anc. Marb. Brit. Mus.*, part II, pl. V. Our scene is purely peaceful, purely musical. For Artemis without attributes, may be cited the black-figured vase of *Élite Cér.*, II, pl. L, where Apollo is mounting a chariot and Artemis is ready to hand him the lyre and plectrum. Leto stands before the horses. The attitude in our relief, each lifting the veil with the left hand, and Artemis resting her right on her hip, is too familiar to need illustration. More of the head of Apollo is preserved than appears from our plate. The head is slightly raised and seems looking into the distance.—A. C. M.]

[46] *Cf.* BIE, *Die Musen*, ch. VI, types, 1.θ; 2.β; 2.η; 3.μ; 4.γ.

Near the woman stands a female attendant; above are cut two rosettes. Height, 0.82 m.; width, 0.40 m. This relief was built into one of the interior walls of the church, and was seen there by Milchhöfer.[47] At the bottom, a few letters of the inscription can be made out. See Inscription No. 14 (p. 107).

XVII.—Torso of a satyr, broken at the waist (*Fig. 7*). The two parts were found separately, one imbedded in the north wall of the church, the other, under the church. Total height, 0.57 m.; breadth of chest, 0.29 m. The root of the tail is distinguishable, behind, and, below it, the place where the tip was attached, curling around.

XVIII.—Breast of a Seilenos with part of right arm and end of the scanty beard, which is divided into four distinct parts (*Fig. 8*). Height of fragment, 0.21 m.; breadth of chest, 0.15 m. Found near the angle made by the peribolos-wall *E* with the later wall *F*.

FIG. 7 (XVII).   FIG. 9 (XIX).   FIG. 8 (XVIII).

XIX.—Head of a child (*Fig. 9*), found in the same place as the last. Height, 0.13 m. The left side of the crown of the head has been worked off flat, and shows that it was part of a group similar to the Eirene and Ploutos of Kephisodotos, or the Hermes and Dionysos of Praxiteles.[48] The face offers a very striking resemblance to that of the Dionysos child in the Hermes group, but is of much inferior workmanship and later date.

[47] *Mitth. Inst. Athen*, 1887, p. 311.

[48] [It will be observed that the inclination of the head is toward the child's left. Its gaze is directed upward and toward some object. In neither of the groups cited, nor in that of the boy in the Peiraieus museum (*Mitth. Inst. Athen*, 1881, pl. XIII), is the position such as to account for the flat surface on the left side of the head.—A. C. M.]

XX.—Head representing an actor in the female tragic mask, with distended eyes, wide-open mouth, and hair in a heavy mass, like a wig. Height, 0.16 m. The hair, which is cut in wide ridges, is drawn up over the middle of the forehead. It is interesting to compare with this an ivory statue of an actor, found at Pompeii.[49]

XXI.—Statue of a girl, of the Graeco-Roman period, head wanting (*Fig. 10*). Height, 1.10 m.

XXII.—Female head of the Graeco-Roman period, found close to the statue just mentioned (*Fig. 10*). It was afterward stolen. The fact that the statue and head were found in close proximity gives a presumption in favor of their belonging together.[50]

FIG. 10 (XXI, XXII).　　　　　FIG. 13 (XXVI).

[49] *Cf. Mon. d. Inst.*, XI, pl. XIII ; *Annali d. Inst.*, 1880, p. 210; also reproduced by BAUMEISTER, *Denkmäler*, under article *Schauspieler*, etc. [This comparison must not be understood as indicating a close parallel. The hair is not arranged in the formal curls of the ivory statue, but falls irregularly beside the face, and the lock on the top of the head runs over the crown to the back of the head, like that seen on many heads of Eros, thus combining, in a way, the arrangement of hair seen on the so-called genius of tragedy from Herculaneum (CLARAC, III, 1132; *Annali d. Inst.*, XVIII, p. 216–22), and the mask held in its hand. On the left side of our head, near the ear, is a fracture which shows that it was here attached to some object.—A. C. M.]

[50] [In *Figure 10*, the head has been set upon the body without any attempt at proper junction or desire to prejudice the question of their belonging together.—A. C. M.]

XXIII.—Portrait-head of Graeco-Roman period. Height, 0.30 m.

XXIV.—Marble slab hollowed out on one side and pyramidal on the other. Width, 1.04 m.; length, as far as preserved, 1.00 m., but originally about 1.24 m., as calculated from the pyramidal side. Found just outside of wall *ac* of *D*, 0.80 m. below top of wall. Along the edge of the side which is hollowed out are five objects which it is difficult to describe, but of which *Figure 11* will afford some idea. Last year, there was found a corner-piece having upon it a similar object, but somewhat larger. This, however, from its dimensions, cannot be one of the missing corner-pieces of the slab found this year, but must have belonged to another similar slab. Along one edge of the slab runs a well-cut moulding. Innumerable suggestions have been put forward as to the nature of the strange objects ranged along the edge of the hollowed side. Animals' feet, birds' tails, *etc.*, must be counted out, owing to the circumstance that one of the objects is intact, and so must be explained, not as a fragment, but as complete. I have attempted to explain the slab as a table for offering sacred cakes to the god, and the mysterious ornaments as representing cakes made with a pine-cone mould. I was led to this by comparing a painting found at Pompeii,[51] in which there is represented, in the midst of woodland and mountain scenery, a statue of Dionysos holding the thyrsos in his left hand and the kantharos in his right; while upon a rough rock-altar is seen a large copper dish within which is a smaller wooden dish containing fruits of various kinds, and beside this wooden dish an object which has the appearance of a pine-cone standing on its base, but which is explained as a cake made in the form of the pine-

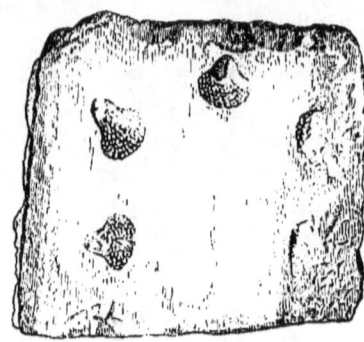

Fig. 11 (xxiv).

Fig. 12 (xxv).

[51] *Musco Borbonico*, vol. VII, pl. XVI; BÖTTICHER, *Baumkultus der Hellenen*, fig. 24.

cone, sacred to Dionysos. Reference is made, here, to the lines of Vergil's *Georgics* (II, 393–5): *ergo rite suum Baccho dicemus honorem | carminibus patriis, lancesque et liba feremus, | et ductus cornu stabit sacer hircus ad aram.* The diameter of the basin in the painting seems to be about equal to the height of the statue, so that we need not feel that our slab is too large to be explained in this way. Nor is it an objection that it is of stone, not of metal. But a serious objection to this theory is found in the pyramidal shape of one side and the cornice with moulding, features which seem inexplicable in connection with such a basin or platter. These may be taken as rather favoring a suggestion which has been made, that the slab was a roof-piece over a niche, the hollow side being underneath and the strange objects some form of ornament.

XXV.—*Figure 12*, from a photograph, represents the head of one of the griffins already mentioned above, p. 68.

XXVI.—Besides the sculptures in marble above described, a few objects in bronze were found, the most important of which is a small anathema with a female figure incised in outline (*Fig. 13*). This is apparently a divinity, perhaps Artemis, holding a flower in her right hand, while her left hand and arm support a sceptre. The head-dress is peculiar, and the whole style archaic.[52]

CARL D. BUCK.

Athens,
February, 1889.

[52] [The bronze is about 0.12 m. in length, somewhat broken away at the bottom and front side below, and is still attached to a narrow ribbon of bronze by which it was affixed originally. A hole pierces the neck. The bronze is cut out to follow the outlines desired, as in the case of the bronze from Olympia noticed by FLASCH (BAUMEISTER, *Denkmäler*, p. 1104s) and that at Metaponto described by A. EMERSON in *Am. Journ. Arch.*, IV, p. 30. The figure faces toward one's left and holds in her right hand her veil of light stuff by the fingers while the thumb is extended straight from the wrist as in the other hand, which does not grasp the staff. The veil extends from the top of the head somewhat in front of the facial outline and probably curved to meet the hand (see GERHARD, *Auserl. gr. Vasen.*, pl. XXIII). A bit of the bronze is lost here and a portion of the hand also. The lines here show the fall of the garment and the folds toward the neck. The dress is the diploïdion, leaving the neck and arms bare. No attributes are visible, except the staff and possibly a wreath on the head. The staff is wound with a fillet. Here, again, I suggest the possibility of a representation of the local heroine. Except in the drawing of the hands, there seems to be nothing more than a slight severity in the style. If the staff be a sceptre and not a thyrsos, this may well have been assigned to Erigone, as it often is given to Triptolemos.—A. C. M.]

DISCOVERIES IN THE ATTIC DEME OF IKARIA, 1888.

SCULPTURE.

STELE OF A WARRIOR.*

[PLATE IX.]

In clearing away the mass of rubbish which had collected in the interior of the church, the workmen, at a depth of twenty centimeters, came upon what was apparently a long marble slab, broken into three pieces, forming the threshold between the narthex and the main body of the church. Upon turning over one of the three fragments, it was found to be sculptured; and, when the other fragments had been carefully taken out and fitted to the first, there appeared a relief which evoked the involuntary exclamation, "Warrior of Marathon!" The material is Pentelic marble. The total height of the slab (of which the upper extremity is wanting), inclusive of the base or κρηπίς, is 1.72 met.; height of κρηπίς alone, 0.165 m.; leaving 1.55 m. for the relief proper. The width of the κρηπίς is 0.485 m.; width of stele at top, 0.41 m.; showing a diminution of 0.075 m. The thickness of the slab is 0.12 m.; highest relief, 0.055 m.; lowest relief, 0.01 m.; width of rim about the relief, 0.01. Wanting in the figure itself are: the head above the neck, the right hand, and pieces of each leg just above the knee. The small fragment which fits in at the waist is not lost, but could not be found at the time the photograph was taken. The κρηπίς bears four finely cut rosettes, but no inscription.

The resemblance of this stele to the "Warrior of Marathon," or "Stele of Aristion," as it is more correctly called, now in the Central Museum at Athens, is very striking; and for purposes of comparison a reproduction of this well-known monument is here given.[1] The

---

* I wish to make acknowledgment of my indebtedness to Dr. Charles Waldstein for assistance in the preparation of this paper, especially in the detailed archæological and artistic comparison between the Ikarian stele and that of Aristion.

[1] KEKULÉ, *Die antiken Bildwerke im Theseion zu Athen*, where are collected the references to all reproductions and descriptions up to date (1869). Of the colored reproduc-

STELE OF A WARRIOR FOUND AT IKARIA.

Stele of Aristion.

stele of Aristion was found in 1838 in the ruined village of Velanideza, which lies at about two-thirds the distance between Spata and the eastern coast of Attika, not, as is frequently stated, on the plain of Marathon, between which and Velanideza intervenes the eastern range of Pentelikon. It comprises three distinct parts: the relief itself, the base proper, and a smooth surface between the relief and the base, which Mr. Kabbadias calls the κρηπίς. The κρηπίς and the base proper (βάθρον) must be distinguished: the κρηπίς, in a sense a base, is the surface upon which stands the figure in relief, and is as essential a part of the representation as the ground upon which stand the figures in a picture. The βάθρον, on the other hand, serves as the base of the whole monument, and is an external feature corresponding to the frame of the picture. The height of the whole monument, inclusive of the βάθρον, is 2.40 met.; the βάθρον itself has a height of 0.30 met., a width of 0.715, and a thickness of 0.435 m. The width of the stele at the bottom is 0.435 m., at the

tions the best, perhaps, is that in the *Revue Archéologique*, 1844, pl. I. *Cf.* MURRAY, *History of Greek Sculpture*, vol. I, p. 193; OVERBECK, *Geschichte d. gr. Plastik* (3rd ed.), vol. I. p. 150; Mrs. MITCHELL, *Hist. of Ancient Sculpture*, p. 218; FRIEDERICHS-WOLTERS, *Die Gipsabgüsse antiker Bildwerke*, No. 101; ΚΑΒΒΑΔΙΑΣ, Κατάλογος τοῦ Κεντρικοῦ Μουσείου, No. 29; PERRY, *Greek and Roman Sculpture*, p. 105; VON SYBEL, *Weltgeschichte der Kunst*, p. 119; COLLIGNON, *L'Archéologie Grecque*, p. 133; PARIS, *La Sculpture Antique*; BAUMEISTER, *Denkmäler des klassischen Altertums*, p. 341.

128   STELE OF A WARRIOR FOUND AT IKARIA.

top, 0.42 m., thus showing a diminution of 0.015 m. The thickness of the stele is 0.14 m. at the bottom, 0.12 m. at the top. Upon the κρηπίς is the inscription, ἔργον Ἀριστοκλέος, showing that the monument is the work of the artist Aristokles; and upon the βάθρον we have Ἀριστίονος, evidently the genitive of the name of the person represented in the relief.[2] The form of the letters[3] is somewhat older than in the inscription on the altar set up by the younger Peisistratos, mentioned by Thoukydides, and found in 1877 on the bank of the Ilissos.[4] The date of this inscription must fall between the death of Peisistratos (527 B. C.) and the expulsion of Hippias (510 B. C.); and, though perhaps some allowance should be made in the comparison of a rural inscription with one from Athens, no one would now venture to date the inscription of the Aristion stele so late as the fifth century; so that the popular designation of it as "The Warrior of Marathon" must be considered ill-founded.[5]

Turning our attention, now, to the relief upon the stele of Aristion, we find represented in profile a warrior armed with cuirass (of either stiff leather or metal, represented according to the older method, i.e., with no indication of the anatomical forms it covers), helmet and greaves, with both feet planted firmly on the ground, the right arm hanging by his side and the left grasping a spear. The crest of the helmet, which was probably of a separate piece, is wanting, as well as the point of the spear; the tip of the beard, also, was of a separate piece set on, probably on account of some flaw in the marble. The lower portion of the cuirass is represented as if made of leather strips over-

---

[2] Some prefer to read it, as one continuous inscription, "Work of Aristokles, son of Aristion:" see MURRAY, Hist. of Greek Sculpture, p. 193, note 1: "The inscription immediately beneath the relief reads EPΛONAPIϟTOKVEOϟ, and continues on the plinth in larger letters, APIϟTIONOϟ. But this separation is a mere necessity of space, and, besides, had 'Aristion' referred to the person of the relief, it would surely have come first."

[3] The letters given by Murray, in the note just cited, are not intended closely to resemble those of the original. The correct forms are given by OVERBECK, Geschichte d. gr. Plastik(3), p. 150; LOEWY, Inschriften griech. Bildhauer, No. 10.

[4] C. I. A., IV (Supplementa voluminis primi) 373e.

[5] Dr. CHARLES WALDSTEIN maintains that, if one were to judge merely from the style, independently of epigraphy, so early a date would not be given to the monument. But, on this point, authorities are not agreed: OVERBECK (Geschichte d. gr. Plastik(3), p. 231, note 63) expresses regret that, whereas in the first edition of his work he had, led by a correct Stilgefühl, given an early date to the stele, in his second edition, yielding to opposing opinions, he had adopted a later date.

lapping each other in such a manner as to leave freedom of movement to the wearer, while furnishing complete protection. The short chiton worn under the armor appears on the shoulder, and about the thighs below the leather strips. The greaves are of the usual flexible and tight-fitting form, following the modelling of the muscles of the calf. The archaic imperfection is illustrated in the ear, which is set too high and too far back; in the eye, which is seen as if almost in full face and does not harmonize with the position of the head in profile; in the hand, the position of the thumb being wholly unnatural with relation to the fingers; in the feet, which rest firmly and flatly on the ground; and in the severity of modelling and awkwardness of attitude in general. The sculptor has evidently been hampered by the narrow limits of the slab within which he had to work, and, in places, he has encroached upon the rim which surrounds and frames the relief.

The stele still exhibits abundant traces of coloring, though the brilliant coloring which it had when found has now in great measure faded away. The background was painted red, and the spear also shows traces of this color; the beard and hair seem to have had a brownish tinge; the shoulder-guard is ornamented with a star, and on the piece below it, of which the ground is red, is the head of an animal, but the colors can no longer be made out; there are traces of dark blue upon the helmet and cuirass; of the three decorative bands painted upon the cuirass, the upper one is a maeander, executed in red, as is also the tassel which hangs over the breast: the $κρηπίς$ shows signs of color, and undoubtedly bore an ornamental design.

The comparison between the Aristion stele and that from Ikaria, which forms the subject of the present article, may be divided under four heads: first, the dimensions and general arrangement of the space; second, the sculpture itself; third, the painting; fourth, their comparative importance.[6]

I. *Dimensions and arrangement of space.*—The total heights of the two monuments do not admit of comparison, since we have not the $βάθρον$ of *I.* and also since much more is missing from the top of *I.* than from the top of *A.* But, measuring[7] on the relief of *A.* from the soles

---

[6] For the sake of brevity, the stele of Aristion will be designated as *A.*, the stele of Ikaria as *I.*

[7] The stele of Aristion is now inclosed in a glass case which cannot be opened, so that I was unable to take measurements from it. In giving the general dimensions, I have taken the figures of Kabbadias and of Rangabé. The first measurement of 1.55 m. was taken from a cast in the Archæological Museum at Cambridge, England.

of the feet to a line drawn across the neck in a position corresponding to the line of breakage in I., I found the height 1.55 m., exactly equal to that of the extant portion of the relief of I., so that the figures were evidently of the same height. The κρηπίς of A. is about eleven centimeters higher than that of I. The width of the steles at the κρηπίς is 0.435 m. in A., 0.485 m. in I.; while the width at the top is 0.42 m. in A., 0.41 m. in I. Thus, the total diminution in A. is only 0.015, while I., though shorter by 0.38 m., shows a diminution of 0.075 m. In A. there is a diminution of 0.02 m. in the thickness of the slab, while in I. the diminution is 0.015 m. The width of the rim on the sides of the relief is the same in both. I. is sculptured in somewhat higher relief than A.

In A., the inscription giving the artist's name is upon a narrow projecting band at the top of the κρηπίς, while in I. there is a band, not projecting, but indicated by a fine line cut below it, on which are four rosettes but no inscription. It is probable, however, that the βάθρον of I., like that of A., bore an inscription giving the name of the person to whom the monument was erected.

The general arrangement of the space is the same in the two reliefs; in I., however, the whole figure above the knees leans further forward than in A. The result of this is, that, while the sculptor of A. is cramped for space in the back of his figure, where it encroaches on the outer rim of the slab, notably at the shoulders, the hips, calf and heel, the sculptor of I. has ample space within the rim for his figure, though he has not profited by it to give to legs and hips their true relations. On the other hand, the variation on the two slabs in the relative positions of the figures causes A. to have more room in front, so that the arm of the hand which holds the spear is visible, whereas in I. the hand alone projects from behind the bust with an awkwardness that calls attention to the cramped space.

II. *Sculpture.*—In I., enough of the beard remains to show that the tip was not, as in A., of a separate piece; furthermore, its projection is far nearer a horizontal than in A. The lower end of the helmet crest which is visible behind the neck of I. shows that this also was not cut from a separate piece. In I., the chiton on the shoulder is not represented in sculpture, as it is in A. In A., the armor below the armpit is cut away to permit free action, while in I. it is fitted tightly around the whole shoulder, not, however, coming so low down over the shoulder as in A. A rude attempt is made in I., not seen in A., to mark, by means of an oblique groove, the projection of the shoulder-muscle, as separated from the biceps. The right forearm is thrown further forward in *I.*, but shows better modelling in *A.* It is impossible to make out clearly the modelling of the hand in *I.*, owing to its mutilated condition, but the fracture leads us to think that the space occupied by it was larger in *I.* than in *A.*;[8] and, though traces of the outlines do not show that the thumb projected below the rest of the closed hand, as is usually the case, there are indications that the hand was better modelled than in *A.* In *I.*, none of the left forearm is shown, as in *A.* In *A.*, the lower border of the cuirass is strongly marked by a projecting band over the hanging strips of leather. For the leather strips of the cuirass, there are, in *A.*, five strips outside, and five in an inner series, without reckoning the edge of a strip in the extreme rear; whereas in *I.* there are only three strips in the inner series, and three over them, if these latter are strips at all and not rather an extension of the cuirass itself, with two wedge-shaped openings cut in it.[9] On the front of the cuirass of *I.* the navel is indicated, not so in *A.* In the modelling of the chiton where it falls below the armor over the thigh, *A.* is undoubtedly far superior to *I.*: whereas in *A.* the conventional stiffness of the archaic folds is relieved by delicate softening of the outlines and varied modelling of the surface—showing, on the part of the artist, a considerable sense for texture, as well as ability to realize it in low relief—all the folds in *I.* stop abruptly on a line parallel with the edge of the cuirass.[10] In the thigh, again, the very delicate modelling of the muscles displayed in *A.* is not found in *I.*, where the surfaces are left comparatively flat, and the outlines hard. The knees likewise are somewhat better in *A.* than in *I.* The indication of the sinews upon the greaves of the right leg is about the same in both figures; it is more wavy in *A.*, but more strongly marked in *I.* Instead of the three parallel ridges that define the muscle of the calf on the inside of the left greave in *A.*, we have, in *I.*, only one strongly marked incised line running along the edge of the shin-bone. The feet in both sculptures have

---

[8] Actual measurement shows the fracture in *I.* to be three centimetres wider than the hand in *A.*

[9] The fact that there is no projecting band above these notches to mark the end of the cuirass, would seem to favor this interpretation, but it must be remembered that the lower border of the cuirass may well have been represented merely in color, and thus have disappeared.

[10] With the general treatment of the chiton in *A.* compare that of the standing warrior on the north side of the Harpy monument, where, however, it is much less refined.

the archaic characteristics of resting flat on the ground, and of being very long and thin with toes somewhat resembling fingers; they are somewhat more delicately modelled in I, and the manner in which the right foot is joined to the ankle is more free. Whereas, in A., the sculptor represented the left heel behind the toes of the right foot, in $I.$, both feet are somewhat more fully shown.

III. *Painting.*—I was not at first able to see on the Ikarian stele any traces of coloring, the marble, owing to corrosion, having lost its original surface; but later, having an opportunity to examine it in Stamata, whither it had been removed, and, in a better light, I found that the outlines of the mæanders which decorated the cuirass are still very plain. I think that traces of painting of the chiton on the right shoulder are almost certain, and faint outlines of a third ornamental band about the flaps of the cuirass seemed to be visible in places, though these cannot be pronounced certain.[11] But, beyond these scanty traces, judgment of the amount of painting on our stele must rest on analogy; and, here, the Lyseas stele is of so great importance that it is worthy of being passed in review.

IV. *Comparative importance.*—But, before leaving the stele of Aristion, I will sum up the results of the comparison, and consider the important but difficult question: Which of the two steles is the earlier? In favor of $A.$ being the earlier may be urged: (1) the less skilful adaptation of the design to the space at the artist's disposal; (2) the inferior modelling of the feet. In favor of the priority in date of $I.$ are: (1) the less developed and refined modelling throughout, the feet excepted; (2) the greater dependence upon painting for details; (3) the much more conventional treatment of the drapery; (4) the more awkward and unnatural manner of holding the spear. There is no doubt that both sculptures belong to very nearly the same time. Several possibilities are open to us: $I.$ may be the earlier, and $A.$ an improvement on it made either by the same hand or by another and superior artist; or $A.$ may be the prototype of which $I.$ is a copy by an inferior artist, or even a careless reproduction by the same artist. It is not impossible, however, that both may belong to a class of analo-

---

[11] A photograph often reveals lines which prove the existence of faded coloring; and, in the present case, Dr. Waldstein, previous to my second examination of the stele, pointed out to me that, in the photograph, there were very plain traces of two wide mæanders about the cuirass. There are also traces on the right shoulder which seem to show that the chiton was represented here in painting. [Professor Rhousopoulos pointed out the mæanders March 7, 1888.—A. C. M.]

gous monuments of which the prototype has yet to be found, and have no more intimate connection than a common type. Dr. Waldstein, judging from the photograph, is inclined to think the Ikarian the earlier. I am disposed to believe that both are the work of the same artist; whether it be that the Ikarian stele was the prior effort, upon which in the Aristion stele he improved, in both style and technique, and, considering the latter his masterpiece, inscribed his name upon it; or that the stele of Aristion was the artist's original work, of which he executed one or more less careful reproductions with trifling variations. The question must rest with the individual judgment of scholars.

Let us now consider the Lyseas stele, to the importance of which in the history of painted steles in general reference has been made. It was found at Velanideza in 1839, and at first presented a perfectly uniform surface, showing, however, to careful observers, traces of coloring. These traces, owing to the crust of lime formed over the surface, remained indistinct until, in 1878, the stele was carefully cleaned by the German architect Thiersch, the result of whose work, as shown in the *Mittheilungen des deutsch. arch. Inst.* of 1879 (plates I, II), is made the basis of two very instructive articles by Loescheke. In the inscription upon the base, the letters are of an older type than those on the altar of Peisistratos son of Hippias, which cannot be dated after 510 B. C.; thus the date of the stele must fall toward the middle of the century. Loescheke does not hesitate to date it from the time of the elder Peisistratos (560–527). Lyseas is represented of life-size, draped in a long himation, with the lustration-branch in his left hand which is raised nearly to the shoulder, and in his right the kantharos from which he is about to pour the libation. In the article referred to Loescheke draws a parallel between painting on marble, as evidenced in this and other steles, and that of the earliest red-figured vases; and he arrives at the conclusion, that the style of the red-figured vases is, in contrast to that of the black-figured, derived from the traditional manner of painting on stone. In addition to the principal figure of the stele of Lyseas, there is on the κρηπίς a design in painting representing a man on horseback followed by another, as if in a race. This seems in itself evidence that the corresponding portion of similar monuments was often painted; and this was very probably the case with the stele at Ikaria, although no traces of color can now be detected. A full list of early Attic steles is given by Loescheke in the second portion of the article cited; but, besides those which have already been mentioned, the only ones of any special interest in connection with the Ikarian stele are two fragments, both belonging to a stele of a hoplite, but, as has been shown by a comparison of measurements, not parts of the same work. The fragment found at the chapel of Hag. Andreas near the village of Lebi and published by Conze,[12] represents a warrior holding his lance in his left hand: in this, not only is the armor of a different nature from that of the Aristion and Ikarian steles, but the whole workmanship is of a more careless and inferior type. The second fragment, which was found at Athens, shows only the legs from the knee downward, and, though of much better workmanship than the last-named fragment,[13] is still far inferior to either the Aristion or the Ikarian stele. As in the former, and not in the latter, the muscles of the calf are indicated by three curved parallel ridges.[14]

The most interesting sepulchral stele found outside of Attika is that of Orchomenos, the work of the Naxian Alxenor, which, though of less finished workmanship than the Aristion stele, belongs to a more advanced stage of art, as is evidenced by the attempt at foreshortening, unsuccessful though it be, and also by the expression shown in the face, in contrast to the totally expressionless face of Aristion.

The series of steles sculptured in relief—instructive, (1) as standing midway between the arts of sculpture and painting and comprising elements of both, (2) as being in the main the work of the early Attic school, (3) as showing a considerable advance toward a perfected style—receives in the Ikarian stele a very important augmentation, second in interest only to the monument of Aristion.

Athens, CARL D. BUCK.
November 10, 1888.

[12] *Arch. Zeitung*, 1860, *Taf.* cxxxv. 2.

[13] This would not, however, be a strong argument against the identity of the two fragments, if it were not disproved by the measurements; for it can be taken as an almost general rule, in early sculpture, that the legs below the knee are much better modelled than any other portion of the figure: witness the so-called Apollo of Tenea in Munich.

[14] At Laurion is the lower part of a similar stele representing two youths one behind the other (*Mittheilungen*, 1887, p. 296, and pl. x.).

[As an example of somewhat later date than the Aristion and Ikarian steles, I would call attention to a fragment preserved in the Collection of Baron Baracco in Rome: it is the lower part of a stele in low relief. It contains the lower limbs of a male figure, and, on the κρηπίς, not a painting but a representation in low relief, if my memory does not play me false, of a chariot with charioteer and horses in rapid motion.—A. L. F., jr.]

GREEK SCULPTURED CROWNS AND CROWN INSCRIPTIONS.*

[PLATES X, XI.]

The following notes are limited to the consideration of a very humble class of the monuments of Greek art. Of the marbles on which crowns are figured not one is noticed by a contemporary author; and there is probably not one made by a known artist. The crown, or wreath of honor, was doubtless developed from a badge of priestly office or a mere ornament, and became a reward conferred by the highest civic authority before the date of the earliest of these reliefs as yet known. From the beginning of the fourth century before our era until the beginning of the fourth century after it, there is now available a tolerably continuous series of such reliefs.

CROWNS.

The crowns are cut upon the flat surface of the marble, and the relief is almost always less than one cm. high. Sometimes the crown is quite without relief, and only the outline is incised on the marble with a sharp point. The koilanaglyphic method, too, is often employed for these reliefs: *i. e.*, the material is cut away from around the crown so as to leave it projecting in a slight depression, but not raised above the general level of the stone. When several crowns occur on the same monument or the same block of stone, they may be upon three sides of it; but more usually they occupy the face alone. When there are several on one side, they are placed at equal distances from one another in vertical or horizontal rows. The more usual arrangement is, however, the latter; and, when two or three crowns occur by themselves, they are almost invariably placed side by side, not one below the other.

* The collection of the material for this paper was encouraged by the following remark in BAUMEISTER's *Denkmäler*, p. 795: *Da über Kränze seit Paschalius* [✝ 1625], '*De Coronis*' (Leyden, 1680) *nicht mehr ausführlich gehandelt worden ist, so verdiente der Gegenstand, namentlich mit Rücksicht auf das in den Denkmälern vorliegende Material, eine erneute Untersuchung.*

The great majority of these crowns appear as though the original wreath had been made out of two pliable sprays or branches. The lower woody ends of these branches are loosely twisted so that one makes a complete revolution around the other, and the tips are then brought together so that the whole forms, approximately, a circle. The fillet (*taenia*) seems to have been the chief, as well as earliest, adjunct of the crown, and emphasized its religious association. Thus, probably in consequence of the sacred character of the national games, crowns given for victory in them are represented in the reliefs as bound with a fillet. On the other hand, crowns conferred on ordinary occasions by the State are always without the *taenia*. A few crowns awarded to the dead, as for instance the crown given to some who died in the Lamian war (*C.I.A.*, II, 1681; PLATE X–2 [1]), and, according to Böckh, certain crowns given by religious associations are, like crowns of victory, also adorned with fillets. Even for crowns of victory the fillet seems to lose its significance, and is sometimes omitted in the Roman imperial period (*Bull. de corr. hellén.*, X, 383; PL. X–3, in part). The figured crowns differ greatly in their position. Some hang down, so that the tips of their sprays are below the twisted stems (PL. X–2, 7, *etc.*) and so appear as if suspended against the stone; others stand erect, the tips of the sprays thus being uppermost (PL. X–3, 5, 6) and the stem-ends downward. In the minor details of the carving there are naturally many differences. The number of leaves that a crown may have varies from twelve up to sixty or more. If the relief is low, the leaves are represented in outline as if they rested flat on the stone. When the relief is higher the leaves are sometimes shown in perspective, some being turned sidewise, or certain leaves may be represented as slightly curled. If the crown has many leaves, they may be more or less bunched together, and thus conceal the stem. In the more carefully designed wreaths, however, the stem is usually visible throughout its length, or is concealed at only one or two points by leaves lying directly upon it. A type peculiar to crowns of small size is that in which the leaves appear in groups of three at every node of the stem (PL. X–10*a*, 11*c*; XI–27). Here the group or whorl is represented as if flattened out so that the middle leaf of the three masks the stem. When the leaves are all separate from one another and the stem is visible in its entire length, more leaves are usually cut on the outside of

---

[1] The crowns figured on PLATES X, XI are phototype reproductions made from squeezes of the reliefs. In every case the reduction is to $\frac{1}{4}$th of the actual size.

the branch than on the inside (PL. XI-17, 19), in order that all the leaves may be at about the same distance apart. In case the leaves are strictly opposite, those on the inside of the branch are made to diverge more from it than those on the outside (PL. X-3, XI-23). A special class of crowns (to be considered further on) have leaves standing out from the circumference of a circle like the rays of composite flowers (PL. X-11*b–d*; XI-25). Certain laurel crowns are arranged with three leaves and two berries at every node of the stem (PL. XI-27). Ivy displays its usual cordate leaf, and sometimes a bunch of berries near the tips of the sprays (PL. X-13*a*, *e*; XI-21, 26*a*). The divided leaf identified as parsley or wild celery is represented in the crowns won in the Nemean games (PL. X-3). The peculiar club-shaped foliage of a crown awarded for victory in the Isthmia is probably intended for pine (PL. X-1). The presence of fruit or berries scattered among the leaves of a crown as well as ravelled threads at the ends of *taeniae*, is subject to no rule, and probably depended on the elaboration desired in the wreath, as well as on the ability of the artist. The same holds true of the carving of a midrib on some of the leaves. Such midribs are made in various ways: as by a single groove or by two small grooves leaving an elevation between them, or by a ridge sloping away on each side toward the margin of the leaf. The tips of the branches where leaves from opposite directions meet, are often finished in a rough manner. Sometimes a mass of small carelessly-made leaves are crowded together in confusion (PL. X-9, 14*c*, *g*). Again, the terminal leaves may be made so that their ends touch each other and inclose a vacant space (PL. XI-23, 30*a*). The stems of the sprays do not usually touch at their tips but sometimes they unite in a sort of button (PL. XI-19), or they may join each other so as to form a circle (PL. X-3, 6*b*, 8).

Besides the crowns in relief, Greek art supplies several instances of wreaths painted on marble. The general principle that decoration in color preceded carving might warrant the supposition that crowns were usually painted in the early periods, and so have been lost to us. The painted crowns that survive (*C. I. A.*, II, 2541, and Ἀθήναιον, VIII, 403) seem, however, to be not earlier than the Macedonian period. This fact, taken together with the comparative rarity of inscriptions which mention crowns before the time of the earliest crown-relief (388 B. C.), may be taken as evidence against a general prevalence of painted wreaths during earlier periods.

The crown occurs in general on two classes of monuments. The first class comprises those which are erected by some civic body or religious association which inscribes its honorary decree on it and accompanies the inscription with a representation of the crown it gives. Such crown-reliefs may from their source be termed public, to distinguish them from the private crowns of the second class, in which the interest lies not so much in the public giver as in the private receiver. This second class consists of the monuments of persons who had their crowns carved in order to record more specifically the honors they had received. Sepulchral steles, monuments dedicated to commemorate victory in the games, and many of those set up for the successful performance of all sorts of civil, military, and sacred duties, come under the second head. At times, both public and private crowns are figured upon the same stone. Thus, in addition to the crowns mentioned in an inscribed decree, other crowns may be sculptured which had been received at other times by the person honored and have no relation to the decree itself. Both classes of wreaths are only another evidence of the vivid plastic sense of the Greek people. The information which the figure of the crown conveyed to them could have been as well told in words, and, indeed, is often set forth in a brief inscription placed in or just above the crown; but it was sought to display the honor in material form to the eye. Public crowns bear, as their inscription, an abridgement of the decree conferring them. Often the name of the giver only is stated; but, when several persons are honored in the same decree, the crown of every one bears his name, and in some cases the name is preceded by the occasion of his receiving the honor—for the most part simply the name of an office or a title. Thus, a full presentation of all three elements would be: ὁ δῆμος τὸν κοσμητὴν Θεόχαριν Ἑστιαίου. The crowns of a private monument, since they usually belong to but one man, contain only the name of the giver and the cause of the honor, in this case generally expressed by a causal participle, as: οἱ ἱππεῖς ἱππαρχήσαντα. These three terms of a crown-inscription—giver, cause, receiver—are, however, rarely all present together. Any one of them, or all, may be omitted; they may be placed within the crown or just above it; and they may occupy different orders in regard to each other. Crowns of victory are characterized by another set of terms, the name of the games and the particular event in which the victory was won. Thus, Ἀμφιάραια τὰ ἐν Ὠρώπῳ πυγμήν is an example of the typical elements of such crown-inscriptions. In the case of public crowns, the material of which the crown is to be made is usually stated in the accompanying decree; but in private crowns it must be inferred from the shape of the leaves or the character of the giver. When the material is mentioned in a decree, it is usually gold. Often, too, its value is added, as 1000, 500, 300 drachmai. Olive or *thallos* stands second in point of frequency. This was given chiefly at Athens, and then by small civil corporations and by religious associations, rarely by the *boule* and *demos*, unless to inferior personages or for trifling services. Ivy crowns usually have some connection with the worship of Dionysos. Laurel or, as it is often called, the "crown of the god" is given at Delphi, Rhodes, and other Doric centres. Myrtle, poplar, and grape-vine crowns seem to have been conferred very rarely, and complete the short list of materials mentioned in the inscriptions.

Any general description of figured crowns would be incomplete, if no effort were made to introduce a chronological standard by which some of the variations which have been noted might be placed in their order of succession. With the object of studying changes of form, a number of crown-reliefs found on the mainland of Greece are classified in TABLE I (pp. 155–7). First come reliefs that can be dated more or less exactly by some historical reference contained in the inscriptions. The others are such as furnish no historical data and are therefore grouped in classes based on differences in the shapes of the letters *alpha* and *sigma*.[2] These latter classes, since they somewhat overlap each other in time, can be expected to indicate only general tendencies. In the narrow column which contains only letters, P denotes that the crown has a pendent position, E that it is placed erect, V that it is a crown of victory: the next column on the right gives the diameter of the crown in millimeters, measured from the stem of one of the sprays to the stem of the other: the third column gives the diameter of the crown in terms of the height of the letters of its inscription.

It will be noticed immediately, on inspecting the table, that the erect wreaths contained in these classes belong exclusively to a period

[2] The general periods in which these forms of *alpha* and *sigma* were used are thus briefly given by REINACH, *Épigraphie Grecque*, pp. 204–7: *L'alpha n'a la barre médiane brisée que dans la deuxième moitié du second et au premier siècle av. J. C. . . . Ce n'est que vers la fin du 1ᵉʳ siècle ap. J. C. que la forme A reparaît avec fréquence, pour dominer de nouveau à l'époque de Trajan et d'Hadrien, sans jamais exclure complètement la forme brisée.*

Le sigma à branches parallèles . . devient fréquent vers 110 av. J. C. et prédomine depuis le commencement du 1ᵉʳ siècle. . . . . . Les formes lunaires du sigma ne commencent à prévaloir qu'à la fin du 1ᵉʳ siècle avant notre ère.

later than the Christian era and to the ΣA and C groups. Among the
earlier dated crowns and in the ≤ groups there is no such erect wreath
to be found. The cause of this alteration in the position of the wreath
seems not to be fully ascertained, but a comparison with wreaths represented on coins appears to throw some light upon it. The reverse
of some of the earliest Attic coins bears a pendent wreath above the
owl. On coins of the period 406–393 B. C. the erect wreath begins to
make its appearance; and on the series of 220–197 B. C. the wreath
has only the erect position. Probably the motive for this change in
the manner of placing the wreath on the coins was merely artistic.
The owl, the amphora, and other symbols seemed better supported if
the wreath about them was erect, or, in other words, closed below. On
certain coins of Sikyon the wreath is placed on its side, and has the
opening in front of the flying dove, as if to avoid impeding its flight.
Thus, the position of the wreath on coins may at first have been the
natural one of suspension, and may have been altered later, to com-
ply with the dictates of taste. On the other hand, in the case of the
reliefs, the letters inclosed in the wreath would not appear to need any
support, and hence the realistic placing of the wreath would naturally
be retained much longer. The change in reliefs to the erect position
of the wreath seems to correspond in point of time to the archaistic
tendency of the second century A. D., and may perhaps be traced to the
influence of the representations on coins. For, since the obverse in
coins of the best period retained archaic types of human feature, it
may have been supposed that the erect crown on the reverse was also
quite as archaic. Thus, the carvers of these archaistic wreaths passed
over all the reliefs of the fourth century B. C. and took as their model
certain wreaths which they supposed to belong to the fifth century, and
which were, in fact, stamped on Attic coins that bore heads of
Athena derived from the fifth century or even earlier.[3] Besides the
erect wreaths enumerated in the above classes, a large number of others
have been found at Teuchira in the Cyrenaica and are published by
Pacho, *Voyage dans la Marmarique et Cyrénaïque* and in the *C. I. G.*,
5249, 5254–5356. It is believed that their system of dates can be

---

[3] Should this theory of archaistic crowns appear untenable, the erect position in the
late reliefs may be explained as due to the increased size of the letters contained in
the crown. The letters would thus have had the same influence in inverting the
crowns of the reliefs as did the owl and amphora much earlier in the case of the
crowns on Attic coins.

referred to the reigns of Augustus and Tiberius, and most of them have the C-shaped *sigma*. Le Bas (III, 358) publishes an erect wreath from Mylasa with the letters ΣA, and in the *Annali* of 1865 (pp. 97, 99) certain victories won in the second half of the second century of our era are recorded within erect wreaths. A very small erect wreath ornaments the pediments of certain steles, such as *Arch. Zeit.*, 1878, p. 98, belonging to 181–85 A. D., and 'Ἀθήναιον, III, 529 ff., of the time of the Antonines.

In the size of the wreaths there is no regular progression. The earliest are generally about 18 or 19 cm. in diameter, but among them are some as small as 14 cm. or even 11 cm. During the second and first centuries B. C. the wreaths are much smaller, averaging not above 11 cm. in diameter. This change is due, at least in part, to the confined space in which the crowns of this time are placed. *C.I.A.*, II, 1217 (PL. X–9) and *Mittheil.*, VIII, 211 (PL. X–8) are good examples of crowding of this kind; though they belong to an earlier period. Late crowns of the time of the Roman Empire exhibit many irregularities, but show a general tendency to increase in size, and, consequently, in this particular approach the earliest reliefs.

But, although the diameter of crowns does not show any regular rate of change, a fondness for enlarging and crowding the letters is noticeable in the later crowns. Many cases occur where there are letters of one size outside the wreath, and of another size within. In such cases, it is evident that the size of the letters within the wreath is governed by the stone-cutter's desire to harmonize the letters and the wreath inclosing them, and not by any general rule prescribing the size of letters in inscriptions. If this feeling for proportion in size given to letters within a wreath was maintained when the letters outside were too large or too small to accord with the wreath, it was doubtless observed also when the letters without happen to be of the same size as those within. A means of expressing this proportion of size of letter to size of wreath is to divide the diameter of the wreath by the average height of the inclosed letters; and it is this ratio which is given in the last column of the table. Two exceptional cases ought, however, to be mentioned, before the general aspect of the column is considered. The first of these is *Mittheil.*, VIII, 211 (PL. X–8), where, owing to lack of space, four crowns are made in such a way that their stems intersect, and thus some crowns lie partly over others. The other case is *C.I.A.*, II, 1158 (PL. XI–30). Here the unusual size (35 to 40 mm.) of the letters outside the crowns seems to have required large letters within, also. Moreover, the letters are not collected near the centre of the wreath, but are extended so that each word runs completely across it, and a line of six letters and one of nine or ten letters are thus made to fill equal spaces. Passing by these two exceptions, the dated crowns show a pretty regular diminution of the ratio from the upper end of the column downward. The ratio averages about 20 in the fourth century B. C., and a little over 10 in the second century, A. D. A considerable change seems to have taken place during the interval which separates the crown of 282/1 B. C. from that of about 150 B. C. An inspection of the ratio with reference to the letter-groups shows that in the ≤A class the ratio averages about 20, and never falls below 16: in the other classes, it averages about 14 and nowhere rises above 19.

Peculiarities in the shape of the wreaths are too various and irregular in their occurrence to admit of illustration by a table of measurements. A wreath of the earlier period, carelessly made but still quite characteristic, is one without any stem and having its exterior leaves strongly divergent. In such crowns the place of the stem is occupied by a course of leaves, so that any radius drawn within the wreath is almost certain to cut at least three leaves. *C.I.A.*, II, 159*b* (PL. XI–24) of about 350 B. C. and three other wreaths of the dated group ending with *C.I.A.*, II, 1291 (PL. XI–28) of 282/1 B. C. show this form, as well as sixteen examples in the ≤A group; but in the other letter-groups it has no representative. A wreath having no stem but with many leaves is found in the latest period also, as *C.I.A.*, III, 1108, and III, 1177 (PL. X–4), of 212–21 A. D. Here, however, the leaves are not divergent but cling closely together and give the wreath a ring-like appearance. This peculiar form seems characteristic of late wreaths. It is well shown in *C.I.A.*, III, 91 (PL. X–5), where, though the stem is visible, the leaves are crowded together, so that their points seem to rest upon concentric circles. A reduction of the stem of a crown to an actual circle occurs quite early, as in *Mittheil.*, VIII, 211 (PL. X–8) of 325/4 B. C.; but rigid regularity in the arrangement of the leaves and the similarity in shape of all of them (PL. X–6; XI–22) are certain indications of decline in artistic spirit. The leaves are first subjected to a geometric regularity in those wreaths in which they are arranged in groups of three. This peculiar arrangement seems to belong to the last two centuries before our era. Among the dated crowns it is represented by Ἀθήναιον, v, 522 (PL. X–10) of 147 B. C., and by *C.I.A.*, II, 465, 467 (PL. X–11e), 481 of 48/2 B. C. The ΣA class supplies two instances, ⪅A only one that is quite certain. The custom of representing laurel with groups of three leaves and two berries at every node of the stem, as seen in *C.I.A.*, II, 552, of about 125 B. C. (PL. XI–27), seems to belong to much the same period. The earlier laurel crown in *C.I.A.*, II, 115 (PL. XI–17b) of 343/2 B. C. is without these groups of three leaves, and differs from the olive wreath placed next it on the same stone (PL. XI–17a) merely in having its opposite leaves cut a trifle broader. At a later date still than the groups of three leaves, there appears in the reliefs a type of wreath in which the leaves are placed exactly opposite each other as far as the tips of the sprays. *C.I.A.*, II, 482 (PL. XI–31), and, better, *Mittheil.*, III, 144 (PL. X–6) are crowns of this form. ΣA supplies two instances, and again ⪅A but one (*C.I.A.*, II, 1347). The earliest crowns show an opposite arrangement of leaves near the butt-ends of the branches, but this system usually becomes alternate or irregular near the tips of the branches by the insertion of an extra leaf or leaves on the outside (PL. XI–17a, 19). In another form exhibited in wreaths of this early period, the exterior leaves are made rather longer than those inside, so that the opposite arrangement can be continued close to the tips of the branches (PL. XI–18, 23). The tips themselves in most of the early crowns bear smaller leaves than the other portions of the branch and the quantity of foliage near the tips is usually diminished, thus avoiding the ring-like appearance of the later examples.

Many crowns are distinguished in the accompanying inscription by the statement that they are of gold, and the question naturally suggests itself, whether there is any peculiar artistic mode of representing a crown of gold. In general, this must be answered in the negative. During the early period, the crowns which are recorded as of gold differ as much among themselves as from those which are stated to be of olive. Their similarity is best observed on such ephebic decrees as *C.I.A.*, II, 470 of 69/2 B. C. and II, 482 of 39/2 B. C. In the former decree (PL. X–13, 14) there are two rows of crowns across the face of the stone. The upper row contains five crowns, of which the three inner ones are, according to the inscription, of gold while the two at the extremities of the row are stated to be of ivy, and are, in fact, sculptured with ivy leaves. The lower row contains seven crowns, all stated to be of olive; but, except in size, these are exactly similar to the three inner crowns of the upper row. In *C.I.A.*, II, 482 (PL. XI-31) even the difference in size is absent. The gold crown conferred upon the *epheboi* is exactly like the olive crowns given to their officers and instructors. In a somewhat earlier class of ephebic monuments the case seems to be different. Certain wreaths which have no leaves on the inner side of their branches, and whose leaves often project like rays, seem to be especially intended to represent gold crowns. Of this type are *C.I.A.*, II, 594 of 127 B. C., II, 467 of about 100 B. C., and II, 471 of just before 69/2 B. C. In the first (*C.I.A.*, II, 594 = PL. XI-25) there is but one wreath, and this is ray-leaved, and is shown by its inscription to be a gold crown: in *C.I.A.*, II, 471 (PL. XI-15 gives the upper row only) the upper row contains five crowns. The first is a ray-crown whose title shows that it was given by the *boule* and *demos* to the *epheboi*; and the resolution according a crown of gold forms part of the inscription above. Similar ray-crowns given by both *boule* and *demos* and by the *epheboi* to the *kosmetes* (Dionysios), are also stated to be of gold. The fourth crown given by the *demos* to the *kosmetes* and *epheboi* jointly is of ivy, and in the inscription above it is mentioned, among the honors of the *epheboi*, a crown given by the *demos* in recognition of a sacrifice to Dionysos. The last crown in the upper row, given by the *boule* and *demos* to the *epheboi*, has olive leaves, but the material of it is not mentioned in the inscription. On the other hand, a gold crown, given to the *epheboi* by the *demos* of the Salaminians, is mentioned in the inscription, but is not distinguished in any way in the relief. In the lower row there are five olive-leaved crowns, all expressly set forth in the decree as of olive. In another ephebic inscription, *C.I.A.*, II, 467 (PL. X-11 gives the upper row only), the decree provides that gold crowns shall be given by *boule* and *demos* to the *epheboi* and to the *kosmetes*, and wreaths of olive to every one of the seven inferior officers. In the plastic representations of these crowns, those of the *epheboi* and the *kosmetes* have ray-leaves, but all the other crowns olive leaves. Besides these two ray-leaved crowns, the upper row contains a third ray-leaved crown given to the *epheboi* and *kosmetes* jointly by the *demos* of the Salaminians. Although this crown is not mentioned in the decree, it must, from the analogy of other crowns given by this *demos*, have been of gold. In *C.I.A.*, II, 469 (PL. XI-29 gives an example from each row) of about 100 B. C., one of the gold crowns given to the *kosmetes*, although not rayed, has no leaves on the inside of its branches, but the olive wreaths of the inferior officers have leaves on both sides of the stem, as on the natural branch. Two crowns in *C.I.A.*, II, 955 (PL. X–12) present another case in point. The crown on the left (the place of distinction) has leaves only on the outside, but the crown on the right has leaves on both sides. Here, as in many other cases, the rayed-crowns are not distinguished by the inscriptions as gold crowns. From the several ephebic decrees examined above, however, it seems clear that at least during a certain period, perhaps limited to the first half of the second century B. C., there was an effort to distinguish crowns of gold from wreaths of olive by differences in their artistic representation. It is highly probable that, if the material of all rayed crowns were known with certainty, every one of them would be found to represent a crown of gold.

CROWN-INSCRIPTIONS.

Crown-inscriptions offer no such characteristic variations as the crowns to which they refer. Their peculiarities pertain to the field of epigraphy; but a cursory examination and classification of them may be of interest. As a basis for this, a table of crown-inscriptions is presented (TABLE II, pp. 157–61). Many of the inscriptions referred to in TABLE I are repeated, and the same division into classes is again used. The remarkable increase in the number of the ΣA class in the latter table is probably due in some measure to inexactness in the copies used for the *C.I.G.* The third column in this table gives the initial letters of the words *giver, cause, receiver*; and places in brackets those of them which are inclosed in the crown. Thus *g*[*cr*] denotes that in the crown in question the name of the giver is outside the wreath, while the cause and the name of the recipient are within. Such collective words as *boule, epheboi, epimeletai*, are classed under receiver and not as cause, when any doubt arises as to which use the word has. A dash in the last column of the table shows that some word does not terminate at the end of its line, but is in part carried over to the line below.

An inspection of TABLE II shows that the placing of the terms with reference to the wreath falls into two classes. Either all the terms are inside the wreath, or some are within and others are without. The crowns of a certain Kassandros (*Arch. Zeit.*, 1855, p. 33) and crowns in *C.I.A.*, II, 1213, II, 480, *Bull. de corr. hellén.*, IV, 516, and *Le Bas*, II, 1338, where the giver is placed above and the crowns themselves are left empty, seem to be almost the only exceptions to these two divisions. Examples in which some of the terms lie outside the wreath are much more rare than those in which all the terms are inside. Terms outside are found mostly in the public and, consequently, dated inscriptions. They seem to begin about 150 B. C., are rare in the ≶A class, more frequent among the ≶A and ΣA classes, but are wholly lacking, later, in the ΣA and C classes; although one instance occurs among the dated crowns as late as about 100 A. D. Most of these terms outside of the crown belong to Attic ephebic inscriptions. A count of the whole TABLE shows that there are 182 instances of a single term inclosed in the wreath; or, to represent the number of terms inside and outside of the wreath by numbers and their position within or without by brackets, there are 182 instances of [1], 51 of [2], 12 of [3], 15 of 1[1], 5 of 1[2], and 6 of 2 [1]. In respect to the kind of term found outside, the following may be stated. The receiver when present is never outside the wreath; the cause is rarely outside (7 cases); but the giver somewhat more often (19 cases). Crowns that have but one term occur as often in the earliest as in the latest periods. Most of them are private inscriptions, and the mortuary crowns from Smyrna and the Cyrenaica constitute a large part.

Many of the earliest crowns that are at present known are not explained by even a single term. From this, the first step of advance was naturally the insertion of one term, the name of the giver. The latest crowns also contain only a single term; but with the difference that this term is not restricted to the name of the giver, but in many instances stands for the receiver. The occurrence of two terms is, generally speaking, contemporaneous with that of three terms, and often both cases are found on the same stone. They occur chiefly in Attic ephebic inscriptions; and, like the cases where terms are placed outside the wreaths, are only another evidence of that general fondness for prolixity and accumulations which these inscriptions exhibit.

In crowns of victory one term, the name of the games, is always present, and sometimes the name of the special event is added as a second term. There are but three instances of a separation of these terms. *C.I.A.*, II, 1318, 1319 place the games outside, and the event inside, the crown; *C.I.A.*, III, 115, on the contrary, places the event outside and the games within. During the Roman imperial period, the name of the town at which the games were celebrated is sometimes added, presumably for the reason that games of the same name were celebrated in more than one place. Examples of this are *C.I.G.*, 5916, Ἔφεσον | ᾿Αδριάνε|ια ά; 5915, Ὀλύμπια ἐν ᾿Αθήναις.

To return to the ordinary crowns; the three terms—giver, cause, receiver—are regularly in this order, and, as any of them can be omitted, the following cases occur in which the terms do not deviate from the regular order, *gcr, gc, gr, cr, c, g, r*. In regard to frequency, *g* stands at the head with 122 instances; then *r* with 51; *gr* with 38; *gc* with 17; *gcr* with 15; *c* with 9; and *cr* with 4. Besides these cases of regular order, a few irregularities are found: there are 6 cases of *grc*, 6 of *rg*, and one of *rc*. The exceptional form *grc* occurs four times on certain Parian inscriptions; here the term *c* is represented usually by the phrase κοσμίως βιώσαντα, so that this order seems to be rather a local peculiarity. One of the instances of *rg* is from a sepulchral inscription at Smyrna, but all the other exceptions to the usual order are Attic.

Two bodies may act in unison in bestowing a crown; as in *Bull. de corr. hellén.*, IV, 433, where the words ὁ δᾶμος | καὶ οἱ ¦ Ῥωμαῖοι appear in one of the crowns: οἱ ἔφηβοι |καὶ οἱ νέοι, *C.I.G.*, 3112, is another example. A psephism of the *boule* and *demos* is also often represented by one crown. More rarely such a decree has two crowns, one inclosing ἡ βουλή, the other ὁ δῆμος, as in *Mittheil.*, VIII, 211 (PL. X–8) and probably in *C.I.A.*, II, 1347. The form in which both words are used in a single crown is especially frequent in ephebic decrees, but it occurs as early as the votive inscription relating to Demetrios Phalereus *C.I.A.*, II, 1217 (in part PL. X–9). When both words belong to one crown, they may stand inside or outside of it, according to convenience. The custom, however, is to place them within; for, putting aside the cases where the position varies on the same stone, the words *boule* and *demos* occur 25 times inside the crown, out of a total of 32 examples. Sometimes the two words are joined by the copula καί, but the omission of it seems to be the older and the Attic usage. *C.I.A.*, II, 1217 (315/12 B.C.), II, 338 (soon after 281 B.C.), and thirteen other examples of ἡ βουλὴ ὁ δῆμος include eight inscriptions belonging to the ϹA class. On the other hand, the earliest approximately dated example of ἡ βουλὴ καὶ ὁ δῆμος is *C.I.G.*, 2270 (soon after 167 B.C.); and, of sixteen other instances of it, only two belong to the ϹA class; while three cases of the C-shaped *sigma* occur among them. Moreover, more than half of the cases of ἡ βουλὴ καὶ ὁ δῆμος are supplied by Paros, Aigina, and other islands; while ἡ βουλὴ ὁ δῆμος is confined to Attika.

When the *demos* alone is the giver, ὁ δῆμος is placed with great regularity within the wreath. In only 14 cases out of 155 does it lie outside, and here its position can almost always be explained by analogy with other crowns in the same row. Boule as giver stands within its crown in 34 cases out of a total of 45. Of the other divisions of the Athenian State, οἱ πρυτάνεις and ἡ φυλή vary in their position, οἱ φυλέται and οἱ δημόται, though occurring but rarely, are always inscribed within the crowns conferred by them. Other associations, also, whether religious or civil or military, when they bestow crowns place their names within, as a rule; but such associations are too numerous to call for separate notice of every one.

In crowns of early periods, the name of the giver is always in the nominative case, the cause and the receiver in the accusative. The verb understood is probably to be supplied from the common formula in decrees, στεφανῶσαι αὐτὸν χρυσῷ στεφάνῳ, but sometimes the verb is expressed. Thus, in several crowns from Paros (*C.I.G.*, 2380, 2381) and in one from Lydia (*Bull. de corr. hellén.*, XII, 473), a complete sentence, ἡ βουλὴ καὶ ὁ δῆμος στεφανοῖ . . ., is brought within the crown. The verb ἐτίμησε is used in *C.I.G.*, 1942, and *Bull. de corr. hellén.*, IV, 68, but the verb is omitted in far the greater number of crown-inscriptions. The nominative case of a proper noun placed within a crown denotes the receiver in *C.I.A.*, II, 1334 and *Bull. de corr. hellén.*, III, 388, as express statements to this effect are added. The nominative, in crowns figured on a large number of sepulchral monuments found in the Cyrenaica, probably stands also for the receiver. A nominative, presumably for the receiver, is found in late ephebic inscriptions, as *C.I.A.*, III, 1042, in dedications to Apollo ὑπ' ἄκραις, as *Mittheil.*, III, 144, and in certain late crowns containing titles of various magistrates, as *C.I.A.*, III, 91 (PL. X–5) πολέ|μαρχ|ος, and III, 1108. The earlier instances of these nominatives come from the Islands, but their occurrence extends over both the Σ and C forms of *sigma*. Crowns connected with the name of a god, such as *Arch. Zeit.*, 1878, p. 98, where a small empty wreath separates the words Διὸρ ἱερά, or where a wreath incloses the word Ζεύς (*Le Bas*, III, 2702), or ἀγαθὴ τύχη (*Le Bas*, III, 2431), belong to a very late and peculiar type of crown-inscription. The meaning of the crown is uncertain, but probably it is used as a sign of consecration. A genitive case in or just above a crown, if it is a proper noun—as in Curtius' *Samos* (p. 34) Σά]μου, Τίμωνος, κ. τ. λ.—denotes the receiver of the crown. The name of an assembly, if in the genitive, belongs presumably to the giver, as γερουσίας, *C.I.G.*, 4152 c, and certainly ὑπὸ τοῦ δήμου,

Le Bas, II, 1338. When a crown-inscription consists of a noun in the dative case, it is naturally to be understood of the receiver. The few cases that occur are late and for the most part from near the outskirts of Greek civilization: στρατηγή|σαντι, *C.I.G.*, 2097 (Tauric Chersonese), 5053 (Nubia), *Bull. de corr. hellén.*, XII, 483 (Phrygia), *C.I.G.*, 3614 (Troad). These irregular nominatives and datives show that the original function of the crown-inscription is becoming obscured. In a small class of equally late inscriptions, the words within the crown lose still more their proper function of explaining the crown to which they belong. Thus, in *C.I.A.*, III, 1177 (PL. X–4*a*, *b*), the lines of the crown-inscription are to be read across from one crown to the other. In *Mittheil.*, III, 144 (PL. X–6*a*), one of the crowns contains a date. *Bull. de corr. hellén.*, VII, 132 gives a case where the last two words of the phrase νεωκόρος | τοῦ Ἀ πόλλ|ωνος are inclosed in a wreath. Perhaps the most peculiar case of irrelevancy in a crown-inscription is *Le Bas*, III, 722. In this, a sepulchral inscription from Asia Minor, the lines of the text run across the crown and lie also on both sides of it, so that the sentence, ὃς ἂν ἀνύξει, θήσει | εἰς τὸ ταμῖον δηνάρ|ια χίλια, has the words ἀνύξει, ταμῖον and the letters -λια inclosed within the crown.

Crown-inscriptions in which a word is divided next call for notice. This division of words has a somewhat close relation with the ratio between the size of the crown and the size of the inclosed letters. For, where a word is placed in an inclosed space, the number of lines it occupies must largely be controlled by the size of its letters, and by the amount of space in which it can extend itself. Consequently, when the ratio, considered above, shows a tendency to decrease, the number of divided words ought at the same time to increase. From the last column of the dated crowns of TABLE II, it can be seen that before 200 B. C. the division of a word is merely sporadic. During the last two centuries before our era it shows considerable increase, and under the Roman Empire becomes almost an established rule. Among the classes of *sigma*, the frequency of divided words is as follows: 65 crown-inscriptions of the ⋞ class give 9 with divided words, 95 of the Σ class give 49, and 17 of the C class give 13; making 14, 52, and 76 per cent. respectively for the three *sigma*-classes. In these instances of the division of a word, the general rules for the separation of syllables in Greek are pretty strictly followed. A single consonant (including a mute + a liquid) goes with the following vowel, as στρατηγή|σαντα, Δημή|τριος. The exceptions to this rule are only 21 against 275 cases of accordance with it. Many of the crown-inscriptions consist of the words ὁ δῆμος, and the usual method of division is then ὁ δῆ|μος (twice, however, ὁ|δῆμ|ος and ὁ δῆμ|ος, and once ὁ|δῆμος). Where two consonants occur at the point of division, one goes with the preceding, the other with the following vowel, as ἄρ|χοντος. This is found in some 57 cases, but to this rule there are 20 exceptions. A mute and a liquid are left undivided in 25 cases out of a total of 26. Such barbarisms as Λαμπτρ|έως (*Mittheil.*, III, 144; PL. X–6a), Φ|λνέα (*C.I.A.*, III, 1297), π|άντες (*C.I.G.*, 3112) belong, as might be expected, to a rather late period; though such divisions were necessarily common enough in the early στοιχηδόν inscriptions.

ARRANGEMENT OF THE CROWNS.

A wider field for investigation than the inscriptions, or even than the forms of the crowns themselves, is found in the order or system of placing the wreaths on the monuments. This arrangement is the question first determined by the stone-cutter on beginning his work. Although the results given below may seem meagre and uncertain, this is not the least important side from which to study the subject in hand. As has been stated, the usual arrangement of crowns on the monuments is in straight lines. Fourteen crowns ranged in two horizontal rows of seven each, and eight in two vertical rows, constitute extreme examples of this system. Besides this linear arrangement, there occur a few instances of crowns placed in other relations. This is shown, especially, when there is an uneven number of wreaths, and they are ranged in two vertical columns, with the odd wreath below the others, thus °°/°, as in *Bull. de corr. hellén.*, III, 388 and *C.I.A.*, II, 1334. A peculiar arrangement of four crowns °8° is found in *C.I.A.*, III, 916, and of seven crowns °8°/°8° in *C.I.A.*, II, 329. The quincunx °/°° seems to occur in but a single example, and this dates from the Roman period. The geometric arrangement of the wreaths, and probably often their number, was to a great extent determined by the shape of the stone and the amount of space left after the inscriptions had been cut upon it. When, however, the crowns are bestowed by different corporations, or received by different persons, there arises a new question concerning the mutual relations of the crowns within their geometric figure. In most cases where this figure, so to speak, has been preserved entire, and information concerning every crown is accessible, the most important crowns seem to occupy the most prominent positions. Two positions may be considered prominent in this sense—either the left-hand extremity of a row of crowns, or the middle. The importance of a crown may be derived from its giver. Thus, in 'Αθήναιον, V, 522 (PL. X-10, in part), two crowns given jointly by the *boule* and the *demos* of Athens precede two given by the *demos* of Troizen. In *Mittheil.*, VIII, 211 (PL. X-8), two crowns given by the *demos* come before two given by the *boule*. In *C.I.A.*, II, 562, the crown given by the *boule* is above one given by the *phyle*. Again, in *C.I.A.*, II, 420, a crown given jointly by the *boule* and the *demos* stands before one given by the *demos* alone. In *C.I.G.*, 2140 a^1, a crown conferred by the *boule* and *demos* jointly, precedes one given by certain οἱ ἐκ τοῦ γυμνασίου. Where the giver is the same but the recipients are different, the relative importance of the latter may determine the order of precedence of the crowns, as in Curtius' *Samos*, p. 34, where the crown received by the *demos* of the Samians stands before those of Samian dikasts. On this principle, the upper row of crowns in many ephebic inscriptions is reserved for the *epheboi* and *kosmetes*, the lower row for the inferior functionaries. The service rendered may also give special importance to a crown, when for two or more crowns both giver and receiver are the same. Thus, a crown containing ὁ δῆμος στρατη|γήσαντα precedes one containing ὁ δῆμος | πολίτας | λυτρωσά|μενον in *C.I.G.*, 2375; and in a monument erected at Athens to an *arrhephoros* (*C.I.A.*, III, 916) her crown for the performance of this duty precedes that given for services in the Eleusinia and Epidauria. In the ephebic inscriptions, the material of the crown influences its position, a condition perhaps due to the scarcity of gold during this period. *C.I.A.*, II, 471 (PL. XI-15) is a good example. In the upper row of crowns the following order is found: (1) a gold crown given by *boule* and *demos* to the *epheboi*; (2) a gold crown by *boule* and *demos* to the *kosmetes*; (3) a gold crown by the *epheboi* to the *kosmetes*; (4) an ivy crown; (5) an olive crown. In *C.I.A.*, II, 465 and 469, a similar arrangement seems to have prevailed, but the information contained in the inscriptions is not sufficient to verify the supposition.

Hitherto, only crowns placed at the left-hand or at the upper end of a row have been examined. *C.I.A.*, II, 470 (PL. X-13) is a case where the more important crowns are placed in the middle of the line. In the upper row the crowns are in the following order: (1) an ivy crown given by the *boule* and *demos* to the *kosmetes* and *epheboi*;

(2) a gold crown by the *boule* and *demos* to the *epheboi;* (3) a gold crown by the *boule* and *demos* to the *kosmetes;* (4) a gold crown by the *demos* of the Salaminians to the *kosmetes;* (5) an ivy crown by the *boule* and *demos* to the *kosmetes* and *epheboi*. On the same principle, in *C.I.A.*, II, 467 (PL. X–11), an ivy crown begins the line, and an olive crown concludes it; while three gold crowns are placed between them. In *C.I.A.*, II, 329, a crown by the *demos* to the *prytaneis* stands between two crowns awarded by less important bodies. *C.I.A.*, II, 454 and *Bull. de corr. hellén.*, IV, 175 seem other examples of this central position of the important crown; and the general principle is also applied in arranging the crowns on the monument described in *Mittheil.*, IX, 49.

When several crowns are equally important, they may be arranged in various symmetrical positions. In *C.I.G.*, 2270, five crowns given by the *boule* and *demos* for services to the State are arranged so as to form the four corners of a rectangle, as well as the middle point of its upper side. The middle points of the other sides and the centre of the rectangle are composed of crowns received for priestly services. In *Bull. de corr. hellén.*, VII, 469, two crowns given by *demoi* form the extremities of the upper row; but the centre of it and the entire lower row are crowns given by an association of certain traders and shippers. In *Bull. de corr. hellén.*, IX, 268, in a long list of services for which crowns were given, an embassy is placed at each end of the upper row and at the centre of the lower one. The quincunx, mentioned above, has in its centre a crown given by the *demos* of the Athenians, and, around it, four crowns given by the *demoi* of several islands.

Thus far, importance in general estimation has been considered. But, when any corporation erected a monument on which were cut crowns given by them, as well as those given by others, they often put their own crowns in the most prominent place. Thus, in the inscription in honor of Demetrios Phalereus (*C.I.A.*, II, 1217), Athenian garrisons stationed at Eleusis, at Panakton, at Phyle, place their crowns even before those of the *boule* and *demos*. In *C.I.A.*, II, 1158, the *boule* places several crowns given by itself to certain individuals before a crown given by the *demos* to the *boule*. Another exceptional arrangement occurs in cases where a crown of the *boule* stands before an exactly similar one of the *demos*. Thus, in *C.I.A.*, II, 1347, a crown contains ἡ βουλή ' Θεομένης Οἰῆθεν εἶπεν, and immediately below it is another inclosing ὁ δῆμος | Θεομένης | Οἰῆθεν εἶπεν. So, also, in *C.I.A.*, II, 1530, the two crowns ἡ βουλή, ὁ δῆμος probably have this relative position, because this was the order in which the resolutions for them were passed. In *Annali*, 1865, p. 97, the crowns of victory are arranged in the order in which they were won. Thus, first come the games for children (παῖδες), then, those for youths (ἀγένειοι), finally, the contests called ἱεραί. Besides such cases, there is little other evidence that the chronological order was ever preferred to that of their relative importance. Often, indeed, there seems to be no possible clew for explaining the order, but in such cases this is for the most part due to lack of information concerning the crowns, or to their incomplete preservation. Thus, it seems difficult to explain the order of victories recorded in Ἐφημερίς, 2558, or in *C.I.G.*, 5919. In the latter instance, however, certain victories διὰ πάντων are observed to form the first and the last of the series. In *Annali*, 1865, p. 99, the uppermost crowns are for games won in Greece, next comes one for a victory in Italy, and at the end are those won in Asia. On other monuments bearing crowns of victory the four great games, Olympian, Pythian, Isthmian, Nemean, occur thus, in the order of their rank. Examples are *C.I.A.*, II, 115, Ὀλύμπια Πύθια, from the year 343/2 B.C.; *C.I.A.*, III, 758a gives the first three and a vacancy is left at the end, to be filled, doubtless, by Νέμεα. In honorary inscriptions at Athens, there is a tendency to place the crowns won in Attic festivals in prominent positions. On the base of the monument of Nikokles (*C.I.A.*, II, 1367), sixteen crowns form a single band around three sides of the stone; on the face are six crowns won in the Pythia; but between the third and fourth, and exactly in the middle of the face, are placed crowns from the Panathenaia and Lenaia. In *C.I.A.*, II, 1319, the Eleusinia, Panathenaia, and Delia are all placed above such Doric festivals as the Olympia, the Soteria at Delphi, and some games held at Dodona; but a great part of the stone is lost. So, also, in the case of some victories won at Ephesos (*C.I.G.*, 5916), local interest probably causes the *Ephescia* to precede the *Hadriancia* and *Barbilleia*.

As a conclusion to this paper, a brief summary of its results may be of service. (1) In regard to the form of the wreaths, it has been shown that only the pendent crown belongs to the better periods of Greek art, and that the erect crown, on stone monuments at least, first appears in the time of Trajan or of Hadrian. The influence of representations on coins has been suggested as a theory to account for this change of position; and a tendency to crowd and enlarge the letters in the later reliefs has been noticed. Certain varieties of form in stem and leaves are found to belong to fixed periods; and a peculiar ray-like arrangement of the leaves has been shown to denote a crown of gold.

(2) An investigation of crown-inscriptions has shown that these consist of one, two, or even three terms placed regularly in the order of *giver*, *cause* of the gift, and *receiver*. Instances where some of the terms are found outside the crown belong mostly to the second or first century before our era, and instances of three terms have been shown to belong to the same period. The use of a verb in a crown-inscription, as well as certain ambiguities that might arise from the use of the nominative and genitive cases of nouns, are of only sporadic occurrence. The division of words in a crown-inscription increases with the advance of time, but in all periods is carried out with considerable attention to the syllables of the word divided.

(3) In the arrangement of crowns on the monuments, two positions, either the left-hand extremity or the middle, have been found to give special emphasis to the crowns placed in them. Moreover, the wreaths which occupy these positions are usually the most important by reason of the rank of their giver, or the value of the service for which they have been conferred.

George B. Hussey.

TABLE I.

(TABLE OF GREEK SCULPTURED CROWNS.)

APPROXIMATELY-DATED CLASS.

REFERENCES.	DATE.	POSITION (pendent or erect).	DIAM-ETER.	RATIO.
C.I.A., II, 1185	about 378/7 B.C.	P	.175	16
II, 51	369/8	P	.185	23
II, 72	353/2	P	.155	22
II, 1174	351/0	P	.200	20
II, 1596	about 350	P	.180	26
II, 1156	343/2	PV	.165	18
II, 872	341/0	P	.195	20
II, 121	338/7	P	.140	18
II, 165	soon after 335	P	.180	26
II, 166	" " "	P	.175	18
Mittheilungen, VIII, 211	325/4	P	.105	14
C.I.A., II, 1681	322	P	.280	25
II, 1187	319/8	P	.180	23
II, 1217	315/12	P	.110	18
II, 243	307/1	P	.180	26
II, 611	300	P	.180	40
II, 613	299/8	P	.180	23
II, 1350	296/5	P	.160	23
II, 300	295/4	P	.250	25
II, 1158	about 285/4	P	.255	13
II, 1291	282/1	PV	.160	24
II, 1642	about 150	P	.170	17
II, 550	soon after 150	P	.130	18
'Αθήναιον, V, 522	147	P	.090	14
C.I.A., II, 594	127	P	.125	14
II, 552	about 125	P	.165	17
II, 465	just before 100	P	.085	17
II, 469	about 100	P	.095	16
II, 467	" "	P	.085, .070	12, 11
II, 471	just before 69/2	P	.100, .080	17, 13
II, 470	69/2	P	.120, .095	16, 14
II, 481	48/2	P	.105	15
II, 482	39/2	P	.085	9
Mittheilungen, III, 144	about 100 A.D.	E	.155	10
C.I.A., III, 735a	" "	P	.100	11
III, 1108	117-29	E	.145	17
Bull. de corr. hellén., X, 383	after 117	EV	.130	10
C.I.A., III, 91	" "	E	.180	9
III, 1177	212-21	E	.110	10

ΣA CLASS.

References.	Position (pendent or erect).	Diam.	Ratio	References.	Position (pendent or erect).	Diam.	Ratio
C.I.A., II, 149	P	.145	24	C.I.A., II, 1367	PV	.150	21
II, 219	P	.190	19	II, 1400	P	.140	18
II, 229	P	.120	20	II, 1449	P	.170	19
II, 298	P	.160	23	II, 1530	P	.190	17
II, 326	P	.130	19	Ἐφημ. '84, p. 187	P	.150	21
II, 420	P	.160	23	Rangabé, 1148	P	.190	19
II, 513	P	.105	18	B. c. h., III, 485	P	.170	24
II, 568	P	.145	21	VII, 471	P	.185	21
II, 604	P	.180	23	* I.	P	.150	21
II, 1334	P	.140 / .190	23	II.	P	.140	23
				III.	P	.145	21
II, 1342	P	.340	16	IV.	P	.160	27
II, 1347	P	.155	22	V.	P	.165	24
II, 1351	P	.125	21	VI.	PV	.150	23

ΣA CLASS.

References.	Position	Diam.	Ratio	References.	Position	Diam.	Ratio
C.I.A., II, 624	P	.150	21	C.I.A., II, 1358	P	.100	17
II, 955	P	.090	11	Ἐφημ. 915	PV	.110	14
II, 1357	P	.135	17	VII.	P	.160	15

ΣA CLASS.

References.	Position	Diam.	Ratio	References.	Position	Diam.	Ratio
C.I.G., 2140a¹	E	.140	13	Ἀθήναιον, VIII, 294	P	.175	19
2322b²⁰	P	.245	13	Arch. Zeit. '79, p. 140	PV	.250	16
C.I.A., II, 1388b	P	.095	12				
III, 115	PV	.100	11	VIII.	P	.115	15
III, 916	P	.125	14	IX.	E	.175	16
Le Bas, II, 1707	P	.150	10	X.	P	.170	15

ΣA CLASS. C CLASS.

References.	Position	Diam.	Ratio	References.	Position	Diam.	Ratio
C.I.A., II, 2169	P	.175	6	C.I.A., III, 3098	P	.220	9
				XI.	EV	.063	4

*The place of publication of crowns marked with Roman numerals is at this time unknown to the writer: a short description of these crowns is therefore added, to assist the reader in their identification.

I. Athens, near the Central Museum, on the face, two crowns inclosing ἡ βουλή, ὁ δῆμος, on the right side, another crown inclosing οἱ δημόται.
II. Athens, Akropolis, crown inclosing Μνησίθεον, οἱ δημόται.
III. Athens, Central Museum, three crowns inclosing Μ[ο]δέστου, Φιλίπ[που, and 'Αντιόχου, respectively.
IV. Athens, southern side of the Akropolis, two crowns, one of which incloses ὁ δῆμος | ὁ Κολοφωνίων | καὶ πολιτεῖαι.
V. Athens, southern side of the Akropolis, two crowns inclosing ὁ δῆμο[ς and οἱ φ]υλέται.
VI. Athens, southern side of the Akropolis, three crowns, each on a different side of the stone, inclosing respectively Δήλια, 'Ελευσίνια, and Παναθήνα[ια]' τὰ μεγάλα.
VII. Athens, Central Museum, crown inclosing τὸν δῆμον | τὸν 'Αθηναίων and, above, τὸ κοινὸν τῶν 'Αμφικτυόν[ων.
VIII. Eleusis, two crowns inclosing .. κα]νηφορήσ a]σαν Μη τρ]ὶ Θεῶν and ἡ βουλὴ | ὁ δῆμος | κανηφορήσα,σαν 'Αφρο[δίτηι 'Αλω πεκῆσι.
IX. Athens, Central Museum, parts of three crowns, one incloses . . . εινος (PL. XI–16).
X. Athens, Central Museum, crown inclosing Σώσανδρον, Φιλίστου | Συπαλλήτ,τιον.
XI. Larissa, two crowns marked respectively 'Αδρι[άνι'a and 'Ολύνπι[a.

TABLE II.
(TABLE OF CROWN-INSCRIPTIONS.)

APPROXIMATELY DATED CLASS.

REFERENCES.	DATE.	GIVER, CAUSE, RECEIVER.
C.I.A., II, 1185	about 378/7 B. C.	[g] —
II, 1174	351/0	[g] —
II, 1596	about 350	[g]
II, 1340	346/5	[gc]
II, 1341	344/3	[g]
II, 1156	about 344/3	[g]
II, 872	341/0	[g]
II, 562	339/8	[g]
II, 121	338/7	[rg]

APPROXIMATELY DATED CLASS—Continued.

References.	Date.	Giver, Cause, Receiver.	
C.I.A., II, 165	soon after 335	[gr]	
II, 166	" " "	[g]	
II, 1216	332/1	[gcr]	—
II, 1186	329/8	[g]	
Mittheilungen, VIII, 211	325/4	[g]	
C.I.A., II, 1187	319/8	[g]	
II, 1217	315/12	[g], [gc]	—
II, 611	300/299	[gr]	
II, 1350	296/5	[gr]	
II, 300	295/4	[g]	
II, 1158	about 285/4	[r], [gr]	
II, 311	286/5	[g]	
II, 1291	282/1	[c], [gc]	—
II, 338	soon after 281	[gr], [gcr]	—
II, 331	about 272	[g]	
Bull. de corr. hellén., IV, 47	soon after 168	[r]	—
C.I.G., 2270	" " 167	[g], [r]	
Bull. de corr. hellén., IV, 164	172/50	[g]	—
C.I.A., II, 550	soon after 150	g[r]	—
Ἀθήναιον, V, 522	147	g[c]	—
C.I.A., II, 594	127	g[rc]	
II, 552	about 125	g[r]	
II, 465	just before 100	g[r], g[c]	
II, 595	" " "	g[r]	—
II, 469	about 100	[gcr], [gr]	
II, 467	" "	g[cr], gc[r], [gr]	—
II, 471	just before 69/2	gc[r], g[r], [r]	
C.I.G., 2349*b*	about 70	[gr]	
C.I.A., II, 470	69/2	g[cr], gc[r], g[r]	
II, 481	48/2	[gc]	
II, 482	39/2	g[r], gc[r]	—
Bull. de corr. hellén., VI, 495	about 7 A. D.	[g]	—
C.I.G., 5249	24 B.C.–36 A.D.	[r]	—
5254	" "	[r]	—
5255	" "	[r]	—
5262	" "	[r]	—
5270	" "	[r]	—
5274	" "	[r]	—
5277	" "	[r]	—
5282	" "	[r]	—
5301	" "	[r]	—
5312	" "	[r]	—
5313	" "	[r]	—
5315	" "	[r]	—

APPROXIMATELY DATED CLASS—Continued.

References.		Date.	Giver, Cause, Receiver.	
C.I.G.,	5331	24 B.C.-36 A.D.	[r]	—
	5337	" "	[r]	—
	5343	" "	[r]	—
	5352	" "	[r]	—
	5353	" "	[r]	—
	5354	" "	[r]	—
	5355	" "	[r]	—
	5356	" "	[r]	
Bull. de corr. hellén., IX,	273	70–80 A.D.	[gc], [c]	—
Mittheilungen, III,	144	about 100	[cr]	—
C.I.A., III,	735a	" "	gc[r]	
III,	1108	117–29	[r]	—
III,	91	after 117	[c]	—
Bull. de corr. hellén., IX,	268	131–53	[c]	—
C.I.A., III,	1042	about 175	[r]	—
III,	1177	212–21	[g], [r]	—

ξA CLASS.

References.		Giver, Cause, Receiver.	References.		Giver, Cause, Receiver.
C.I.G.,	1687	[g]	C.I.A., II,	1312	[g]
C.I.A., II,	149	[g]	II,	1331	[gr]
II,	157	[g]	II,	1334	[r]
II,	209	[g]	II,	1342	[gr]
II,	218	[g]	II,	1344	[g]
II,	219	[rg]	II,	1345	[gc] —
II,	220	[gr]	II,	1346	[gr]
II,	298	[gr]	II,	1347	[g]
II,	326	[g]	II,	1351	g[rc]
II,	331	[g]	II,	1352	[r]
II,	369	[g]	II,	1355	g[c]
II,	400	[gr]	II,	1431	[g] —
II,	420	[ger], [gr] —	II,	1449	[r]
II,	513	[cr] —	II,	1530	[g]
II,	568	[gr]	II,	1968	[r]
II,	587	[g]	Ἐφημ., No. 995		[g]
II,	861	[r], [cr], [ger]	1884, p. 187		[gr]
			Rangabé, 1148		[g]
II,	869	[rg]	Hermes, VIII, 417		[g]
II,	987	[r]	B. c. h., III, 62		[g]
II,	1199	[g]	III, 372		[g]

≶A CLASS—Continued.

References.	Giver, Cause, Receiver.	References.	Giver, Cause, Receiver.
B. c. h., III, 388	[r]	*Mittheil.*, XIII, 389	[g]
III, 485	[gcr]	I.	[g]
VII, 69	[gr]	II.	[rg]
X, 102	[gr]	III.	[r]
XIII, 370	[gr]	IV.	[g]
Mittheil., VI, 360	[g]	V.	[g]
XIII, 339	[g]		

≶A CLASS.

C.I.A., II, 454	g[r]	—	*B. c. h.*, IV, 173	[r]	—
II, 624	[gr]	—	IV, 213	[g]	
II, 1358	g[c]	—	IV, 285	[gr]	
II, 1388	g[c]		IV, 433	[g]	
II, 1419	[g]				
B. c. h., III, 372	[g]	—	VII.	g[r]	

ΣA CLASS.

C.I.G., 1942	[gr]		*C.I.A.*, III, 1297	[r]	—
2140*a¹*	[gr]	—	LE BAS, II, 1707	[g]	—
2380	[grc]	—	III, 13	[g]	—
2427	[gr]	—	III, 14	[g]	—
3073	[g]	—	III, 50	[g]	—
3098	[g]	—	III, 117	[g]	
3105	[g]	—	'Αθήναιον, VIII, 403	[gcr]	—
3157	[g]		*B. c. h.*, II, 489	[g]	—
3219	[g]		IV, 176	[r]	
3232	[g]		IV, 285	[gr]	
3234	[g]		IV, 447	[g]	
3253	[g]	—	IV, 516	[g]	
3254	[g]		XIII, 412	[gc]	—
3256	[g]		*Mittheil.*, I, 237	[g]	—
3613	[g]		XI, 278	[g]	—
C.I.A., II, 473	g[cr]		XII, 245	[g]	—
II, 874	gc[r]		XIV, 100	[g]	—
II, 477*b*	[gr]		*Bullett.*, 1873, p. 226	[g]	—
II, 1359	[gc]		*P.Sch.Ath.*, I, p.26, No.9	[g]	—
II, 1388*b*	[c]		*Arch. Zeit.*, 1875, p. 47	[g]	—
III, 916	[gc], [c]		CONZE, *Lesbos*, p. 12	[g]	—

GREEK CROWNS AND CROWN INSCRIPTIONS.

ΣA CLASS—Continued.

References.	Giver, Cause, Receiver.	References.	Giver, Cause, Receiver.
Δελτίον, 1888, p. 183	[cr]	VIII.	[gc]
		X.	[r]

ΣA CLASS.

References.	Giver, Cause, Receiver.	References.	Giver, Cause, Receiver.
C.I.G., 259	[g]	C.I.G., 3240	[g]
2097	[c]	3249	[g]
2197	[g]	3251	[g]
2206	[g]	3299	[g]
2219	[g]	3614	[g], [r]
2271	[g]	2384b	[grc]
2375	[gc]	4152c	[g]
2873	[c]	C.I.A., II, 329	[gcr], [gr]
3034	[g]	II, 1197	[g]
3065	[r]	III, 835	[rg]
3079	[g]	III, 852	[r], [g]
3086	[g]	III, 921	[gc]
3101	[g]	III, 95a	[r]
3103	[g]	Le Bas, II, 1706	[g]
3125	[g]	Conze, Imbros, p. 93	[g]
3214	[g], [gr]	Annali, 1842, p. 144	[g]
3217	[g]	B. c. h., IV, 175	[g]
3220	[g]	VII, 278	[rg], [g]
3224	[g]	VII, 469	[g]
3226	[g]	VII, 470	[g]
3228	[g]	XI, 473	[g]
3229	[g]	Mittheil., XII, 251	[g]
3231	[g]	XII, 370	[g]
3235	[g]	XIII, 74	[g]
3237	[g]	XIII, 80	[g]

C CLASS.

References.	Giver, Cause, Receiver.	References.	Giver, Cause, Receiver.
C.I.G., 2381	[grc]	C.I.A., III, 92	[r]
3112	[g]	III, 740	[r]
3221	[g]	III, 1203	[rc]
5053	[r]	III, 3926	[r]
5269	[r]	Le Bas, II, 1697	[g]
5279	[r]	III, 235	[c]
5339	[r]	B. c. h., IV, 68	[grc]
5348	[r]	XI, 483	[r]
6480	[r]		

THE NEWLY DISCOVERED HEAD OF IRIS FROM THE FRIEZE OF THE PARTHENON.

[PLATE XII.]

In the successful excavations that have been carried on during the last few years on the Akropolis at Athens, now brought to a close, the closing days were peculiarly fortunate for the excavators. I must refer the readers to the Δελτίον for an account of these excavations; but I wish to publish one discovery which may perhaps be considered the crowning event in this series of fortunate finds, though it merely consists of a fragment of marble not more than a foot in size. It will be shown in the following remarks—it is to be hoped, conclusively—that the fragment is a most interesting portion of the Frieze of the Parthenon.

"As is well known, the Frieze of the Parthenon formed a continuous band of sculpture in low relief which ran round the outer wall of the *cella*, with its two smaller halls in front and back, the *pronaos* and the *tamicion*. Like every peripteric temple, the rectangular temple proper, with its halls closed in by walls on all sides, was surrounded by a colonnade which supported the roof and projected over the walls of the actual temple. The distance from the walls to the columns (exclusive of these) varies from 2.96 to 3.57 m. (9.7 to 11.7 ft.). This space was paved with white marble and afforded shady walks to the visitors to the Akropolis. The plain wall is bounded above by a slightly projecting band (ταινία) under which are small blocks, called by Vitruvius *regulae*, which in the Doric order to which the temple belongs would lead us to expect above them the triglyphon, a frieze subdivided by metopes (μετοπαί, *metopae*) and triglyphs (τρίγλυφοι). Instead of this triglyphon, however, we here have a continuous frieze (ζωφόρος, διάζωμα) which ran round the four sides of this outer wall like a belt, or rather like a band uniting its two ends on the forehead of a victor. It was 11.9 m. (39 ft.) above the pavement of the colonnade, and above it a painted ornamentation after the manner of a cornice completed the decorations of the wall, which was joined, above, to the entablature of the outer colonnade by a ceiling, just as, below, the marble pavement joined the base of the columns with the wall. The length of the frieze was 159.42 m. (522.8 ft.), of which 21.18 m. (69.5 ft.) covered each of the narrower walls of the front and back, while 58.53 m. (191.9 ft.) decorated each longer side of the rectangular building. It consists of numerous slabs carefully joined together, almost exactly 1 m. (3 ft. 3.95 in. according to Stuart) in height."[1]

The subject represented on this frieze is generally acknowledged to be the procession on the occasion of the Panathenaic Festival. The participants in this procession started at sunrise on the last day of the Festival, the birthday of Athene, from the outer Kerameikos, passed through the Dipylon, the Dromos, and the chief street of the Inner Kerameikos, to the market-place, then to the Eleusinion, to the north-east corner of the Akropolis, to the west, and through the Propylaia to the Temple of Athene Polias, upon whose altar the hecatombs offered by Athens and its dependent states were sacrificed, and a great festive meal concluded the whole celebration. Accordingly, in the frieze on the narrow west end of the Temple is represented a scene of preparation for the procession. There are groups of horsemen, many of them already mounted, others in the act of mounting, another forcing the bit into the mouth of his restive horse, another drawing on his boots, another again trying to hold back a rearing horse, and so on. The long north and south sides present the procession proper. In it are not only the divisions of horsemen, the chariots with charioteers and hoplites; but also groups of men and youths and maidens on foot carrying branches or vases, or musical or sacrificial instruments of which in ancient life the authors give us an account. Finally there are the sacrificial cows and sheep which bring us to the narrow east or front side where the advancing maidens are met by the magistrates supposed to be awaiting them on the Akropolis. With this the procession is brought to a close, but the scene has only reached its climax; for in the central portion of this frieze forming the front of the Temple are represented the gods and goddesses who are supposed to be witnessing the display in honor of Athene. Accordingly, Athene heads the right-hand division of gods, as Zeus heads the left-hand division; and these two divisions are kept apart by the introduction of a scene supposed by many to represent

[1] WALDSTEIN, *Essays on the Art of Pheidias*, p. 191.

the dedication of the Peplos to Athene, by others the preparation on the part of the Priest and Priestess to perform the sacrifice of the hecatombs offered to the goddess.

The gods, grouped on either side of the central scene, are seated in dignified repose beside one another. After Athene we have, according to Flasch,[2] Hephaistos, then Poseidon, then Dionysos, and then Demeter (called by others, perhaps correctly, Peitho). This last figure and Dionysos fortunately have their heads preserved, and they form two of the most perfect works that have come down to us from antiquity. After Demeter we have Aphrodite, against whose knee the youthful Eros is leaning, with whom the series of gods on this side comes to an end. On the other side, next to Zeus, who is seated upon a more elaborate throne, is his divine spouse, Hera, beside whom stands as an attendant a youthful female figure, according to Flasch, Iris, according to others, Hebe or Nike. Then follows Ares, then Artemis, then Apollo, and the gods on this side are brought to a close by Hermes.

The bodies of all these figures are in comparatively good preservation; but the heads of all, with the exception of the two above mentioned, have been so strongly corroded and worn or broken away, that no trace of modelling remains. The central marble slab, beginning with Iris and including the central scene, ended on the other side with Hephaistos. The upper corners of this slab were at some period broken away and carried with them the head and neck of Iris, which figure was thus found by Lord Elgin without a head and is to be seen in this state in the British Museum.

The excavations carried on to the southwest of the Akropolis, laying bare the wall built by Kimon, and descending to great depth to the primeval rock of the Akropolis, showed that after the Persian invasion Kimon levelled the surface of the Akropolis and filled in all those portions where the rock sunk to considerable depth below the highest point. His wall, surrounding the entire Akropolis, binds the whole compactly together and joins the rocky bosses into the complete unity of the levelled citadel as it has now come down to us. All the objects found in the excavations carried on along this Kimonian wall in this and other portions of the Akropolis, date from a period preceding the Persian invasion when the enemy destroyed the buildings and monuments on the citadel. And there can be no doubt that these objects

---

[2] *Zum Parthenonfries:* Würzburg, 1877.

were thrown in during the operation of filling up and levelling the surface of the Akropolis when Kimon undertook the restoration of the Athenian citadel.

But above the wall of Kimon, which is built with massive blocks of careful masonry, there is another wall of nondescript character, which projects to the present day above the surface of the Akropolis and forms a kind of parapet. This wall is composed of stones, Roman brick, and earthwork, and has been considered a barbarian wall. We shall recur presently to the date of this structure.

Sticking in this wall, just where it joins the wall of Kimon, was found the marble fragment with which we are now concerned. It is a piece of Pentelic marble 0.275 m. in the widest portion, and 0.22 m. in height in the highest portion; the slab is 0.155 m. thick in the thickest part exclusive of relief, and the highest relief is 0.05 m., the fracture in the back being very uneven, comparatively thin at the back of the head, and thickest at the top left angle: at this corner there is a facing of about an inch in width running round the edge of the left side that is not visible in our plate and surrounding the rougher surface within it. It thus formed part of a frieze block, and has the same working of the sides where block joined block as is found in the slabs of the Frieze of the Parthenon which are 54 centimetres in thickness. The face of this marble fragment (PLATE XII) contains a head in low relief turned to the left, where a curved flattish elevation, rising from the back and shoulder of the figure, runs upwards to the left edge of the fragment. The left edge and top are thus cleanly cut, and therefore this fragment formed the top corner of some relief. The head, in excellent preservation (only the tip of the nose has been broken away), shows that simplicity and breadth of style and that marked technique of low relief (the edges almost undercut running straight down to the background) which distinguish the work of the Parthenon Frieze; and Mr. Kavvadias, the Director General of Antiquities, and Mr. Staïs conjectured that it was a piece of the Parthenon Frieze. They asked me to examine the fragment, and I at once felt assured that it was the head belonging to Iris in the East Frieze of the Parthenon, the slab to which it belongs now being among the Elgin marbles in the British Museum (*Figure 1*). When a cast of this slab was produced the identification was placed beyond all doubt.

The head and neck are turned towards the left, worked in profile, with a very slight turn towards the front as if to make room for a flat elevation rising beside the head. This elevation was evidently a wing, and in the original was no doubt painted to indicate its detail drawing. The modelling of the head and neck are of that broad simple character which mark Pheidian art, and yet with this large style the artist has been able to add a singular grace and charm to the nobility of character. The modelling of the hair is not over elaborate, in simple broadish ridges, and yet varied in the flow of line, conveying well its peculiar texture. It is similar, in this respect, to the excellent head of Demeter in this same frieze; yet the whole

FIGURE 1.—*Slab from the East Frieze of the Parthenon (in the British Museum) representing Zeus, Hera, and Iris, to which belongs the newly discovered head of Iris.*

peculiar mode of wearing the hair is one which marks a more youthful figure. The hair falls over the brow in short curls and over the temples, and it had been hanging loosely down the back till, with her left hand, Iris collected it into a knot at the back of her head. This is the action of the figure in the moment represented by the sculptor. There are several instances in the frieze in which male figures are raising their hands to their heads, tying the taenia, or otherwise arranging their hair. So, in the West Frieze (Michaelis), Plate IX, Fig. 2; North Frieze, Plate XI, Fig. 38,[3] Plate XIII, Figs. 97, 125; South Frieze,

[3] In this figure we have the complete motive of the Diadumenos, both hands placed up tying the taenia, the right hand higher than the left hand; and, when we remem-

Plate XI, Fig. 121 (a similar motive to the preceding one), and West Frieze, Plate IX, Fig. 2.

In general, this head, which may well be compared to the head of Demeter, is a youthful translation of the same type. As its dimensions (the head of the fragment is 0.09 m. from brow to chin, that of Demeter 0.10. m; from bend of nostril to the lobe of the ear in the fragment 0.06 m. and in Demeter 0.07 m.) are comparatively smaller, the proportions being exactly those that obtain between the figure of Iris and the figure of Demeter.

In the extant marble in the British Museum (*Fig. 1*), we see, on the right side of Iris, traces of a wing and the uplifted left arm. Now the wing here corresponds exactly to the right wing on our fragment; and, when the fragment was placed on the cast of the relief from the British Museum, the wrist of the upraised left hand of Iris naturally continued to the extant remains of the fingers of the hand clearly to be seen collecting the hair into a knot on the head of the fragment. The little finger and the third finger have been injured somewhat, but the middle finger is quite intact. They are distinctly seen when looked at from above, but can be distinguished with sufficient clearness in the front view here given on PLATE XII.

In the restorations made by Stuart and copied by Worsley, the head is wrongly turned towards our right; but, when the slight remaining fragment of the neck in the Iris of the British Museum is examined, it will be seen that the head was turned to our left, and this our fragment now places beyond a doubt. Henning's restoration is more correct in this respect. I am now awaiting the arrival of the cast of the fragment in its thickness, which Mr. Kavvadias has kindly promised me. This will be sent to the British Museum, and I hope to place it on the figure in the original frieze, when the identification, which really needs no further confirmation, will be settled beyond all dispute.

The question of the history of this central slab and of our head must be dwelt upon in a few words. As is known, the Parthenon remained in its original condition until the close of the fifth or beginning of the sixth century A. D., when it was converted into a Christian church. Some authorities now hold that this was done under Constantine. The

---

ber the statue of a youthful Anadumenos by Pheidias mentioned by Pausanias (VI. 4, 5), we may be justified in conjecturing that this subject, repeated in the famous statue of Polykleitos, and applied to graceful female figures of which so many adaptations have come down to us, may have been the invention of Pheidias.

alteration then made in the structure was the transference of the main entrance from the east to the west, and in the east end an apse was built. This probably necessitated the taking down of the central slab. Carrey, in 1674, did not see it, and omits it from the drawings of the frieze. Pierre Babin, in his letter to the Abbé Pécoil⁴ in 1672, after describing the Frieze, mentions one slab as being not in its place, but behind the door of the Temple (then Mosque). In Chandler's time (1765) it was let into the wall of the fortress. He refers to it as the piece which probably ranged in the centre of the cell and contained " a venerable person with a beard reading in a large volume which is partly supported by a boy."⁵ No doubt the priest with the boy and the cloak. In 1785, Worsley saw it lying on the ground before the east front of the Temple; while, according to Visconti, it is again immured in a house whence Lord Elgin's workmen took it.⁶ Thus, the slab remained for about thirteen centuries detached from its place on the Akropolis. But in taking down this heavy block the top corners were probably chipped off; the right one contained no figure, the left one this head of Iris. Now it is unlikely that this small fragment would have remained about in such excellent preservation for any length of time. And thus, shortly after the removal of the slab, it was probably used in the building of the wall in which it was found, which wall is thus likely to belong to the Byzantine period. Now the central figures of the Eastern Pediment of the Parthenon were not extant when Carrey made his drawings in 1674, fourteen years before the destruction of the Temple by the Venetians under Morosini. These were, in all likelihood, removed to make some large windows or similar structures in the east front of the temple, when it was converted into a church. And, if these figures were then thrown from their places and reduced to fragments on the ground, it is likely that portions of them are also immured in this wall, which ought therefore to be taken down and examined. It can easily be erected again in its present picturesque condition; and I am happy to say that the Commission recently appointed to consider what remains to be done on the Akropolis, unanimously decided to examine this wall.

By the discovery of this fragment, another important light is thrown upon the question of the genuineness of reduced Roman casts of the

⁴ F. MICHAELIS, *Der Parthenon*, Anhang III, p. 336, 31.
⁵ *Travels in Greece:* Oxford, 1776, p. 51.
⁶ WALDSTEIN, *ibid.* p. 264.

Frieze, the bearings of which upon the genuineness of the terracotta plaques at Paris, Copenhagen, and Rome I have discussed in Note F of Essay VII of my *Essays on the Art of Pheidias*. On page 265, I put the question, "Are the Roman casts, which have certainly been in existence since 1840, reductions taken by Collard precisely from the early casts of Choiseul-Gouffier, reduced perhaps by Andreoli?" and I inclined then to answer in the affirmative. But the fragment shows this not to have been the case: for in the Roman cast the head of Iris is turned towards our right, and has thus evidently been influenced by the restoration of Stuart. The Roman cast of the Frieze is thus not connected with the originals in a more perfect state than Lord Elgin forwarded them to London. Though this does not yet finally prove the terracottas I found, to be forgeries, it goes far to make this probable. It is by such discoveries that this question will finally be decided, and not by mere assertions on the part of those who have not carefully studied all the points and have in no way contributed by unwarrantable expression of opinion to the settling of the problem.

Finally, I should like to mention that I desired in treating of this head to dwell upon the method of representing the eye in the heads from the Parthenon. In a note to an article on a head in Madrid published by me in 1884,[1] I pointed to the peculiar treatment of the upper eyelid, which treatment forms a conclusive chronological landmark for Greek sculpture. In all the eyes of the Archaic period down to, say, the year 460 B. C., the eyelids join at their outer angle on one plane. After this period, owing, no doubt, to the influence of pictorial art, and the consideration of the shadows thrown by the brow on the upper eyelid in real life, the upper lid is carried beyond and over the lower lid at the outer angles. In the sculptures of the Parthenon we have the first indication of this innovation, some eyes having the old treatment, others the new; and after that period the projecting upper eyelid becomes the rule. I have for a long time examined eyes of ancient statues with this consideration, and what was conjecture has taken the form of a law. I hope, with the aid and co-operation of Mr. C. D. Freeman, to publish the results of this investigation with numerous illustrative instances.

CHARLES WALDSTEIN.

American School, Athens,
January, 1889.

[1] *Journal of Hellenic Studies*, vol. v, p. 174.

THE DECREES OF THE DEMOTIONIDAI.
A STUDY OF THE ATTIC PHRATRY.

In the Athenian State as constituted by Kleisthenes, every citizen belonged to three subordinate political corporations; he was member at once of a tribe, a deme, and a phratry. Of these three, the last was the least conspicuous. The phratry did not rival the deme in the frequency of its meetings and the importance of its affairs; nor did it enter, like the tribe, into the political and military organization of the State. But it had in its keeping an important trust, that of preventing the intrusion of illegitimate members into the body politic. This trust it shared in a measure, it is true, with the deme; but inasmuch as both male and female children were received into the phratry, and that, as a rule, in their earliest years, while the deme enrolled in its register only males, receiving them at the age of seventeen, we can hardly go wrong in regarding the phratry as the chief guardian of the purity of Athenian citizenship. An acquaintance with it is thus essential to an understanding of Athenian political life.

Our principal literary sources of information on the subject are as follows:[1] (1) Aristotle, in the 'Αθηναίων Πολιτεία, gave an account of the organization which he conceived to have existed at Athens before the profound reforms of Kleisthenes. The passage is preserved in a more or less garbled form by Harpokration, Pollux, and other lexicographers, and is given verbatim in the Patmian Scholia published in the *Bulletin de Correspondance Hellénique* (vol. I, p. 152). According to this, each of the four original tribes consisted of three phratries, each phratry of thirty gentes, and each gens of thirty men. This account is so artificial in its numerical symmetry, and so fanciful in the reasons assigned for it, as to excite the gravest doubts of Aristotle's competence as a witness for the period in question. Where, indeed, could he have obtained full and trustworthy information? As to whether the phratries were affected by the reforms of Kleisthenes, Aristotle has

---

[1] See especially PLATNER, *Beiträge zur Kenntniss des attischen Rechts*; MEIER, *De gentilitate attica*; BUSOLT, *Griechische Staats- und Rechtsaltertümer*, § 159, in Iwan Müller's *Handbuch der klassischen Altertumswissenschaft*, Bd. IV. I have not been able to see SAUPPE, *De phratriis atticis* (Göttingen, 1886/7).

left us two unfortunately ambiguous notices. One is in the *Politics* (VI. 4 : Bekk.) and seems to say that the phratries, as well as the tribes, were then remodelled and increased in number. The other is in the recently discovered fragments of the 'Αθηναίων Πολιτεία (II, a *Landwehr*) and seems to say just the contrary.[2] (2) Several writers of the fifth and fourth centuries B. C. refer to the phratries of their own day. The most instructive of these references are in Isaios and the private orations of Demosthenes (genuine and spurious). These are the chief basis of our knowledge. (3) Scraps of relevant information, and of misinformation as well, are preserved by scholiasts and by the lexicographers, Harpokration, Pollux, Hesychios, Suidas, *etc.*

Inscriptions have until lately yielded little to supplement this scanty literary evidence. That little may be classified thus : (1) the decrees of the Ekklesia conferring citizenship on a foreigner, regularly authorize him to be enrolled as a member of such tribe, deme and phratry as he may choose (εἶναι φυλῆς καὶ δήμου καὶ φρατρίας ἧς ἂν βούληται, or some similar formula. This is the regular order of mention. Only in *CIA*, II, 115[b] do we find δήμου καὶ φυλῆς καὶ φρατρίας[3]). (2) Two temenos boundary-stones give us names of phratries, the only names indisputably known, and one of these in a mutilated form, viz., the 'Αχνιάδαι[4] and the Θερρικ .... αι.[5] Two other boundary-stones, one of the Ζακυάδαι[6] and one of the 'Ελασίδαι,[7] give names with regard to which it is impossible to decide whether they belonged to gentes or phratries. (3) Two short fragments of phratrial decrees, eulogizing deserving members, are given in *CIA*, II, 598, 599. The Dyaleis of 600, who enact a decree in reference to the lease of a piece of real estate, are probably to be regarded, not, with Köhler, as a phratry, but, with Buermann,[8] Gilbert,[9] and Busolt,[10] as a union of two phratries.

Such was, in outline, the material available for the study of the Attic phratries down to 1883. In that year there was found at Tatoï, the

---

[2] The difficulty of dealing with these two statements is illustrated by the case of BUSOLT, who in his *Griechische Geschichte*(pp. 394–5), published in 1885, decides that Kleisthenes did not meddle with the phratries, but in his *Griechische Altertümer* (p. 144[(1)]), published in 1887, reverses this decision.

[3] *Cf.* BUERMANN, *Jahrb. für Phil., Suppl.*, IX, 643; DITTENBERGER, *Sylloge Inscr. Graec.*, 43, note 7.

[4] DITTENBERGER, *Sylloge*, 302; *CIA*, II, 1653.   [5] *CIA*, II, 1652.

[6] DITTENBERGER, *Sylloge*, 303.   [7] *Classical Review*, III, p. 188.

[8] *Op. cit.*, 645, Note.   [9] *Griech. Staatsaltertümer*, I, 199[(3)].

[10] *Griech. Staats- und Rechtsaltertümer*, 145[(5)].

site of the deme of Dekeleia, a stele, on the front of which were preserved 57 lines of a phratrial decree, dated in the year 396/5 B.C. and dealing with the phratry's most vital duties. This was published by Koumanoudes in the Ἐφημερὶς Ἀρχαιολογική (1883, 69 ff.) and by Köhler in the *Addenda* to the second volume of the Attic Corpus (841ᵇ). It has been made the subject of special articles by Szanto in the *Rheinisches Museum* (1885, 506–520) and by Gilbert in the *Jahrbücher für Philologie* (1887, 23–28). Szanto's paper is ingenious and suggestive, but is pervaded by a most improbable view of the relation of phratry to gens, and marred besides by some downright and inexcusable blunders. Gilbert corrects Szanto on one important point, the question as to where that portion of the decree which was intended to be of permanent application begins, but hazards a theory of his own which is now demonstrably false. For in the summer of 1888 the stone bearing this inscription was cleaned, with the result that the back also was found to be inscribed. Of the new text, published by Pantazides in the Ἐφημερίς (newspaper) of Sept. 1/13, 1888, and by Lolling in the Ἀρχαιολογικὸν Δελτίον for August, lines 1–55 were engraved at the same time with the portion previously published and form its continuation. These lines, like those on the front, are engraved στοιχηδόν, with occasional aberrations. Two or three lines are apparently all that is lost at the end of the part on the face of the stone. Lines 56–68 were added many years afterward. So far as I can judge from an excellent squeeze (I have not seen the stone), this portion would belong to the third cent. B.C. or the first part of the second. The letters are extremely irregular and unevenly spaced, which makes a more exact determination of the date peculiarly difficult. Δεκελεές for Δεκελεεῖς in *B*, 65 is probably only a blunder of the stone-cutter. I give below the text of the whole document, with the restorations of Köhler and Lolling, followed by a translation. The foot-notes do not touch upon orthographical peculiarities, of which there are several.

TEXT.

Face A.

Διὸς Φρατρίο
ἱερεὺς Θεόδωρος Εὐφαντίδο [11] ἀν|έγραψε καὶ ἔστησε τὴν στήλην. |

---

[11] The words Θεόδωρος Εὐφαντίδο are engraved *in rasura*. The letters, if regularly distributed, would have just filled the space. Instead of this, the letters of Θεόδωρος

5   ἱερεώσυνα τῶι ἱερεῖ διδόναι τ|άδε· ἀπὸ τô μείο[12] κωλῆν, πλευ-
    ρόν, ὀ|ς,[13] ἀργυρίο'||· ἀπὸ τô κορείο κωλῆ|ν, πλευρόν, ὅς, ἐλατῆρα
    χοινικια|ῖον, οἶνο ἡμίχον, ἀργυρίο ⊦.|
10 τάδε ἔδοξεν τοῖς φράτερσι ἐπὶ| Φορμίωνος ἄρχοντος 'Αθηναί-
    οι|ς, φρατριαρχôντος δὲ Παντακλέ|ος ἐξ Οἴο·|
    Ἱεροκλῆς εἶπε· ὁπόσοι μήπω διεδικάσ|θησαν κατὰ τὸν νόμον
15 τὸν Δημοτιωνιδ|ῶν, διαδικάσαι περὶ αὐτῶν τὸς φράτερ,ας αὐτίκα
    μάλα, ὑποσχομένος πρὸς τô Δ|ιὸς τô Φρατρίο, φέροντας τὴν
    ψῆφον ἀπ'ὸ τô βωμô·[14] ὅς δ' ἂν δόξῃ μὴ ὢν φράτηρ ἐσα|χθῆναι,
20 ἐξαλειψάτω τὸ ὄνομα αὐτô ὁ ἱερ|εὺς καὶ ὁ φρατρίαρχος ἐκ τô
    γραμματεί|ο τô ἐν Δημοτιωνιδῶν[15] καὶ τô ἀντιγράφ|ο·[16] ὁ δὲ
    ἐσαγαγὼν τὸν ἀποδικασθέντα ὀφε|ιλέτω ἑκατὸν δραχμὰς ἱερὰς
25 τῶι Διὶ τ|ῶι Φρατρίωι· ἐσπράττεν δὲ τὸ ἀργύριο|ν τοῦτο τὸν
    ἱερέα καὶ τὸν φρατρίαρχο|ν ἢ αὐτὸς ὀφείλεν. τὴν δὲ διαδικασίαν|
    τὸ λοιπὸν ἐναι τῶι ὑστέρωι ἔτει ἢ ὧι ἂ|ν τὸ κόρεον θύσηι, τῆι
30 Κορεώτιδι 'Απατ|ορίων· φέρεν δὲ τὴν ψῆφον ἀπὸ τô βωμô. ἐ|ὰν
    δέ τις βόληται ἐφεῖναι ἐς Δημοτιων|ίδας, ὧν ἂν ἀποψηφίσωνται,
    ἐξεῖναι αὐ|τῶι· ἑλέσθαι δὲ ἐπ' αὐτοῖς συνηγόρος τ|ὸν Δεκελειῶν
    οἶκον πέντε ἄνδρας ὑπὲ|ρ τριάκοντα ἔτη γεγονότας, τούτος δὲ |

are crowded, with the result of leaving a blank space sufficient for two letters after Εὐφαντίδο. I conjecture that, after the name had been once engraved, the priest desired to add his *demotikon*, and that this was attempted and found impracticable.

[12] That the μεῖον was the offering for a young child and the κούρειον that for an [adopted] lad [or man], as AUGUST MOMMSEN conjectured (*Heortologie*, 308) and as LIPSIUS, even after the publication of the first part of this text, was disposed to believe (*Meier und Schömann's Attischer Process*,[2] 3tes Buch, Note 165), is now definitively disproved. See B, 57–60. I can suggest nothing better than the explanation of KÖHLER, which has been generally adopted, that the μεῖον was the offering for a daughter, and the κούρειον that for a son.

[13] This is the reading of Koumanoudes. Köhler's κωλῆν πλευρόνος is to me unintelligible. [Compare the sacrificial calendar from Kos, *Journ. Hellen. Studies*, 1888, p. 335: θύει ἱερε[ὺς καὶ ἱερὰ] παρέχει· (γ)έρη δὲ οὖατα.—A. C. M.]

[14] A solemn mode of voting, perhaps the usual one in the phratries; cf. HEROD., VIII. 123; PLUT., *Themist.* 17; PLUT., *Per.* 32; DEM., XLIII. 14 (ed. Bekker).

[15] This construction occurs elsewhere only with deme-names of gentile form, and indicates that the Demotionidai were a local body. See MEISTERHANS, *Gram. d. att. Inschriften*[(2)] § 83, 19(b).

[16] The copy, it is implied, was not kept in Demotionidai; perhaps in Athens. I conjecture that the copy was intended as a protection against tampering with the record and against the confusion which would result if the register should be injured or lost. That such a safeguard was desirable may be seen from DEM., XLIV. 41; LVII. 26, 60.

35 ἐξορκωσάτω ὁ φρατρίαρχος καὶ ὁ ἱερε|ὺς συνηγορήσεν τὰ δικαιότατα καὶ ὀκ | ἐάσεν ὀδένα μὴ ὄντα φράτερα φρατρίζ|εν· ὅτο δ' ἂν τῶν ἐφέντων ἀποψηφίσωντα|ι Δημοτιωνίδαι, ὀφειλέτω χιλίας
40 δρα|χμὰς ἱερὰς τῶι Διὶ τῶι Φρατρίωι· ἐσπρ|αττέτω δὲ τὸ ἀργύριον τοῦτο ὁ ἱερεὺς | τὸ Δεκελειῶν οἶκο ἢ αὐτὸς ὀφειλέτω. ἐ|ξεῖναι δὲ καὶ ἄλλωι τῶι βολομένωι τῶ|ν φρατέρων ἐσπράττεν τῶι κοι-
45 νῶι·¹⁷ ταὖ|[τα] δ' ἔναι ἀπὸ Φορμίωνος ἄρχοντος.¹⁸ ἐπὶ|[ψ]ηφίζεν δὲ τὸν φρατρίαρχον περὶ ὧν ἂ|ν διαδικάζεν δέηι κατὰ τὸν ἐνιαυτὸν | ἕκαστον·¹⁹ ἐὰν δὲ μὴ ἐπιψηφίσηι, ὀφελέτ|ω πεντακοσίας δραχμὰς
50 ἱερὰς τῶι Διὶ | [τ]ῶι Φρατρίω[ι· ἐ]σπράττεν δὲ τὸν ἱερέα | [κ]αὶ ἄλλο[ν τὸν βο]λόμενον τὸ ἀργύριον | [το]ῦτ[ο τῶι κοινῶι]. τὸ δὲ λοιπὸν ἄγεν τὰ | [μεῖα καὶ τὰ κόρει]α ἐς Δεκέλειαν ἐπὶ τ|[ὸν
55 βωμόν· ἐὰν δὲ μὴ θ]ύσηι ἐπὶ τὸ βωμὸ, ὀφ|[ελέτω πεντήκοντ]α δραχμὰς ἱερὰς τῶ|[ι Διὶ τῶι Φρατρίωι· ἐσ]πραττέτω δὲ ὁ ἱερ|[εὺς τὸ ἀργύριον τοῦτο ἢ] αὐτὸς ὀφει]λέ|τω. — — —

Face B.

ἐὰν δέ τι τούτων διακωλύηι, ὅποι ἂν ὁ ἱ|ερεὺς προγράφηι, ἐνθαῦθα ἄγεν τὰ μεῖ|α καὶ τὰ κόρεια· προγράψεν δὲ πρόπεμπ|τα τῆς
5 Δορπίας ἐν πινακίωι λελευκωμ|ένωι μῆλαττον²⁰ ἢ σπιθαμιαίωι ὅπο ἂν Δ|εκελειῆς προσφοιτῶσιν ἐν ἄστει.²¹ τὸ δ|ὲ ψήφισμα τόδε καὶ τὰ ἱερεώσυνα ἀναγ|ράψαι τὸν ἱερέα ἐν στήληι λιθίνηι πρ|όσθεν

¹⁷ *The common fund; cf.* Theoph., *Char.* xxx. 5. The fund of Zeus Phratrios was the fund of the phratry.
¹⁸ According to Szanto, everything preceding ταῦτα δ' εἶναι (except the sentence τὴν δὲ .... βωμῶ, lines 26–29, which he regards as standing out of its proper connection) belongs to the provisions for the immediate future, and the ταῦτα δ' εἶναι marks the beginning of the permanent law. But, as Gilbert pointed out, if the pronoun referred to what follows, it would probably be τάδε. More decisive is the presence, in the next clause, of δέ, which is irreconcilable with Szanto's view. The permanent law begins with τὴν δὲ διαδικασίαν in line 26. The aorists ἐλέσθαι, ἐξορκωσάτω, make no difficulty; *cf. B*, 29 and Meisterhans, *op. cit.*: Anm. 1638.
¹⁹ Szanto twice (pp. 507, 518) gives the sense of this as being *dass der Phratriarch jedes Jahr die Abstimmung darüber einzuleiten habe, wer diadikasirt werden solle*. As if ὦν ἂν δέῃ could be an indirect question!
²⁰ This crasis would not occur in a decree of the Ekklesia; Meisterhans, *op.cit.*, § 24.
²¹ Lolling refers to Lysias, xxiii. 3, which mentions "the barber's shop near the Hermae" as the place ἵνα οἱ Δεκελεῖς προσφοιτῶσιν. Blass says that we have no indications as to the date of this oration (*Att. Beredsamkeit*, I, 632). But, surely, the presence of Plataeans in Athens implies a date prior to 387 or not much later; see Paus., ix. 1. 4. This was probably, then, the place in 396/5. But the wording of the clause ὕπο .... προσφοιτῶσιν provides for possible changes.

10 τὸ βωμὸ Δεκελειᾶσιν τέλεσι το|ῖς ἑαυτὸ. Νικύδημος εἶπε· τὰ
    μὲν ἄλλα κατ|ὰ τὰ πρότερα ψηφίσματα ἃ κέται περὶ τ|ἒς εἰσα-
    γωγῆς τῶν παίδων καὶ τῆς διαδ|ικασίας, τὸς δὲ μάρτυρας τρὲς,
15 ὃς εἴρη|ται ἐπὶ τῆι ἀνακρίσει, παρέχεσθαι ἐκ τ|ῶν ἑαυτὸ θιασωτῶν
    μαρτυρόντας τὰ ὑπερωτώμε(να)²²| καὶ ἐπομνύντας τὸν Δία τὸν
    Φράτριον· | μαρτυρὲν δὲ τὸς μάρτυρας καὶ ἐπομνύ|ναι ἐχομένος
    τὸ βωμὸ· ἐὰν δὲ μὴ ὦσι ἐν τ|ῶ(ι) θιάσωι τύτωι τοσῦτοι τὸν
20 ἀριθμὸν, ἐ|κ τῶν ἄλλων φρατέρων παρεχέσθω. ὅταν| δὲ ἦι ἡ
    διαδικασία, ὁ φρατρίαρχος μὴ π|[ρ]ότερον διδύτω τὴ(ν) ψῆφον
    περὶ τῶν παί|δων τοῖς ἅπασι φράτερσι πρὶν ἂν οἱ αὐ|τὸ τὸ εἰσα-
25 γομένο θιασῶται κρύβδην ἀ|[π]ὸ τὸ βωμὸ φέροντες τὴν ψῆφον
    διαψηφ|ίσωνται· καὶ τὰς ψήφος τὰς τότων ἐναν|τίον τῶν ἁπάντων
    φρατέρων τῶν παρόν|των ἐν τῆι ἀγορᾶι ὁ φρατρίαρχος διαρ|ιθμη-
30 σάτω καὶ ἀναγορευέτω ὁπύτερ' ἂν| ψηφίσωνται· ἐὰν δὲ ψηφισα-
    μένων τῶν θ|ιασωτῶν ἔναι αὐτοῖς φράτερα οἱ ἄλλο|ι φράτερες
    ἀποψηφίσωνται, ὀφειλόντ|ων ἑκατὸν δραχμὰς ἱερὰς τῶι Διὶ τῶι
35 Φ|ρατρίωι οἱ θιασῶται, πλὴν ὅσοι ἂν τῶν | θιασωτῶν κατήγοροι
    ἢ ἐναντιόμενοι | φαίνωνται ἐν τῆι διαδικασίαι· ἐὰν δὲ | ἀποψηφί-
    σωνται οἱ θιασῶται, ὁ δὲ εἰσά|γων ἐφῆι εἰς τὸς ἅ[π]αντας, τοῖς δὲ
40 ἅπασ|ι δόξει ἔναι φράτηρ, ἐνγραφέσθω εἰς τ|ὰ κοινὰ γραμματεῖα.²³
    ἐὰν δὲ ἀποψηφίσω|ντ[α]ι οἱ ἅπαντες, ὀφειλέτω ἑκατὸν δρα|χμὰς
    ἱερὰς τῶι Διὶ τῶι Φρατρίωι· ἐὰν δὲ | ἀποψηφισαμένων τῶν θια-
45 σωτῶν μὴ ἐφῆ|ι εἰς τὸς ἅπαντας, κυρία ἔστω ἡ ἀποψήφ|ισις ἡ
    τῶν θιασωτῶν· οἱ δὲ θιασῶται με'τὰ τῶν ἄλλων φρατέρων μὴ
    φερόντων τὴν | ψῆφον περὶ τῶν παίδων τῶν ἐκ τὸ θιάσο | τὸ
    αὐτῶν. τὸ δὲ ψήφισμα τόδε προσαναγ|ραψάτω ὁ ἱερεὺς (ε)ἰς τὴν
50 στήλην τὴν λι.θίνην. Ὅρκος μαρτύρων ἐπὶ τῆι εἰσαγω|γεῖ τῶν
    παίδων· μαρτυρῶ ὃν εἰσάγει ἑα|υτῶι υἱὸν ἔναι τὸτον γνήσιον ἐγ
    γαμετ|ῆς. ἀληθῆ ταῦτα νὴ τὸν Δία τὸν Φράτριο|ν. εὐορκὸ(ν)τι μέν
55 μοι πολλὰ καὶ ἀγαθὰ ἔν|αι, εἰ δ' ἐπιορκοίην, τἀναντία.²⁴

---

²² According to LOLLING, lines 11–15 are written *in rasura*, which may partly account for the awkward and ungrammatical expression. τοὺς μάρτυρας τρεῖς is anomalous for τοὺς τρεῖς μάρτυρας; cf. KEIL, *Zur Syll. inscr. Boeot.*, p. 620. παρέχεσθαι does double duty, being needed in both relative and antecedent clauses. I do not see the force of ὑπό in ὑπερωτώμενα, but it seems to have been thought important, since, by omitting it, the ἐρωτώμενα could have been written entire, whereas, as it is, the last two letters had to be omitted altogether.

²³ These were called, above, τὸ γραμματεῖον τὸ ἐν Δημοτιωνιδῶν καὶ τὸ ἀντίγραφον.

²⁴ The wording of this oath is extremely muddled; probably the work of Nikodemos, who seems to have been exceptionally illiterate and bungling.

Μενέξενος ειπεν· δεδόχθαι τοις φράτερσι περί | της εισαγωγής τωμ παίδων, τα μεν άλλα κα|τα τα πρότερα ψηφίσματα, όπως δ'
60 αν ειδώσι οί | φράτερες τους μέλλοντας εισάγεσθαι, άπο|γράφεσθαι τωι πρώτωι [25] έτει ή ωι αν το κούρεο|ν άγει το όνομα πατρόθεν και του δήμου και τή|ς μητρός πατρόθεν και του δήμου προς τον |
65 φρατρίαρχον· τον δε φρατρία[ρχον άπογραψ]|αμένων αναγρά- ψαντα εκ[τιθέναι όπου αν Δεκ]|ελεές προσφοιτώσι, εκτιθ[έναι δε και τον ιερέα] | αναγράψαντα εν σανιδί[ωι λευκώι εν τωι ιερ]|- ωι της Λητούς.[26] το δε ψ[ήφισμα τόδε προσαναγράψαι | εις τη]ν στήλην [την λιθίνην.]

TRANSLATION.

Theodoros, son of Euphantides, priest of Zeus Phratrios, had this stele engraved and erected.

The sacrificial portions due to the priest are as follows: from the *meion*, a haunch, a rib, an ear, and three obols of money; from the *koureion*, a haunch, a rib, an ear, a quart-cake, a half-chous of wine, and a drachma of money.

The following decrees were passed by the phraters in the archonship of Phormion at Athens [396/5 B. C.] and the phratriarchate of Pantakles of Oion:

On the motion of Hierokles: For all who have not yet been subjected to a *diadikasia* according to the law of the Demotionidai, the phraters, having promised in the name of Zeus Phratrios so to do, shall hold a *diadikasia* immediately, taking their ballots from the altar. And, whoever be found to have been introduced illegally, the priest and the phratriarch shall erase his name from the register kept in Demotionidai and from the copy thereof. And he who introduced the rejected member shall be fined 100 drachmas, to be devoted to Zeus Phratrios. This money the priest and the phratriarch shall collect, or be responsible for the amount.

In future the *diadikasia* shall be held in the year following that in which the *koureion* is sacrificed, on the Koureotis of the Apatouria, the ballots being taken from the altar. And, if any disfranchised member

---

[25] πρώτῳ for προτέρῳ is extraordinary. It may help to prop up the three similar examples given by Kühner, *Griech. Gramm.*, II, 22 (Arist., *Birds*, 824 should not have been cited), two at least of which have been corrected by critics. *Cf.* the cases of πρῶτος with genitive quoted in Stephanos, *Thesaurus*, s. v. πρῶτος.

[26] Probably in Dekeleia.

wishes to appeal to the Demotionidai, he shall have the right. In these cases the house of Dekeleians shall choose five men above thirty years of age as advocates, to whom the phratriarch and the priest shall administer an oath to be absolutely just in their advocacy and not to allow any one illegally to belong to the phratry. And every appellant rejected by the Demotionidai shall be fined 1000 drachmas, to be devoted to Zeus Phratrios. This money the priest of the house of Dekeleians shall collect, or be responsible for the amount. And it shall also be permissible for any other phrater who wishes to collect this for the common fund. These provisions shall be in force from the archonship of Phormion.

The phratriarch shall every year put to vote the cases of those for whom a *diadikasia* is required. Otherwise, he shall be fined 500 drachmas, to be devoted to Zeus Phratrios. This money the priest, or any one else who wishes, shall collect for the common fund.

In future the *meia* and the *koureia* shall be taken to the altar in Dekeleia. And, if they be not sacrificed on the altar, the offender shall be fined 50 drachmas, to be devoted to Zeus Phratrios. This money the priest shall collect, or be responsible for the amount. . . . And, if any of these causes prevent, the *meia* and the *koureia* shall be taken to whatever place the priest may advertise, the said advertisement to be made four days before the Dorpia on a whitewashed board not less than a span broad at the usual resort, for the time being, of the Dekeleians in the city.

This decree, together with the priest's portions, the priest shall have engraved at his own expense on a stone stele in Dekeleia before the altar.

On the motion of Nikodemos: The earlier decrees in force in regard to the introduction of children and the *diadikasia* are hereby amended as follows:

The three witnesses whom it has been required to produce for the examination shall be fellow-thiasotes of the applicant, testifying to the matters of inquiry and confirming their word by an oath in the name of Zeus Phratrios. And the witnesses shall touch the altar during their testimony and oath. And, if there be not so many in the thiasos in question, they shall be furnished from the other phraters.

At the *diadikasia* the phratriarch shall not permit the whole body of phraters to vote in regard to the children, until the fellow-thiasotes of the candidate himself have voted secretly, taking their ballots from the altar. And the phratriarch shall count their ballots before the whole body of phraters present at the meeting and proclaim which way they have voted. And if, when the thiasotes have voted favorably, the rest of the phraters vote adversely, the thiasotes, except those who openly denounce or oppose [the child] at the *diadikasia*, shall be fined 100 drachmas [apiece], to be devoted to Zeus Phratrios. On the other hand, if the thiasotes vote adversely and the applicant [*i. e.*, father or guardian] appeal to the whole body and the whole body decide that the child belongs to the phratry, he shall be enrolled in the general registers; but, if the whole body vote adversely, he [*i. e.*, the father or guardian] shall be fined 100 drachmas, to be devoted to Zeus Phratrios. And, if, when the thiasotes have voted adversely, no appeal is taken to the whole body, the adverse vote of the thiasotes shall be decisive. And the members of any thiasos shall not vote with the rest of the phraters on the children of their own thiasos.

This additional decree the priest shall have engraved on the stone stele.

Oath of witnesses at the introduction of children: I testify that this child whom he introduces as his son is the legitimate child of a lawful wife. This is true, by Zeus Phratrios. [I pray] that much good may befall me if I swear truly, and the contrary if I swear falsely.

On the motion of Menexenos: Resolved by the phraters to amend the former decrees in regard to the introduction of children, as follows: In order that the phraters may know those who are to be introduced, there shall be presented to the phratriarch, during the year before the *koureion* is brought, a written statement of the name [of each child], with the father's name and deme, as well as the mother's name, with her father's name and deme. And, when the statements have been made, the phratriarch shall inscribe them and post them up at the usual resort, for the time being, of the Dekeleians, and the priest also shall inscribe them on a white board and post it up in the temple of Leto.

This additional decree shall be engraved on the stone stele.

COMMENT.

The foregoing document is difficult of comprehension especially for two reasons. In the first place, the subjects of εἰσαγωγή and διαδικασία, with which these psephisms deal, are not here taken up for the first time. As regards the *diadikasia*, to be sure, Szanto[27] and Busolt[28]

---

[27] *Op. cit.*, 507. [28] *Griech. Alt.*, § 160.

are (or were) of another opinion. Regarding the Demotionidai as a gens, with which our phratry was intimately connected, either as contained in it (Szanto) or containing it (Busolt), they see in the "law of the Demotionidai" a recent enactment of the gens, and suppose that the *diadikasia* was in the archonship of Phormion first introduced into our phratry and presumably into others as well. Now, it may be, as Szanto and Busolt have assumed, that the first of our phratrial psephisms is symptomatic of the same movement which found expression in the archonship of Eukleides in the revival of the law, that only those should be citizens both of whose parents were citizens, though the interval of time, eight years, is hardly favorable to such an assumption. But, at any rate, the psephism of Hierokles does not introduce a new practice. If the "law of the Demotionidai" had been a recent enactment, it would almost certainly have been called a ψήφισμα: and the language, "all who have not yet been subjected to a *diadikasia* according to the law," implies that some have already passed that ordeal. The law is not a novelty, but it has been laxly observed, and is now to be again enforced. Furthermore, as we now know, there have been one or more earlier psephisms of the phratry in regard to εἰσαγωγή or διαδικασία or both. The πρότερα ψηφίσματα to which Nikodemos refers (*B, 11*) may include the psephism of Hierokles, but imply at least one besides. The measures now enacted presuppose the immemorial νόμος and the previous legislation, of whose precise nature we are ignorant.[29]

In the second place, the style of our document is extremely clumsy and inexact. Attention has been called above to the illiterate syntax of certain passages. What is far more serious is the inconsecutiveness, the incompleteness and the ambiguity in statement of principles. It requires talent and training of a high order to frame a good law, and these the legislative methods of the Athenians did not tend to develop. Least of all were such qualities likely to be found in the subordinate, rural corporations, as these psephisms bear witness. Hence it is useless to bring to bear upon them strict rules of interpretation.

In consequence of these difficulties, a complete and certain explanation of these decrees is impossible so long as our materials remain what they are. The way in which the newly discovered text has thrown

---

[29] The words οὓς εἴρηται ἐπὶ τῇ ἀνακρίσει παρέχεσθαι seem to me to refer to a previous psephism. The novelty in Nikodemos' measure was not the requirement of witnesses, but the requirement that they should be of the thiasos of the candidate.

some ingenious theories to the winds is a warning against over-confidence in dealing with riddles still unsolved. Nor, even if the constitution and procedure of this particular phratry lay clearly before us, would it be safe to assume that all the Attic phratries were cut out on the same pattern and pursued the same methods. There was of course a fundamental likeness between phratry and phratry. The conditions of membership must have been the same for all,[30] being none other than the conditions of Athenian citizenship. But beyond this the variation may have been wide. Our stele shows us one phratry modifying its rules and regulations. If the same phratry performed its duties in different ways at different times, how much more is such difference likely to have existed between different phratries. Yet, in spite of all these difficulties and limitations, the new text sheds enough additional light to justify a review of the whole subject.

One thing which is now put beyond a peradventure is, that the members of this phratry did not all belong to one deme. Szanto, who regards the phratries in general as subdivisions of the demes, saw no difficulty in supposing that all the members of this phratry were of the deme Oion, to which the phratriarch Pantakles belonged, in spite of the facts that the inscription was found at Dekeleia and the meetings for the admission of children were required to be held in that deme (A, $52\,ff$.). This view, always improbable enough, is now shown to be certainly false. It is scarcely conceivable that the rendezvous of the Dekeleians in Athens should have been selected as the place to post notices intended to reach all members of the phratry (B, 5–6, 64–65), unless there had been Dekeleians in the phratry. A still more cogent proof is supplied by the provision of B, 61. If the members had all belonged to one deme, it would have been idle to require the mention of the father's *demotikon*. But, besides Dekeleia and Oion, we cannot name any deme represented in this phratry, nor can we say whether there were any others. If there were, they were probably, like Oion (*i. e.* no doubt Οἷον Δεκελεικόν) in the immediate vicinity of Dekeleia. At least, the presumption, derived from other sources, that the phratries were unions of neighbors, receives some confirmation from our inscription. It looks as if this phratry were localized in and near Dekeleia, not, indeed, in the sense that all the members actually lived in that neighborhood, but that they belonged to that group of demes. But, whether *all* the

---

[30] Except that some phratries were by law not open to δημοποιητοί; see BUERMANN, *Jahrbücher für Philologie*, Supp., IX, 643.

members of these demes or of any one of them belonged to the phratry, we cannot tell. If the Dyaleis of *CIA*, II, 600 are rightly regarded as a union of two phratries, then, as the two phratriarchs there mentioned were both Myrrhinusians, it follows that members of the same deme might belong to different phratries. The same inference has been drawn by Buermann from the formula of the decrees conferring citizenship, εἶναι φυλῆς καὶ δήμου καὶ φρατρίας ἧς ἂν βούληται, which suggests that, as after the choice of a tribe there was still open the choice of a deme, so after the choice of a deme there was still open the choice of a phratry. It may be then that the demesmen of Dekeleia and Oion were not all enrolled in our phratry. And thus we are as far as ever from being able to estimate even approximately the size of an Attic phratry, or, what comes to the same thing, the number of phratries in the State. Between the twelve commonly accepted until lately and the three hundred and sixty once proposed by Buermann, there is still room for indefinite guessing.

Nor does the new text supply any decisive answer to the important question raised by Szanto, Are the Demotionidai a gens or a phratry?[31] and answered by him in favor of the former. It should be premised that the Demotionidai, if a gens, are to be regarded, not with Szanto as a wider organization including the phratry, but rather with Busolt as the nucleus around which non-gentiles were grouped to form the phratry. Now the first two occurrences of the name do not favor the view that the Demotionidai are a gens. The "law of the Demotionidai" is the law of the phratry (*A*, *14*); ergo, one naturally infers, the Demotionidai *are* the phratry. Busolt,[32] to be sure, asserts, *Die Satzungen des Geschlechts galten auch für die Phratrie*, but the passage in Isaios to which he refers affords no confirmation of the assertion, and the general impression produced by the psephisms before us is that the phraters were a law unto themselves. Again, as the phratry as a whole has control of the register (*B*, *39–40*; *A*, *19–20*), it is hard to see why a gens, and not the phratry, should be named as the body with whom the register is kept (*A*, *27*). But the "appeal to the Demotionidai" (*A*, *30*) makes a difficulty. How, asks Szanto, not without

---

[31] There is a third alternative possible, viz., that both gens and phratry were called Demotionidai. In that case, we could understand the phratry in the first two instances and the gens in the third. I should prefer this to Szanto's view, but do not think it necessary.

[32] *Griech. Alt.*, §159, with references to this inscription and Isaios, VII. 15.

force, can there be an appeal from a body to the same body again? On the other hand, we may ask, Why should the phraters, who in general manage their affairs collectively, abdicate in favor of a section of their number in the most important of their proceedings? The question is more forcible now than before, because, in the detailed regulation of the *diadikasia* by the psephism of Nikodemos, we find no disposition to accept as final the decision of any subordinate body. On the whole, therefore, I am disposed to see in the Demotionidai the phraters, and the phraters only. If this be right, the word "appeal" is indeed not strictly appropriate, but perhaps the interpretation suggested below for the passage in question may make the employment of the word more intelligible.

If our inscription teaches nothing about the relation of gens to phratry, it redeems this silence by the proof it brings that every member of the phratry belonged also to some one or other of a number of religious associations or *thiasoi*. We can with some confidence go a step further. If any dependence is to be placed on the literal meaning of *B, 23–48, all* the members of any thiasos were expected to take part at the *diadikasia* of the child of one of their own number, and were *all* liable to be fined; in other words, the *thiasoi* were subdivisions of the phratry. Further, according to the present wording of our text, these *thiasoi* were, at least in some instances, very small bodies; the possible case is considered of the membership being less than four (*B, 18–19*). But it may be that in the first version of lines 11–15 a larger number of witnesses than these was prescribed. As to the nature of these *thiasoi*, we learn nothing beyond what the name itself implies, nor do other sources of information have much, if anything, to say of such associations, at least under that name.[33] But, inasmuch as θιασῶται and ὀργεῶνες are practically synonymous, it seems permissible to bring these *thiasoi* into connection with a much debated statement of Philochoros. His words, as quoted by Photios and Souidas, κ. τ. Ὀργεῶνες, are as follows: τοὺς δὲ φράτορας ἐπάναγκες δέχεσθαι καὶ τοὺς ὀργεῶνας καὶ τοὺς ὁμογάλακτας, οὓς γεννήτας καλοῦμεν. Opinions have differed as to whether οὕς here refers to both ὀργεῶνας and ὁμογάλακτας, or only to ὁμογάλακτας. But, even without the context, the latter alternative seems to me almost certain,[34] and those who

---

[33] The "*thiasoi* of Herakles," mentioned in Isaios, ix. 30 may be analogous.
[34] *Cf.* Busolt, *Griech. Gesch.*, i, 395(1).

had the context so understood it.³⁵ See Harpokration s. v. Γεννῆται, and Bull. de Corr. Hellén., 1, 152, from which we learn further that the sentence in question was taken from the fourth book of Philochoros' *Atthis*. This book covered the latter half of the fifth century B. C., so that the statement quoted probably referred to the phratries of the post-Kleisthenean period. We thus learn that a phratry consisted of two classes of members, γεννῆται or members of a gens (or gentes) based upon real or fictitious kinship and ὀργεῶνες or members of a religious union or unions, perhaps not laying claim to kinship. Conformably to the statement of Philochoros, we find admission to a phratry coupled with admission to a gens in Isaios, VII. 16 and Dem. LIX. 77, and with admission to a body of ὀργεῶνες in Isaios, II. 14. But now, although ὀργεῶνες might be contrasted with γεννῆται, and were so contrasted by Philochoros, yet the name in its broad sense is applicable to any religious association. A gens was a religious association; hence a body of gentiles could be called ὀργεῶνες. Such at least is the clear statement of the *Etymologicum Magnum*, s. v. Γεννῆται,³⁶ and I see no ground for doubting it. The combined testimony of these passages may be summed up by saying that a phratry consisted of two or more religious associations, one at least of which was or might be a gens. Probably then, by the *thiasoi* of our inscription, we are to understand any gens (or gentes) included in the phratry and a number of non-gentile associations. Possibly the οἶκος Δεκελειῶν may have been a gentile or quasi-gentile thiasos.³⁷

So much for the constitution of the Demotionidai. What, now, were the special circumstances which evoked the psephisms of 396/5? As I conceive the situation, there had been in our phratry three closely connected abuses, to the reform of which the psephism of Hierokles was directed. (1) Meetings for the reception of children had been held elsewhere than at Dekeleia. This is a certain inference from *A, 52* ff., and that the practice was considered an abuse is almost equally certain. I think we can plausibly conjecture how the abuse arose. During the years 413–404, Dekeleia had been continuously occupied by a Spartan garrison, and the residents of the neighborhood had been shut up in

---

³⁵ Except perhaps POLLUX, in III. 52; see BUSOLT, *loc. cit.*

³⁶ The confused words of the same lexicon, s. v. Ὀργεῶνες: Σύνταγμά τι ἀνδρῶν, ὡς τῶν γεννητῶν καὶ φρατόρων, seem to point the same way.

³⁷ That the οἶκος Δεκελειῶν was a religious association is evident from its having a priest (*A, 41-42*). Whether this priest was identical, as some suppose, with the priest of the phratry, is not clear.

Athens. During these years, whatever meetings the Demotionidai held must have been held in the city. Moreover, when the war was over, it is likely that many, habituated to city life, did not return to their country homes, but remained in the capital. What more likely than that the Demotionidai, having got into the way of it, should have found it convenient to continue meeting and transacting business in Athens? (2) But the irregularity went further than is implied in the mere substitution of one meeting-place for another. These meetings had been held without the presence and sanction of the priest of Zeus Phratrios. This is clear from the priest being appointed to collect the fine from future offenders—an unintelligible provision if he were an aider and abettor in the offense. Naturally, if the priest was not present, he did not receive the sacrificial portions to which he was entitled. The instructions of B, 7, and the consequent announcement of the ἱερεώσυνα at the head of the stele, bear witness to an attempt to restore neglected rights. Henceforth the priest is made the judge as to whether circumstances necessitate a meeting elsewhere than at Dekeleia, and it falls to him, if need be, to choose and advertise another place. In fact, all that part of the first decree which relates to εἰσαγωγή was passed in the interest of the priest—a fact which may explain the requirement that he shall bear the expense of the stele. (3) The names of new members had been entered in the register without the διαδικασία. This was simply part and parcel of that confusion into which the affairs of the phratry had fallen. The psephism of Hierokles aimed at correcting these laxities and restoring the traditional order. That of Nikodemos, on the other hand, bringing the θίασοι into prominence and making them jointly responsible for their members, seems to introduce innovations. What the occasion of this move was I am unable to say.

Let us now attempt to realize, step by step, the process established by the decrees of 396/5 for seeking admission to the phratry of Demotionidai. There is probably no fixed rule as to the age at which a child shall be presented, but the ceremony under ordinary circumstances takes place within the first three or four years of the child's life.

The regular occasion, according to the evidence of several scholiasts and lexicographers, is the Koureotis, the third and last day of the Apatouria-festival. This statement has been disputed by August Mommsen,[38] who assumes that the presentation began on the Dorpia,

[38] *Heortologie*, 308–310.

the first day of the festival, on no better ground than that it would have been a bad arrangement to postpone the serious business till the last. But the evidence of the grammarians receives some confirmation from our inscription, which fixes the *diadikasia* upon the Koureotis. And it may well be doubted whether an attendance of the scattered phraters sufficient to transact business could have been secured for more than a single day. Unless insuperable obstacles, such as war, intervene, the meeting is held at Dekeleia. Thither are brought the children,[39] male and female, and with them the victims and other offerings which law or custom prescribed. Schoemann conceived such meetings as being held in the φράτριον, which according to Pollux (III. 52) was τὸ ἱερὸν εἰς ὃ συνῄεσαν (sc. οἱ φράτορες). It is noteworthy that Stephanos of Byzantion (s. v. φατρία) and Eustathios (ad. Il., 239. 30 and 735. 50) know the φράτριον only as a τόπος or τόπος ὡρισμένος. At all events, the Demotionidai meet in the open air for the εἰσαγωγή as well as for the διαδικασία: for they are in presence of the altar,[40] and that this was not in a covered building we may infer, not only from its use for burnt sacrifices, but also from the phraseology of *B, 9*; one would not say "in Dekeleia before the altar," if this altar were in a building. The meeting is presided over by the phratriarch. Each applicant presents his child, and is subjected to an examination, searching or perfunctory according to circumstances. Then, while the sacrificial portions assigned to Zeus Phratrios burn upon the altar, he takes oath that the child he presents is γνήσιος ἐγ γαμετῆς. Following the oath of the father or guardian, comes the examination of the three witnesses whom he produces from among the members of his thiasos. They testify with one hand upon the altar and confirm their testimony with an oath. We should expect, then, to find the phraters proceeding at once to vote on the application, and, in case of acceptance, to enter the name of the child in the register. Such was the practice in other phratries, so far as known to us:[41] but the practice of the Demotionidai, as regulated by the psephism of Hierokles, seems to have been different.

[39] That the candidates were presented in person appears from ISAIOS, VII. 16; DEM., LVII. 54: cf. ANDOK., I. 126, for admission into a gens.

[40] See, especially, *B, 17-18*.

[41] ISAIOS, VII. 16-17; DEM., XLIII. 13-14; DEM., LIX. 59: cf. ANDOK., I. 127. The phratry of DEM., XLIII, might be the Demotionidai, since Eubulides was of the deme Oion. But this may have been Οἷον Κεραμεικόν; or, if it was Οἷον Δεκελεικόν, the phratry, as shown above, may have been different. The apparent difference of practice points to a different phratry.

For a year later the child is still ὁ εἰσαγόμενος (B, 24) and the father or guardian ὁ εἰσάγων (B, 37–38), and not till after a favorable issue of the διαδικασία does registration take place (B, 29). I would suggest, therefore, that the *diadikasia* of the Demotionidai, instead of being a procedure otherwise unknown to us, was nothing more or less than the trial and vote which every well-conducted phratry held on the admission of each new child, the peculiarity lying solely in the interval of a year required between the first presentation and the vote. The object of this arrangement would be to secure due advertisement of the names and alleged antecedents of the candidates, and thus to prevent fraud. At the meeting on the Koureotis of the next year following, the phratriarch is required to bring up each case in turn. There is opportunity, for whoever will, to make objections (B, 34–36). Then follows the vote, which may result in any one of five ways. (A) If the child's fellow-thiasotes vote favorably, the case must then go before the remaining phraters. (1) If they vote favorably, the child's name is enrolled in the two registers (this case, as being self-evident, is not mentioned by Nikodemos). (2) If the phraters vote unfavorably, the child is rejected and each thiasote (or the thiasos collectively?) including presumably the father or guardian (unless the latter should not belong to the thiasos), but excluding any who may have opposed the candidate in the previous discussion, is fined 100 drachmas. (B) If the child's fellow-thiasotes vote unfavorably, then an appeal may or may not be taken to the remaining phraters. (3) If no appeal is taken, the child is rejected, but there is, apparently, no fine. If an appeal is taken and (4) the action of the thiasos is sustained, the child is rejected and the εἰσάγων is fined 100 drachmas; but (5), if the decision of the thiasos is reversed, the child is accepted and his name enrolled. For cases (2) and (4) there remains the possible appeal to the Demotionidai. The subject is beset with difficulties, and I do not pretend to clear them away. But it is noteworthy that, whereas, in case a child is rejected at the ordinary *diadikasia* by his fellow-thiasotes, it is the εἰσάγων who is said to appeal (B, 38), and, whereas at the extraordinary *diadikasia* of 396/5 it is the εἰσαγαγών of a rejected member who is fined (A, 22–23), here the rejected person is himself authorized to appeal, and, in the event of failure, the fine is said to fall upon him (A, 30–31, 38–39). Is this a mere carelessness of language, as Gilbert thought? Possibly so. But may we not take the language literally? In that case, this paragraph provides that one who had been rejected in infancy may, as an adult, seek admission again in his own person. He refers his suit anew to the phratry; the years that have elapsed since he was on trial before disguise a little the inappropriateness of the word ἐφίημι. Such a renewed application, made when proof would be harder than ever to obtain, would be a serious matter and would call for great caution. The οἶκος Δεκελειῶν, which holds a position of dignity in the phratry, appoints five *synegoroi*, whose duty it is to oppose the claims of the applicant. The case is brought to trial before a meeting of the phraters. If the applicant succeeds in securing a majority vote, he is of course at once admitted; if he fails, he is visited with a heavy fine, 1000 drachmas, and remains what he was, a metic.

At a much later day, in the Macedonian period, it was thought desirable to make still ampler provision than had existed for the advertisement of the names of candidates. It was now required that, at some time during the year preceding the Apatouria at which application was to be made, the name of each child should be reported to the phratriarch. When the time allowed had elapsed,[42] the list was posted at the rendezvous of the Dekeleians in Athens and in the temple of Leto in Dekeleia, each name being announced in the form, Μένων Μενεξένου ἐξ Οἴου καὶ Νικαρέτης Καλλίππου Πλωθέως. Perhaps, at this time, the meetings of the phratry were so thinly attended that the mere presentation of a child did not constitute a sufficient advertisement. At any rate, the psephism of Menexenos gives us a fresh glimpse of laxity in the conduct of the affairs of the phratry, and of an effort, probably ineffectual, to secure reform.

POSTSCRIPT.—The *Berliner philologische Wochenschrift* for Feb. 16 and 23, 1889, containing a short discussion by Buermann of the new part of this inscription, reached me as I was finishing the foregoing article. Buermann's interpretation differs from mine on some important points. The most serious divergence concerns the εἰσαγωγή, which, by implication, he puts in the year following the offering of the *koureion*, and consequently immediately before the *diadikasia*. Conformably to this, he takes τῷ πρώτῳ ἔτει ἤ. in B, 60, as equivalent to τῷ ὑστέρῳ ἔτει ἤ. The phrase is a strange one, but I do not

---

[42] Of course, if the announcement was to be of any use, it must be made some time before the εἰσαγωγή, but, with characteristic carelessness, that point is not made clear in the psephism. The language used would allow the presentation of names to the phratriarch up to the date of the Koureotis; or should we understand τῷ πρώτῳ ἔτει as meaning, in the preceding *civil* year, *i. e.*, before midsummer?

believe it can be so understood. Apart from this, I think my view preferable. That εἰσαγωγή and διαδικασία are two distinct acts appears from A, 13–19, B, 12–13, 20–21, in spite of εἰσαγομένο and εἰσάγων (B, 24, 37–38). As far as that goes, they might both come on the same day. But the dissociation of the εἰσαγωγή from the offering of the victim on behalf of the child creates great difficulties. I will not press the argument, that Hierokles ought to have written τὴν δὲ εἰσαγωγὴν καὶ τὴν διαδικασίαν τὸ λοιπὸν εἶναι τῷ ὑστέρῳ ἔτει κ. τ. λ., if such was his intention. But what meaning could the sacrifice have, if the child was not presented at the same time?

Buermann infers from the terms of the oath (B, 52) that only sons, and not daughters, were enrolled. He might have quoted, further, A, 28 and B, 60. But, for the admission of daughters, we have the evidence, not only of the Scholiast on Aristophanes, *Acharnians* 146, but also of Isaios, III. 73–76. I therefore think it more likely that the omission of reference to daughters in the oath and the psephisms is due to carelessness.

Through the courtesy of Professor Pantazides, I have seen also, at the last moment, the advance sheets of his discussion of the inscription, shortly to appear in the Ἐφημερὶς Ἀρχαιολογική, and have been able to appropriate from him two or three valuable suggestions in regard to minor points.

F. B. TARBELL.

American School, Athens,
 March 12, 1889.

REPORT ON EXCAVATIONS NEAR STAMATA IN ATTIKA.

[PLATE XIII.]

While the excavations were going on at Dionysos (Ikaria) in November, 1888, Mr. H. S. Washington and Mr. C. D. Buck spent an afternoon in investigating some ruined churches near Stamata, a village situated to the north of Pentelikon about midway between Kephisia and Marathon. These churches seemed likely to yield interesting material, especially for the identification of one or two demesites. It was decided by the Directors of the American School to begin excavations at once, especially as Mr. Washington was ready to take charge of the work and generously provided the necessary money. Permission having been obtained from Mr. Heliopoulos, the owner of the land, and from the Greek Government, the work was begun on December 27. The present report is an abstract of Mr. Washington's notes.

The first site excavated was a small ruined Byzantine church, the *débris* of which were visible above the ground at Palaio-Stamata, about a quarter of a mile south by west from the present village of Stamata (see above, p. 50). Six days were spent in clearing the interior of this church down to the virgin soil, which was reached a few centimetres below the rough slabs of the pavement, and in making trenches in all directions from the outside walls. The church had three apses. As is generally the case with these Byzantine churches on ancient Greek sites, the material, collected indiscriminately from what was nearest at hand, consisted of stones of all descriptions, including pieces of sculpture and inscribed blocks. The lowest course of the wall of the north apse consisted of four cleanly worked stones, all of the same dimensions. Thickness, from front to back, 0.62 m.; height, 0.49 m.; inner circumference, 0.98 m. This gives an inner arc of 3.92 m. for the semicircle, and an inner diameter of 2.50 m.

SCULPTURES.

The following objects found on this site deserve mention.

I.—Torso of a female statue of Pentelic marble (PLATE XIII); found built into the wall at the north end of the semicircular row of blocks mentioned above, upright and facing inward, 0.50 m. below the surface. Head, fore-arms, and all below the knees wanting, otherwise in a good state of preservation. Height, 0.98 m.; greatest width, 0.60 m.; thickness from chest to back, 0.35 m. Mr. Washington's careful description is as follows: "To judge from the drapery and the general appearance, a female figure is represented, though the breasts are not prominent. The small of the back is deeply hollowed, the thickness from front to back being here only 0.28 m. The chiton, which appears on the right shoulder and back, has its texture indicated by narrow wavy ridges, and is finished off, round the neck, by a smooth, slightly raised border 0.03 m. wide. It appears also below the himation, round the thighs, and shows, though not as prominently as the himation, the straight folds parallel to a central one. There are also indications of its having been held up by the right hand. The himation is supported by a strap passing over the left shoulder and under the right elbow. The himation is folded over this in short zigzag folds, except at the back of the left shoulder, where the strap is smooth and uncovered. Below the strap the himation hangs, both in front and in the back, in stiff, straight, parallel ridges on each side of a central fold with slightly divergent edges, being carried further down at the sides of the figure. Part of it is draped over the left fore-arm and falls below in a stiff sheet, the space between this and the body being deeply undercut. The hair is represented by four curls in front and a square mass behind. Two curls fall in front of each shoulder. They are wavy and the texture is indicated by small ridges parallel to the general curves. In the back, the oblong plait of hair has almost square corners. It is in quite high relief (0.02 m.) and has a surface of fine wavy ridges." It was not possible for me to examine the statue during my last visit to Greece, and I must, therefore, for the present, leave it an open question whether the work is archaic or archaistic.

II.—Graeco-Roman torso of a youth: marble. Height, 0.60 m. Draped on the left side.

III.—Portion of a slab, 0.44 m. high, 0.39 m. wide, 0.14 m. thick, with a rough and much-worn relief. It represents a male (?) figure with bare legs, extending his arm toward two smaller figures in front of him. The foremost of these figures is partly hidden behind a rounded object in higher relief, while, from the head to the outstretched hand of the larger figure, a circle is described by a slightly raised ridge, perhaps the edge of a shield carried on the left arm. No inscription is to be seen on this relief.

IV.—Fragments: (1) portion of an archaic, draped, female (?) statue: height, 0.60 m.; width, 0.17 m.; thickness, 0.22 m.; in bad state of preservation: (2) front portion of a life-sized, sandaled, right foot; several parts of small arms and legs: (3) part of a small acroterium.

On January 2, Mr. Washington began exploring a small hill, covered with loose stones and a few plain Byzantine columns, about ¾ of a mile N. E. of Stamata, a few minutes to the right of the Marathon road. This hill, as well as some ruins near it, is known to the peasants by the name of Amygdalesa. A Byzantine church was laid bare, but without much result. In one corner there was found part of a 16-channeled Doric column, 1.20 m. high, 0.38 m. across the broken upper end.[1] A late Doric capital was also found. Four Ionic capitals of good style, one larger than the others, were found here. The circle of the larger capital is 0.38 m. in diameter, while the other three measure 0.32 m.; height of the larger, 0.14 m., of the smaller, 0.12 m. Two marble vases, 0.20 m. high, with an upper diameter of 0.39 m., were on the same site. A slab with an amphora in relief was found among the loose stones on the surface. The church was paved with slabs, none of which bore reliefs or inscriptions.

Digging was also carried on in a small square building on the same site, and a trench was dug at the church at Palaio-Stamata, but with no further result.

CHARLES WALDSTEIN, *Director*.

---

[1] In a small ruined church across the Marathon road, about five minutes to the north, are two pieces of Doric shafts which correspond exactly to this one, but are a little longer.

INSCRIPTIONS.

The following inscriptions were found in the first church described above. The measurements were taken by Mr. Washington.

I.—Rectangular marble block, with mouldings at top and bottom, and a small hole in the upper surface near the front. Height, 0.82 m.; breadth, 0.91 m.; thickness, 0.72 m. Height of lower moulding, 0.08 m., of upper moulding, 0.17 m.; thickness of each, 0.08 m. Height of letters, 0.02 m.

ΛΛΛΙΓΓΟΣΓΛΩΘΕΥΣΑΦΡΟΔΙΤΗΙΤΟΝΔ=...ΟΙ

Apparently a hexameter verse. Mr. E. A. Gardner suggested

Κά]λλιππος Πλωθεὺς 'Αφροδίτῃ τόνδε [ἀνέ](θ)[ηκεν,

which is probably right. For the rather unusual use of τόνδε alone, referring to a statue above, compare Löwy, *Inschriften griechischer Bildhauer*, Nos. 47, 50.

The inscription may date from the fourth cent. B. C.

II.—Rectangular marble base without mouldings. Height, 0.34 m.; breadth, 0.625 m.; thickness, 0.61 m. In the middle of the upper surface there is a shallow cavity, 0.46 m. long by 0.35 m. wide. Height of letters, 0.025 m.

ΙΛΛΙΑΣΚΑΛΛΙΟΥΙ'ΛΣ.ϽΕΙ
ΑΝΕΘΗΚΕΝ

Κα]λλίας Καλλίου Πλω[θ]ε[ὺς
ἀνέθηκεν

The inscription may date from the third century B. C.

III.—Rectangular marble base without mouldings. Height, 0.435 m.; breadth, 0.65 m.; thickness, 0.63 m. On the upper surface, back of the middle, there is a shallow cavity, 0.42 m. long by 0.38 m. wide. Height of letters, 0.019 m.

ΑΡΙ...ΩΝΓΛΩΟΕΕΥΣΑΝΕΘΗΚΕΝ

'Αρι[στί]ων Πλω(θ)εεὺς ἀνέ(θ)ηκεν

The inscription may date from the third century B. C.

The foregoing dedications, taken together, afford almost convincing proof that the deme of Plotheia had its deme-seat near the site of this church.

IV.—Rough boundary-stone, rounded and smoothed on one side. Height, 0.35 m. ; breadth, 0.12 m. ; thickness, 0.11 m.

ΟΡΟΣ
Γ

There are two or three illegible characters after the Γ'.

F. B. TARBELL.

DISCOVERIES AT ANTHEDON IN 1889.

[PLATE XIV, PLAN.]

REPORT ON EXCAVATIONS AT ANTHEDON.*

In the winter of 1888–9, the Director of the American School at Athens decided to conduct excavations at one or two ancient sites in Boiotia, and invited me to take charge of the work. As early in the spring as the weather permitted, work was begun among the ruins of Anthedon.

Anthedon is first mentioned by Homer (*Iliad*, II. 508), who speaks of it as the furthest town in Boiotia. The pseudo-Dikaiarchos (Βίος Ἑλλάδος, 17) tells us that it was situated on the shore of the Euripos, 70 stadia from Chalkis and 160 from Thebes. Pausanias (IX. 22.6) adds that it lay on the left side of the Euripos (as he came from the eastward) at the foot of Mt. Messapion. This is all the information that the ancient writers give us about the location of the town, but it is enough to identify, as the ancient site, the remains on the shore of the Euripos, about a mile and a half to the north of the little village of Loukisi, and this identification has never been questioned. The remains consist of a city-wall "of the most regular kind of masonry,"[1] an acropolis hill with remains of fortification-walls, the foundations of two breakwaters enclosing a small harbor, and "part of the platform of a great public building, thirty-four yards long, founded in the sea."

About the city itself our information is scanty. The pseudo-Dikaiarchos (*l. c.*) tells us that it was a town of no great size, and that it had an agora surrounded by a double stoa and planted with trees. Strabo

---

* For the plans which accompany this article, I am indebted to Mr. Robert Weir Schultz, of the British School at Athens. Mr. Schultz visited Anthedon with me after the excavations were completed, and was on the ground less than a day and a half. For this reason his plan, though rendering accurately the appearance of the foundations as a whole, does not attempt to give the exact dimensions and levels of the remains. The walls are rougher at the edges in some places than might be inferred from the plan.

[1] LEAKE, *Travels in Northern Greece*, vol. II, p. 272.

(*Geog.*, 404) and Athenaios (I. 56, VII. 47, 99, XV. 24) give us no additional information of importance. Pausanias (*l. c.*), however, tells us that "somewhere about the middle of the city" there was a shrine of the Kabeiroi, and, close by, a temple of Demeter and Kore, containing their statues in white marble. On the land-side of the city, according to the same authority, lay a temple of Dionysos, containing a statue of the god. There were also at Anthedon the tombs of the sons of Iphimedeia and Aloeus, slain by Apollo, and near the sea the so-called Leap of Glaukos. The last, as Mr. Buck has suggested, " was probably a natural cliff like the numerous Lover's Leaps on our eastern coast." If so, it can only be the steep cliff on the seaward side of the acropolis. Ovid refers twice to Anthedon (*Met.*, VII. 232-3, XIII. 903 ff.) in connection with Glaukos, and Stephanos of Byzantion (Ἐθνικῶν, s. v. Ἀνθηδών) quotes Lykophron (*Alex.*, 754) for the statement that it was founded by Thracians. Finally, we know from inscriptions (Larfeld, *Syll. Inscr. Boeot.*, 15, 181, 274) that in the last years of the fourth century B. C. and toward the end of the third, Anthedon was a member of the Boiotian League, a fact which was further testified to by one of the inscriptions unearthed by us. As to the name of the town, it seems natural to connect Ἀνθηδών with ἄνθος. Stephanos of Byzantion (*l. c.*) tells us that the place got its name διὰ τὸ πασῶν ἀνθηροτάτην εἶναι, a view which a visitor to Anthedon in late February or early March would certainly be inclined to favor.

Our work at Anthedon began March 5, and continued for three weeks, during which time only one day was lost through bad weather. The number of men employed varied from fourteen to thirty-five, the average being about twenty-five. Mr. Carl D. Buck remained with me during the greater part of the three weeks, and by his suggestions aided me much. Through the kindness of Mr. Ree, director of the English company which is draining Lake Copais, we were allowed, without charge, to use one of the company's buildings half-an-hour's walk from the acropolis of Anthedon. With the aid of the sketch-plan given by Col. Leake (*l. c.*), we were able to trace the course of the city-walls over their whole extent. We found rather more remains of the walls than Leake had indicated, and at one point traces of a tower. Leake's plan seems inaccurate in some respects. The depth of the town from north to south is greater than would be inferred from it, and a comparison of the accompanying sketch of the harbor

with his plan will show that he did not accurately give the relative
positions of the breakwater and the "public building" (*Fig. 1*).

We were disappointed to find that nearly the whole area of the city
was planted with grain, for, as the only point at which a building
could confidently be looked for was at the platform by the sea, we
had counted on doing a great deal of experimental digging; but,
while we should not have hesitated to dig through grain fields if we
had had undoubted indications of important remains, it seemed hardly
justifiable to do so on an uncertainty. Work was begun at the platform already mentioned. There were visible, besides the platform, an
outer foundation-wall of poros blocks, with a few blocks of an upper
course of a rough conglomerate. The wall was well built and the
blocks were regular. Four trenches were dug inward from the sea
at different parts of the platform. All these, at a depth of 0.56 m.,

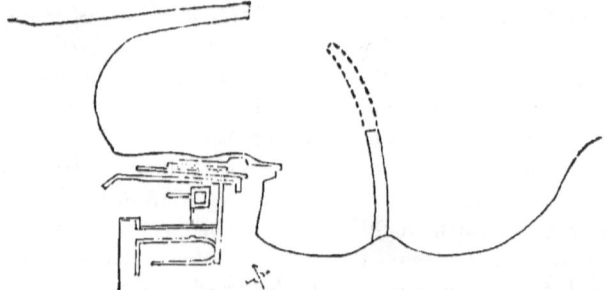

FIG. 1.—*Harbor and Foundations at Anthedon.*

ran into a second foundation-wall composed of large regular blocks of
poros. The average size of the blocks is as follows: length, 1.20 m.;
breadth, 0.80 m.; thickness, 0.47 m. The wall, which is evidently of
Greek workmanship, runs nearly east and west, parallel to the outer
wall and to the sea. Eight days were spent in the work at this place,
and the foundations of a very extensive structure, or combination of
structures, were laid bare (see PLAN). During this work there were
found: near the junction of the walls *c* and *c'*, the top of an inscribed
stele of poros, and, close to the most southern wall *a*, an inscribed basis
of blue limestone; near the stele, a small Doric capital of poros, 0.36
m. in diameter, with twenty channels and with a dowel-hole in the top;
in the part of the structure furthest from the sea, considerable remains
of a Roman mosaic pavement with a rather complicated and pretty

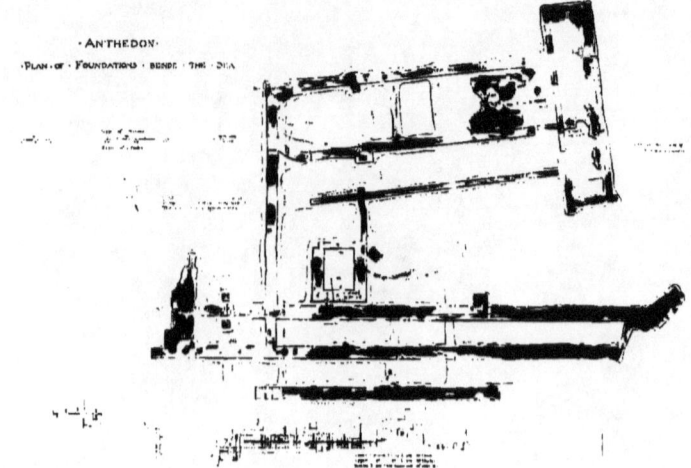

pattern in several colors; besides various small objects of no special interest or value.

As the space included in these foundations was so great, and the excavations so barren of epigraphic results or of sculpture, it was deemed best to do only so much work as was necessary to show the ground-plan clearly, without attempting wholly to explore the interior.

The work at Anthedon was, as has been said, merely experimental, and confined to a comparatively small area. Our next trial was made on the acropolis, a hill near the sea and the eastern wall of the city. It descends abruptly into the sea in rocky cliffs, and on its brow are considerable remains of fortification-walls of regular masonry. The top of the hill consists mainly of bare or scantily covered rock, but on the side toward the sea there is a level terrace with a considerable depth of soil. Across this terrace a trench was dug from east to west, and two others were made at right angles to the first; but nothing was found except two walls roughly built of small, irregular stones.

The third trial was made on a hill just outside the city-walls to the southeast, between them and the dry bed of a stream. Excepting the acropolis, this is the most considerable elevation in the immediate neighborhood of the site, and it commands an extensive view, including the acropolis and the greater part of the area of the city. Surreptitious digging for tombs, which has been carried on to a great extent at Anthedon, had previously been done there, and the ground was littered with fragments of pottery. A small portion of a fairly good wall, running about east and west, projected above the surface of the ground on the southern side of the hill. It seemed a promising place at which to look for the temple of Dionysos. Three trenches were dug into the northern side of the hill, and the wall mentioned above was followed. As this proved to form part of a foundation, work was abandoned in two of the three trenches, and the men were transferred to the walls, which in the course of the day were completely laid bare. The foundation seemed to be that of a very small temple, with some irregularities of structure, built of well-cut blocks of the local poros. Though trenches were dug in all directions about the walls, nothing was found except a small Doric unchanneled capital (0.36 m. in diameter) and a long unchanneled drum, both of poros.

Meanwhile, in the trench which had been continued, we found, at a depth of only 0.28 m., a collection of over twenty-five bronze implements and small ornaments, together with a great quantity of sheet bronze and bronze slag. Four men were kept at work the rest of the day at this point, but found nothing more except some small rough vessels of unpainted clay, and, at a considerable distance, some Byzantine graves. The bronze implements were taken to the National Museum at Athens.

We decided next to make an attempt to find the temple of the Kabeiroi, which Pausanias (*l. c.*) says was in the middle of the city. A very long trench was dug from the southern slope of the acropolis toward the southern city-wall, with two shorter ones at right angles to it. These trenches ran for their whole length through a grain field, the owners of which received compensation. In the upper part of the long ditch, bed-rock was very soon reached; in the lower part, the depth was about a metre. A great many tombs were found, but no walls of any other kind. In the upper part of the trench, on the south-

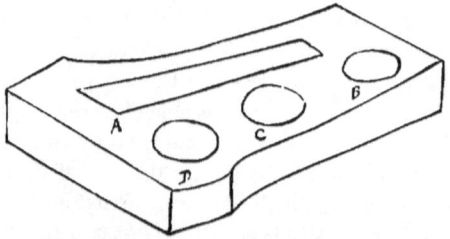

FIG. 2.—*Object in poros found at Anthedon, perhaps a* σήκωμα.

ward slope of the acropolis, we found an object in poros which is reproduced in *Figure 2*. It is 0.58 m. long, 0.38 m. wide at one end and 0.265 m. at the other. The four cavities, *A, B, C, D*, have the following dimensions:

A, 0.39 m. by 0.095 m.; depth, 0.07 m.; capacity, 1.5 litre.
B, 0.135 m. in diameter; " 0.074 m.; " 0.725 "
C, 0.13 m. " " " 0.065 m.; " 0.5 "
D, 0.125 m. " " " 0.06 m.; " 0.425 "

In many ways it resembles the σηκώματα which have been found in different parts of Greece and Italy. It differs, from any of those I know, in its small size, in having the rectangular cavity *A*, and in the small size of the three circular cavities. It bears no inscription. It is finished smooth except on the bottom, which is left rough. It is now in the church-yard at Loukisi, where were deposited the less important objects found at Anthedon. Further down in the same trench was what appeared to be a very small tomb, made of two pieces of stone hollowed out into a double coffer. It is 1.40 m. long by 0.80 m. wide, and 0.19 m. deep. It somewhat resembles a coffered ceiling-piece, except that it is made of two pieces of stone.

The fourth and last trial was made at a low hill some distance east of the city, beside the road to Chalkis. Here there had been found a sacred boundary-stone of rough conglomerate, not *in situ*, but in a Byzantine grave; and there were visible above ground two architectural fragments, a small Doric frieze-block of poros, with triglyphs, and a small poros cornice-block with denticular ornamentation. There were also, projecting from the surface, some good walls, which, however, proved to be tomb-walls. At this point a great many trenches were dug in all directions, but no trace of a temple-foundation was found. A number of architectural fragments were brought to light, some of which showed traces of blue and red. Of these, a Corinthian capital, rather prettily ornamented but evidently of late workmanship, was taken to the museum at Thebes. In one of the trenches, at a depth of 0.81 m., were found two dedications to Artemis Eileithyia, and what may perhaps be a fragment of a third dedication to Artemis. A great many Byzantine graves were found, one of which was covered by a large inscribed stele of marble, now in the museum at Thebes. At a depth of 2.60 m., was found a grave which was cut in a circular shape in the virgin soil. In this grave were glass beads, bits of bronze, and fragments of terracotta figurines, besides a number of small objects of gilded terracotta with bronze eyelet-holes, which had evidently formed a necklace. They consisted of pear-shaped and crescent-shaped pendants, beads, and small button-like disks, two of which bore well-executed heads.

ARCHITECTURAL DISCOVERIES AT ANTHEDON.

THE FOUNDATIONS BY THE SEA.

Between the outer wall and the water's edge lies an extensive platform of poros blocks. This platform, which projects beyond the wall for some distance, is at present 48.50 m. long, and its greatest width is 7.10 m. It appears to have originally run some distance further to the westward. It is cut by grooves 0.11 m. wide and 0.08 m. deep, which are represented in accompanying PLAN. These grooves may have been used in fastening on an upper course of stones, or, more probably, they may have served merely to let the water run off when the waves dashed over the platform, as must have occurred if the platform was originally of its present height.[2] The wall c shows no trace of further extension toward the east, but apparently ran some distance further toward the west. The length of the existing portion of the wall is 26.25 m. It is built of regular, well-squared blocks of poros. The wall d is 0.40 m. higher, and runs parallel to c. Its eastern portion is very regular. Toward the west, although it is firmly built and averages over a metre in breadth, the edges are very irregular. There is no trace of a continuation of this wall further to the west. Its total length is 50 m. The wall e is parallel to c and d until it reaches a point just beyond the end of d, when it bends sharply. It greatly resembles d in every respect; like d it is regular and even at the eastern end, but it soon grows irregular at the edges and is more irregular than d. Its total length is 47 m. These two walls are crossed at right angles by a third, é, which corresponds in all respects to d and c. Where it intersects d and c it is regular and even, but it soon becomes ragged at the edges, and is the most irregular of the three walls. This irregularity may perhaps be explained by the nature of the material, which is soft and friable, but, at and near the junction of d, e, and é, the walls, though of the same material, are as regular and even as if built of marble. From c is built a slightly sloping, regular foundation of blocks a little over a metre in width. It appears to be the foundation of a sloping entrance into the structure. It is flanked by two blocks of limestone about 0.80 m. square, on which are marks of columns about 0.50 m. in diameter. Directly across the end of this entrance run the remains of a wall f, which was probably a supporting wall, not rising much above its present level. The length of this wall, as it now exists, is 11 m.

All the walls so far described are very much alike, and seem to have belonged, with the platform, to a single structure. What this structure was it is difficult to say. It certainly was not a temple. Now the only building not a temple which our literary authorities speak of,

---

[2] Mr. Schultz believes that the platform was originally much higher, reaching the level of the foundations.

unless the enigmatic Leap of Glaukos was a building, is the double stoa around the agora mentioned by the pseudo-Dikaiarchos; and the long parallel walls *d* and *e* might very well belong to such a structure. The agora in a town of fishermen and mariners would naturally be situated near the port, around which the town evidently clustered. All that Leake says (*l. c.*) about the supposed temple might apply equally well to the agora. The entrance, if it be an entrance, descends to the port, as would be expected.[3]

Of the other walls, the next in order, *m*, is probably Greek. From the fact that it does not run parallel to *d* and *e*, and because it is of poorer and rougher construction, it probably belonged to a different structure. The dressed stones of the plan are of blue limestone and stand on the outer (southern) edge of the wall *m*: when uncovered they appeared in shape like the top of a stele, formed of a large central stone and two smaller ones at the sides. Between the central and the eastern stone was a bit of a Doric column of poros, showing channels.

The small structure between this wall and *e* is of extraordinary irregularity. The blocks composing the walls are good, and the foundation is firm and broad, but the edges are very irregular, hardly any two blocks being of the same width. A small and narrow wall of very poor construction connects it with *m*. Through the western wall is carried a v-shaped water-trough, formed of grooved lengths of stone. This comes abruptly to an end after running a short distance.

The walls *n* seem to form the foundation of a Roman building. The curved portion of this wall, which rests upon *e*, contains mortar. At the western end are considerable remains of a Roman mosaic pavement. The greater part of this was covered with a thin layer of plaster, which revealed the individual stones composing the mosaic but hid the pattern. To the west is a rectangular flooring, with remains of a similar mosaic pavement. This flooring seems to have been surrounded by a foundation-wall, of which there are but scanty remains. At the northern end of this rectangle are some exceedingly irregular walls. All these walls are built of blocks of poros, and we found no traces of mortar anywhere except at the curved part of the wall *n*. It is quite possible that these foundations extend still further toward the

---

[3] Mr. Schultz is of the opinion that the end of the walls *d* and *e* has not been reached, though, as has been said, there is no trace of their further extension. It may be mentioned as a curiosity that there is a tradition, among the villagers of Loukisi, of a palace of Alexander in that neighborhood.

south and west, but there is no trace of a continuation of any of the walls represented in the PLAN, and the general results were not such as to lead me to excavate at this point more than was necessary to make a complete piece of work.

THE SMALL TEMPLE AT ANTHEDON.

I have ventured to call this building a temple, from its general form and because its position seems to correspond with that of the temple of Dionysos, as Pausanias describes it. It is very small, its extreme length being only 10.47 m., and its breadth, 6.05 m.; but, according to the pseudo-Dikaiarchos, Anthedon was in his time only a small fishing-village. The walls are certainly Greek, and of a good period.[4] The walls of the pronaos are the best and most regular, those at the back are rougher. The walls within (B and the wall at right angles to it) I cannot understand (see PLAN). There appears to be no reason for considering them earlier or later than the other walls. It will be noticed that the building faces almost exactly east. It lies on a slight slope, the eastern end being somewhat higher than the western. To the west there is a stream, dry while I was at Anthedon, whose banks at this point are strengthened by regular masonry. The building lies very near the road from Anthedon to Thebes, as is indicated by the line of opened graves. Absolutely nothing was found by which the building could be identified. The bronze implements were found less than a hundred feet away.

BRONZE IMPLEMENTS FOUND AT ANTHEDON.

These implements comprise the following objects (PLATE XIV):

I.—Double-edged axe-head, with a hole for inserting a handle. Length, 0.225 m.; width at edges, 0.08 m.; width at middle, 0.04 m.; greatest thickness, 0.025 m. The edges of the sides are beveled toward the hole in the centre, which is 0.038 by 0.017 m. It shows no signs of use.

II.—Another axe-head of the same general shape, but smaller, and broader in proportion to its length. It shows evident marks of use

---

[4] Mr. Schultz agrees with me in this opinion.
[5] I am indebted to Mr. W. J. Stillman for the excellent photograph from which PLATE XIII is made. The photograph was taken after I left Athens, and, as all of the objects could not be represented, some of those to which I wished to call special attention happen to be omitted.

ANTHEDON·

·PLAN·OF·FOUNDATIONS·OF·A·TEMPLE·

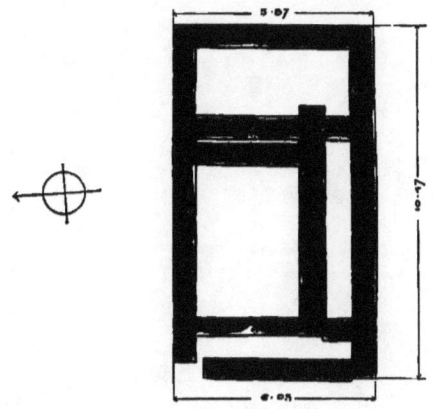

·R·W·S· APRIL·1889·

in the nicked edges. Length, 0.135 m.; width at edges, 0.066 m.; width at middle, 0.038 m.; greatest thickness, 0.024 m.; hole in the middle, 0.035 by 0.02 m.

III, IV.—Fragments of similar tools. Length of first, 0.076 m.; width at edges, 0.062 m.; width at break, 0.037 m.; greatest thickness, 0.024 m. Length of second, 0.08 m.; width at edges, 0.052 m.; width at break, 0.04 m.; greatest thickness, 0.027 m. The break in each is through the hole in the middle, but the two fragments evidently do not belong to the same axe-head.

Axe-heads very like all these have been found in the excavations on the acropolis at Athens, at a depth of 14 m.

V.—Implement consisting of a tube, apparently for inserting a wooden handle, and a short blade beveled to a sharp edge from the under side. Total length, 0.145 m.; length of tube, 0.055 m.; diameter of tube, 0.056 m. Similar objects were found with the axe-heads in the excavations on the acropolis at Athens, but their use has not been satisfactorily explained. A bit of sheet bronze is fastened to the under side of our specimen, which led to the suggestion that a bronze plate had been soldered on, forming a shovel. This view is hardly tenable, and it seems clear, especially from the sharp beveled edge, that the instrument is complete as it is. It may have been used for grubbing roots, or as a kind of gouge. Our specimen is slightly heavier, and rather more carefully made, than the one from the Athenian acropolis.

VI.—End of the blade of a similar instrument (not represented in the PLATE). Length, 0.05 m.

VII.—Piece of bronze resembling a hollow horn. It appears to have been part of some ornament, rather than of an implement of any kind. A bit of sheet bronze is attached to this near the end.

VIII.—Fragment of a narrow, slightly curved band, with raised edges, ornamented with the figure of a stag in repoussé. There are traces of the hind legs of a similar animal going in the opposite direction. The stag's head is thrown back almost upon its haunches, while the horns project in front.

IX.—Drill resembling those now used in working stone. Length 0.13 m.; width at large end, 0.025 m.; at small end, 0.011 m.

X.—Smaller tool somewhat like an awl, with four flat sides, and with a tang for inserting into a wooden handle. Total length, 0.095 m.;

without handle, 0.057 m.; width, 0.07 m. It is barely possible that these two implements may have been used in cutting stone.[6]

XI.—Chisel, with a flaring edge, consisting, in one piece, of two parts, the chisel proper, and the part to be inserted in a wooden handle. These are separated by a projection on each side. Total length, 0.21 m.; length of chisel proper, 0.12 m.; of handle, 0.075 m.; width of edge, 0.042 m. It shows no signs of use.

XII.—Sickle, ornamented with lines, the edge beveled on one side. Length of arc, 0.31 m.; greatest width of blade, 0.035 m. It is broken across the middle. It has a tang to be inserted in a wooden handle, pierced with a hole for receiving a rivet. It appears to have been used, for the edge is nicked and the point blunted.

XIII–XXVI.—Blades and fragments of blades, mostly of knives of various shapes and sizes, the longest of which measures 0.19 m. Nearly all of these show signs of long use, some being nearly worn through by constant whetting and wear; one is bent nearly double; many of them still bear the rivets by which they were fastened to the handles. One blade (not represented in the PLATE) appears to be serrated, but it may be that it is only nicked, although the nicks are remarkably regular.

XXVII.—Fragment resembling a bundle of reeds or rods. Length, 0.068 m.; circumference, 0.073 m.; width of each reed, 0.010 m.

XXVIII.—Handle of a large vase or caldron with a fragment of the side (not represented in the PLATE).

XXIX–XXXI.—Three smaller handles.

XXXII.—Fragment, apparently of a lance-head, consisting of a thick central shaft, with a thinner blade. Length, 0.05 m.; greatest width, 0.04 m. This is not represented in the PLATE.

XXXIII.—Oval piece of bronze, with indistinguishable ornament in relief.

XXXIV.—Ring of bronze wire (perhaps a bracelet), 0.056 m. in diameter.

XXXV.—Two fragments of a flat-sided bronze rod.

Besides these were found a great quantity of sheet bronze, and large masses of bronze slag, some fragments apparently of the vessel to which the large handle belonged (XXVIII), and a number of small objects.

As has been said, these implements were not deposited in a tomb.

---

[6] W. J. Stillman says, decidedly, that they could not have been used for that purpose.

The character of the collection—including implements of various kinds, some new and some bearing marks of long use, fragments of ornaments, together with the presence of masses of bronze slag (thirty or forty pounds, at least)—suggests that we may have come upon the shop or stand of a maker of bronze tools, and that the old implements and fragments were collected to be worked over, while the apparently unused ones may or may not be products of his skill. This theory would account for what seems to be the case, that we have, in the collection, objects of different epochs. It seems more than doubtful that the axe-heads and the object described under No. V can belong to the same time as the ornament with the stag in relief.

JOHN C. ROLFE.

DISCOVERIES AT ANTHEDON IN 1889.

INSCRIPTIONS FROM ANTHEDON.

Some of the following inscriptions were brought to light in the course of the excavations carried on at Anthedon in March 1889. A few others were found above ground by Mr. Rolfe and Mr. Buck among the graves of the neighborhood. A good number of others had been unearthed by peasants in their illicit digging for graves, and had been taken to their houses in the neighboring village of Loukisi. These last were collected by Mr. Koromantzos, the government overseer of the excavations, and were deposited in the church-lot at Loukisi. The others, unless the contrary be specified below, were taken to the same place.

Except in the case of No. V and of two or three trifling details elsewhere, Mr. Buck has the sole credit and responsibility for the text of these inscriptions, so far as contained on the stones, as well as for the measurements. The notes on dialect are also exclusively his.

By a "new name," below, we mean a name not to be found in the dictionary of Pape-Benseler or in the indexes to Collitz' *Sammlung der griech. Dialekt-Inschriften*, Bd. I and II[(1)], the *Corpus Inscriptionum Graecarum*, the *Corpus Inscriptionum Atticarum I, III*, the *Inscriptiones Graecae Antiquissimae*, the *Bulletin de Correspondance Hellénique* 1877–1886, and the *Mittheilungen des deutschen archäologischen Instituts zu Athen*, Bd. I–X.

LIST OF RECRUITS.

I.—Gable-top stele of poros, broken off at the right and below, the first two lines only of the inscription being complete. Height of fragment, 0.415 m.; width, 0.355 m.; height of letters, 0.13 m.

ΚΤΕΙΣΙΑΟΑΡΧΟΝΤΟΣΒΟΙΩΤΟΙΣ   Κτεισίαο ἄρχοντος Βοιωτοῖς,
ΕΓΙΔΕΓΟΛΙ   ΡΙΩΝΟΣ   ἐπὶ δὲ πόλι[ος Ἡσχ?]ρίωνος,
ΓΕΛΤΟΦΟΡΗΑΓΕ   ᐵΑΨΑΝ   πελτοφόρη ἀπε[γ]ράψαν[θο
ΑΦΗΣΤΙΩΝ   Ἀφηστίων   – – –
ΓΟΛΙΚΛΕΙΣΔ   Πολικλεῖς   Δ – – –

```
TYXΩNΣ             Τύχων Σ - - -
KΛ   ΣΙΛ           Κ[αφι]σία[ς - - -
ΑΡΙΣΤΙΩ            'Αριστίω[ν  - - -
Α    <T            'Α (or 'Α) - - στ - - - - -
ΑΡΙΣ               'Αρισ[τ - -      - - -
ΑΡΙ<               'Αρισ[τ - -      - - -
```

Translation.—When Ktesias was archon of the Boiotian League and Aischrion (?) archon of the city, (the following) enrolled themselves as peltophori : Hephaistion [son of —], etc.

Comment.—This inscription belongs to the large class of lists of recruits which have been found in cities of the Boiotian League—Lebadeia, Orchomenos, Hyettos, Thespiai, Chorsia, Kopai, Akraiphia, Megara and Aigosthena. The archon Ktesias is mentioned in two other inscriptions, one of Orchomenos,[1] the other of Hyettos ;[2] and his date has been approximately determined as falling at the end of the third or beginning of the second century B. C.[3]

The various lists of recruits to which reference has been made exhibit marked local differences in phraseology, nearly every city having a stereotyped form of its own. It will therefore be well to examine our inscription in this respect, as being the only representative of Anthedon in this class of documents, and to observe in what particulars it differs from the others. We first note that, while the names of the archon of the Boiotian League and the archon of Anthedon are given, there is no mention of the three polemarchs or of the secretary. The practice in the matter of citing officials may be seen from the following table.[4]

	Archon of League.	Local Archon.	Polemarch.	Secret.ry.
Orchomenos	×	×	×	×
Hyettos	×	×	×	×
Kopai	—	×	×	×
Akraiphia	—	×	×	×
Megara	×	×	×	—
Lebadeia	×	×	—	—
Anthedon	×	×	—	—
Thespiai	—	×	—	—
Aigosthena (in two instances)	×	—	—	—

[1] COLLITZ, *Sammlung der griech. Dialekt-Inschriften*, 483.   [2] COLLITZ, 535.
[3] See COLLITZ, under 482.   [4] × denotes mention, — denotes omission, of the name.

In the lists of Aigosthena, as well as of Chorsia, there are two forms. Of those from Aigosthena, two have the form last given in the table, while eight have that given under Lebadeia and Anthedon. Of the two lists from Chorsia, one has the form given under Thespiai, the other, that given under Lebadeia and Anthedon. We must not assume the non-existence of officials in cases where their names are omitted. The constitutions of the various members of the league were probably the same.[5]

The order of words in ἐπὶ δὲ πόλιος is not the usual one. We find, rather, ἐπὶ πόλιος δέ in all the previously known Boiotian lists in which the phrase occurs, with one exception,[6] while in the lists of Aigosthena the order is the same as in our own. The phrase πελτοφόρη ἀπεγράψανθο is, in this form, unique, though ἀπεγράψανθο ἐν πελτοφόρας is exceedingly common. The various corresponding phrases in the lists of the other cities have been collected and tabulated by Foucart.[7]

As regards the dialect, we note that while we have the earlier and invariable orthographic peculiarities of Boiotian vocalism, such as ει=η and η=αι, the etymologic spelling is preserved in those cases where the Boiotian spelling is either of comparatively late introduction or was never absolutely fixed. Thus, we have Βοιωτοῖς, not Βοιωτῦς, and Τύχων, not Τούχων. In the other two inscriptions of the archonship of Ktesias, υ is written for οι, but in the Nikareta inscription (COLLITZ, 488), which belongs approximately to the same period, the proportion between οι=οι and υ=οι is nearly even. In the third line the squeeze does not show whether the penultimate letter is θ or τ. The regular form of the endings -ντι, -νται, -ντο, -ντω is in Boiotian -νθι, -νθη, etc., but forms with τ are found occasionally. Thus, among thirty-two occurrences of the word ἀπεγράψαντο in the lists of recruits, twenty-six have -νθο, but six have -ντο.

Πολικλεῖς is a new name.

DEDICATIONS.

II.—Fragment of a base with cornice, broken at the bottom and back. Height, 0.19 m.; width, 0.29 m.; height of letters, 0.014 m.

ΜΑΤΡΩ ΔΙΩΝΙΟΥΣΙΟ   Μάτρω[ν] Διωνιούσιο[ς
ΕΙΡΑΙΔ ΑΡΤΕΜΙΔΙ   Εἰραίδ[α] Ἀρτέμιδι
ΕΙΘΙΟΥΙΗ   Εἰλ]ειθιουίη

[5] Cf. FOUCART, in LE BAS, Voyage archéol., II, 34a.   [6] COLLITZ, 736.
[7] Bull. de corr. hellén., IV (1880), p. 87.

Translation.—Matron son of Dionysios (dedicates this statue of) Heraïs to Artemis Eileithyia.

Comment.—This inscription may be more closely dated on dialectic than on palaeographic grounds. For, as one approximate limit, we have the middle of the third century B. C., when occurs the earliest example of the spelling ιου=ου=Attic υ, and, as the other limit, the end of the same century, when the patronymic adjectives disappeared. Διων—— is the usual Boiotian spelling, though Διον—— is occasionally met with.[8] The form 'Ἀρτέμιδι, repeated as it is in the next inscription, is worthy of note. In all other Boiotian inscriptions the form is 'Ἀρταμι-,[9] and the occurrence of 'Ἀρτέμιδι in these two inscriptions of Anthedon, so thoroughly Boiotian in their orthography, seems to indicate one of those interesting local divergences which are not uncommon within the dialect. The related names, 'Ἀρτέμεις, 'Ἀρτέμων, 'Ἀρτεμισία, occur, however, elsewhere in Boiotia.

The worship of Artemis Eileithyia is shown by inscriptions to have existed at Tanagra, Orchomenos, Chaironeia, and Thisbe. Including Anthedon, then, we know of five seats of worship of this divinity in Boiotia, and yet not one of them is mentioned by Pausanias.[10] Eileithyia appears in a great variety of spellings, as may be seen from the following: at Tanagra and Orchomenos, Εἰλεθυία; at Chaironeia, Εἰλειθία and Εἰλιθία; at Thisbe, Εἰλειθεία; at Anthedon, Εἰλειθουία[11] and Εἰλειθιουία. According to the general principles of Boiotian vocalism, we should have expected 'Ἰλιθουία or 'Ἰλιθιουία, but we see, from the preceding forms, that the etymologic spelling was retained, always in the first syllable, with one exception in the second, and in one case also in the third. In the Anthedonian forms, the third syllable is written phonetically, showing the regular preservation of the old u-sound, together with that affection of it which is denoted by ιου. From the fact that the inscription in which Εἰλειθουία occurs is later than that with Εἰλειθιουία, we must not conclude that in the first instance the old pronunciation was preserved without the affection. It is impossible to believe, with Larfeld,[12]

---

[8] *Cf.* MEISTER, *Die griechischen Dialekte*, I, p. 230.
[9] GUSTAV MEYER's statement (*Gr. Grammatik*(2), p. 64), that "Ἀρταμις is *allgemeindorisch*, is incorrect. "Ἀρτεμις is the only form in Kretan, and examples of it can be found in nearly every one of the Doric dialects.
[10] *Cf.* ΚΟΥΜΑΝΟΥΔΗΣ, 'Ἀθήναιον, IV, p. 294.   [11] See inscription No. III.
[12] *Sylloge Inscriptionum Boeoticarum*, p. xxv.

that, in cases where both spellings occur in the same inscription, the inconstancy of spelling is caused by inconstancy of pronunciation. The affection of the pronunciation which came about in the third century was constant. Its representation, on the other hand, was often neglected by the stone-cutters. In regard to the form Εἰλειθεία from Thisbe, M. Foucart, who published the inscription in which it occurs,[13] has made a mistake to which attention ought to be called. Speaking of Εἰλειθείη, he says: *M. Larfeld a fait remarquer que, dans les textes de Chéronée et de Lebadée, ει est souvent employé à la place de υ. La dédicace de Thisbé fait connaître la même altération dans une troisième ville.* The change referred to by Larfeld (*op. cit.*, p. xviii) is between ει and υ representing οι, and to bring into connection with this a change from an original υ to ει is entirely misleading. It is an impossibility for original υ to become ει in Boiotian, the very dialect which shows the greatest tenacity in preserving the old open sound. We have nothing to do with a phonetic change from one to the other. The two forms are distinct and dependent on a play between strong and weak suffix-forms. The relation of Εἰλειθεία to Εἰλειθυία is the same as that of γεγονεῖα to γεγονυῖα (suffix −Fεσ-ια to υσ-ια).[14] In the form Εἰλειθία from Chaironeia, the ει has become ι, as regularly in Boiotian.

III.—Six fragments of bluish stone, fitting together. Total length, 1.015 m.; height, 0.20 m.; height of letters, 0.02–0.025 m.

    ιν-ιsΛC   ΣΙΜΑΧΩΤΑΣΘΟΥΙ\ΤΕΡΑΣΚΑΡΑΙΔΑΚΗ
              ΜΕΛΛΝΟΙΔΑΑΡΤ ΕΜΙΔΙΕΙΛΕΙΘΟΥΙΗ

. . . . . . - ν[ε]ις Λο[υ]σιμάχω τὰς θου[γα]τέρας Καραΐδα κὴ
            Μελ[α]νθίδα Ἀρτέμιδι Εἰλειθουίῃ.

Translation.— - - nos, son of Lysimachos, (dedicates) to Artemis Eileithyia (these statues of) his daughters, Karaïs and Melanthis.

Comment.—The name Καραΐς has been hitherto met with, so far as we know, only at Chaironeia (*Bull. de corr. hellén.*, VIII, p. 55); Μελανθίς, as a woman's name, only at Tanagra (COLLITZ, 987). One of the breaks in the stone runs through the fourth letter of Ἀρτέμιδι, but the remaining marks can belong only to an E, not by any possibility to an A. The inscription shows the customary Boiotian orthography, ex-

---

[13] *Bull. de corr. hellén.*, 1884, p. 415.
[14] MEYER, *Gr. Grammatik*(2), p. 308; BRUGMANN, *Gr. Grammatik* in *Iwan Müller's Handbuch*, § 73.

cept in the name of the divinity, which has already been commented on. The letters are of the Roman period.

IV.—Block of blue limestone, broken at the back. Height, 0.25 m.; width, 0.81 m.; greatest thickness, 0.67 m.; height of letters, 0.025 m.

ΘΙΟΓΙΤΩΝΤΟΝΠΑΤΕΙΑΚΗΔΑΜΟΚΛΕΙ
ΑΤΟΝΑΝΔΡΑΕΥΡΟΥΦΑΟΝΤΑ
ΟΙΟΓΙΤΟΝΟΣΤΥΣΘΙΥΣ

Θιογίτων τὸν πατέ[ρ]α κὴ Δαμοκλεί|α τὸν ἄνδρα Εὐρουφάοντα | Θιογίτονος τῦς θιῦς.

Translation.—Theogeiton and Demokleia (dedicate) to the gods (this statue of) their father and husband Euryphaon, son of Theogeiton.

Comment.—In the first line the sixteenth letter, which is perfectly distinct, is shaped like an I with an excessively broad top.

LIST OF MAGISTRATES.

V.—Gable-top marble stele, unearthed in the excavations and taken to the museum of Thebes. Height, 1.11 m.; width, 0.515–0.545 m.; letters irregular and of various heights. Edited from an imperfect squeeze.

ΑΓΑΘΗΤΥ
ΧΗ

ΑΡΧΟΝΤΩΝΣΤΕΦΑΝ
ΑΝΑΓΡΑΦΗ ΔΕΥΤΕΡΑ

ΤῙ ΤΕΡΤΥΛΛΟΣ ΑΥΡΖΩΣΙΜΟΣ
ΛΕΩΝΑΣ   ΑΥ
ΛΕΟΝΤΑΣ   ΑΥΡΠΑΡΑΜΟΝΟΣ
ΜΕΓΙΣΤΙΩΝ   ΑΥΡΕΡΩΤΑΝΟΣ
ΖΩΠΥΡΟΣ   ΛΕΟΝΤΑΣ
ΕΥΦΡΑΣ   ΠΡΟΣΔΟΚΙΜΟΣ
ΜΑΡΚΟΣ   ΖΕΥΘ
ΖΩΣΙΜΟΣ   ΜΑ ΙΜΟ
ΦΛ̄ΠΡΕΙΜΟΣ   ΘΑΛΛΟ
ΕΠΑΦΡΑΣ   ⊊
ΖΩΣΙΜΟΣ
ΘΕΟΔΟΣΙΟΣ

INSCRIPTIONS FROM ANTHEDON.

```
Γ Ι ΚΛΕΟΠΑΤΡΟC
    ΑΤΤΙΚΟC
    ΕΠΙΚΤΑC
    ΖωCΙΜΟC
   ΦΛ ΠΡΕΙΜΟC
    ΑΡΜΟΔΙΟC
   ΦΛΤΥΧΙΚΟC
    ΖωCΙΜΑC
    ΓΙΟΥ
    ΚΑΛΛΙΝΕΙΚΟC
    ΖωCΙΜΑC
    ΓΙΟΥΛΙΟCΕΡΜΗC
    ΑΥΡΗΛΙΟCΖω  ΑC
    ΑΑΥΡΗΛΙCΥΡΕΙΝΟC
    ΦΛΕΥΦΡΑC
    ΔΙΟΓΕΝΗC
    ΙCΕΙΔω              ///////
    CωΠ             ΑΥΡΕΥΙΝΕΤΟC
    ΗΡΑΚΛΕΙΔΗC      /////////////
    ΛΟΥΚΙΟC               ΓΙCΤΙωΝ
    //////////      Α         ΚΛΗC
    /////////       ΑΥΡΖωCΙΜΟC
    ////////
    ////////
    ΓΑΙΟC
    ΖωCΙΜΟC
```

Ἀγαθῇ τύ-
χῃ.

Ἀρχόντων στεφαν [ηφόρων?
                 [ωθέντων?

ἀναγραφὴ δευτέρα.

Τι(βέριος) Τέρτυλλος   Αὐρ(ήλιος) Ζώσιμος
Λεωνᾶς   Αὐ[ρ](ήλιος) - - -
Λεοντᾶς   Αὐρ(ήλιος) Παράμονος
Μεγιστίων   Αὐρ(ήλιος) Ἐρω[τ]ιανός
Ζώπυρος   Λεοντᾶς
Εὐφρᾶς   Προσδόκιμος
Μᾶρκος   Ζευθ(?) - - -
Ζώσιμος   Μά[ξ]ιμο[ς

INSCRIPTIONS FROM ANTHEDON. 213

Φλ(άουιος) Πρεῖμος   Θάλλο[ς
Ἐπαφρᾶς
Ζώσιμος
Θεοδόσιος
Γ(άιος)'Ι(ούλιος) Κλεόπατρος
Ἀττικός
Ἐπικτᾶς
Ζώσιμος
Φλ(άουιος) Πρεῖμος
Ἁρμόδιος
Φλ(άουιος) Τυχικός
Ζωσιμᾶς
Γ(άιος) Ἰού[λιος - -
Καλλίνεικος
Ζωσιμᾶς
Γ(άιος) Ἰούλιος Ἑρμῆς
Αὐρήλιος Ζω[σ]ᾶς
Μ(ᾶρκος) Αὐρήλι[ος] Συρεῦ ος
Φλ(άουιος) Εὐφρᾶς
Διογένης
Ἰσείδω[ρος   - - - -
Σωπ - - -   Αὐρ(ήλιος) Εὐ[α]ίνετος (?)
Ἡρακλείδης   - - - - - -
Λούκιος   Με]γιστίων
- - - - - -   Ἀ - - -κλῆς
- - - - -   Αὐρ(ήλιος) Ζώσιμος
- - - - -
- - - - -

Γάιος
Ζώσιμος

Translation.—With the blessing of Fortune. Second register of crown-wearing (or crowned) archons: Ti. Tertullus, *etc.*

Comment.—The names down to Φλ. Πρεῖμος or thereabouts look as if they might have been engraved at one time. The rest, in letters of various sizes and in some cases sprawling carelessly, would seem to have been added at intervals. Why the series should have been brought to an end by the leaf in the second column and then resumed below is a mystery. The numerous Aureliuses in the latter part of the list enable us to assign the document to the latter part of the second and the beginning of the third century A. D.

In restoring line 3, we have been unable to choose between the possible alternatives, στεφανηφόρων and στεφανωθέντων. Στεφανηφόρος was the title of an eponymous magistrate in several cities of Asia Minor and elsewhere.[15] The combination ἄρχων στεφανηφόρος, though unexampled, is likely enough. If στεφανωθέντων be read, the list would be one of archons who had received the honor of a crown.

INSCRIPTIONS IN THE EPICHORIC ALPHABET.

VI.—Poros slab. Height, 0.45 m.; width, 0.40 m.; height of letters, 0.04–0.06 m.

ΒΙΟΓΙΤΟ   Θιογίτο

The chief interest of this inscription lies in the peculiar form of the *theta*, of which there is only one other example in the whole mass of early inscriptions. This is in a short dedication of Elis,[16] where we find ΑΝΕΒΕΚΑΝ. The corresponding rounded form Θ is found three times in early Boiotian inscriptions,[17] once at Corinth,[18] and once at Selinous,[19] while from Amorgos[20] we have a similar form in which the cross-bar comes to an end in the centre of the circle (Θ). Hinrichs, in his table of the Greek alphabets,[21] has given Β as a Boiotian as well as an Elean variety, but this is now for the first time substantiated, as there is no such form in any previously published Boiotian inscription. Both Β and Θ appear again in Roman times as developments of Θ, but are distinguished from the similar archaic forms by the style of cutting. The letters of our inscription are large, bold, and deeply cut. Λ is the more usual form of *gamma* in Boiotian inscriptions in the epichoric alphabet, but, in the fine example of archaic epigraphy

---

[15] See the list of cities in REINACH, *Épigraphie Grecque*, p. 349.

[16] RÖHL, *Inscriptiones Graecae Antiquissimae*, 120; ROBERTS, *An Introduction to Greek Epigraphy*, 299; KIRCHHOFF, *Studien zur Geschichte des gr. Alphabets*(4), p. 163.

[17] At Kriëkouki in the district of Plataia (LARFELD, 271; RÖHL, 144; ROBERTS, 223 b), at Tanagra (RÖHL, 125; ROBERTS, 215 b), and in a dedication by an Orchomenian found at Delphi (ROBERTS, 204). Roberts, apparently following Kirchhoff, attributes the form of the *theta* in the third instance to an error of the copyist, though he gives the other two forms without remark, and in the Elean inscription calls especial attention to the simplified form of the *theta*. But, if once the form be well attested, there is no necessity for attributing certain instances of it to error.

[18] RÖHL, 20⁸².

[19] RÖHL, 514, ε, δ.

[20] *Museo Italiano*, vol. I, p. 225.

[21] *Handbuch d. klass. Alter.*, vol. I, p. 416.

found at Haliartos,[22] we have Γ. At Orchomenos, Thebes, and Tanagra Γ and Λ were used indiscriminately.[23] The *omicrons*, especially the second, are smaller than the other letters, but this is common in early inscriptions of nearly all parts of the Greek world. The change of ε before vowels to ι, of which we have an example in our inscription, took place in Boiotia at a very early period, as we find ι written in some of the oldest inscriptions, although there was no consistency even in the same locality.[24] The change of the original diphthong ει to ι, which is represented in the third syllable of Θιογίτο, was also accomplished in very early times. Thus, we have in the epichoric alphabet Καλλιγίτων,[25] Πισιδωρίδας,[26] Θειογίτα,[27] Ἀθανογιτίς.[28]

VII.—Poros slab, broken on the right and at the bottom. Height of fragment, 0.43 m.; width, 0.44 m.; height of letters, 0.06-0.09 m.

ORRO   oppo

VIII.—Poros tombstone with beveled top. Height, 0.87 m.; width, 0.37 m.; height of letters, 0.35 m.

ANOYLLIS   Ἀνθυλλίς

This name occurs in *C.I.G.*, 2201. The form of the *lambda* shows that the inscription belongs to a period preceding the introduction of the Ionic alphabet, but more than that one cannot say. The form of the *sigma*, which is a valuable criterion in Attic inscriptions, cannot serve as such in Boiotia, where the choice between the three-barred and four-barred forms is often dependent on individual preference.[29]

IX.—Rough boundary-stone of conglomerate. Height, 0.28 m.; length, 0.51 m.; thickness, 0.40 m.; height of letters, 0.125-0.13 m. On one end is HI, on the other OP. ὅρ(ος) ἱ(εροῦ). The stone must have rested on its long side, the two ends with the letters being exposed. It is strange that the aspirate, which is expressed in ἱ(εροῦ),

---

[22] RÖHL, 149; ROBERTS, 224.
[23] Compare ΕΓΙΘΡΕΓΟ, RÖHL, 133, with ΑΘΑΝΟΛΙΤΙΣ, RÖHL, 137, ROBERTS, 216 f.
[24] Compare ΤΙΜΑΣΙΘΕΟΣ and ΘΙΟΜΝΑΣΤΑ at Tanagra, RÖHL, 136 and 139; cf. MEISTER, p. 243.
[25] COLLITZ, 461, but with ει as rar. lect.   [26] COLLITZ, 579.
[27] COLLITZ, 677.   [28] COLLITZ, 891, RÖHL 137 with ⊕.
[29] Cf. KIRCHHOFF, *Alphabet*, p. 142.

should be omitted from ὅρος, a word which in Attic shows such tenacity in keeping the aspirate-sign.

X.—Rough poros slab. Height, 0.665 m.; width, 0.45 m.; height of letters, 0.05 m.

ΦΕΡΕΣ   Φέρες

XI.—Tombstone of poros with a rude and one-sided gable top. The slab is broken at the bottom. Height, 0.27 m.; width, 0.30 m.; height of letters, 0.03–0.055 m.

ΣΓΙΝΘΕΙΡ   Σπίνθειρ

There is nothing in the form of the letters to show decisively that this inscription belongs to the period preceding the introduction of the Ionic alphabet, but the style of cutting favors placing it in that period. The representation of ē by ει is no objection to this, as we have undoubted instances of this in inscriptions of the epichoric alphabet, such as Μέννει, - - κράτεις, Ἱ]σμεινοτέλεις,[30] Ἀ]μεινοκλείαε.[31] These cases show that the change in pronunciation had taken place before the introduction of the Ionic alphabet, while the representation in writing was still fluctuating.

XII.—Poros slab in the museum at Thebes, said to have been found at Anthedon. Height, 0.96 m.; width, 0.57 m.; height of letters, 0.04 m.

MARSYAS.   Μαρσύας

EPITAPHS AND FRAGMENTS IN THE IONIC ALPHABET.

XIII.—Tombstone of poros, broken at the bottom. Height, 0.58 m.; width, 0.40 m.; height of letters, 0.05–0.06 m.

ΒΑΤΤΙΣ   Βαττίς

XIV.—Poros tombstone with gable top and rosettes; broken at the bottom. Total height, 0.82 m.; width, 0.36 m.; height of letters, 0.028 m.

ΚΑΝΘΙΣ   Κανθίς

A new name; cf. Κάνθος.

XV.—Poros tombstone, complete, but much weather-worn. Height, 0.88 m.; width, 0.39 m.; height of letters, 0.035 m. There are traces of red color in the letters.

ΕΥΝΑΝΘΙΣ   Εὐνανθίς

[30] Röhl, 300; Roberts, 200.   [31] Röhl, 155.

A new name. A Eunanthus occurs in Mommsen's *Inscriptiones Regni Neapolitani*, No. 7177.

XVI.—Poros tombstone with gable top. Height, 0.73 m.; width, 0.31 m.; height of letters, 0.03 m.

   ΓΟΥΡΡΙΣ Πουρρίς

This name is found also at Tanagra (COLLITZ, 1080).

XVII.—Poros slab. Height, 0.38 m.; width, 0.39 m.; height of letters, 0.045 m.

   ΓΟΥΡΡΙΧΟΣ Πούρριχος

XVIII.—Slab of very coarse poros. Height, 0.38 m.; width, 0.39 m.; height of letters, 0.03 (O)–0.07 (Y).

   ΙΩΓΥΡΟΣ Ζώπυρος

Ζώπυρος occurs in an inscription of Thespiai (COLLITZ, 814), which shows a mixture of Boiotian and Attic dialects; Ζωπυρίνα occurs at Tanagra (COLLITZ, 1106, 1107, 1108). The genuine and usual Boiotian forms are Ζώπουρος, Ζωπούρα, Ζωπουρίνα, etc.

XIX.—Poros slab. Height, 0.70 m.; width, 0.42 m.; height of letters, 0.045 m.

   ΞΕΝΝΩ Ξεννώ

There was no regular gemination of liquids in Boiotian as in Lesbian, but the doubling of any consonant in the abbreviated forms of proper names is frequent (*cf.* FICK, *Die griechischen Personennamen*, lix ff.; MEISTER, I, p. 266).

XX.—Poros tombstone with gable top. Height, 0.72 m.; width, 0.48 m.; height of letters, 0.03–0.05 m.

   ΦΙΛΛΩ Φιλλώ

This name occurs also once at Tanagra (COLLITZ, 1065).

XXI.—Poros tombstone with gable top. Height, 0.69 m.; width, 0.33 m.; height of letters, 0.03 m.

   ΔΙΔΥΜΜΕΙ Διδύμμει

The short forms of proper names in –εις=Attic –ης are especially prone to drop the nominative sign ς in Boiotian (*cf.* MEISTER, I, p. 272; BLASS, *Rheinisches Museum*, 1881, pp. 604 ff.).

XXII.—Tombstone of poros. Height, 0.54 m.; width, 0.30 m.; height of letters, 0.035 m.

   ΒΙΩΝ Βίων

XXIII.—Poros slab. Height, 0.66 m.; width, 0.38 m.; height of letters, 0.04 m.

    ΑΝΤΙΦΙΛΗ Ἀντιφίλη

The form is Attic.

XXIV.—Poros slab, broken at bottom. Height, 0.52 m.; width, 0.47 m.; height of letters, 0.03 m.

    ΑΥΤΟΒΩΛΟΣ Αὐτόβωλος

XXV.—Poros tombstone. Height, 0.70 m.; width, 0.32 m.; height of letters, 0.025 m.

    ΑΓΟΛΛΩΝΙΔΑ Ἀπολλωνίδα
    ΝΙΚΟΒΩΛΑ Νικοβώλα[ς

XXVI.—Fragment of poros tombstone. Height, 0.29 m.; width, 0.29 m.; height of letters, 0.023 m.

    ΓΟΛΛΩΝΙΔΑΣ Ἀ]πολλωνίδας

XXVII.—Poros slab. Height, 0.70 m.; width, 0.44 m.; height of letters, 0.03-0.04 m.

    ΣΙΜΩΝΙΔΑΣ Σιμωνίδας

XXVIII.—Fragment of poros tombstone. Height, 0.33 m.; width, 0.49 m.; height of letters, 0.05 m.

    ΜΝΑΣΙΓΙΤΑ Μνασιγίτα

A new name, analogous in formation to Θιογίτα (COLLITZ, 1044).

XXIX.—Poros tombstone, widest at the top. Height, 0.86 m.; greatest width, 0.0375 m.; height of letters, 0.04 m.

    ΚΑΛΛΙΓΙΤΩΝ Καλλιγίτων

XXX.—Rough poros slab. Height, 0.32 m.; width, 0.52 m.; height of letters, 0.045 m.

    ΚΑΛΛΙΑΣ Καλλίας

XXXI.—Rough poros block. Height, 0.33 m.; width, 0.53 m.; height of letters, 0.055-0.08 m.

    ΕΥΦΑΣΙΑ Εὐφασία

A new name.

XXXII.—Rough poros block. Height, 0.185 m.; width, 0.415 m.; height of letters, 0.06 m.

ΚΑΦΙΣΙΑΣ   Καφισίας

The stone-cutter has apparently attempted to strike off the excessively long right-hand stroke of the first *alpha*. The *sigmas* are decidedly sprawling.

XXXIII.—Poros tombstone, broken at the bottom and top. Height, 0.29 m.; width, 0.455 m.; height of letters, 0.035 m.

ΝΕΣΤΙΔΑ   'Ο?]νεστίδα

If correctly supplied, a new name, patronymic from 'Ονέστας.

XXXIV.—Long bar-tombstone of poros with cornice at top and rosettes at the ends. Length, 1.09 m.; height, 0.25 m; height of letters, 0.05 m.

ΑΡΙΣΤΩΝΥΜΟΣ   'Αριστώνυμος

Attic: the Boiotian form would be 'Αριστώνουμος.

XXXV.—Marble tombstone with gable top. Height, 0.37 m.; width, 0.255 m.; height of letters, 0.015 m.

ΑΡΙΣΤΩΝ   'Αρίστων
ΚΝΩΣΙΟΣ   Κνώσιος

Ariston son of Knosos, or Ariston of Knosos (?).

XXXVI.—Poros tombstone with gable top. Height, 0.73 m.; width, 0.41 m.; height of letters, 0.04 m.

⁻ₙΡΝΕΙΑΣ   Π?]αρνείας

A new name.

XXXVII.—Poros tombstone. Height, 0.71 m.; width, 0.35 m.; height of letters, 0.025 m.

ΑΡΙΣΤΟΜΕΝΕΙΣ   'Αριστομένεις

XXXVIII.—Poros tombstone with gable top. Height, 0.45 m.; width, 0.45 m.; height of letters, 0.03 m.

ΕΝΩΝ   Μ]ένων or Ξ]ένων

XXXIX.—Fragment of poros. Height, 0.20 m.; width, 0.40 m.; height of letters, 0.03–0.035 m.

ΜΕΝΕΣΤΡΟΤ   Μενέστροτ[ος

The Boiotian and Aiolic change of α to ο in the group ρα=ρ̥ is seen in στροτός and the proper names of which it forms a part, as Δ]ινόστρο[τ]ος (COLLITZ, 476), Τιμόσστροτος (COLLITZ, 485), etc. There are, however, many instances of --στρατος, doubtless due to Attic influence, and among these is Μενε[σ]τράτω (COLLITZ, 501). Μενέστροτος is now met with for the first time.

XL.—Poros tombstone with gable top. Height, 0.77 m.; width, 0.45 m.; height of letters, 0.035 m.

   ΓΟΛΥΞΕΝΑ Πολυξένα

XLI.—Poros tombstone with gable represented in relief. Height, 0.64 m.; width, 0.43 m.; height of letters, 0.05 m.

   ΕΥΗΣΧΡΟΣ Εὔησχρος

This name, which is new, is a peculiar compound, but cf. Κάλλαισχρος.

XLII.—Marble tombstone, at the village spring of Loukisi. Height, 1.70 m.; width, 0.45 m.; height of letters, 0.03 m.

   ΣΩΚΡΑΤΕΙΣ Σωκράτεις
   ΓΕΤΑΣ   Πέτας

The name Πέτας is not found elsewhere, but is probably a short form of Πέταλος, which occurs in Thessalian (COLLITZ, 358) and on one of the lead plates of Styra (BECHTEL, *Inschriften des Ionischen Dialekts*, p. 33, No. 404).

XLIII.—Marble tombstone with gable top. Height, 0.38 m.; width, 0.165 m.; height of letters, 0.015 m.

   ΟΝΑΣΙΜΟΣ 'Ονάσιμος
   ΟΝΑΣΙΜΑ   'Ονασίμα

XLIV.—Poros tombstone with gable top; broken below. Height, 0.88 m.; width, 0.43 m.; height of letters, 0.025 m.

   ΝΟΥΜΗΝΙΣ Νουμηνὶς
   ΟΝΑΣΙΜΙΔΟΥ 'Ονασιμίδου

Attic, except the second syllable of 'Ονασιμίδου. The name Νουμηνὶς occurs in *C.I.A.*, III, 2905.

XLV.—Marble tombstone with gable top; broken below. Height, 0.25 m.; width, 0.265 m.; height of letters, 0.018 m.

   ΓΑΥΣΙΛΛΑΝ Παύσιλλαν

A new name. The simple accusative upon tombstones is rare. Examples in KEIL, *Zur Sylloge Inscr. Boeot.*, p. 535 at bottom; LE BAS, *Voyage arch.*, II, No. 654; *Mitth. Inst. Athen.*, XII (1887), p. 357; COLLITZ, 1053, 1074. This list makes no pretence to completeness.

XLVI.—Poros slab. Height, 0.59 m.; width, 0.43 m.; height of letters, 0.055 m.

ΔΗΤΑ   Δήτα

Probably the genitive of Δήτας (=Attic Δαίτης).

XLVII.—Marble tombstone with gable top and rosettes. Height, 0.95 m.; width, 0.40 m.; letters, 0.02–0.04 m.

ΕΠΙ   Ἐπὶ
ΦΙΛΟΞΕΝΩΙ   Φιλοξένῳ
ΜΝΗΣΙΚΛΕΟΥΣ   Μνησικλέους

The letters are cut in a slovenly fashion and badly arranged.

XLVIII.—Marble tombstone, built into the wall surrounding the church at Loukisi. Height, 1.21 m.; width, 0.44 m.; height of letters, 0.04 m.

ΕΠΙ   Ἐπὶ
ΦΙΛΙΠΠΩΙ   Φιλίππῳ

XLIX.—Marble tombstone with akroterion and rosettes, in wall surrounding the church at Loukisi. Total height, 1.34 m. (of which akroterion alone = 0.55); width, 0.44 m., height of letters, 0.03 m.

ΦΙΛΙΠΠΟΣ   Φίλιππος

Below are represented in relief various tools, including a knife, axe, and chisel.

L.—Block of rough poros. Length, 0.46 m.; width, 0.285 m.; height of letters, 0.05 m.

ΗΡΑΚΛΕ   Ἡρακλε[ί]-
ΔΗ   δη

The stone-cutter omitted the Λ and inserted it afterwards. There is no trace of an Ι at the end of the line, but Ἡρακλέδη would be an impossible form. Ἡρακλείδη would be a good Boiotian dative, but is probably to be regarded as Attic, the *iota subscript* being omitted, as often in late inscriptions. The simple dative is rare on gravestones, but not unexampled. Two or three cases are referred to by FRANZ (*Elementa Epigraphices Graecae*, p. 340), and three cases of the name in the dative with ἥρωι are quoted by Keil (*Sylloge Inscr. Boeot.*, pp. 155, 169). Possibly we ought to restore Ἡρακλε[ί]δη[ς.

LI.—Fragment of poros slab with cornice. Height, 0.19 m.; width, 0.24 m.; height of letters, 0.025 m.

ΕΝΑΝΔΓ   Μ]ένανδρ[ος

LII.—Fragment of poros. Height, 0.24 m.; width, 0.23 m.; height of letters, 0.028 m.

ΝΤΡΟΦΙ∠   Σου]υτροφίς

A new name.

LIII.—Marble tombstone with gable top represented in relief. Height, 0.31 m.; width, 0.40 m.; height of letters, 0.025 m.

ΤΑΓΟΝΙ⌒   --ταγόνιο[ς

LIV.—Poros tombstone with gable top. Height, 0.50 m.; width, 0.45 m.; height of letters, 0.035 m.

ΑΝ..ΚΙΜΟΣ

Nearly all the letters are very uncertain.

LV.—Poros slab, broken at the bottom and on the left. Height, 0.35 m.; width, 0.26 m.; height of letters, 0.045 m.

ΗΡΙΔΑΣ   Φιλετ?]ηρίδας

A new name.

LVI.—Poros block with cornice at the top. Height, 0.48 m.; width, 0.22 m.; thickness, 0.205 m.; height of letters, 0.018 m.

ΑΡΙΣΤΗ—
ΤΙΣ

There are traces of three or four lines, but the stone is so badly worn that it was found impossible to make out more of the letters than are given above.

LVII.—Fragment of marble tombstone, broken at the bottom and left side. Height, 0.54 m.; width, 0.22 m.; height of letters, 0.05 m

ΕΙΝΙΣ   -εινίς

LVIII.—Fragment of poros, found near Nos. II and III. Height, 0.19 m.; width, 0.14 m.; height of letters, 0.025 m.

ΡΤΑ
ΤΗ
Ε

LIX.—Fragment of poros tombstone with gable in relief. Height, 0.30 m.; width, 0.24 m.; height of letters, 0.0225 m.

ΩN

LX.—Fragment of poros with cornice. Height, 0.34 m.; width, width, 0.20 m.; height of letters, 0.04 m.

ΣΚΑ

LXI.—Fragment of poros slab. Height, 0.32 m.; width, 0.18 m.; height of letters, 0.04 m.

```
I I K E
M A P
  X A
```

LXII.—Small poros fragment. Height, 0.38 m.; width, 0.18 m.; height of letters, 0.03 m.

ΣΩΤ

BILINGUAL INSCRIPTIONS.

LXIII.—Marble slab, now used as threshold for the entrance to the church lot at Loukisi. Length, 1.01 m.; width, 0.21 m.; height of letters, 0.04 m.

M⋅ARELLIVS⋅Q⋅F⋅POM   M(arcus) Arellius Q(uinti) F(ilius)
                                    Pom(ptina)
ΜΑΡΚΟΣΑΡΕΛΛΙΟΣΚΟΙΝΤΟΥ   Μᾶρκος Ἀρέλλιος Κοίντου
  ΥΙΟΣΠΩΜΕΝΤΙΝΑ   υἱὸς Πωμεντίνα

On the form Πωμεντίνα, see MOMMSEN in *Ephemeris Epigraphica*, IV, 221.

LXIV.—Marble slab, in same position as preceding. Length, 1.01 m.; width, 0.21 m.; height of letters, 0.04 m.

Q⋅ARELLIVS⋅M⋅L⋅XSENO
\OINTOΣAPEΛΛIOΣMAPKOY
      ΞΕΝΩΝ

Q(uintus) Arellius M(arci) L(ibertus) Xseno
Κ]όιντος Ἀρέλλιος Μάρκου (ἀπελεύθερος)
        Ξένων

There is a similar omission of ἀπελεύθερος in the inscription published in the *Bull. de corr. hellén.*, I, 284–5.

                                      C. D. BUCK,
                                      F. B. TARBELL.

DISCOVERIES AT THISBE IN 1889.

REPORT ON EXCAVATIONS.

Between March 18 and 21, I made a trip to Kakosia, the work of laying bare the foundations by the sea, at Anthedon, being meanwhile superintended by Mr. Buck. The village of Kakosia lies between two peaks of Mt. Helikon, not far from the sea. On the hills which immediately surround it, and in the village itself, are well-preserved remains of the walls of an ancient town, built of regular blocks of bluish limestone and strengthened by numerous towers. The walls are of Leake's " fourth order," consisting of a double line of well-cut, regular blocks, the interval between them being filled in with loose stones. In the village are clear traces of one of the gates, and just outside it, in a wheat field, traces of the foundations of a large building. There are also the remains of a mole (now serving as a road) across a marshy plain to the southward, evidently to protect the plain from inundation. It seems to be certain that this village stands directly on the site of ancient Thisbe, as was concluded by Leake and others (from Strabo, *Geog.*, 411, and Pausanias, IX. 32. 3). The only building which Pausanias mentions in Thisbe is a temple of Herakles, with a standing statue of the god. Judging from the great number of churches (twenty-three in all, I was told), Thisbe must have been an important place in Byzantine times. Since the modern village stands directly on the ancient site, extensive excavations must involve considerable expense. I found, however, a great number of Byzantine churches in ruins, and I judged that a few days of work in and around these might yield good results. I returned to Anthedon, finished the excavations by the harbor and cleared off the walls, and on March 27 began work at Thisbe with fifteen men, a number which was afterward increased to twenty. Trenches were first dug in and around the church "Ὅσιος Λουκᾶς, within the limits of Kakosia, but just outside the ancient walls. In front of the church we found a Byzantine pillar of fine white marble, apparently for supporting a screen or curtain. It is ornamented in front with a conventional design in relief, and has a smooth, pear-shaped top, separated from the main shaft by a narrow neck. The dimensions are as follows: height, 1.77 m.; breadth, 0.20 m.; thickness, 0.135 m. The top is 0.17 m. high and 0.47 m. in circumference. In the pavement of the church we found six inscribed tombstones. An examination of the walls of the church, with as little damage as possible, yielded no inscriptions.

In the pavement of the church 'Αγία Τριάς, which was next examined, were found three inscribed tombstones. As the walls of this church were mainly composed of rough masses of stone, and were without architectural or artistic interest, and as they evidently contained inscriptions, I felt justified in tearing down a part of them. Four fragments of inscriptions were found here. The arched entrance was left standing, but was afterward thrown down by the boys of the village. In a third church ('Αγία Κυριακή or "Αγιος 'Ηλίας), of which nothing but the foundations remained, four inscribed bases and tombstones were found. Two of the former, though we found them underground, prove to have been published.

At this point, the Directors of the School, Dr. Waldstein and Professor Tarbell, arrived at Kakosia, and decided to concentrate all our energies at Plataia.

JOHN C. ROLFE.

INSCRIPTIONS FROM THISBE.

The following inscriptions were found by Mr. Rolfe at Thisbe (Kakosia) in March, 1889. Those to which *R* is prefixed are edited on the basis of Mr. Rolfe's copies alone; to him also the measurements are chiefly due.

I.—R. Marble slab, used in the pavement of the ruined church 'Αγία Τριάς. Height, 0.77 m.; breadth, 0.45 m.; thickness, 0.30 m; height of letters, 0.03 m. In the upper surface there is a round hole with a diameter of 0.14 m.

   ΕΥΘΥΝΙΔΑΣ   Εὐθυνίδας

II.—Marble slab in pavement of same church. Height, 0.765 m; breadth, 0.525 m.; thickness, 0.28 m.; height of letters, 0.023 m.

   ϜΙΣ ΛΑΟΣ   Ϝισ[ό]λαος

The letters have the forms characteristic of the Hellenistic period. They are regularly, though very widely, spaced. A rectangular cut has removed a single letter, the fourth. Fισόλαος, of which the Attic equivalent would be 'Ισόλεως, is a new name, comparable to 'Ισόδημος.

III.—R. Stone slab in pavement of same church. Height, 0.78 m.; breadth, 0.49 m.; thickness, 0.19 m.; height of letters, 0.03 m.

ΙΩΠΟΥΡΟΣ   Ζώπουρος

IV.—R. Slab of red stone in the wall of the same church. The height could not be exactly ascertained, as the stone was not taken from the wall; it was apparently about 0.75 m. Breadth, 0.44 m.; thickness, 0.34 m.; height of letters, 0.03 m.

ΜΑΟΜΕΙΛΟΣ   (Σ)αόμειλος

The first letter must have been erroneously copied. The name occurs at Orchomenos and Lebadeia in the form Σαύμειλος, and the same contraction is found in other Boiotian proper names beginning with the same element;[1] but, in view of the Boiotian retention of ao in compounds of λαός and in some other words, Σαόμειλος seems a possible local form.

V.—R. Fragment of limestone, complete at the left, in the wall of the same church. Height, 0.33 m.; breadth, 0.28 m.; thickness, 0.28 m.; height of letters, 0.05 m.

ΚΛΑΥΔ   Κλαυδ[ίαν ὁ ἀνὴρ (?)
ΚΑΙΗΘΥΙ   καὶ ἡ θυ[γάτηρ.
ΔΙΩΝΕΠΟ   Δίων [ἐ]πο[ίησεν.

"This statue of Claudia (?) was erected by her husband (?) and daughter. The sculptor was Dion."

VI.—Four fragments of limestone (A, B, C, D), apparently belonging together, taken from the walls of same church. Fragment A is complete at the top and at the left; the others are broken on all sides. Dimensions of B; height, 0.30 m.; breadth, 0.33 m.: of C; height, 0.19 m.; breadth, 0.18 m.: of D; height, 0.23 m.; breadth, 0.49 m. The thickness of each is about 0.175 m.; height of letters, 0.01 m. and (in the last five lines of D) 0.016 m. There are numerous ligatures, and the inscribed surface is defaced in spots, so that the decipherment of the text is difficult, and the results in some places uncertain. Fragment A, the inscribed face of which was always visible, was published

---

[1] MEISTER, Die griechischen Dialekte, 1, p. 246.

by PITTAKES as No. 3061 in the 'Εφημερὶς 'Αρχαιολογική and by VON VELSEN in the *Archäologischer Anzeiger*, XIV (1856), p. 288; by both, as we now see, most inaccurately. Unfortunately, we took no squeeze of this fragment, and are not able to give a thoroughly trustworthy text of it. What is given below in majuscules, as *A*, is simply Von Velsen's text, with some corrections and additions introduced from Mr. Tarbell's hastily made copy.

Fragment A.

```
         ΜΟΥΛΠΙΟΣ
  ΟΒΟΥΛΟΜΕΝΟΣΘΙΣΒΑΙΩΝΧΩΡΙΟΝΔΗ
  -------ΝΕΠΕΜΟΥΓΕΩΡΓΟΥΜΕΝΩΝ
  ΒΙΒΛΙΟΝΓΡΑ---ΝΑΥΤ--ΟΠΟΗΤΕΟΝΙΣ
  --ΛΑΙ-ΙΟΝΥΠΕΡΕΚΑΣΤΟΥΠΛΕΘΡΟΥ
  --ΛΗΣΗΕ-----ΣΟΝΤΑΤΟΔΕΔΟΜΕΝΟ
               ϽΝΚ--ΙΜΕΝΤΙΣ
               ΕΙΤ----ΘΕΚΚ
                    ΩΕΙΣ
```

Fragment B.

```
  Κ/
  ϽΝΚΑΙ
  ΠΕΡΕΚΑ
  ΩΝΠΕΝΤ
  ΑΤΑΛΑΜΒΑΝΟΜ
  ΙΟΙΔΕΜΗΠΠΡΑΞΑΝΤΕΣ(
  ΑΞΑΝ   ΕΙΔΕΤΙΣΛΑΒΩΝ--ΤΟΣ
  ΤΑΠΩΛΗΣΟΥΣΙΝΟΙΚΑΤΑΛΑΜΒΑΝ
  ΓΟΝΠΠΡΑΞΟΥΣΙΝΠΑΡΑΥΤΟΥΤΗΣι
  ΑΞΙΟΝΤΟΥΦΟΡΟΥΤΩΝΠΕΝΤΕΕΤ
  ΤΟΧΩΡΙΟΝΠΟΛΕΙΤΗΚΑΙΤΟΑΡΓΟΝΚΑ
    ΕΦΥΤΕΥΜΕΝΟΥΕΙΣΚΟΜΙΣΘΗΝΑΙΤΗΠΟ/
  ΕΝΙΑΥΤΟΝΟΣΟΝΤΕΛΕΣΘΗΚΑΙΟΠΡΟΤΕΡΟ
  ΟΤΟΥΦΟΡΟΥΤΗΣΠΕΝΤΑΕΤΙΑΣΥΠΕΡ
    ΤΗΣΕΚΑΣΤΟΣΜΗΠΛΕΟΝΠΛΕΘΡ(
    ΤΟΙΣΠΛΕΟΝΠΩΛΗΣΟΥΣΙΝ
  ΚΑΙΘΚΤΟΥΤΟΥΣΩΖΕΣΘΑΙ⁻
  ΩΜΟΛΟΓΗΣΕΝΥΠΕΡΕΚΑΣΤΣ
  ΕΝΤΟΣΤΟΝΓΕΙΝΟΜΕ
     ΞΛΤΟ[uncut]
```

Fragment C.

```
ΘΡΟΝΙͺ
ΑΜЄΝΟΣΚΑι
ΟΥЄΞΟΣΟΥΤ
ΑΡΑΤΗΣΠΟΛЄ ͼ
ΙϢΚΑΙΤΑΑΛΛΑΚΑ
ΟΜЄΝΟΥΤΟΥΦΟΡΟΥ
ЄΙΤΗΔΑΝЄΙΣΤΗϢΣΚΛ
ΟΣΙΟΥΧϢΡΙΟΥΗΔ
ΗΜΟΣΙΟΥΚΑΘΗΜ
ΥΤΟΣΓΡΑΦЄΤͼ
ΝΤ--ΟΙЄΚΑ
ΠΟΣΟΝΗΟΤ
ΑΤΟΣΥ
```

Fragment D.

```
    ΓΟΤЄΟΝͺΜΑ  ͺ
    ЄΙΔЄΤΙΣЄΞΑΠΑΤΗΣΑ----ΟΦЄΙΛΟΝ
    ͺΝΔΗΜΟΣΙϢΝΚΑΙΤΟΥΤΟЄΛЄΝΧΘЄΙΗΑΦΑΙΡЄ
    ΗΠΟΛΙΣΟΔЄΔΑΝЄΙΣΤΗΣΟΞЄΝΟΣЄΚΤϢΝΑΛΛ
  5 ЄΝΤΟΣΤΗΝЄΙΣΠΡΑΞΙΝΠΟΙЄΙΣΘϢΤΟΥΟΦЄΙΛΟΜЄ
    ΑΙΣΚΑΤΑΛΙΠΟΙΞЄΝϢΣΥΝΓЄΝЄΙΗΦΙΛϢΤΟΥΤϢΝΤΙΤϢΝ
    ΥΤΟΥΗΔϢΡЄΛЄΣΤϢΔЄΤΗΣΠΟΛЄϢΣΤΟΧϢΡΙΟΝ ЄΙΔ
    ΘΗΚΑΣΤЄΛЄΥΤΗΣΑΙϢΜΗЄΙΣΙΝΝΟΜΙΜΟΙΚΛΗΡΟΝΟΜΟΙΠ
    ΟΤЄΡΑΚΛΗΡΟΝΟΜΟΣΤΟΥЄΑΥΤΗΣΚΤΗΜ/-ΟΣΗΠΟΛΙΣ
 10 ΜΙΝΙΟΣΜΟΔЄΣΤΟΣΑΝΘΥΠΑΤΟΣ      ΘΙΣΒ
    ΤΗΒΟΥΛΗΚΑΙΤϢΔΗΜϢ ΧΑΙΡЄΙΝ   ΙΚΑΝΟΝ
    ΚΥΡΙΑΤΑΔΟΞΑΝΤΑΥΜЄΙΝΠЄΡΙΤΗΣΠΡΟΤЄ
    ΓЄΓЄΝΗΜЄΝΗΣΚΑΙΤΟΤΟΥΑΞΙΟͷ
         ͷΙͷΤΟͷЄΠΙΧϢΡΙΟΥΚΑΙ
```

A

Μ(άρκος) Οὔλπιος ⸺

Ὁ βουλόμενος Θισβαίων χωρίον δη[μόσιον - - -
- - - - τῷ]ν ἐπ' ἐμοῦ γεωργουμένων - - - - - -
βιβλίον γρα[φ - -]ν αὐτ - - ὃ πο[ι]ητέον (ἐ)σ[τί; -
- - λαι. ιον ὑπὲρ ἑκάστου πλέθρου - - - - - -
πω]λήσῃ ε - - - - -σοντα τὸ δεδομένο[ν - - - -
            νκ[- - ε]ἴ μέν τις
            ειτ - - - - τῇ ἐκκ[λησίᾳ
                 ωεις

B

κα
-ον καὶ
ὑ]πὲρ ἑκά[στου πλέθρου
τ]ῶν πέντ[ε ἐτῶν
κ]αταλαμβανομ[εν-
-ι. οἱ δὲ μὴ πράξαντες
-αξαν. εἰ δέ τις λαβὼν - - τος
ταῦ(?)]τα πωλήσουσιν οἱ καταλαμβαν[ο
-τον πράξουσιν παρ' αὐτοῦ τῆς
ἄξιον τοῦ φόρου τῶν πέντε ἐτ[ῶν
τὸ χωρίον πολείτῃ καὶ τὸ ἀργὸν κα[ὶ τὸ πεφυτευμένον
π]εφυτευμένου εἰσκομισθῆναι τῇ πο[λει
ἐνιαυτὸν ὅσον τελεσθίῃ καὶ ὁ πρότερο-
-ο τοῦ φόρου τῆς πενταετίας ὑπὲρ
-της ἕκαστος μὴ πλέον πλέθρο[υ
τοῖς πλέον πωλήσουσιν
καὶ (ἐ)κ τούτου σώζεσθαι
ὡμολόγησεν ὑπὲρ ἑκάστο[υ πλέθρου
-εντος τὸν γεινόμε[νον
-ξατο.

C

πλέ]θρον
-άμενος καὶ
-ου ἐξ ὅσου τ-
π]αρὰ τῆς πόλεω[ς
-ίῳ καὶ τὰ ἄλλα κα-
-ομένου τοῦ φόρου
πολ ?]είτῃ δανειστῇ ὡς κα-
δημ]οσίου χωρίου ἡ δ[ωρεὰ
δ]ημοσίου καθ' ἡμ[έραν ?
α]ὐτὸς γραφέτω
-οι ἑκα[στ
ποσον(?) ἢ ὀπ-
ατοσυ

D

- - - - - - - τό τε ὄνομα - - - - - - - - - - - - - - -
- - - - - - εἰ δέ τις ἐξαπατήσα[ς τὸν ?] ὀφείλον[τα - - - - - -

- - - - - τῶ]ν δημοσίων καὶ τοῦτο ἐλενχθείη, ἀφαιρε[ίσθω - - - - -
- - - - - ἡ πόλις· ὁ δὲ δανειστὴς ὁ ξένος ἐκ τῶν ἄλλ[ων - - - - - -
- - - - ἐντὸς τὴν εἴσπραξιν ποιείσθω τοῦ ὀφειλομέ[νου.   εἰ δέ τις
διαθήκ]αις καταλίποι ξένῳ συνγενεῖ ἢ φίλῳ τούτων τι τῶν [χωρίων, ἄκυρος
ἔστω το]ύτου ἡ δωρεά, ἔστω δὲ τῆς πόλεως τὸ χωρίον.   εἰ δ[έ τις μὴ καταλι-
πὼν δια]θήκας τελευτήσαι, ᾧ μή εἰσιν νόμιμοι κληρονόμοι, π[- - - - κατ'
ἀμφ]ότερα κληρονόμος τοῦ ἑαυτῆς κτήμ[ατ]ος ἡ πόλις.

Φλα ?]μίνιος Μόδεστος ἀνθύπατος   Θισβ[αίων τοῖς ἄρχου-
σι καὶ]τῇ βουλῇ καὶ τῷ δήμῳ χαίρειν.   Ἱκανὸν - - - - - - -
- - - - - κύρια τὰ δόξαντα ὑμεῖν περὶ τῆς προτέ[ρας - - - - - - - -
- - - - - - - - γεγενημένης καὶ το[ύ]του?   ἄξιον - - - - - - - - - -
- - - - - - - - - - τον ἐπιχωρίου καὶ - - - - - - - - - - - -

The document seems to consist of a series of enactments relating to the public lands, followed by the ratification of the proconsul, Modestus.

VII.—Fragment of limestone, found in same church ; complete at the left only. Height, 0.19 m. ; breadth, 0.27 m. ; height of letters, 0.014 m. and (in the last line) 0.036 m.

NYNΔE   νῦν δὲ
ΦΟΥΣΚΟΝ   Φοῦσκον
ΠΑΡΕΧΟΜΕΝ   παρεχομεν-
ΤΟΙΣΠΡΟΔΟΞΑ   τοῖς προδόξα[σι
ΣΤΕΙΛΑΤΕΒΕΒΑΙΟ   στείλατε βεβαιο[- - - - βε-
ΒΟΥΛΕΥΜΕΝΑΚΑΙΔ βουλευμένα καὶ δ[όξαντα
.ΙΣΦΟΥΣΚΟΝΤΕΙΜΗ   . . ς Φοῦσκον τειμη-
. . ΙΚΑΓΩΠΡΟΣΕΠΙΚ . . . κἀγὼ προσεπικ[τήσομαι
ΨΗΦΙΣΜ   Ψηφίσμ[ατι Βουλῆς

VIII.—Marble slab, used in the pavement of the ruined church Ὅσιος Λουκᾶς. Height, 0.83 m. ; breadth, 0.49 m. ; thickness, 0.37 m. ; height of letters, 0.04 m.

ΚΑΛΛΙΓΙΤΙΣ   Καλλιγιτίς

IX.—Marble slab in same position. Height, 0.98 m. ; breadth, 0.52 m. ; thickness, 0.34 m. ; height of letters, 0.04 m.

ΚΛΗΝΕΤΟΣ   Κλήνετος

The name occurs in the same form at Hyettos (COLLITZ, *Sammlung der griech. Dialekt-Inschriften*, 537) ; in the form Κλιήνετος, at Tanagra (COLLITZ, 950). It is the Boiotian equivalent of the Attic Κλεαίνετος.

X.—Marble slab in same position. Height, 0.82 m.; breadth, 0.475 m.; thickness, 0.33 m.; height of letters, 0.03 m.

ΑΓ.ΛΛΟΔΩΡΟΣ   'Απ[ο]λλόδωρος

XI.—Marble slab in same position. Height, 0.87 m.; breadth, 0.5 m.; thickness, 0.34 m.; height of letters, 0.04 m.

ΟΕΟΦΑΝΙ/   Θ]εοφάνι[α

The name is new, though the corresponding masculine name (Attic Θεοφάνης) is common. The Attic equivalent would be Θεοφάνεια (MEISTER, Die griech. Dialekte, I, p. 229), like 'Αριστοφάνεια, etc.

XII.—Marble slab in same position. Height, 0.8 m.; breadth, 0.45 m.; thickness, 0.34 m.; height of letters, 0.03 m.

ΑΓΓΙΣΙΑΣ   'Αγ[ε]ισίας

XIII.—Basis of blue limestone, in the ruined church 'Αγία Κυριακή (or "Αγιος 'Ηλίας, as the name was given by some). At the top there is a cornice, on which the inscription is cut. The upper right-hand corner has been broken off, but the breadth can be easily obtained from the back. Height of basis, 1 m.; original breadth at top, 0.455 m.; height of letters, 0.03 m.

ΔΕΥΞΙΑΣΑΣΚΛ   Δευξίας 'Ασκλ[απιῦ κὴ
ΟΥΓΙΗ   Οὐγίη

" Deuxias to Asklepios and Hygieia."

Although this stone was found lying on its face under a considerable accumulation of rubbish, it had been seen a few years before, and ι squeeze of the inscription had been submitted to M. FOUCART. See the *Bulletin de correspondance hellénique*, VIII (1884), p. 401, No. 2. M. Foucart's reading and note are as follows:

ΔΕΙΞΙΑΣΑΣΚΛΑ
ΟΥΓΙΗ

La pierre est brisée à droite; à gauche l'inscription paraît complète, les deux premières lettres ne sont pas très-distinctes. Δειξίας 'Ασκλα[πιοδώρω] Οὐγίη. *Dédicace à la déesse Hygia. Les lettres qui terminent la première ligne se prêteraient à la restitution* 'Ασκλα[πίω]. *Asklépios est souvent associé à Hygia, mais dans ce cas les noms des deux divinités seraient rapprochés. Οὐγίη étant isolé à la seconde ligne, je crois plutôt que* 'Ασκλα *est le commencement du nom du père de celui qui a faitla consécration.* On this MEISTER remarks (COLLITZ, *Sammlung*, 747ª): Δειξίας, *mir unverständlich; etwa* [Μ]ιξίας *oder* Δεξίας?

Our reading of the first name may be taken as certain, although we found the third and fourth letters not easy to make out, owing partly to the presence in their places of accidental marks which bear a delusive resemblance to the letters ΩΔ. Δευξίας is the regular Boiotian equivalent of Ζευξίας.

As for the restitution of the first line, five letters following Λ (at the edge of which the break at present begins) would leave as much uncut space at the end of the line as at the beginning, while seven letters would extend to the edge. M. Foucart's restoration gives eight letters. A shorter name might be substituted, as Ἀσκλαπίχω or Ἀσκλάπωνος. But, considering the extreme rarity of dedications to Hygieia alone[2] and the frequency with which, in joint dedications, the names of the two divinities stand in different lines,[3] we have preferred without hesitation the restoration given above.

XIV.—R. Stone slab in same church. Height, 0.9 m ; breadth, 0.49 m. ; thickness, 0.21 m. ; height of letters, 0.04 m.

ΑΦΡΟΔΙΣΙΑ   Ἀφροδισία,
ΧΑΙΡΕ   χαῖρε

XV.—R. Rough stone basis with rectangular hole in the top; found in same church. Height, 0.99 m ; breadth, 0.44 m. ; thickness, 0.24 m ; height of letters, 0.025 m.

ΩΝΟΣ
ΑΡΤΑΜΙ
ΟΣΑΓΡΟ
ΕΡΑΣ

The stone is badly defaced, and only so much could be made out. It is perhaps a dedication to Artemis. Two dedications to that goddess, published by M. FOUCART in the *Bulletin* (VIII, 1884, pp. 401–2, Nos. 3, 4), are in this same church.

F. B. TARBELL,
J. C. ROLFE.

---

[2] We can cite only *CIA*, III, 185, and BAUNACK, *Studien*, I, 1, *Inschriften aus Epidauros*, No. 40.

[3] See, for example, *CIG*, III, 2390, 2396, 2428, 2429 b; *CIA*, II, 1504; III, 132 b, c, d, e, f, i, 181 a, 183.

DISCOVERIES AT PLATAIA IN 1889.

A NEW FRAGMENT OF THE PREAMBLE TO DIOCLETIAN'S EDICT, "DE PRETIIS RERUM VENALIUM."

The preamble to Diocletian's Edict *De Pretiis Rerum Venalium* has been known hitherto from two copies, one (.1) found in Egypt and brought in 1807 to Aix in Provence, where it is now preserved in the museum, the other (*S*) still *in situ*, inscribed on the wall of a Roman edifice in Stratonike in Karia. The latest and best editions of these two inscriptions are given by Waddington in Le Bas, *Voyage Archéologique*, vol. III, pp. 145 ff., and by Mommsen in the *Corpus Inscriptionum Latinarum*, vol. III², pp. 801 ff.

In the course of the excavations carried on at Plataia in April 1889, under the direction of Dr. Waldstein, there was found, in the most western of the ruined Byzantine churches situated within the walls of the northern half of the city, a marble stele, bearing an inscription which proved to be a fragment of this preamble. The stone formed part of the pavement of the church, the inscribed face being uppermost, and the upper end, including part of the inscription, being imbedded in the wall. The back is rough. There are traces of an original moulding on the sides and front, but this has been hacked away, with the result of totally obliterating the first line of the inscription. On the right-hand side about half of the letters have been worn away, as if by the tread of feet. As this is true of the part imbedded in the wall, the stone must have been used, but in a different position, in the pavement of an earlier building. When found, it was broken irregularly across the middle. It has since been conveyed to Athens, and is now in the National Museum. In the course of transportation two small

233

234 *DIOCLETIAN'S EDICT,* "*DE PRETIIS RERUM VENALIUM.*"

pieces were chipped off and lost, one containing the last twelve letters of line 34, as given in our text below, the last eleven of 35, and the last three of 36; the other containing the first letter of 49, the first two of 50, the first two of 51, and the first three of 52. Mr. Rolfe's copy and squeeze were made at Plataia; Mr. Tarbell's, at Athens.

Length of stele, 1.35 met.; width at bottom, 0.835 m., at top, 0.80 m.; thickness, 0.18 m.; height of letters, 0.006–0.013 m.

Specimen letters; rare forms in ( ):

Λ(Λ), b ϐ, C, δ d(ΔΔ), ε, Ϝ, Ϛ; h, I(inverted), ι, m, NN, O, P, Ϙ, R, Υϝ, τ, U[ᵛafter Ϙ], X

With the help of the two copies of this text previously known (*A* and *S*), the original contents of our stone can be restored. Letters between parentheses, ( ), are those which appear on this stone, but not on *A* or *S*; those in italics and not between brackets, [ ], are either lacking in our text and supplied from *A* or *S*, or substituted from *A* or *S* for the reading of our text; letters between brackets, [ ], are conjectural restorations, *i. e.*, do not appear on any of the three stones. In the latter no great confidence can be felt; in no case where a gap in *A* and *S* has been filled by the Plataian copy has the conjecture of a previous editor been exactly verified. In numbering the lines, the original first line has been counted. The sign § is used to indicate uncut spaces. Three of these (those in lines 12, 28, 44) are in the legible portions of the inscription, and all correspond with similar vacant spaces in *A*. We have therefore assumed that, if our inscription were complete, the correspondence would hold throughout, and have inserted, on the testimony of *A*, the sign § in lines 18 and 24. We have inserted it also at the beginning of lines 40 and 52, where *A* fails us, because the number of letters in the preceding lines is insufficient to fill the space. It will be seen that we thus get a § at the beginning of every sentence, except in line 6, where there is no evidence for one (though one is not impossible, the size and distribution of letters being irregular), and in line 35. Nothing was inscribed below line 55, and the remainder of the preamble must therefore have been on a second stele.

FRAGMENT OF THE PREAMBLE TO DIOCLETIAN'S EDICT, "DE PRETIIS RERUM VENALIUM," DISCOVERED AT PLATAIA IN 1889.

```
  . . . . . . . . . . . . . . . . . . . . . . . . . . . . . . .  ͝A
  . . . . . . . . . . . . . . . . . . . . . . . . . . . . . . .  TE
  . . . . . . . . . . . . . . . . . . . . . . . . . . . . . . .
  . . . . . . . . . . . . . . . . . . . . . . . . . . . . . . .
                                                    CIA͡P
  . . . . . . . . . . . . . . . . . . . . . . ͝
5.PRAETE    RAPINASGENTRUMBARBA   ͝     PL
  SUNDAT⌐   IETEMDIBITUMIUSTICIAEMUNIME  ͞AEPIAMUS
  BIFINAEPR    SITOARDATAAUARITIADESAEUIENSQUISINE    ECTOGENI
  UELMENSIBUSAUTDIEBUSSEDPAENHORISIPSISQUEMOM  ͞A
  TINATALIQUAEONTINENTIAERATIOFRENARETUELSIFORTUN
10.BACCANIDILIGENTIAMQUAPESSIMEINDIESEIUSMODISURTAEIAC
  DERELICTUSLOCUSUIDERETURCUMDETESTANIAM
  MUNISANIMORUMPATIENTIATEMPERARET  SĒDQUI
  NECESSITUDINISAHBEREDILECTUMETGLICENTISABAR
  RELIGICAPUDINPROBUSETINMODESTUSEXISTIMATUP
15.AMUOLUNTATEDESTITUIADQUAEULTRAQUONIUERENO
  EXTRAEMATRAXERUNTCUNUENITPROSPICIENTIBUSN
  TERUENIREIUSTITIAMUTQUODSPERATUMDIUHUM/
  PERAMENTUMREMEDIISPROMISIONISNU TRAETCUNF
  OMNIUMCONSCIENTIAMRECOGNOSCITETIPSARUMR
20.CEPECONSILIAMOLIMURAUTREMEDIAINUENTACOHIB
  ISSIMISDEPRAEHENSADILICTISIPSASEEMENDARE
  AREDIREPTIONISNOTASACUMMUNIBUSIUDICII
  EINPEIORAPRAECIPITESETINPUALICUMNEFASQUA
  GULESETHUNIUERSISREOSATROCISSIMAEINHUMANi
25.AMDIORERUMNECESSITATEDESIDERATAPRORUMPI
  BOAUTSUPERILLOUMEDILLAENUSTRAEINTERUEN
  TURQUITTANNORUMRETICENTIAMNUSTRAMI
```

```
LUERUNT    QUISENIMADEOOATUMSIPECTOR
POSSITINMONONSENSERITINUENALIBUSRE
30. CONUERSATIONEMTRACTANTURINTANTUMSE'
RAPIENDINE  RERUMCOPIANECANNORUMUERTATIB
OFFICIAEXERCITUS_ HABENTDUBIUMNONSITSE
SASCENPESTATISQUAECAPIARENEQUEINIQUITATISUA
SUPERISINDRIBUSARUAFELICIAUTQUIDETRIMENTL
35. DANTIAMREBUSPROUENIREETQUIBUSSENPERSTUDIUM
PUALICAEFELICITATISFLUENTIAMSTRINGERERUR
EINSTITUTORUMOFFICISNONDINARIQUISINGULIMA
TIMEXPLEREPOTUISSENTCONSENCTENTURPECUL
RUMADARITIAEMODUMSCATIIPROBINCIALESNUSTRI
40. SEDIAMETIAMIPSASCAOSASQUARUNE  ESSITASTAMDE
 IREDEBEMUSOTQUAMBISDPSIP/OACOTOORBAE
FACTOPOTIUSDROTOELARIIUSTIORTAMENINTEPL
TISSIMIHOMINESMENTIORNSUARUMINDOMITASCUPII
TURACNOSDEBE   QUISERGONESCIATUTILITAI
45. EXERCITUSNOSTROSIDIRIGICOMMUNISOMNIUMSA
MNIITINEREANIMOSECTIONISOCCURREREPRAETIAUI
TAEXTORQUEREUTNOMINAESTIMONISETFACTIEX
INTERDAMDISTRACTIONEHUNIUSREIDONATIBUMILIT
TINENDOSEXERCITUSCOLLATIONEDETESDANDIS
50. SSEMMILITIAESUAEETEMCRITUSLAUORESMILITESNOSTRISE(ONIUSUMNIU
IDEPRAEDATORESIPSIUSREIPUBLICAETANTUMINDIESRAPIANTQUANTUMHABER
HISOMNIBUSQUAESUPRACONPREHENSASUNTIUSTIACMERITOPERMOTICUMIAMIPSAHU
DERETURNONPRETIAUENALIUMRERUMNEQUEENIMFIERIIDIUSTUMPUTATORCUMPLu
BINCIAEFELICITATAEOPTATAEUILITATISETUELUTQUODAMAFLUENTIAEPR
55. MODUMSTATUENDUMESSECENSUAMUSUTCUMUISALIQUACARITATISEMERGERE,
```

DIOCLETIAN'S EDICT, "DE PRETIIS RERUM VENALIUM." 237

TEXT.

Fortunam reipublicae nostrae, cui iuxta immortales deos bellorum memoria quae feliciter gessimus, gratulari licet tranquillo orbis statu et in gremio altissimae quietis locato, etiam paris bonis, propter quam sudore largo laboratum est, disponi fideliter adque ornari decenter, honestum publicum et Romana dignitas maiestasque desiderant, ut nos, qui benigno favore numinum aestuantes de

5. praeterito rapinas gentium barbararum ipsarum nationum clade compressimus, in aeternum fundatam qui(etem debitis institiae numine)[oti]s saepiamus. Etenim si ea, quibus nullo si-
li finae proposito ardet avaritia desaeviens, quae (or qui) sine respectu generis humani, non annis modo vel mensibus aut diebus, sed paene horis ipsisque momentis ad incrementa sui et augmenta fes-
tinat (or tinant) aliqua continentiae ratio frenaret, vel si fortunae communes aequo animo perpeti possent hanc de-

10. bacandi licentiam, qua pessime in dies eiusmodi sortae faecerentur; dissimulandi forsitan adque reticendi relictus locus videretur, cum detestandam immanitatem condicionemque miserrandum communis animorum patientia temperaret. § Sed quia una est cupido furoris indomiti nullum communis necessitudinis habere dilectum, et gliscentis abaritiae ac rapidis aestuantis ardoribus velut quaedam religio apud improbos et immodestos exi)stimatur in lacerandis fortunis omnium necessitate potius qu-

15. am voluntate destitui, adquae ultra quoniuvere non possunt quos ad sensum miserrimae condicionis egestatis extraema traxerunt ; convenit prospicientibus nobis, qui parentes sumus generis humani, arbitram rebus in-t(ervenire institiam), ut, quod speratum diu humanitas ipsi praestare non patuit, ad commune omnium tem-peramentum remediis provisionis nostrae conferatur. § Et huius quidem causae, quantum communis omnium consequentia recognoscit et ipsarum rerum fides clamat, paene sera prospectio est, dum hu-

20. c spe consilia molinur aut remedia inventa cohibemus, ut quod expectandum fuit per iura naturalia, in gravissimis depraehensa delictis ipsa se emendaret humanitas; longe melius erstimantes non ferud-ae direptionis notas a communibus indiciis ipsorum sensu adque arbitrio submoveri, quos restitui-e in potiora praecipites et in publicum nefas quadam animorum caecitate erogades inimicos sint-gulis et luniversis reos atrocissimae inhumanitatis generis noxa debiterat. § Ad remedia igitur i-

25. am diu rerum necessitate desiderata prorumpimus, et securi quidem querellarum, ne ut intempesti-ba aut superflua medellae nostrae intervendus vel apud improbos levior aut vilior estimare-tur, qui tot annorum reticentiam nostram praecipuinem modaestiae sentientes sequi tamen no-

238 DIOCLETIAN'S EDICT, "DE PRETIIS RERUM VENALIUM."

luerunt. § Quis enim adeo obtunsi pectoris et a sensu humanitatis extorris est, qui ignorare
possit, innuo non senserit in venalibus rebus, quae vel in mercimoniis aguntur vel diurna urbium

30. conversatione tractantur, in tantum se licentiam diffusisse pretiorum, ut effrenata libido
rapien(di nec re)rum copia nec amorum ubertatibus mitigaretur? ut plane eiusmodi homines, quos haec
officia exercitos habent, dubitum non sit semper pendere animis, etiam de siderum motibus auras ip-
sas tempestatesque captare, neque iniquitati sua perpeti posse ad spem frugum futurarum innodari

super(is in/ri)bus arva felicia; ut qui detrimentum sui existiment caeli ipsius temperamentis abun-
35. dantiam rebus provenire. Et quibus semper studium est in quaestum trahere etiam beneficia divina, ac
publicae felicitatis affluentiam stringere rursusque tuni steril[itate de seminum] iactibus, adqu-
e institorum officiis vendinari; qui singuli mariuis divitis diffluentes, quae etiam populos adfatim explere potuissent, consectentur peculia et lucratrices centesimatis prosequuntur; co-
rum ataritiae modum statui, probinciales nostri, communis humanitatis ratio persuadet.

40. § Sed iam etiam ip-as causas, quarum necessitas tamden pro[ferre nimis] diu prolatan patientiam compulit, explicare debemus, ut—quamlis difficile sit toto orbae avaritiam saevientem speculi argumento vel
facto potius revelari—iustior tamen intelegatur remedii constitutio, cum intempera-
tissimi homines mentium suarum indomi(tas cupi)[ditus desig]nationem quadam et notis cogni-
tur agnoscere. § Quis ergo nesciat utilitatibus publicis insidiatricem audaciam, quatencunque

45. exercitus nostros dirigi commums omnium salus postulat, non per vicos modo aut oppida, sed in o-
mni itinere animo sectionis occurrere, praetia venalium rerum non quadruplo aut oc[tuplo, sed i]-
(ta extor)huere ut (nomina estim)[rat]onis et facti explicare humanae linguae ratio non possit? denique
interdum distractione luminis rei donatiho militem stipendioque privari?, et omnem totius orbis ad sus-
tinendos exercitus collationem detestandis quaestibus diripientium cedere! ut [universum me]-

50. (sem m)ilitiae suae et emeritos labores milites nostri sectorius omnium conferre videantur, quo
depraedato(res) ipsius reipublicae tantum in dies rapiant, quantum habere s[tat]uant.
§ His omnibus, quae supra comprehensa sunt, iuste ac merito permoti, cum iam ipsa humanitas deprecari videretur, non pretia venalium rerum—neque enim fieri id iustum putatur, cum (p)lurimae interdum probinciae felicitatae optatae viliatis et velut quodam affluentiae privilegio glorientur—sed

55. modum statuendum esse censuimus; ut, cum vis aliqua caritatis emergeret—quod dii omen avertent!—

TRANSLATION.*

The national honor and the dignity and majesty of Rome demand that the fortune of our State—to which, next to the immortal gods, we may, in memory of the wars which we have successfully waged, return thanks for the tranquil and profoundly quiet condition of the world—be also faithfully administered and duly endowed with the blessings of that peace for which we have laboriously striven; to the end that we, who under the gracious favor of the gods have repressed the furious depredations, in the past, of barbarous tribes by the destruction of those nations themselves, may hedge about this peace, established forever, with the defences which justice demands. For, if those practices by which raging avarice, that knows no bounds, is inflamed, an avarice which, without regard for the human race, not yearly or monthly or daily only, but almost hourly and even momently, hastens towards its own development and increase, were checked by any spirit of self-restraint; or if the common weal could with patience endure this reckless madness, by which, under its unhappy star, it is from day to day outrageously wounded; peradventure there would seem to be room left for shutting our eyes and holding our peace, since the common patience of men's minds would ameliorate this detestable enormity and pitiable condition.

But, since it is the sole desire of untamed fury to feel no love for the ties of our common humanity; and since among the wicked and lawless it is held to be a religious duty, as it were, of avarice which grows and swells with fierce heats, in harrying the fortunes of all, to desist of necessity rather than voluntarily; and since they whom extreme poverty has driven to a sense of their most wretched condition cannot longer keep their eyes shut; it suits us, who are the watchful parents of the whole human race, that justice step in as an arbiter in the case, in order that the long hoped for result, which humanity could not achieve by itself, may be conferred on the common disposition of all by the remedies which our forethought suggests.

And of this matter, it is true, as the common knowledge of all recognizes and indisputable facts themselves proclaim, the considera-

---

* The style of this preamble is in the last degree verbose and obscure; à peine intelligible dans certains passages, as Waddington says. There are some clauses which we do not pretend to understand. We have had the benefit, in our translation, of several suggestions from Professor J. B. Greenough, who is, however, in no way responsible for our work.

tion is almost too late, since we form plans or delay discovered remedies in the hope that, as was to be expected from natural justice, humanity, detected in most odious crimes, might work out its own reformation; for we thought it far better that the censure of intolerable robbery should be removed from the court of public opinion by the feeling and decision of those men themselves, who rush daily from bad to worse, and in a sort of blindness of mind tend towards crimes against society, and whom, enemies alike to individuals and to the community, guilty of most atrocious inhumanity, their gross criminality had exposed to punishment.

Therefore we proceed promptly to apply the remedies long demanded by the necessity of the case, and that too, feeling no concern about complaints, lest our corrective interference, as coming unseasonably or unnecessarily, may be considered cheaper or less valuable even in the eyes of the wicked, who, seeing in our silence of so many years a lesson in self-restraint, nevertheless refused to follow it.

For who has so dull a breast, or is so alien to the feeling of humanity, that he can be ignorant, say rather that he has not seen with his own eyes, that in commodities which are bought and sold in markets or handled in the daily trade of cities, extravagance in prices has gone so far that the unbridled lust of plunder could be moderated neither by abundant supplies nor fruitful seasons? so that there is clearly no doubt that men of this sort, whom these occupations have engaged, are always mentally calculating and even anticipating from the motions of the stars the very winds and seasons, and by reason of their wickedness cannot bear that the fruitful fields be watered by the rains of heaven, so as to give hope of future crops, since they consider it a personal loss for abundance to come to the world by the favorable moods of the sky itself. And to the avarice of those who are always eager to turn to their own profit even the blessings of God, and to check the tide of general prosperity, and again in an unproductive year to haggle about the sowing of the seed and the business of retail dealers; who, individually possessed of immense fortunes which might have enriched whole peoples to their heart's content, seek private gain and are bent upon ruinous percentages;—to their avarice, regard for common humanity persuades us, people of our provinces, to set a limit.

But now, further, we must set forth the reasons themselves, whose urgency has at last compelled us to discard our too long protracted patience, in order that—although an avarice which runs riot through the whole world can with difficulty be laid bare by a specific proof, or rather fact—nevertheless, the nature of our remedy may be known to be more just, when most lawless men are compelled to recognize, under a certain name and description, the unbridled desires of their minds.

Who therefore can be ignorant that an audacity that plots against the good of society presents itself with a spirit of speculation, wherever the general welfare requires our armies to be directed, not only in villages and towns, but on every march? that it forces up the prices of commodities not four-fold or eight-fold, but to such a degree that human language cannot find words to express the valuation and the transaction? finally, that sometimes by the outlay upon a single thing the soldiery are robbed of their largesses and the pay which they receive? and that the entire contributions of the whole world for maintaining armies accrue to the detestable gains of plunderers, so that our soldiers seem to yield the entire fruit of their military career, and the labors of their entire term of service to these universal speculators, in order that the plunderers of the commonwealth may from day to day seize all that they resolve to have?

Being justly and duly moved by all these considerations above included, since already humanity itself seemed to pray for release, we resolved, not that the prices of commodities should be fixed—for it is not thought just that this be done, since sometimes very many provinces exult in the good fortune of the low prices they desire, and as it were in a sort of privileged state of abundance—but that a maximum should be fixed; in order that, when any stress of high prices made its appearance—which omen we prayed the gods might avert—[avarice might be checked, etc.]

COMMENT.

6. The substitution of *debitis* for the DIBITUM of the stone is violent, but seems almost certain. The S before *saepiamus* in *S* is given by both Waddington and Mommsen. According to Bankes's facsimile of *S*, for whose accuracy Waddington vouches, the neighboring lines of that text have, in the space corresponding to that between *qui*- and *saepiamus*, from 23 to 28 letters; in *–etem debitis iustitiae munimentis* there are 30 letters.

14. *existimatur: S* has ---*matur*. *A* has, according to Waddington, --*stimatur*; according to Mommsen, ---*estimatur*.

17–18. *intervenire:* wanting in *S*. *A* has, according to Waddington, INTO---; according to Mommsen, INTO---.

34. *inbribus arra:* wanting in S. A has been read by all editors ---*ros arra.* ROS is, on that stone, an easy blunder of the lapidary for BUS. Or possibly the letters have been misread.

37. *institorum:* substituted from S for the nonsensical INSTITUTORUM of the stone.

37–38. *adfatim:* S has ad---. A has *adfaciam.* Mommsen restored *adfatim* in *C.I.L.*, III².

47. *extorquere:* S has, according to Waddington, --- *uere;* according to Mommsen, ---*atuere.* Wanting in A.

estimationis: wanting in S. A has, according to Waddington, ---*ionis;* according to Mommsen, ---*monis.*

49–50. *messem:* suggested by Professor J. E. B. Mayor. We had thought of *assem,* which is not so good.

52. *cum:* S has *ut cum.* The *ut* is not wanted.

The orthography of the foregoing inscription differs considerably from the classical standard, and it should be noted that the three copies of this preamble now known present numerous variations in the spelling of individual words. Following is a list of the non-classical spellings in the legible portions of our stone, the frequency of which in the inscriptions of this period justifies their retention in our minuscule text:

e for *ae:* estima*ti*onis (47). *ae* for *e:* extraema (16). *ae* for *e:* finae (7), sortae (10), adquae (15), deprachensa (21), quae (33), orbae (41), praetia (46), felicitatae (54).

h wrongly added: huniversis (24), hunius (48). *h* omitted: debaecandi (10).

b for *v:* abaritiae (13), intempestibo (26), abaritiae, probinciales (39), quambis (41), donatibo (48), probinciae (54). *v* for *b:* lavores (50). We have ventured to write *ucertatibus* (31) and *sectoricus* (50), thinking that the omission of a letter adjacent to *u* was thus most easily explained.

qu for *c:* quonivere (15).

np for *mp:* inprobos (14), tenpestates (33), senper (35), conprehensa (52). *nb* for *mb:* inbribus (34). *nm* for *mm:* inmodestos (14), inmo (29). *nd* for *nd:* tandem (40). *ns* for *ns:* obtumsi (28). *n* inserted: consenetentur (38).

d for *t:* adquae (15).

The substitution of *i* for *e:* dibitum (6), dilictis (21), medillae (26), tenpestatis (33), iusti (52); of *e* for *i:* reticende (11), singules (24); the improper addition and omission of final *m:* conscientiam

(19), conversationem (30), collatione (49); and the omission of *n* in desiderant (4) and festinant (? 9), can be extensively paralleled and need not be set down as mere lapidary's blunders; but we have not ventured to retain these spellings in the minuscule text. So also some of the many cases of *u* for *o* and *o* for *u* have a considerable justification in contemporary usage; but, as the forms of *u* and *o* rendered them liable to confusion and, as several unquestionable instances of confusion occur on our stone, we have thought it best to restore in all cases the standard spelling. iusticiae (6) may afford an early instance of *ei* for *ti*, but is most safely regarded as a blunder. On all these points see Seelmann, *Die Aussprache des Latein*.

The following blunders are easily explained: *n* for *o*: nus (4), inprobus, inmodestus (14), exercitus (32), emeritus (50), nustra (18), nustrae (26), nustram (27), nustri (39), cunvenit (16), cunferatur (18), cummunibus (22), surtae (10), donatibu (48). *o* for *u*: dio (25), nondinari (37), caosas (40) ot (41), mentiorn (43), putator (53).

s for *f*: sundatam (6).

c for *t*: iusticiae (6), coto (41), cenpestatei (33), seatui (39). tcunferatur (18) is due to the stone-cutter's mistaking *c* for *t* and then discovering his mistake before beginning the next letter.

e for *o*: religie (14). *e* for *g*: acnoscere (44). *e* for *c*: emeritos (50). *e* for *c*: continentiae (9). *y* for *e*: ligentiam (10).

a for *b*: pualicum (23), oatumsi (28), pualicae (36). *d* for *b*: indribus (34), adaritiae (39). *i* for *d*: detestaniam (11). In debaccanidi (10), idirigi (45) and idepraedatores (51), *d* was probably mistaken for *i* and the mistake at once discovered; *cf.* tconferatur (18).

Letter doubled: aearitia (7). Double letter reduced to single: *tranquill orbi statu* (3), *officis* (37), and perhaps *aertatibus* (31) and *sectorius* (50).

Other omissions: *pacn* (8), *glicentis* (13), *tt* (27) for *tot*, *fluentiam* (36) for *afluentiam*, *estimonis* (47) for *estimationis*.

Letters transposed: *ahbere* (13), *superflou* (26).

The following blunders are more flagrant:

gentrum (5) for *gentium*, *dibitum* (6) for *debitis*, *ardat* (7) for *ardet*, *qui* (7) for *quae* or *qua*, *promisionis* (18) for *provisionis*, *epe* (20) for *spe*, *ferendare* (22) for *ferendae*, *superillou* (26) for *superfluo*, *institutorum* (37) for *institorum*, *seatii* (39) for *statui*, NN (10) for MN, *inteplegatur* (42) for *intellegatur*, *mentiora* (43) for *mentium*, *aenosdeBe*[1]

---

[1] The penultimate letter seems to have been first made as a *b* and then changed to a *p*, or *vice versa*.

(44) for *agnoscere, interdam* (48) for *interdum, detesdandis* (49) for *detestandis, censuamus* (55) for *censuimus*. Add the meaningless characters, some of which are not even letters, in lines 41 and 42, in place of *difficile sit* and *revelari*, and the meaningless leaf in line 32.

Some of these monstrosities look as if the stone-cutter knew little or no Latin.

It deserves notice that the fragments of this edict previously found in Greece, viz., at Gythion, Geronthrai, Megara, Karystos, Thebes, Lebadeia, Thespiai and Elateia,[2] are all in Greek.

J. C. ROLFE,
F. B. TARBELL.

REPORT ON EXCAVATIONS AT PLATAIA IN 1889.

In December 1888, the Greek Government granted to the American School a concession to carry on excavations in Boiotia, at Plataia, Anthedon and Thisbe. Work was to begin in the latter half of February 1889. Accordingly, Professor Tarbell, Mr. Buck and Dr. Rolfe examined the sites, and decided to begin work at Anthedon and to proceed next to Thisbe.

On March 29, I set out with Professor Tarbell for Thebes and Thisbe, at which latter place Dr. Rolfe was at that time digging. From Thebes I visited the site of ancient Plataia and decided upon beginning trial excavations at once. The drawback of Plataia as a field for excavation is the great extent of the ground and the confusing number of vestiges of ancient remains. But, though this adds to the uncertainty of making definite finds, it also increases the probability of discovering some objects of interest. Moreover, I felt that our efforts could in no event be wasted; as, even if no objects of artistic or epigraphic importance should be discovered, a careful study of the site would be a great addition to topography, as it soon became evident that all previous work in this direction had been insufficient. With this in reserve, I have set as my highest aim the discovery of the ancient temple of Hera or of some other edifice of similar importance, such as the temple of Athena Areia, or the temple of Demeter. Meanwhile, through the exertions of Mr. Wesley Harper, Dr. Lamborn and Mr. H. G.

[2] See *C.I.L.*, III², pp. 812-23; *Ephemeris Epigraphica*, IV, p. 180, and V, pp. 87-91; *Bull. de corr. hellén.*, IX (1885), pp. 222-39.

Marquand, a sufficient sum had been collected to warrant the undertaking of this work.

On March 31, I joined Professor Tarbell and Dr. Rolfe at Thisbe, and the next day we proceeded to Plataia and began work on April 2 with 63 men. Our plan was to dig at numerous points in the hope of finding some index for concentrated work in the future. There are, on the upper and lower portions of this extensive site, nine Byzantine churches. As, in the building of such churches, fragments of earlier structures and monuments were generally used, we decided to dig in and about these ruins. We therefore divided the workmen into three parties. Professor Tarbell and Dr. Rolfe will give their notes in their own words. The objects found were chiefly inscriptions, which will be published separately by these two gentlemen.

April 2. I began by clearing away the *débris* from the ruined church just below the lower city on the north side facing Thebes, by digging a trench between two rocky projections on the hill near the church, which, it appeared to me, might have occupied the site of a gate. In digging here, as indeed, in all of the churches, care was taken not needlessly to destroy traces of Byzantine work—a practice which future explorers ought rigorously to maintain. One fragmentary inscription was found among the *débris* of this church; but no trace of further antique work; nor was there any trace of a gate at this spot. Work at the first church was continued, and then a church within the city-walls on the north side, nearest the northern limit, was examined. In the latter was found a fragmentary inscription of a few letters on dark stone; and trenches dug about this church showed extensive Byzantine walls.

April 3. We began to clear a church about the centre of the lower city toward the east, where inscriptions (already known) on drums of columns were above ground: no results. Work was interrupted by rain. An hour in the evening was utilized in clearing away rubbish from a small church by the well on the road leading to the village on the west of the city-wall. A small sepulchral relief of Graeco-Roman period was found here, but no further work of art.

April 4. We continued digging to a considerable depth in the central church, and cleared some Byzantine walls around it. In the afternoon, took all the workmen to top of lower city to work in and about the church where Professor Tarbell had previously dug. I was subsequently joined by Dr. Rolfe. On the following day, we cleared away and dug down to the pavement, occasionally below it, in this church. The ground-plan here published (see *Fig.*) has been kindly drawn by Mr. Schultz of the British School at Athens. The only additions I have to make to his plan of this interesting three-apsed church is a staircase, which could be distinctly made out during the digging, leading down to the southeast corner of the southern apse. The egg-and-dart pattern on the *geisa* used as door-posts on the west and south sides is of good workmanship and belonged to an earlier classic building, probably the same as the one from which came a fine marble moulding immured in the well on the road. The marble architrave-blocks are also of good workman-

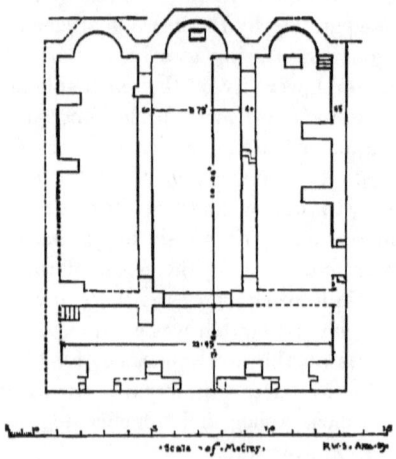

Plataia. *Ground-plan of Byzantine church.*

ship. There had probably been an extensive classic building near this site. But I am inclined to believe that the church in its present condition was built in Frankish times, as a fine piece of Byzantine marble screen-work was immured in the southwest corner of the wall. The inscriptions here found will be published subsequently. The inscription recording the heroization of Moscheina was found in an upright position in the west wall; while the fragment of the Edict of Diocletian was part of the pavement running under the southern wall at the beginning of the middle apse.

CHARLES WALDSTEIN.

April 2. I began work, with eighteen men, at a ruined Byzantine church to the N. E. of the city, outside the walls. Trenches were dug both within and without, but nothing of importance was found. On the same day, I made a beginning of clearing the westernmost of the churches in the lower (northern) division of the ancient city, but without results.

April 3. After working an hour on the last-named church, I moved to another, just outside the upper division of the city on the east side, said to be named "Ἅγιος Δημήτριος. Some late inscriptions were found here.   F. B. TARBELL.

April 2. I began work, with twenty-one men, in a ruined Byzantine church, situated on a low elevation east of the city-walls as usually defined, but within the long eastern wall extending from the northern slope of Kithairon. The name of the church was given me as "Ἅγιος Νικόλας. In the interior of the church, were found two inscribed tombstones and some fragments of inscriptions. In the apse of the church, digging was carried as far as the pavement, which was examined. At the sides, where the pavement was gone, a depth of 3 m. was reached, and some graves, with human bones, were found. Trenches were also dug up to and around the church on the northern, southern, and western sides.

April 3. Work was continued at the same church until noon, when it was suspended on account of rain. In the front of the church, at a depth of 2 m., were found two fragments of reliefs of poor Roman workmanship; also a fragment of a marble plinth with the toes of one foot, fairly well executed.

April 4. Work proceeded during the morning at a church west of the city-walls, close to the spring, which had been cleared of *débris* the day before. Trenches were dug around the church and the interior was cleared out, but we were unable to go very deep on account of the water, which was reached at the depth of half a meter. Nothing was found in this church. At noon, I took my men to the southern part of the town, where trenches were cut until (at 4 p. m.) I joined forces with Dr. Waldstein.

                                                                J. C. ROLFE.

DISCOVERIES AT PLATAIA IN 1889.

INSCRIPTIONS FROM PLATAIA.

The following inscriptions were found at Plataia in April 1889. Those to which *R* or *T* is prefixed are edited on the basis of Mr. Rolfe's or Mr. Tarbell's copies alone.

I.—Marble stele with akroterion and two rosettes, found in the foundation-walls of the ruined church "Ἅγιος Νικόλαος, outside the city-walls, to the east. Height, including akroterion, 0.88 m.; breadth, 0.53 m.; thickness, 0.17 m.; height of letters, 0.03 m.

   ΛΙΓΥΡΟΝ   Λίγυρον

The name occurs, with the regular Boiotian spelling, at Tanagra, and there also, as it happens, in the accusative (Λίγουρον : COLLITZ, 1053). For examples of the simple accusative on gravestones, see *Inscriptions from Anthedon, No. XLV.*

Just below the ΛΙΓΥΡΟΝ a second inscription is carelessly cut by another hand, and probably at a considerably later date. The letters are about 0.02 m. in height.

   ΕΠΙ
   ΟΡѠΑΕΔΕΙ

Repeated examination of the stone and of a squeeze has convinced us that this reading is certain in every letter. That there were other letters at the beginning or end of the last line is not impossible, but no distinct traces of any can be seen. This line should give a proper name, but is wholly unintelligible to us.

II.—R. Slab of coarse marble, found in same church. Height, 0.64 m.; breadth, 0.51 m.; thickness, 0.25 m.; height of letters, 0.05 m.

   ΕΠΙ   Ἐπὶ
   ΣΩΤΑ   Σωτᾶ

III.—Marble block, found in the most western of the ruined churches within the walls of Plataia. Height, 0.335 m.; length, 0.94 m.; thickness, 0.525 m.; height of letters, 0.0475 m. The block had been hollowed out into a trough on the reverse side. On one of the narrow sides is a builder's mark, Σ.

ΗΠΟΛΙΣ ΗΡΩΙΣΣΑΝ
ΜΟΣΧΕΙΝΑΝΑΡΙΣΤΙΩΝΟΣ
Ἡ πόλις ἡρῶσσαν | Μοσχεῖναν Ἀριστίωνος

" The city (erected this statue of the) heroine (i. e., demi-deified lady) Moscheina, (daughter) of Aristion."

IV.—R. Part of marble block, hollowed out into a trough on the inscribed side; found in same church. Height, 0.53 m.; length, 0.77 m.; thickness, 0.7 m.; height of letters, 0.03 m.

ΑΝΔΡ   ἀνδρ-
ΕΛ   ἐλ-
ΤΥΜΕ   τύμ(β)[ο-
ΚΟ   κο-

Fragment of sepulchral distichs.

V.—T. Block of white marble, found in central apse of same church. The upper right-hand corner and the lower end are gone. The front is ornamented with a simple panel. The inscription is at the top. Height, 1.16 m.; breadth, 0.4 m.; thickness, 0.16 m.

ΥΣ ΤΟΝΙΩ   Ὑς τὸν [τῶν
ΚΑΝΚΕΛΛΩΝΚΟΙ   κανκέλλων κό[σ-
ΜΟΝ   μον

" For the adornment of the screen."

The first two letters are twice as high as the rest. The spelling ὑς for εἰς would point to a date not earlier than the ninth century A. D.[1]

VI.—R. Marble slab, found in pavement of same church.

Ε   Ἐ[πὶ
ΚΑΛΛΙ   Καλλι-

VII.—T. Fragment of white marble, found in a heap of stones near this church; complete at top, surface chipped away to the extent of three or four letters at left, broken off at right and below; letters very indistinct. Height, 0.26 m.; breadth at top, 0.26 m.; thickness, 0.06 m.

[1] BLASS, Aussprache d. griech.(3), p. 42, Note 108a.

OK I M I O Σ
Σ OM I KOY Ϛ
uncut] Δ O Λ I X ␣
Π A Ϝ Θ E N O
\ H A Π E P I
uncut] T
/////OY
////////
uncut]//
Λ Y Σ I

Apparently a list of victors in gymnastic contests. The word in the sixth line, therefore, was probably πάλην, παγκράτιον, or πένταθλον.

VIII.—T. Fragment of white marble, found near same church; complete at left only. Height, 0.14 m.; breadth, 0.145 m.; thickness, 0.06 m.

Π I C Ω   Ἐ]πὶ Σω-
E Π I E B I '   Ἐπὶ Ἐ-

IX.—Marble block, found face uppermost in the apse of the ruined church "Άγιος Δημήτριος, just outside the city-wall on the east, near the upper (southern) end; broken off at the left. Height, 0.58 m.; length, 1.45 m.; thickness, 0.19 m.

A Γ Y N A I K ω N   -α γυναικῶν
Λ A M A I C Π O C I O C   πα]λάμαις πόσιος
ˉE P A C A Ξ I O N ω M E Γ A . A I P I C   γ]έρας ἄξιον, ᾧ μέγα [χ]αίρις
X O N E Y P A M E N H   -χον εὐραμένη
Ξ ω C A N Θ E . N I Λ A C K O N T O   -ς ὡς ἂν θε[ὸ]ν ἱλάσκοντο
T E Δ A M N Ϟ M E N H N   τε δαμναμένην
\ Π A N T F . E I N O Δ E I T A I C   -ν πάντε[σσ]ιν ὁ δείταις
E K Λ E I C E ␣ / P A C   ἔκλεισε [θ]ύρας.

These are the ends of sepulchral distichs. Professor F. D. ALLEN has kindly furnished the following, as a suggestion of the general sense of the original:

μνῆμα τόδ' εὔτυκτον, Κλεοβούλη, δί]α γυναικῶν,
εἴργασται κεδνοῦ ταῖς πα]λάμαις πόσιος.
εἰκόνα δ'ἔστησεν, γ]έρας ἄξιον, ᾧ μέγα [χ]αίρις,
τιμὴν σῆς ἀρετῆς δίπτυ]χον εὐραμένη.

πάντες γάρ σε βροτοὶ ζ]ῶσαν θε[ὸ]ν ἱλάσκοντο,
νῦν δὲ σέβουσι νόσῳ κηρί] τε δαμναμένην,
τύμβον ἀγαζόμενοι δῆλο]ν πάντε[σσ]ιν ὁδείταις,
τοῦ γαμέτης στυγναῖς χερσὶν] ἔκλεισε [θ]ύρας.

X.—T. Marble block, found in same position as No. IX; broken off at the right. Height, 0.51 m.; length, 0.51 m.; thickness, 0.13 m.

ΕΝΠ
ΠΟ
ΟΣΜΕ
ΘΗ

The beginnings of distichs, similar to the foregoing.

XI.—Marble stele, with anthemion and rosettes; found in same church. Height of letters, 0.35–40 m., and, in fourth line, 0.25–30 m.

Above the rosettes:

  ΕΠΙ   Ἐπὶ
 ΑΦΡΟΔΙΣΙΑ   Ἀφροδισίᾳ

below the rosettes:

 ΔΙΟΝΥΣΙΟΥ   Διονυσίου.
 ΑΘΑΝΙΧΑ   Ἀθανίχα.

"Over Aphrodisia, (daughter) of Dionysios."
The name *Athanicha* was added subsequently.

XII.—T. Marble fragment, found in same church.

  ΤΥΧΙΚΟΥΣ
   ΣΜΟΝ

        F. B. TARBELL,
        J. C. ROLFE.

AN INSCRIBED TOMBSTONE FROM BOIOTIA.

The tombstone which is described below was shown me by a peasant of the village of Charadrás, on the road from Thebes to Thisbe. He had found it near the village, and removed it to his house; the inscription, he said, had not been copied.

The stone, which is of marble, is of a peculiar shape, consisting in one piece of a base, 0.23 m. high and 0.28 wide, surmounted by a circular stele, with a rounded top, 0.34 m. high, and 0.495 in circumference, as here represented.

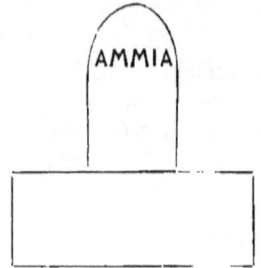

The inscription, in letters 0.02 m. high, is cut on the stele as follows:

AMMIA   Ἀμμία

The name occurs frequently in Attic inscriptions (*C.I.A.*, III, 712a, 2891, 2986a, 2897, 2898), and in a list of names found at Hermione (*C.I.G.*, 1211).

Rounded steles are very common. Of these Ross (*Arch. Aufsätze*, I, p. 26) says: *Vielleicht Andeutung des Phallos? Die böotischen Grabsteine, in Form viereckige Altäre, sind häufig mit einem Phallos gekrönt, z. b. in Thisbe und Lebadeia.* I saw nothing of the kind at Thisbe, and I have been able to find no representations or descriptions of tombstones like this one. Professor Merriam has called my attention to a vase-painting represented in Schreiber's *Bilderatlas* (PL. XCIV, 6), but, as he remarks, the round-topped base, on which a stele shaped like ours stands, is evidently a mound on which the stele was placed.

JOHN C. ROLFE.

DISCOVERIES AT PLATAIA IN 1890.

[MAP.]

GENERAL REPORT ON THE EXCAVATIONS.

The Excavations at Plataia which were carried on during the Spring of 1890 under my direction were the continuation of our work on the same site in the preceding year. The funds for these excavations during the two seasons were procured for me by personal friends in America, namely, Dr. Lamborn and Mr. Wesley Harper. The students of the School who took part in the work were Messrs. W. I. Hunt and H. S. Washington of Yale, J. P. Shelley of Findlay College, Ohio, H. D. Hale of Harvard, C. M. Washington of Yale, and J. F. Gray of Harvard.

As stated in my Report last year, the immediate aim of the expedition for this year was not so much actual excavation as topographical work. I desired, in the first place, to make a careful and final survey of the walls enclosing the ancient city of Plataia, and also to study the site of the battle-field of Plataia. The survey of the walls was carried on chiefly under the direction of Mr. H. S. Washington, the maps being drawn by Mr. H. D. Hale. Mr. Hale's map together with Mr. Washington's Report of the work will follow this introduction.[1] A paper on the topography of the battle-field of Plataia

---

[1] On the whole, we have found our own investigations as regards the site of ancient Plataia and the relations of the various walls to one another to agree most with VISCHER'S views (*Erinnerungen und Eindrücke aus Griechenland*, pp. 219, 543). There is also some probability in favor of the hypothesis, recently expressed by FABRICIUS (*Theben, etc., Akademisches Antrittsprogramm*, Freiburg i. B., 1890, p. 17), that the stone walls as now standing were surmounted by fortifications of unburnt brick. That the whole wall (stone and brick) was covered with a uniform stucco is possible, but, I think, not probable; as I do not remember to have seen on the stones themselves traces of stucco, which would in all likelihood have survived. I may also add that one of the best maps of the Plataian district is that made by Spencer Stanhope (*Topography illustr. of the Battle of Plataea*, by JOHN SPENCER STANHOPE, London, 1817). The copy of this map in the library of the museum of archæology at Cambridge (which contains the whole of Col. Leake's library) is of especial interest, as it contains additions and corrections in pencil by Col. Leake himself.

has been written by Mr. W. I. Hunt, who, with Mr. Hale, studied the question on the spot. Mr. Hunt's paper and the results of the survey of the site, illustrated by a map drawn by Mr. Hale, will also be embodied in this Report. Professor Theodor Mommsen of Berlin, who has for years devoted himself to the study of the numerous fragments of Diocletian's Edict, and is now producing a revised edition of the whole material, was naturally the fittest person to publish the new fragment which we discovered this year in our excavations. He has consented to edit it for us, and this publication also will be included in this Report. Finally, my colleague for the coming year in the School at Athens, Professor Richardson, will, I hope, publish an interesting votive inscription to some female deity discovered by us on the same site.

It was my intention to begin work at Plataia early in February; but, as the weather was particularly unfavorable during the whole season, we had to defer our departure from day to day. I finally yielded to the enthusiastic eagerness of Mr. Washington, who left Athens on February 14, and on the 19th began digging with 22 men at the church where last year the Preamble of Diocletian's Edict was found. He was soon joined by Mr. Hunt and Mr. Shelley, and subsequently by the other students. During this time the party had to contend with great difficulties, the most trying of which was the severe weather, with snow and cold winds, in houses that were not even provided with glass windows; and I cannot sufficiently commend the self-sacrificing perseverance of all concerned. Owing to stress of weather, work had to be suspended for some days. In the first week of March, I joined the party. When not engaged in the excavations, the walls, over $2\frac{1}{2}$ miles in circumference, were carefully measured and surveyed. Mr. Hale also drew the ground-plans of six Byzantine and Frankish churches at which we dug.

Our corps of workmen was increased to a number averaging 40 men, and with these we dug at a promising site at the southeast wall of a Byzantine church and monastery, which I thought might mark an important entrance to the ancient city. Here Messrs. Hunt and Shelley came upon an interesting aqueduct or drain covered with large stones, light yellow in color, at a depth of 1.20 metre below the surface. Mr. Washington describes the stone as somewhat like *poros*, very soft when first found, but hardening on exposure. It is apparently a limestone containing gypsum and a small quantity of tale. These large stones covered terracotta drain-tiles, which are laid in trenches cut through very solid soil. The tiles are made of well-baked red clay, are 0.20 m. deep and 0.15 wide (interior measurements), and about 0.03 thick. They were joined together end to end, not overlapping, by a grey cement very neatly applied. The tiles have apparently a very gentle slope down toward the city, which is a confirmation of the supposition that they served as an aqueduct. Mr. Hunt and I explored the neighborhood for the possible source; and there is some probability that he discovered this, outside and to the south of the city-wall, at some considerable distance from the point at which we found the tiles. The aqueduct runs under the city-wall and under the church, a block of the aqueduct being cut away obliquely. It is probable that the wall was the earliest, the aqueduct the next in date, and the large church the latest.

Several inscriptions had already been found; but at this church we discovered, in a grave below the east wall, two large inscriptions used as covering stones. One turned out to be another slab of the Diocletian Edict, giving, in Greek, the prices of textiles. This contains a large portion of the 17th Chapter in Waddington's edition of the known texts, with some interesting variations, as well as a column and a half of material hitherto unpublished and unknown, constituting the beginning of the chapter. It appears to me not unlikely that the Preamble found last year and this text, though they were found within the city about a mile apart, are portions of the same document. The marble slabs are of the same material, and must originally have been of the same dimensions; and it appears probable that the Preamble remained in the original Latin, while the text, which was of practical importance to the people at large, was here posted in the Greek translation. The other Greek inscription records a dedication to some goddess on the part of women, with a list of interesting female names. From the frequent mention of a torch (δαίς), it seems not unlikely that the goddess was either Demeter or Artemis Eukleia, both which goddesses had temples at Plataia.

We continued to dig at various sites outside the city-walls, hoping to find some clue for discovering either the Temple of Demeter (and in this we followed Mr. Hunt's suggestion) or the Temple of Hera. We did not succeed in fixing these sites; though several objects of interest were discovered. Thus, for instance, on Mr. Hunt's site, a fragment of an inscription undoubtedly referring to some hippic contest, may possibly refer to the games called Eleutheria which were celebrated outside the city-walls (*cf.* Pausanias, IX. 2. 4). It may be desirable to make one more attempt, next season, upon this site, and to search again for the Temple of Hera inside the city-walls, at the church where last year we found the Edict of Diocletian. It is true that we came upon the native rock in digging in this church, but it may be desirable to continue trenches around the church, cutting them to the rock throughout. When this has been done, these explorative excavations may be considered as completed.

What seems to stand in the way of important discoveries of temples and sculptures at Plataia, is the fact of its evident importance in Byzantine and Frankish times. Our exploration has certainly taught an historical fact which seems to have been previously overlooked: for it is generally supposed that, after the classical period, Plataia sank into insignificance and oblivion. Our excavations, together with the existence of the numerous Byzantine and Frankish churches (there are over twelve scattered about the site), certainly prove that, in Byzantine and Frankish times, this must have been a densely-populated and important city. The people were probably attracted thither by the situation, which commands the Boiotian Plain; possibly, too, its walls may have remained standing. It appears to me also that Plataia must have been a centre of considerable importance in Roman times.

CHARLES WALDSTEIN.

American School of Classical Studies, Athens.
April, 1890.

DETAILED REPORT ON THE EXCAVATIONS.

Work was begun Feb. 19 with 22 men at *Church No. I* (see MAP), where two days were spent in partially clearing out the church and sinking a trench, running north, about 40 m. long. The paving-stones of the church (about 70 × 60 cm., and 20 cm. thick), of good white marble, were examined on the under side, but no sculptured work was found on them—they probably formed the pavement of a temple. Two late walls built with small stones laid in mortar were crossed by the trench, and at its northern end a low arch of brick-work, probably Byzantine, was laid bare. The trench was sunk to a depth (in places) of 2.70 m., but, with the exception of a fragment of

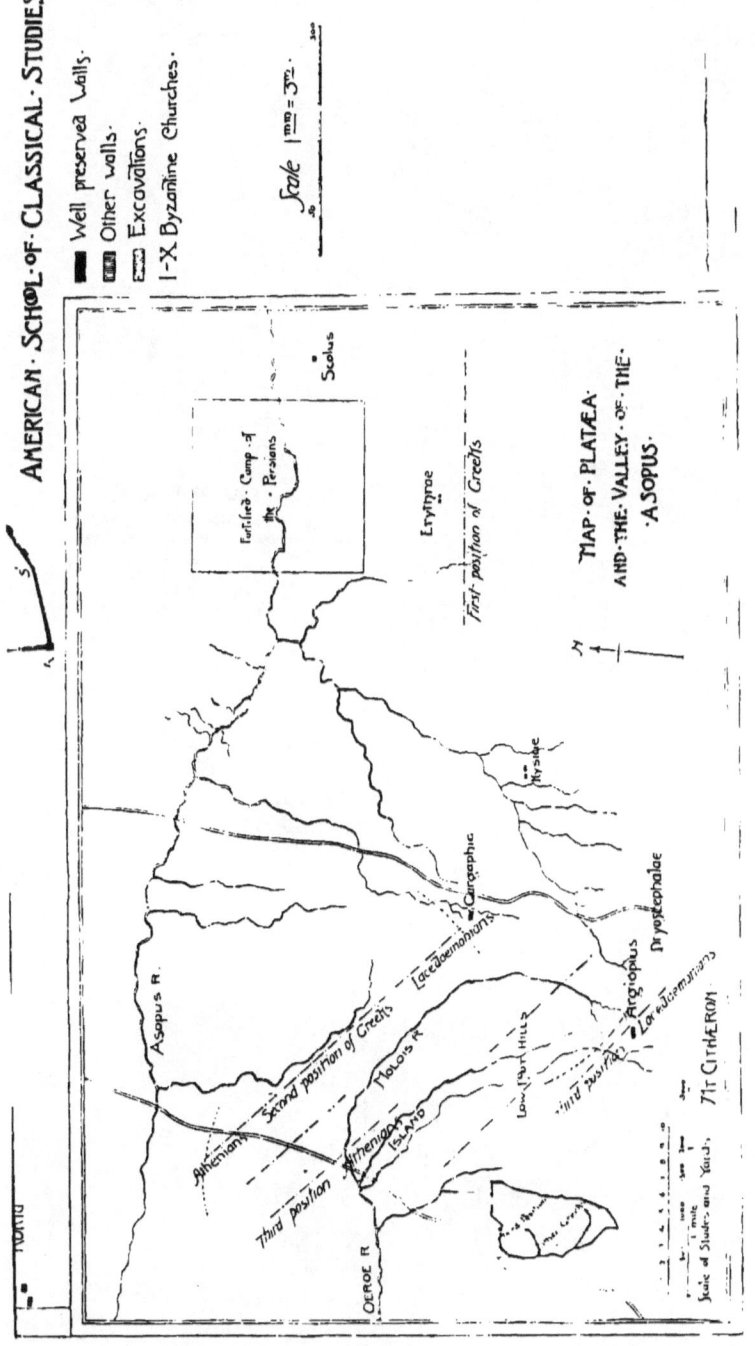

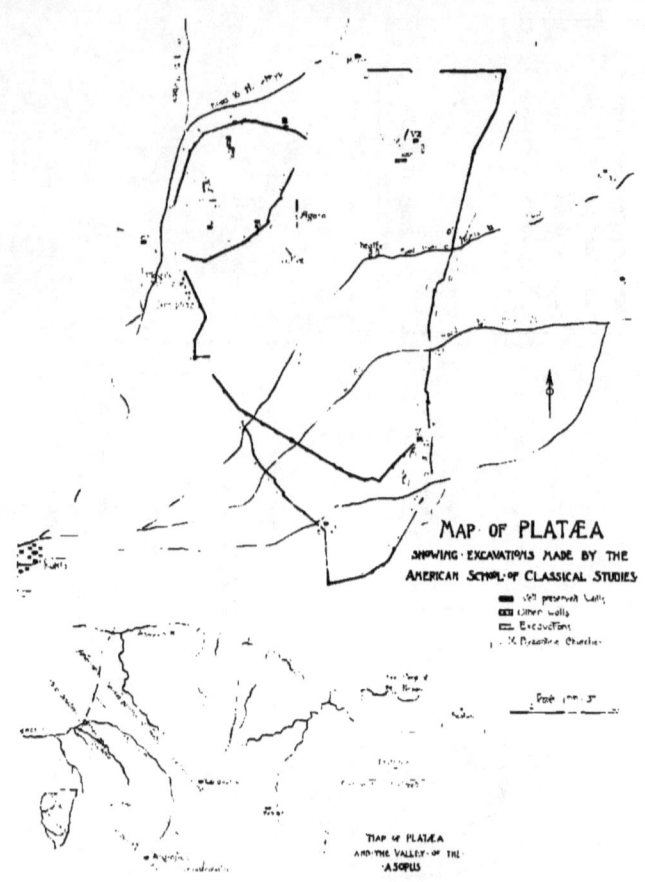

DISCOVERIES AT PLATAIA. 257

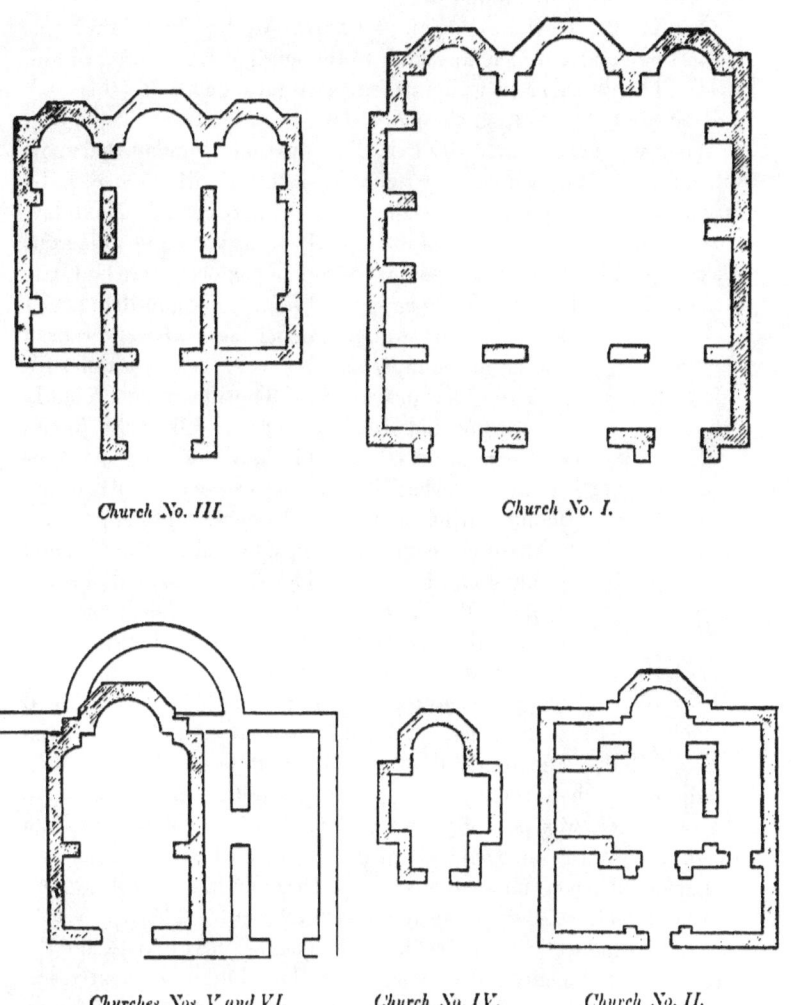

FIGURE 1.—*Ground-Plans of Byzantine Churches at Plataia* (Scale, .01 = 1 metre).

a small sepulchral stele of late Roman work, representing a man and his wife, nothing was found.

On Feb. 21, work was begun at *Church No. V*. The church was cleared out, and a trench was sunk to the south of it running east and west. The upper cross-wall was traversed (at a depth of 50 cm.) at a distance of 37 cm. from the point *W'*.

Work was not resumed till Feb. 25, a feast-day, Sunday, and snow intervening. We then went on upon the same site with 25 men, and a larger apse, surrounding the smaller one, was uncovered.[1] Next day, with 30 men, the church-walls were partly torn down and numerous graves opened. The covering-stones of the "aqueduct" were laid bare (1.20 m. below the surface) for the space of 8 m. The aqueduct passes under the city-wall and under the southeast corner of the larger church, running W. S. W. A section of it is here given (*Figure 2*). The top stones, roughly cut (of unequal size, but averaging about 60–70 cm. each way, and 40 cm. thick), are of a light yellow stone, somewhat like the *poros:* very soft when first found, but hardening on exposure. It is apparently a limestone, containing gypsum and a little talc, and comes doubtless from a ridge on which stands a small chapel, about two kilometers to the east of the city, toward the north from the Vergoutiani spring, near Argiopios. These covering-stones are not closely fitted, in places the holes left at the joints being filled with stones. Several have their edges bevelled, and apparently they were brought from some building.

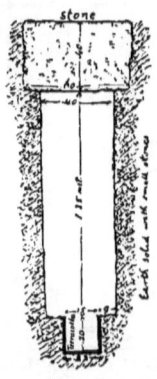

FIG. 2.
Section of Aqueduct.

At the place where the aqueduct passed under the upper cross-wall, the cavity left was partially protected against earth falling in by a rough block of the same stone tilted against the wall; while at the west end, where it passes under the corner of the church, the block was cut away obliquely to make room for the church-wall. This apparently proves that the wall was the earliest, the aqueduct next in date, and the larger church the latest. The trench was followed up subsequently, but to the west of the church only three of the covering-stones were found,

---

[1] There were two churches at the point where the aqueduct was found, the smaller one built on the site of the larger one. The builders of the smaller church knew of the larger, for the chord subtending the apse was the same in both churches (see *Figure 1, Churches Nos. V and VI*).

which apparently had fallen in, as they were lying irregularly. The aqueduct could be traced, however, by the terracotta drain-tiles at the bottom, and by its sides in the hard soil. It had no made walls, being cut through a very solid soil, composed of small irregular stones cemented by a clay-like earth, apparently virgin soil. The drain-tiles at the bottom are of well-baked red clay, like three sides of a rectangle in section (⊔), the pieces being 60 cm. long, 20 deep and 15 wide (interior measurements), and about 3 cm. thick. These tiles were joined together, end to end (not overlapping), by a gray cement, very neatly applied. The aqueduct was filled with earth to a depth of something like 80 cm., and when this was cleared out was found to have a very gentle slope down toward the west, i. e., into the town.

The next day (Feb. 27), with 30 men, work was proceeded with at the same place, and bed-rock was found at a depth of 3 m., in the larger apse. Several graves were opened, and in them were found quite a number of rough Byzantine lamps and small jars and vases. No further work was done until March 6 (owing to bad weather, feast-days and strikes), on which date 21 men came from Kriekouki and two trenches were sunk, at right angles, inside the ruined church above the Vergoutiani spring, and an inscription was found. Work was also done at *Church No. V.* Next day we worked at a spot north by west from Vergoutiani, where lie a number of large cut blocks (about 1.20 × 1.00 × 0.30 m.) of a coarse marble breccia. Three or four trenches were cut to virgin soil, but with no result. In the afternoon, two trenches were sunk at the ruins of a small church of St. Demetrios to the east of Plataia and northwest of Vergoutiani. The only thing found was part of a small and late smooth column (24 cm. high, 15 wide, and 8 thick) with an inscription. The same day a tombstone was found at *Church No. V.* Two days were spent in sinking two trenches 50 m. long to the south of *Church No. VIII*, running east and west. They were carried (one 1.20 m. and the other 1 m.) to virgin soil, but with no result except the exposing of three or four Byzantine walls of small stones and mortar. Lying on the surface, near the middle of the northern one, was found a block of cut stone (90 × 50 × 30 cm.) with the characters ΔΓ roughly cut on its upper surface near the middle. The characters are about 10 cm. high. To the south of this trench was uncovered part of a rough platform, a few centimetres below the surface, probably of Byzantine origin. A trench running north and south was dug to the east of

Church No. VIII, and uncovered a corner of the wall of some building, made of large roughly-cut stones, one of which measured 1.20 m. long, 70 cm. deep, and 40 cm. thick. They were only one course deep, however, and, after a few blocks in each side, became merged in a late wall of smaller stones. Some additional work was done in clearing out *Church No. I*, where a well was discovered, the brim being beneath the floor-level (about 6 m. deep and 1 wide), and also in sinking two small trenches at a spot which may have been the theatre. A flat piece of white marble (23 cm. high, 15 wide, and 5 thick) was found here with an inscription. Bad weather coming on, the expedition returned finally to Athens on March 13.

HENRY S. WASHINGTON.

Madrid, Spain;
April 22, 1890.

DESCRIPTION OF THE SITE AND WALLS OF PLATAIA.

The ancient city stood on a fan-shaped ridge or plateau, about 1.4 km. long, from north to south, and 1 km. in its greatest width, stretching down from the north slope of Mt. Kithairon toward the plain of the Oëroë. This plateau has its highest point at the southern end, where a shallow ravine, 50 m. wide at its narrowest point, separates it from the lower rocks of the mountain. From this point the plateau slopes down rather sharply at first, but toward the upper cross-wall very gently, the ground becoming almost level inside the lower cross-wall and rising again near its northern edge. In the northeast corner it is split by two small ravines, formed by a couple of little brooks running north. The question whether these existed in ancient times, will be considered below. The soil for the most part inside the walls is cultivated and fairly deep, at *Church No. V* bed-rock being reached at a depth of 3 m., and at *Church No. I* at about the same depth. In many places, however, especially to the west and south, the rock crops out, the soil being very thin. This is especially the case to the south of the north cross-wall, between it and the outer wall as far as *Church No. VII*, and to the north of it, about parallel with its general direction as far as the point *M* of the outer wall. In the northern, or lower, part no rock crops out except along the western wall, as far as the point *T*, and near the so-called votive cuttings. The rock is a coarse gray marble, much corroded into deep holes and channels where exposed to the weather. All the walls are built of this rock, which forms the ridge of Kithairon to the south, and could be quarried either on the mountain slopes or on the plateau itself. The soil is a rather clayey lime earth, very loose when dry, but exceedingly clinging and sticky when wet—the mud making the plain of the Oëroë and Asopos almost, if not quite, impassable in winter.

The sides of the plateau are not precipitous and rocky, except at a few points. As a rule, they slope gently down to the plain below. The slope has, of course, been decreased during our era by the washing down of earth from the plateau above. It is probable that the sides were never high or precipitous enough to make good defenses *per se*, and that walls must always have been needed to make the plateau a tenable position.

The remaining walls appear to be assignable to five periods. The earliest is characterized by a polygonal style of masonry, though not of the earliest type. The blocks are of fairly uniform size, the form seldom hexagonal, quite often pentagonal, step-cutting common on the upper edge to fit the superincumbent stone, with joints very neatly made. This style is similar to the oldest part of the walls of Lepreon, in Arkadia. The portions of wall exhibiting this style are the worst preserved of all, the stones being much corroded and weatherworn.

The style of the second period—that most largely represented—is intermediate between the first and third. The walls of this period are better built than those of the former, with scarcely any polygonal blocks, but are not so well made as those of the latter period, to which, however, they bear a closer resemblance and for which they probably served as a model.

The third period or style comprises work which is much the best built as well as the best preserved. It is seen in the upper crosswall, which is entirely of this period, and in the northeast corner. The blocks are larger than those of the first two periods, about 1 m. high, from 1 to 3 m. long, and about 60 cm. thick. They are four-sided, laid in horizontal courses, with the edges neatly and accurately fitted. The vertical joints are very commonly, in fact generally, not perpendicular, but slanting or oblique—never more than 20° off from the perpendicular, however. The adjoining block in almost every case fits closely, with the same slope, except in one or two instances where the slopes are opposite and a well fitted wedge-shaped block is inserted. The separate courses do not run along continuously at the same level, but, after varying distances (generally from 5 to 10 blocks) the upper course is lowered (or raised) by the upper side of the block below being cut into a step shape, the difference between the level of the two steps being only a few centimetres, never over five. The outer surface of the blocks, rather rounded or bulging, is cut vertically into wide and rather deep furrows or grooves. The whole is a very good piece of work, the blocks of good size, the joints accurate, and the workmanship everywhere careful.

The fourth period is represented only by the lower cross-wall. It can hardly be said to represent a distinct style, the wall being built of blocks from earlier walls (of the second and third periods), of building-blocks and of other architectural fragments, all of the common, coarse gray marble, no white marble being observed in this wall or in any other. The blocks are not used with much system or care, sometimes the furrowed side being out and as often not. The joints are not close, the blocks not having been recut after their removal from their original positions, and little pains having been taken in fitting them. Mortar and tiles were used at one time to fill up the crevices, as can still be seen in the third tower from the west; but whether or not this was subsequent to the building of the wall cannot be made out.

The last period, including the worst-built masonry of all, is represented by a few fragments and stretches of Roman, or more probably Byzantine, wall, built of rubble and tiles laid in mortar. It is seen only at a few scattered points on the north and west sides.

The walls of the first four periods are very uniformly 3.30 m. in thickness, very little variation from this figure having been noted anywhere. The outer facing is the better of the two, built of larger stones and better finished, but the difference is not great. In all the walls the space between the outer and inner faces was filled with smaller rough stones and earth. How the walls were finished on top, whether battlemented or not, cannot now be determined, nor can any calculation be made, from the *débris*, of the probable height, the fallen stones having been scattered all over and below the plateau, and having disappeared in various ways. In many places, notably at the northwest from Q to S and at the southwest from C to H, the wall could be traced only by the smoothing of the natural rock as a bed on which to lay the wall-stones. The rock was rather carefully cut away so as to present a level surface in many places, and several of the step-cuttings were observed in the native rock. At two points, C

and between *S* and *T*, the natural rock has been cut away so as to leave a smooth vertical fall.

In order to take up and describe *seriatim* the various parts of the city-walls, we will begin at the point *A*, the southwest corner, and proceed toward the north. This point is the highest and most southerly of the plateau, and from it may be had a fine view of the whole site and the plain of the Oëroë and Asopos rivers stretching away to the north toward Thebes, which is entirely hidden by a low range of hills separating the valleys of the two rivers. Behind us, and to the right and left, runs the ridge of Mt. Kithairon ; to the northwest can be seen Mts. Helikon and Parnassos, and to the northeast the mountains of Euboia. A ravine, about 50 m. wide and about 5 m. deep, separates the plateau from the lowest point of the slope of Kithairon. This ravine was much deeper in former times, a great deal of earth having been washed down from the mountain, especially since the destruction to a great extent of the forest growth. It is wide and deep enough, however, to prevent any earth from being washed down from the mountain onto the plateau, and we may safely say that this part of the plateau has been steadily losing earth since it became uninhabited, and consequently for centuries diminishing in height.

There is little left of the wall above ground (merely one course of blocks, inside and out), but enough by which to determine the period, presumably the earliest. A tower, square in plan, 5.50 m. on each side, stood at the angle, and from this point the wall runs down the slope, toward the north, very well defined till it turns to the west near *Church No. VII*, and thence runs irregularly in a general northwesterly direction till it meets the upper cross-wall. All along this stretch, a single course above ground in a few places constitutes the best-preserved remains, the whole being of the first period. The wall has been traced, for the most part, by the rock-surfaces smoothed for the reception of the masonry. Along a great part of this stretch, notably from *C* to *G*, the wall runs along the edge of a rough and jagged rocky cliff, nearly vertical, but now only a few metres high. Below the point *D*, on the outside, there is a rectangular sarcophagus-like cavity cut in the rock.[1] The point of junction of this outer and older wall with the upper cross-wall cannot be clearly made out, but is probably not far from *H*.

[1] The two branches of the road from Kokla to Kriekouki cut this section of the wall, as shown on the MAP.

We now turn toward the east and follow the upper cross-wall. This is by far the best built of all the walls; it is of the third period, and is in places in a very good state of preservation. It runs for 407 m. toward the southeast in a line almost straight, at one point making a bend of less than 2° and at another of 10°, and there turns to the northeast and runs toward *Church No. V*. The wall is everywhere 3.30 m. wide, both faces carefully finished (the outer one, that toward the south, the better) and the space between filled with rubble of earth and stones. The present height of the ruins varies greatly; at places they barely appear above ground, while at their highest point, the third tower from the west end, the structure is 3.80 m. above ground.* Along the outer, *i. e.*, the southern, side of the wall there are remains of eight towers of rectangular plan, measuring 6.70 m. in length (*i. e.*, along the wall) and 5 m. in breadth. The variations are only a few centimetres either way from these averages. The towers are distant from one another 42.50 m., and form an integral part of the wall, not added to the outer face but built at the same time and continuously with it. The best-preserved example is the tower above mentioned, and it offers a few points of interest. The main courses rest on a foundation-wall, projecting 10 cm. beyond them, the blocks of which measure only 40 cm. high instead of 1 m., as in the courses above. This foundation is carefully worked with vertical or very slightly oblique joints, and furrowed facing. In this tower at present three courses of the foundation are above ground, while a similar foundation runs beneath the wall proper, though not visible at present, except at one or two points, owing to the accumulation of earth. The corners of the towers present a striking peculiarity. The rough, bulging sides have been cut in from both sides, so as to leave a sharp right-angled ridge along the vertical edge, finished smooth and clean. This right-angled ridge, which measures 10 cm. on each side, is carried along the whole angle of the tower and is continued in the foundation. It occurs in every tower on all the walls of the first three periods, its use in this upper cross-wall being probably copied from the older walls. The towers, as far as can be judged, were solid, filled up within, like the walls. Another peculiarity of the upper cross-wall (also occurring once in the extreme south wall) is that there are several "platforms," as they have been called, built on the inside of the wall. These are thickenings of the wall, about 10 m. long and 1 m. thick, and were probably buttresses to strengthen the main wall, though too

---

* See PLATE XVII.

little is left of them to determine this definitely. At one place in the upper cross-wall two of these platforms occur, one on each side of a tower, while at another place one is found between two towers.

Returning to *II*, we continue toward the north along the western outer wall. The stretch *III*, distinctly traceable, but not projecting much above ground, is of the second period; it is similar to the wall of the third period, that of the upper cross-wall, but is not so carefully built. It disappears at *I*, and the wall begins again at *K*, where there are traces of a square tower. A wall running east from this point was traced for some 50 m. The main wall, of the same masonry as *III*, continues to the point *M*, where it makes a sharp angle, turns to the northwest, and thence to *N* is traceable mostly by rock-cutting. From *II* to near *M*, it runs along the edge of the plateau, the ground sloping down gently toward the plain. At *M* is a tower, and the wall from this point on to *N* overhangs a steep and rocky cliff, from 3 to 8 m. high. Inside the tower to the north of *M*, there run for a few metres the remains of an apparently polygonal wall, probably of the first period, as in the extreme southern part, but perhaps earlier still. Below the wall *MN*, perched on the rocks, are half a dozen sarcophagi, hewn in one piece out of the common, coarse gray marble, and separate from the rock on which they rest. The dimensions of the most northerly one are as follows: length (exterior) 2.40 m., width 1.20, height 1.25, thickness of sides, 0.20. These sarcophagi are surrounded at top and bottom by a simple moulding. The interior is sloping at the bottom. The monolithic cover of the sarcophagus measured lies further down the slope; it has the shape of a long, obtuse wedge. To the south of the sarcophagi lie some graves of less importance, hewn in the rock, in the shape of rectangular pits; all these are empty. Of two of the sarcophagi only halves remain, and all the covers with the one exception have disappeared. At a distance of 98 m. from *N*, there are traces of a path leading down through the wall and between the sarcophagi—very faint however. At *N* this wall disappears, though blocks are still scattered about the slope in large numbers, and many are built into field-walls below.

At *O*, begins the lower cross-wall, almost the latest of all. It is built entirely, as stated above, of blocks taken from other structures. The remains of seven towers, measuring 6.20 m. in length by 5.50 in width, are visible in its southern or outer side, joined to and forming part of the main wall, as in the upper cross-wall. The third tower from the west end is the best-preserved, its extreme height being 3.85 m.* The wall makes a rather sharp turn at Z', and thence runs almost due north, with a few slight angles, for over 150 m., finally being lost amid a tangle of blocks and house-walls, which contiaue till within 50 m. or so of V. The wall runs throughout on almost level ground, and no traces of a gate appear. Below the point O, near the road, are 19 m. of the inner facing of a wall, built of large cut blocks, apparently of the second period. No connection could be made out between it and the main western wall, and it is probably all that remains of a wall figured in Stanhope's map, but of which all other traces are now lost. At P, there are scanty remains of a wall of the same period, half-way down the rather steep, earth-covered slope, and above this is a right angle, apparently a corner of a tower, built of small stones and mortar, while a little further north there is a large mass of the same material.

From O to Q the main wall is lost, but at this latter point we come upon rock-cuttings, and hence to R the line of the wall can be made out, in a straight line, by the leveling of the tops of the rocks for the reception of the blocks. All along this part of the west wall the side of the plateau is fairly steep and quite high, perhaps 15 m. above the road to Thebes. The slope, except toward the top, is not rocky, but of earth. Below the stretch QR, at two points appear short lengths of what at first sight looks like early polygonal masonry; but a closer examination shows that it is late work. The stones are very roughly fitted, and in one or two cases have apparently been taken from an early wall of cut blocks. One block shows a hole, apparently made for an iron anchor or clamp. Just below the point R is a grave-cutting.

From the point R, the northwest angle, till half-way between S and T, the wall remains are short lengths of rough wall made of small stones and tiles laid in mortar. No trace exists of an earlier wall except at S, where there are two pathways cut a few centimetres deep in the rock, meeting in the line of the wall at an obtuse angle, just outside which a large rock projects, its top cut away flat and level. This may have been a small gate where met two paths, coming up from below. A little to the west of T, the rock has been cut away perpendicularly for a few metres, the wall running along its edge. Hence to U, the wall, 3.30 m. thick, can be seen just above ground, and belongs apparently to the second period. The remains of one or

* See PLATE XVII.

two towers can just be made out. From U to V the wall runs east, down hill. Very little is left of it, and that little is mainly of small, rough stones, without mortar—very late work. No trace could be found of the wall figured to the north of this by both Leake and Stanhope. 30 m. south of V, there are 4 m. of a wall running north and south, apparently of the same style as the lower cross-wall, and a continuation of it. But there are so many late house-walls in this region that this is not certain. At V, all traces disappear, and the next sight of the wall is at W, 234 m. to the northeast of V, on the east slope of the western valley. Hence the wall runs in a straight line about due east for 150 m., disappears where it formerly cut across the eastern valley and brook, reappears 50 m. further on, and thence runs 187 m. to the northeast angle of the plateau. This wall, though barely projecting above ground, can easily be seen, especially at its eastern end, where the outer or northern face projects a metre or more above the surface. It is built in almost exactly the style of the upper cross-wall, the oblique up-and-down joints, the step-cuts, the peculiar tower-angles, and the wider foundation being all present; the stones large, well-fitted, and with furrowed, bulging faces. From X westward to near the brook, the courses, though horizontal, descend step by step, following the gentle slope of the small ravine, thus proving that this ravine existed when the wall was built. As the valley to the west is the larger, we can infer, though there is no wall there to prove it, that it also existed at the same period. The slope down from all this stretch of wall (east of V) to the plain is gentle and entirely of earth. At the northeast angle, X, there was a round tower, about 10 m. in diameter. Only four such towers appear; there being one between S and T, on the north wall, and two on the east wall, to be noted later. This one at X is built in the same style as the rest of this part, but very little of it remains.

From X, the wall, fairly well preserved, and for some distance overgrown with bushes, runs due south, then turns a little toward the west and disappears near A', just beyond a small ilex tree, some 5 m. high, the only tree on the plateau. All this stretch of wall is of the second period, not as well built as WX. Hence to near *Church No. V*, the wall can be traced running a little west of south, sometimes entirely destroyed, and again fairly well preserved. All the remains are of the second period. At B', a wall, 2.80 m. thick, runs almost at a right angle for 27 m. down the slope toward the brook, here distant 35 m.

from the main wall. This offshoot-wall is of rougher and apparently late masonry. Inside the main wall, due west of B' at a distance of 17 m., are remains of a square building, measuring about 8 m. each way, with a small threshold—probably a late Byzantine structure. At E', traces of a round tower can be made out. The slope down to the brook all along this east wall is very gentle, no rock crops out, and the soil is apparently deep. At K', near Church No. V, all traces disappear, but at L' we make out a bit of wall, and hence trace it, at intervals, to P'. The only rock along all this stretch is a narrow ridge running from L' to N', along the top of which the wall was built, as shown by the cuttings. At O' there are traces of a round tower. Too little remains of this stretch, south of L', to determine its period; but it probably belongs to the first, that of the extreme southern part. At P', both faces of the wall can be seen, and hence to A it is fairly preserved, though not high above the surface—less than a metre. It is all 3.30 m. through, and of the same period, the first, as that near A, described above. At a point 37 m. from A, there is a cutting in the wall—traces of what may have been a threshold. The slope to the south down into the small ravine which separates the wall from Mt. Kithairon is very gentle, though in one or two places the wall runs along rather steep rocks. At P, the wall is nearly 150 m. from the mountain slope, while at A, as stated above, it is only 50 m.

This completes the survey of the walls, and a few remarks may be made as to the area included within them. It seems probable, from the apparently greater age of the walls there and from its height above the rest of the plateau, that the extreme south end was the original acropolis. Search was made for an old north enclosing-wall, but no trace of such a wall was found. Such a wall probably existed near where the upper cross-wall now stands, but running more east and west. The plateau, as has been said, sloped down to the north, the northern half being comparatively level. The southwestern part is very rocky, the natural rock here jutting out in large rough masses, while the southeastern part is almost free from rock, except the ridge between L' and N'. The middle zone (between the north and south parts) is rocky on its western side, while to the east it is mostly good soil. The northern third is entirely free from projecting rocks except along its western and northwestern edges. Inside the lower cross-wall (to the north of it), and for a little distance to the east, the ground is entirely uncultivated, owing to the circumstance that it is covered with potsherds, broken tiles, and small stones, while to the east, on both sides of and between the two ravines, the soil is deep and fertile.

Apart from the ruined churches, there are few objects of interest above ground on the plateau. East of *D*, in the southwest, there is cut in the rock what is probably a threshold, facing west, 2 m. in length. Beyond this, to the east, there is a semicircular area in the rocks, some 15 to 20 m. across; and about 3 m. lower than this, to the north, there is a similar area. Both areas are level and apparently made by the hand of man. Southeast of *Church No. IV*, appear what are called on the map, "Votive Cuttings." These consist of seven or eight small rectangular holes or niches cut in the rock for the reception of votive or other tablets. To the south of them is a small level plateau, with some roughly hewn wall-stones. The wall to the east of *Church No. IV* is a very well built and preserved one of rubble and mortar. It is 32 m. long by 1.15 wide, and runs almost due north and south. To the south of this extends in the same line a series of eight square piers, 1.15 m. square, of the same materials, the first one distant 15.40 m. from the south end of the wall. The first seven piers are uniformly distant from one another 1.75 m., and from the spacing we judge that four are probably missing between the seventh and eighth remaining piers. No traces are left above ground of any wall to the south, but the broad level space to the east of the wall makes it seem probable that a large building, or some such feature as an agora, once existed here.

There are four springs and brooks in the immediate vicinity of the plateau, besides the two very small ones in the northeast part. One brook on the east side rises in a spring a short distance due south of *P* and flows northerly along the whole east side, at a distance from the wall varying from 20 to 100 m. The brook on the west begins at a point southwest of the older wall, flows northwest, is joined by the water from Megale Brysis, below *O*, and thence flows to the northwest away from the city into the Oëroë. Some 250 m. to the east of the plateau is another spring called Kondati, where are two inscriptions and some architectural fragments. Between this and the brook to the east of the walls is a ridge on which are the ruins of a small church and a number of large hewn blocks.

On the whole plateau there is a remarkable lack of white marble. The pieces remaining are confined almost entirely to the ruined Byzantine churches, *Churches Nos. I, IV, V, VII* and *VIII* being the richest in them. The greater number are Roman architectural pieces, architraves, capitals and bases, *etc.* There are some Greek slabs and other marbles, some with inscriptions, all built into the church-walls, and some reworked into Byzantine forms. A few fragments of white marble, small pieces of cut and sculptured work, are found on the ground on the northwest part; and to the east of *Church No. I* lies a portion of a Roman plain white marble column. The two springs of Megale Brysis to the west and of Kondati Brysis to the east have walls made of ancient fragments of white marble. All this marble is much like the Pentelic, but undoubtedly comes from a much nearer quarry.

I will close with a few remarks as to the different periods of settlement of the plateau. As already stated, it seems probable that the extreme southern end was the earliest citadel, if not the only part occupied before the time of the battle of Plataia. Then, later, a town was built lower down in the northern part (the upper citadel probably being abandoned), the upper cross-wall being built for its defense. This town very probably covered the whole of the plateau to the north of the wall. The apparently greater age of the walls to the east and west makes it seem likely, however, that the whole plateau was inhabited and fortified before the shrinkage within the upper cross-wall, which is probably of about the time of Alexander. At a much later date, in Byzantine times perhaps, the lower cross-wall was rather hastily and carelessly built to surround the much shrunken town. The fact that the ground inside this wall is deeply covered with tiles, *etc.*, and the number of house-walls, point to the conclusion that a densely populated town once occupied this part of the plateau. The great number of churches on and in the immediate vicinity of the plateau, ten in all, also tends to prove the same, and is a circumstance important in the later history of the place, and one which may explain the great scarcity of white marble, this probably having been burned to make mortar.

HENRY S. WASHINGTON.

Tarragona, Spain,
May 23, 1890.

NOTES ON THE BATTLEFIELD OF PLATAIA.

Those who admire the greatness of ancient Athens cannot fail to feel an interest in Plataia, the gallant little city which stood by the side of Athens on the field of Marathon and was equally faithful in the still darker hour of the Peloponnesian war. It would be of interest to follow at length the fortunes of Plataia. But the aim of this paper is more limited; its purpose is to examine the statements of ancient writers that throw light on the topography of the battlefield, where the victory of Salamis was made complete.

Diodoros, Strabo, Plutarch, and Pausanias have been consulted, but the authorities by which all others have been tested are Herodotos and Thoukydides; for they stand nearest to the battle of Plataia, and their works bear most clearly the marks of simple truth.

The story of the battle as told by Herodotos (IX. 15 ff.) is in brief as follows: After Mardonios had captured Athens for the second time, and had flashed the news to the Persian king by beacon-fires, he retired from Attika through Dekeleia to Skolos in the Theban country. He extended his forces along the Asopos from Erythrai, past Hysiai, into the Plataian territory and strengthened part of his camp by means of a wooden fort, ten stades square. The Greek forces came to Erythrai and took their stand on the skirts of Kithairon opposite the enemy; but the Persian cavalry harassed them. The Megarians, who were in a place easily accessible to cavalry, suffered most until a volunteer band of three hundred Athenians went to their aid. In a skirmish which followed, Masistios, the commander of the Persian cavalry, was slain, and his body was captured by the Greeks. The Persians in their mourning shaved themselves, their horses, and their cattle, and filled Boiotia with their lamentations. The Greeks bore the body in triumph through their ranks, and were encouraged to take a more convenient position for their camp, where they would have a better water supply. They advanced along the skirts of Kithairon, past Hysiai, into the Plataian district, and took their stand near the spring Gargaphia and the sacred enclosure of the hero Androkrates, their line extending over low hills and level ground. The Lakedaimonians held the right, and the Athenians, after a dispute with the troops from Tegea, occupied the left. The Tegeans were solaced with a position next the

STORY OF THE BATTLE.

FIRST POSITION OF THE GREEKS.

SECOND POSITION.

Lakedaimonians, and the Plataians stood next the Athenians. The rest of the Greeks held the centre. The enemy were soon at hand and formed their line of battle. Opposite the Lakedaimonians were the Persians; then came the subject nations; and at the other end of the line were the medizing Greeks. The Asopos divided them,[1] and the prophets on both sides advised acting on the defensive. For eight days the armies faced each other, and the Greek force continually grew stronger. On the night of the eighth day, Mardonios sent to the pass Dryoskephalai[2] a troop of cavalry, which captured a large supply-train on its way to the Greek camp.

On the eleventh day Mardonios, not wishing that the Greek forces should be further strengthened, resolved upon giving battle. This purpose was communicated to the Greeks that night, and the Lakedaimonians asked the Athenians to change places with them, because the Athenians had already faced the Persians at Marathon. This change was made; but, in the morning when the enemy observed it, Mardonios moved the Persians to his right wing, so that they once more faced the Lakedaimonians. Pausanias, the Lakedaimonian commander, seeing that he had gained nothing by the change, went back to his former position and the Persians did the same. Mardonios, after sending a taunting challenge to the Spartans, ordered a cavalry charge. The cavalry captured the spring Gargaphia and choked it up. This cut off the water supply of the Greeks; for it was unsafe to go to the Asopos on account of the horsemen and bowmen. They

THIRD POSITION.

determined to move that night to the Island, where they would have water in abundance and be free from the assaults of the Persian cavalry. When the time came, the Greeks in the middle of the line did not march to the appointed place, but were glad to flee from the enemy's cavalry toward Plataia, and came to the Heraion before the town. The Lakedaimonians on the right were detained by the obstinacy of Amompharetos, who refused to retreat before the enemy, while the Athenians on the left remained where they were, because they did not think the Lakedaimonians

---

[1] Part of the Persian forces may have been south of the Asopos. The Persian cavalry were continually active on the south side of the river. *Cf.* HERODOTOS, IX. 40.

[2] Also called Treiskephalai; because one looking south from the valley of the Asopos can distinguish three peaks of Kithairon in the neighborhood of the pass, through which the road from Athens to Thebes now passes. There was another pass from Megara. *Cf.* XENOPHON, *Hell.*, v. 4. 14; VISCHER, *Erinnerungen aus Griechenland*, p. 533.

meant to carry out the arrangement in good faith. As dawn approached, Pausanias left his obstinate captain, who soon followed him, and retired ten stades to a place called Argiopios on the banks of the Moloïs, where there was a temple of Demeter. On the retreat the Lakedaimonians kept to the hills, but the Athenians turned down into the plain. When the Persians saw the Greek position deserted, they set out to pursue, as they supposed, a fleeing enemy. They advanced on the Lakedaimonians, for the Athenians in the plain were hidden from them by the hills. The sacrifices were unfavorable for the Lakedaimonians, and they were being wounded without striking a blow, until Pausanias looked away toward the Heraion and prayed that they might not be disappointed in their hopes. Here by the temple of Demeter the battle was fought and the Persians were routed. The Boiotians kept the Athenians employed till they too were routed and fled to Thebes. The Persians had fled to their wooden fort. When the Greeks at the Heraion learned that the Persians were fleeing, they set out in two detachments. One passed among the hills at the base of the mountain on the way which led up straight toward the shrine of Demeter; the other moved through the plain till it fell in with the Theban cavalry, which charged it and drove it into the mountain. The Persian fort was soon stormed and great slaughter followed.

This outline shows that Herodotos gives three positions of the Greek troops, which we shall endeavor to determine. But first let us fix the more permanent features, such as the Island, the spring Gargaphia, the temple of Demeter, the Heraion, and the shrine of Androkrates.

The ruins of Plataia[3] lie on a plateau at the foot of Kithairon about two miles and a half from the Asopos, which flows at this point in a comparatively straight line toward the east. This is enough to form the basis of our investigation. To begin with the Island. Herodotos (IX. 51) says: "This Island is before the city of the Plataians, distant ten stades from the Asopos and the spring Gargaphia, at which they were then encamped." And under the following circumstances there would be an island in a continent. The river branches and flows down from Kithairon into the

POSITION OF THE ISLAND.

---

[3] See the MAP above. For other maps, see LEAKE, *Travels in Northern Greece*, vol. II; STEIN, *Herodotus*, vol. V; GROTE, *History of Greece*, ch. 42; STANHOPE, *Topography of the Battle of Plataea*; BOCAGE, *Travels of Anacharsis*, pl. 6.

plain, with its streams about three stades apart, and then comes together. Its name is Oëroë, and the natives call it 'the daughter of Asopos.'"

Again Herodotos (IX. 51) speaks of the Island as the place "which Oëroë forks about as it flows from Kithairon." From this we gather that the Island was: (*a*) before the city of Plataia; (*b*) ten stades from the Asopos and Gargaphia; (*c*) three stades wide; and (*d*) that it ended in the plain. And in the plain before Plataia, ten stades from the Asopos, we must accordingly find one point of the Island.

The statement of Herodotos, that the island is "ten stades from the Asopos and the spring Gargaphia, at which they were then encamped," makes it important to fix the position of the troops at this time. Herodotos (IX. 25) says the forces went "from Erythrai past Hysiai to the Plataian territory, and on arriving took up their position by nations near the spring Gargaphia and the sacred enclosure of the hero Androkrates, over low hills and level ground."[4] Later, Herodotos (IX. 49) says the Persian cavalry choked up the spring Gargaphia, from which all the Greek army procured water. "Now the Lakedaimonians alone were posted at the spring, while for the rest of the Greeks the spring was distant as every contingent happened to be drawn up, and the Asopos was near; but being kept back from the Asopos they continued to resort to the spring, for it was not possible for them to get water from the river on account of the horsemen and arrows." The left, then, held by the Athenians, was near the Asopos, and the line extended away from the river to the spring Gargaphia, where the Lakedaimonians held the right. When Herodotos (IX. 51) says that the Island to which they proposed to retreat was ten stades from the Asopos and from the spring Gargaphia, he seems to imply that each end of the line would fall back ten stades to the Island; in which case the new line would be about parallel to the old. Acting on this supposition, we draw, from the part of the Island which we have fixed, a circle with a radius of ten stades, and the left of the Greek line will lie on this circle near the Asopos.

SECOND POSITION OF GREEK TROOPS.

At the other end of the line was Gargaphia—(*a*) ten stades from the Island,[5] (*b*) near low hills and level ground, accessible to cavalry,[6] (*c*) ten stades from the temple of

GARGAPHIA.

[4] DIODOROS says (XI. 30) that the Greeks, in their second position, had on their right a high hill and on their left the Asopos, and here they won their victory.
[5] HERODOTOS, IX. 51.   [6] IX. 25, 49.

Demeter,[7] and (d) twenty from the Heraion.[8] We cannot allow less than twenty-four stades for the length of this line. There were 110,000 men in all.[9] Of these, 38,700 were heavy-armed troops. Supposing these heavy-armed men to be drawn up eight deep, as was common in the fifth and fourth centuries B. C.,[10] and, allowing three feet front for every man with his shield, we shall have a line about twenty-four stades long. That the estimate of twenty-four stades is not far from right, will be evident when one considers that this line was supported by 71,300 light-armed troops. Gargaphia will then be on the circumference of a circle whose radius is twenty-four stades, and whose centre is the Athenian position. Our line must not swing too far to the south away from the river, or the spring Gargaphia will not be twenty stades from the Heraion, which is near Plataia.[11] On the other hand, it must not swing to the north toward the river; for it must be within ten [12] stades of the temple of Demeter, which, as we shall show, was on high ground; and we have seen that the spring was distant from that part of the line which was near the river. We therefore place the spring east of Plataia among the "low hills" of the Asopos valley, where are several springs, one of which Leake names Gargaphia.[13]

Taking Gargaphia as a centre, we draw a circle with a radius of ten stades to find the temple of Demeter about which the battle was fought. Herodotos (IX. 57), speaking of the retreat of Pausanias from Gargaphia, says: "This column, drawing off about ten stades, waited for the company of Amompharetos, taking position on the banks of the Moloïs, and in a place called Argiopios where stands a temple of Eleusinian Demeter." Just before the battle, Pausanias "looked away toward the Heraion of the Plataians."[13a] When the Persians were put to flight, the Corinthians and others at the Heraion "turned along the skirts of Kithairon and the hills on the way which led up straight toward the shrine of Demeter."[14] The temple of Demeter, then, was on the circumference of the circle—(a) ten stades from Gargaphia, (b) on the river Moloïs, (c) up hill from the Heraion, (d) so situated that an observer standing near it could see the Heraion, and (e) at a place

TEMPLE
OF DEMETER.

---

[7] HERODOTOS, IX. 57: cf. 49.   [8] IX. 52.   [9] IX. 29, 30.
[10] HANS DROYSEN, Die griechischen Kriegsalterthümer, in K. F. Hermann's Lehrbuch der gr. Antiquitäten, II, 2te Abt. p. 44.
[11] HERODOTOS, IX. 52.   [12] IX. 57: cf. 49.
[13] Op. cit., II, 332 f. PAUSANIAS (IX. 4. 3) says that the spring was restored.
[13a] HERODOTOS, IX. 61.   [14] IX. 69.

called Argiopios. This name, "White Rock,"[15] may help to identify the spot. We cannot place it very far to the south, for the troops from the Heraion passed to it over the foot-hills of Kithairon. We may suppose that it was west of Gargaphia, for Pausanias originally intended to go to the Island, and Plutarch[16] says that he retired toward Plataia. We therefore place the temple of Demeter on high ground southeast of Plataia at a point where are now the foundations of a large Byzantine church.[17] Back of it rises a wall of rock which is visible for miles in the valley, and may have given to the place the name of Argiopios. The Lakedaimonians who were at this point could be seen easily by the Persians in the valley of the Asopos; while the Athenians in the plain north of Plataia would be hidden by the foothills northeast of the town.[18] From the rising ground a few rods east of the church one can see the lower half of the ruins of Plataia where the Heraion may have stood. The conclusion with regard to the position of the temple of Demeter, which we reach from our study of Herodotos, receives a curious confirmation from a statement of Pausanias. Pausanias comes down from Kithairon to Plataia, and, after speaking of the monuments[19] of those who fought against the Mede, and the altar of Zeus "just about opposite the entrance to Plataia," he says (IX. 2. 6): "But the trophy which the Greeks set up for the battle at Plataia stands about fifteen stades further from the city." The trophy ($\tau\rho o\pi a\hat{\imath}o\nu$) was set up on the battlefield in memory of the turning of the enemy to flight ($\tau\rho o\pi \acute{\eta}$). In this case the battlefield was about the temple of Demeter. Herodotos (IX. 62) says: "The battle waxed hot right by the temple of Demeter," and again (IX. 65): "It is a marvel to me how not a single one of the Persians, who fought beside the grove of Demeter, appears to have gone into the sacred enclosure or to have died within it, though very many fell about the temple on the unconsecrated ground." Measuring from the en-

---

[15] Pape, *Wörterbuch der griechischen Eigennamen*.   [16] *Aristides*, 17.

[17] About six minutes walk east of the spring Vergoutiani. Here have been found Greek sepulchral steles, inscriptions, bits of Roman mosaic, and numerous fragments of marble. No doubt the temple became popular after this battle, and continued so down to Roman times. Plutarch describes it as "under the projecting foot of Kithairon in places rough and rocky." *Arist.*, 14; *cf.* 11.

[18] Herodotos, IX. 59: ὑπὸ τῶν ὄχθων.

[19] Plutarch (*Arist.*, 20) mentions one set up by the Lakedaimonians, and one by the Athenians. Leake (II. 366) wrongly places the trophy at the gate of Plataia beside the tombs.

trance to Plataia "about" fifteen stades, we find the point which we had already fixed for the temple of Demeter.

THE ISLAND. The so-called Island was ten [20] stades from Gargaphia, and so must touch the circle on which the temple of Demeter stood. A number of streams flow down from Kithairon on the east of Plataia, and turn to the west, where they unite to form the Oëroë which flows into the Korinthian Gulf.[21] The modern traveller is unable to discover any such island as Herodotos seems to describe. Leake [22] and Vischer [23] are inclined to think that it was rather a narrow peninsula formed by two of these branches, which was popularly called by the inhabitants the "Island," a name misleading to one not acquainted with the place. Herodotos does not speak as if he had verified the statement that it was entirely surrounded by water. He prefaces his description (IX. 51) with : "and there would be an island in a continent under the following circumstances." It would not be difficult to find parallels for such a use of the term "Island." Long ridges run out from Kithairon between the water-courses; and on one of these ridges, which the Plataians called the "Island," the Greeks proposed to take their stand. On rising ground with a stream in front they could defend themselves from the enemy's cavalry, while the stream behind them would furnish water.

THE HERAION. It is important that we should fix the position of the Heraion. The language which Herodotos uses seems to associate it closely with Plataia. He calls it (IX. 61) the "Heraion of the Plataians," and, like the Island, it is "before the city of the Plataians,"[24] an expression which seems to point toward the valley. It was distant twenty [25] stades from Gargaphia. It will therefore be on the circumference of a circle whose centre is Gargaphia and

---

[20] HERODOTOS, IX. 51.   [21] Cf. VISCHER, op. cit., p. 547; LEAKE, II, p. 324.
[22] II, p. 357 ff.
[23] P. 547 f. LEAKE claims that this is all that Herodotos means; but περισχίζεται, and Herodotos' general treatment of the subject exclude this view. VISCHER thinks it possible that such an island existed in antiquity.
[24] HERODOTOS, IX. 52; cf. 51. PLUTARCH (Arist., 11) calls Hera Kithaironian. PAUSANIAS (IX. 2, 7.) saw in her temple a large standing statue of the goddess by Praxiteles. Plataian coins of the time of Praxiteles bear the head of Hera. Cf. IMHOOF-BLUMER and GARDNER, Numismatic Commentary on Pausanias, pp. 110-111. The same temple contained a Rhea and a Kronos by Praxiteles, and a seated statue of Hera by Kallimachos.
[25] HERODOTOS, IX. 52. LOLLING, in Baedeker's Greece, places the Heraion twenty stades outside the city (?). On a circle of twenty stades radius from Gargaphia, within

whose radius is twenty stades. Herodotos says that the Greeks in the middle of the line were "glad to flee from the cavalry, and in their flight came to the Heraion, which is before the city of the Plataians, twenty stades from the spring Gargaphia;" and "these encamped about the Heraion." The Heraion was therefore in the direction of Plataia from the middle of the line, and the site was probably unfavorable for a cavalry attack, or the Greeks would not have halted so comfortably. If it was in the northern part of the plateau upon which Plataia lies that they halted, they would be protected on the west and north; for at this point the plateau rises somewhat abruptly from the plain. Leake and Vischer place the Heraion in the northern part of the present walls of Plataia. Both [26] note the statement of Thoukydides, that the ancient city was small, and observe that the walls at the south angle are the most ancient. The present ruins of Plataia are not less than two miles and a half in circumference. Leake and Vischer conclude that the later walls were extended from the south so as to include the temple of Hera, which was outside the city at the time of the Persian war. Pausanias seems to place the Heraion within the city, though his statement is not definite. After describing the altar and statue of Zeus Eleutherios near the entrance to Plataia, he says:[27] "In the city itself..... is the heroön of (the divinity) Plataia, and I have already told what is said with regard to her, and what I myself surmised; and (δέ) the Plataians have a temple of Hera notable for its size and the beauty of its sculptures." If Pausanias saw a temple of Hera within the city, it was not necessarily the Heraion of Herodotos; for, when the Peloponnesians captured Plataia, they razed the city;[28] and built near the Heraion a large inn, which they dedicated to Hera. They also built to her a temple one hundred feet long, which was probably the large temple seen by Pausanias. Vischer finds traces of a quadrangular building within the northern part of the city, and concludes that there is scarcely any doubt that this is the temple of Hera. But, in truth, there is abundant room for doubt. This part of

the northern part of the present walls of Plataia, is a ruined Byzantine church containing numerous fragments of a large Ionic temple (MAP, *Church No. 1*). A fragment of a decree by Diocletian was found here in 1889 by the American School of Classical Studies at Athens. Several other sites would satisfy the conditions of Herodotos' account.

[26] LEAKE, II. pp. 325 f., 360 f., 364.   VISCHER, p. 543 ff.
[27] PAUSANIAS, IX. 2. 7.   [28] THOUKYDIDES, III. 68. 3–5.

the city is covered with foundation-walls, and the mere fact that there had been a large temple in any place would prove nothing; for Pausanias speaks of a temple of Athena at Plataia,[29] a heroön of Plataia,[30] and a temple of Eleusinian Demeter,[31] which may however be the one referred to by Herodotos. Plutarch (*Arist.*, 20) mentions a shrine of Artemis Eukleia. Successful excavation alone can fix the exact position of the temple of Hera.

The heroön of Androkrates[32] was somewhere on the line of battle which we have determined. Thoukydides (III. 24) says that those who escaped over the besieging walls of the Peloponnesians "went on the way leading to Thebes, having on their right the heroön of Androkrates." They saw the enemy pursuing them with torches toward Kithairon and Dryoskephalai. "They proceeded for six or seven stades on the way toward Thebes, then turning back they advanced on the road leading toward the mountain to Erythrai and Hysiai, and getting into the mountains they escaped to Athens." If the fugitives travelled only seven stades toward Thebes, and had the heroön of Androkrates on their right, this heroön must have been nearer to Gargaphia than to the Asopos. Stein[33] and Grote say that the spring was on the right of the Greek line of battle, and the heroön on the left, which is impossible, for the left was near the Asopos, almost twenty stades from Plataia. Plutarch places the heroön at the foot of Kithairon, near the temple of Demeter.

HEROÖN OF ANDROKRATES.

Our next task is to fix the positions occupied by the forces. Of the Persian position Herodotos (IX. 15) says: "Mardonios, bivouacking for the night in Tanagra, and turning on the next day to Skolos, was in the country of the Thebans. .... He let his camp extend from Erythrai along by Hysiai, and

PERSIAN POSITION.

---

[29] PAUSANIAS, IX. 4. 1; PLUTARCH, *Arist.*, 20. This temple, according to Pausanias, was built from the spoils of Marathon. It contained a colossal gold and marble statue by Pheidias, and was adorned with paintings, "Odysseus after the slaughter of the suitors," by Polygnotos, and "The Seven against Thebes," by Onasias. Before the feet of Athena was a portrait of Arimnestos, the Plataian commander at Marathon and Plataia. Plutarch says the temple was built from the Plataian share of the spoils.

[30] PAUSANIAS, IX. 2. 7.

[31] PAUSANIAS, IX. 4. 3. Pausanias may use ἐν Πλαταιαῖς loosely for ἐν Πλαταιΐδι γῇ. *Cf.* HERODOTOS, IX. 25; ἐς Πλαταιάς, 31. 41; ἐν Πλαταιῆσι. Pausanias seems to be thinking of the account of Herodotos; for in the next sentence he speaks of the restoration of Gargaphia, which Mardonios and his cavalry destroyed.

[32] HERODOTOS, IX. 25. A hero of Plataia; *cf.* PLUTARCH, *Arist.*, 11.

[33] *Note on Herodotos*, XI. 25, l. 18; *cf.* GROTE, *History of Greece*, vol. V, p. 19, Note 2.

advanced it along the Asopos river into the Plataian territory. However, he did not make his entrenchment so large, but made each side about ten stades." [34]

Skolos, Erythrai, and Hysiai were towns on the skirts of Kithairon; Skolos on the east, and Hysiai on the west, with Erythrai between. Skolos [35] was on rough ground near the Asopos, forty stades below the point where the road from Plataia to Thebes crossed the river. Hysiai and Erythrai [36] were near together, a little to the right of the road which crossed Kithairon from Eleutherai to Plataia. Plutarch (*Arist.*, 11) says: "Near to Hysiai is an ancient temple called the temple of Eleusinian Demeter and Kora." He further describes the place as near the heroön of Androkrates in the foot-hills of Kithairon. That the temple of Demeter and the heroön of Androkrates were not far apart is possible from what Herodotos and Thoukydides say; but that they should be near Hysiai would be inconsistent with the account of Herodotos. For, when the Greeks moved from Erythrai, their first position, to their second position, they passed Hysiai.[37] Then, when the Lakedaimonians fell back ten [38] stades from this second position, they came to the temple.[39]

SKOLOS,
ERYTHRAI, AND
HYSIAI.

The camp of Mardonios occupied the plain of the Asopos, and extended past Hysiai into Plataian territory. At least part of the camp was south of the Asopos, and there is nothing to show that the wooden fort was north of

CAMP OF
MARDONIOS.

[34] DIODOROS (XI. 29, 30) says Mardonios came from Thebes.
[35] STRABO, 408, 409; PAUSANIAS, IX. 4. 4; LEAKE, II, 330 f, 369. Pausanias saw here an unfinished temple of Demeter and Kora.
[36] PAUSANIAS, IX. 2. 1; STRABO, 404; LEAKE, II, 327–329. HERODOTOS (v. 74) mentions Hysiai with Oinoë as a frontier-deme of Attika. At Hysiai, Pausanias saw a half-built temple of Apollo and a sacred well.
[37] HERODOTOS, IX. 25.   [38] IX. 57.
[39] PLUTARCH may use "Hysiai" loosely for "the district of Hysiai" (see Note 31). At the foot of Kithairon, near Kriekouki, east of the road from Athens to Thebes, are remains of an ancient acropolis. Along the brow of the rock one can follow the wall with some difficulty. On the other side of the road is an ancient well, now dry, which was perhaps the sacred well of Hysiai. Near here were found two dedicatory inscriptions to Demeter, belonging to the first half of the fifth century. *Cf.* FOUCART, *Bull. de corr. hellén.*, 1879, p. 131, N. 1; ROBERTS, *Epigraphy*, 223. One objection to placing the Plataian temple of Demeter here has been pointed out above. Moreover, Pausanias, who speaks of the Plataian temple of Demeter, saw Hysiai in ruins. It is not impossible that Hysiai also had a temple of Demeter, as had Skolos (PAUSANIAS, IX. 4. 4). PLUTARCH himself says that the temple of Demeter, at which the Greeks halted, was near the shrine of the Plataian hero Androkrates, which must have been nearer Plataia.

the river. The camp of the Medes extended "along by Hysiai into the Plataian district."[40] Exactly the same expression is used of the Greeks who went from Erythrai across the skirts of Kithairon "along by Hysiai into the Plataian district." The expression "into the Plataian district" could hardly have been used, if part at least of the Persian forces had not been south of the Asopos. There is no proof that the Plataian territory ever extended north of the Asopos; on the contrary, there is proof that at first it did not extend as far as the Asopos. Herodotos tells[41] us that when the Athenians espoused the cause of the Plataians against the Thebans, they passed over the bounds which had been fixed for the Plataians, and "made the Asopos the boundary between the Thebans and the Plataians." Pausanias (II. 6. 1; IX. 4. 4) speaks of the Asopos, which forms the boundary between the Theban and the Plataian land; and again he says: "Even yet the Asopos separates the land of the Plataians from the Thebans." We are told that the Persians fled to their wooden fort in the Theban territory;[42] but this does not prove that the fort was north of the Asopos. We have seen that, before the Athenians interfered, the Theban territory extended across the Asopos opposite Plataia. This was doubtless the case at Erythrai; for Strabo (409) tells us that all the villages along the Asopos at this point were under the Thebans; though he adds that some say that Skolos, Eteonos, and Erythrai are in the country of the Plataians. Herodotos himself (IX. 15) places Skolos in the Theban territory.

While Mardonios was encamped here in the plain of the Asopos, the Greeks came to Erythrai, and, as Herodotos says,[43] observed that the barbarians were encamped on the Asopos; and perceiving this they took their stand on the skirts of Kithairon facing the enemy (ἀντετάσσοντο);"[44] and Mardonios, as the Greeks did not descend into the plain, sent against them all his cavalry. Masistios, commander of the cavalry, was slain, and the Greeks bore his body along their ranks on a wagon, a circumstance which throws light on the nature of the ground.

FIRST POSITION OF GREEKS.

[40] HERODOTOS, IX. 15; cf. 25. The wooden fort may have been extended across the river for the sake of a better water supply. The valley widens conveniently at this point.   [41] HERODOTOS, VI. 108: 519 B. C. Cf. THOUKYDIDES, III. 68.
[42] HERODOTOS, IX. 65.   [43] IX. 19 ff.; cf. DIODOROS, XI. 29, 30.
[44] LEAKE, who places the Persians on the other side of the Asopos, bases his view on this ἀντετάσσοντο, which can have no more definite meaning than we give to it. See *Northern Greece*, II, 340, Note.

The Greeks moved to their second position which we have fixed; and, "when Mardonios and his barbarians had finished mourning for Masistios, they, too, were at hand at the Asopos which flows here."[45] Most of the Persian forces were north of the river;[46] for "the sacrifices were favorable for the Greeks, if they kept on the defensive, but unfavorable, if they were to cross the Asopos and begin the battle." "The barbarians advanced as far as the Asopos to make trial of the Greeks, but neither side crossed."[47] On the day of the battle, Mardonios led the Persians across the Asopos on the run.[48] With regard to the position of the forces on the day of battle but a word remains to be said.

SECOND POSITION OF FORCES.

THIRD POSITION OF LAKEDAIMONIANS, ATHENIANS, AND OTHER GREEKS.

The Lakedaimonians, as we have seen, were at the temple of Demeter.[49] The Athenians were down in the plain where they fell in with the medizing Greeks. Plutarch says[50] that the Athenians, while advancing across the plain to the aid of the Spartans, were attacked by the medizing Greeks. Of the Greeks at the Heraion, one detachment went eastward to the temple of Demeter; and the other marched north or northeast through the plain till it fell in with the Boiotian cavalry.[51]

After the battle, according to Herodotos (IX. 84), the body of Mardonios disappeared. Several claimed to have buried him, and were rewarded by the son of Mardonios. Pausanias (IX. 2. 2) saw a monument "said to be that of Mardonios." on the right of the road from Athens to Plataia, a little beyond Hysiai.

MONUMENT OF MARDONIOS.

The Greeks buried their dead in large tombs or *polyandria*.[52] The Spartans set up three, one for every class of citizens; the Athenians one; the Tegeans one; and the Megarians and Phliasians one. Others, as the Aiginetans,[53] who took no part in the battle, erected cenotaphs. In the Peloponnesian war, when Plataia had been captured by siege, the Plataians pointed to these tombs,[54] and implored the Spartans to spare them for the honors which they had shown every year to the graves of "those who fell fighting against the Mede." Pausanias (IX. 2. 5) says: "Opposite the entrance to Pla-

TOMBS OF GREEKS.

[45] HERODOTOS, IX. 31.   [46] IX. 36 f.; PLUTARCH, *Arist.*, 11, 15.
[47] HERODOTOS, IX. 40.   [48] IX. 59.   [49] IX. 57, 62.
[50] *Arist.*, 18 : *cf.* HERODOTOS, IX. 59, 61.   [51] HERODOTOS, IX. 69.
[52] HERODOTOS, IX. 85.   [53] The Aiginetan tomb, it is said, was built ten years later.
[54] THOUKYDIDES, III. 58, 59.

taia are the tombs of those who fought against the Medes. The rest of the Greeks have a common monument; but the Lakedaimonians and Athenians who fell have separate tombs, and on them are inscribed epitaphs by Simonides. Not far from the common tomb of the Greeks is the altar of Zeus Eleutherios." Plutarch relates that this altar was dedicated to the Zeus of Freedom in honor of the battle for freedom at Plataia;[55] and, in describing the ceremonies which were performed every year at these tombs, he uses language which seems to place them near the city. He says: "They form a procession, which the trumpeter, sounding the charge, leads on at dawn. Wagons, loaded with myrtle and garlands follow. A black bull is led in the procession, and free-born youths advance bearing drink-offerings of wine and milk, vessels of olive-oil and myrrh. No slave is allowed to touch any of the things connected with that service because the men died for freedom. Finally, the archon of the Plataians, who is not allowed at any other time to touch iron,[56] or to put on any but a white garment, then clad in a purple tunic, and armed with a sword, taking up a water-jar from the place where the records are kept, leads on through the midst of the city. Then, taking water from the spring,[57] he himself washes the steles,[58] and anoints them with myrrh. Slaughtering the bull upon the altar for burnt sacrifice, and, praying to Zeus and Hermes Chthonios, he invites the brave men who died in behalf of Greece to the banquet and the offering of blood. Then mixing a bowl of wine and pouring it out, he says : 'I drink to the men who died for the freedom of the Greeks.' "

W. IRVING HUNT.

[55] PLUTARCH, *Arist.*, 19-21. Inscription on the altar:

Τόνδε ποθ' "Ελληνες νίκας κρατεῖ, ἔργῳ "Αρηος,
εὐτόλμῳ ψυχᾶς λήματι πειθόμενοι
Πέρσας ἐξελάσαντες, ἐλευθέρᾳ 'Ελλάδι κοινὸν
ἱδρύσαντο Διὸς βωμὸν ἐλευθερίου.

STRABO speaks of it as a ἱερόν, which Leake translates "temple." Here they celebrated games called the'Ελευθέρια. STRABO, 412; PLUTARCH, *Arist.*, 21; PAUS., IX. 2. 6.

[56] Perhaps it would be better to say "a weapon of iron ;" *cf.* σιδηροφορέω in THOUKYDIDES; or simply "a weapon."

[57] DODWELL (*Tour through Greece*, vol. I, p. 280) makes this spring Gargaphia (?). The tombs were just at the entrance to Plataia, as Pausanias came from Megara. Hence the spring referred to by Plutarch is probably that on the eastern side of the ruins of Plataia, which flows out of a terrace wall, in which are Greek sepulchral steles and a piece of an Ionic cornice. The spring a mile southeast of Plataia, now called Vergoutiani, has been confounded with Gargaphia, but it is probably the spring of Artemis. LEAKE, *Northern Greece*, II, 333 f.

[58] Of bronze, PAUSANIAS, IX. 2. 5.

THE MANTINEIAN RELIEFS.*

[PLATES XV, XVI.]

In the year 1887, M. G. Fougères of the French School at Athens, while digging at Mantineia, came upon three slabs of marble basreliefs. These M. Fougères published in a very interesting article in the organ of the French school,[1] in which he endeavored to identify these slabs with the reliefs decorating the base of the statues of Leto, Apollo and Artemis in their temple at Mantineia as described by Pausanias (VIII. 9), thereby greatly enhancing the undoubted value of his important discovery. Since then Professor Overbeck,[2] supported by several other authorities, has denied M. Fougères' identification. It is the object of this paper to adduce further reasons for the ascription of these remains to the reliefs mentioned by Pausanias, and it is hoped that the identification may become conclusive.

The three slabs were found among the ruins of a Byzantine church at Mantineia in which they served as pavement, the face bearing the reliefs fortunately having been turned downward. They are of white marble, according to M. Fougères possibly from Doliana near Tegea, and are now deposited in the National Museum at Athens where they have been put together carefully under the direction of M. Kabbadias. The plates illustrating M. Fougères' article are from photographs from the originals taken in the museum; but, owing perhaps to insufficient light, and to spots and corrosions which disfigure the marble and interfere more or less with the lines and modeling, they are not as good as

---

*The substance of this paper was read at the opening meeting of the American School of Classical Studies at Athens, Jan. 17, 1890.

[1] *Bull. de corr. hellén.*, XII, 1888, pp. 105 seq., pls. I, II, III. His view is shared by RAVAISSON, *Compte-rendu de l'acad. des inscript., etc.*, 1888, p. 83; LÖSCHCKE, *Jahrbuch d. Instit.*, 1888, p. 192; FURTWÄNGLER, *Philolog. Wochenschrift*, 1888, p. 1482.

[2] *Bericht. d. Königl. Sächs. Gesell. d. Wissensch.*, 1888, pp. 284 seq.; *Gr. Kunstmythologie*, III, pp. 454, 457, where also a full list of other representations of Apollo and Marsyas is given.

they might be. In such cases casts which give all the lines and do not reproduce the accidental staining of the marble may supplement the accurate appreciation of works of antiquity. The authorities of the museum generously made a set of casts which they presented to the American School to illustrate the present paper when read at one of our meetings.

The three slabs are practically of the same dimensions: slab I is 1.35 m. wide by 0.96 m. in height, while slabs II and III are 1.36 m. wide by 0.96 m. and 0.98 m. in height.

The first slab bears three figures of which the first is seated: a dignified male figure with long curls dressed in the long-sleeved talaric chiton, and himation, and holding a large lyre resting upon his knee. There can be no doubt that this figure represents Apollo. At the other end of this slab is a nude bearded older man playing the double pipes, in an attitude half-retreating, half-advancing, which from the well-known type of the Myronian Marsyas will at once be identified as Marsyas. Between these two figures stands a bearded younger man with a head-dress something like a combination of a veil and a Phrygian cap, wearing a chiton with sleeves, *anaxyrides*, and shoes. He holds in his right hand a knife. From this foreign costume, as well as from the type and evident function of the figure, no archaeologist can fail to see in him the Scythian slave charged with the execution of Marsyas. The scene suggested by this slab is beyond doubt the first stage in the story of the flaying of Marsyas. It is equally evident that the six female figures holding musical instruments, rolls, and papyri represent six of the nine Muses, and it appears evident that one slab is missing which must have contained the other three Muses. Now, in the passage cited above, Pausanias, in describing Mantineia which he enters by the southeast gate, mentions first a double temple of which one half was dedicated to Asklepios; and he continues: Τὸ δὲ ἕτερον Λητοῦς ἐστὶν ἱερὸν καὶ τῶν παίδων. Πραξιτέλης δὲ τὰ ἀγάλματα εἰργάσατο τρίτῃ μετὰ Ἀλκαμένην ὕστερον γενεᾷ. τούτων πεποιημένα ἐστὶν ἐπὶ τῷ βάθρῳ Μοῦσα καὶ Μαρσύας αὐλῶν. We thus learn that Praxiteles made the three statues of the second half of the temple, namely, Leto with her two children Apollo and Artemis, and that on the base of these statues was portrayed a story of Marsyas and the Muses.

Literally, Pausanias speaks only of "a Muse and Marsyas playing on the pipes;" and M. Fougères solves the difficulty in interpreting this passage, which even before his discovery had been felt, by amending it and substituting the plural Μοῦσαι for Μοῦσα. Many years ago, De Witte[3] suggested that the one Muse who could accompany Marsyas would be Euterpe, who presides over flute-playing; but there is no archaeological or literary instance of the conjunction of these two figures known to me, and, as we shall see, this very slab disproves it. It appears possible that Pausanias, who never was a careful and accurate observer of the monuments which he describes loosely, mistook the seated Apollo for a female figure, a Muse, and rapidly noted what he hastily saw, characterizing the whole scene by two figures which he could identify. And this possibility was increased to my mind when I heard that, at the first glance, the discoverers themselves were misled in the same way. Still, perhaps M. Fougères' emendation is the better suggestion, as it includes the figures of all the other slabs,— and as the omission of the letter ι at the end of a word is easily made by any scribe.

With this definite passage of Pausanias to go upon, it seemed to me strange that there could be much hesitation in identifying the slabs found at Mantineia with the reliefs decorating the base of the Praxitelean statues; I was therefore astonished to find that most of the leading archaeologists here at Athens agreed with Professor Overbeck, for, even before I had read M. Fougères' article and was aware of the provenience of the slabs, I had pointed out these works as important specimens of fourth-century relief work of Praxitelean character.

M. Fougères, rightly assuming that there must have been one more slab bearing three Muses, restores the base of the statues by placing one slab upon each of the four sides of the pedestal, and this restoration has been in the minds of archaeologists as the only possible one, ever since the publication of these works. Starting from this conception of their distribution, Professor Overbeck and those who agree with him direct their strongest criticism against the identification on this ground. But, besides this, he and they also maintain that the reliefs themselves, in the posing of the figures and their relation to one another, and in the modeling of every one, as well as in the general character and artistic feeling of the grouping and of the separate figures, are either Roman or late-Hellenistic in style. Now Professor Overbeck, though he holds that M. Fougères has put it beyond all

[3] *Élite Céramogr.*, II, pl. 70, p. 213, Note 3.

doubt that the three slabs belong together, and is right in maintaining that they were not part of a continuous frieze, denies that they could have been arranged on the four sides of the *bathron*, inasmuch as this base would have been decidedly too small for the three statues which stood upon it. Though it might be urged, even against this, that we do not know how large the pieces on either side were, into which each one of these slabs may have been set, just as a picture hangs with space about it upon our walls, still it would be hard to conceive of this base as a whole, if so decorated, and supporting the three large temple-statues. Yet, if we can, as I propose, show that all the four slabs formed a continuous composition and decorated only the front of the base, all the weighty arguments of Professor Overbeck and his supporters against the attribution of the reliefs, so far as these arguments depend upon the arrangement formerly proposed, fall to the ground. Now, I will say at once, though it hardly needs much argument, that the reliefs are more likely to have decorated a *bathron* than anything else. As, from the nature of the subject represented, the whole composition consisted of but four slabs, they are not likely to have formed part of an extended architectural decoration, such as a continuous frieze or single metopes. Nor are they likely, for the same reason, to have formed part of a balustrade or screen; nor could they have been fixed upon a sarcophagus. Four slabs of this dimension, evidently belonging together, are structurally most likely to have decorated the large base of some sculptural monument.

The first mistake in judging these works appears to have been made in that an analogy for the base of the three statues by Praxiteles was unconsciously found in the numerous existing open-air *bathra* discovered at Olympia, Epidauros, and other places. But these interesting bases of statues are chiefly those of athletic and votive figures, and are therefore much smaller in dimensions. They can in no way give us an adequate notion of the size, form, and decoration of the bases belonging to great temple-statues and groups of statues.

Now, as regards the bases of great temple-statues, so far as ancient literary records are concerned, the two about which most was written in antiquity are those of the Olympian Zeus and the Athena Parthenos by Pheidias. As regards the base of the statue of the Olympian Zeus, we learn from Pausanias (v. 11. 8) that it was decorated in relief, that the scene represented the birth of Aphrodite in the presence of all the chief divinities, the action bounded on one side by Helios, rising with his steeds, and, on the other, by Selene descending to the realms of night. The base of the Athena Parthenos was similarly decorated with scenes portraying the birth of Pandora. Fortunately for us, the so-called Lenormant statuette in the British Museum, giving a free copy of the Athena Parthenos, has on the base an imperfect rendering of this scene; but, imperfect as it may be, it shows that the decoration in relief occupied only the front of the base, and did not extend round the four sides. This, moreover, we should naturally have surmised before, inasmuch as it could not have been intended that the visitors should walk round the back of such sacred statues, generally placed toward the west end of the cella, without sufficient space left free at the back for proper appreciation of a relief on the base.

Among extant bases, I would specially draw attention to one decorated with reliefs representing pyrrhic dancers,[4] now in the Acropolis Museum at Athens, to which my attention was drawn by Mr. Loring of King's College, Cambridge, and the British School at Athens. I shall have occasion to recur to these reliefs for further comparison with the works under discussion. For the present, I merely wish to point out that, though this base belonged to what must have been a much smaller group of figures than ours, as the figures in the relief, cut into the solid stone of the base, are less than half the size of our Muses, it is still instructive as showing sculptured decoration similarly disposed only on the front side.

The most important light, however, upon the disposition of these slabs and the base which they ornamented, is thrown by the important discovery at Lykosoura in the autumn of 1889 of the temple-statues of Damophon of Messene by Messrs. Kabbadias and Leonardos. The temple and the statues there found are beyond a doubt those described by Pausanias (VIII. 38). The date of these works cannot be far removed from that of Praxiteles. Now, there were four statues on this base, while there were three on that of Mantineia. By computation, the width of the Lykosoura base would be about eight metres, and on this ratio, a base for only three statues would be about six metres wide. Four slabs of the dimension of our Mantineian reliefs would measure

[4] BEULÉ, L'Acropole d'Athènes, II, pls. III and IV; RANGABÉ, Antiq. hellén., pl. XXI; vide, also, MICHAELIS in Rhein. Mus., XVII. 217, and Mittheil. d. deutsch. Arch. Instit. Athen, I, 295. The inscription is published CIA, II. No. 1286.

about 5¼ metres. Hence, so far as actual measurements would go, four such slabs would suffice, when placed continuously side by side, to decorate the front of the base of a group of temple-statues such as the Leto, Apollo and Artemis at Mantineia in all likelihood formed. Accordingly the arguments of Professor Overbeck, so far as the ordinary dimensions and decoration of such bases are concerned, fall to the ground, and leave unshaken the probability of such an arrangement of the reliefs from Mantineia.

A careful consideration of the composition of these reliefs, necessarily leads us to the same conclusion. There can hardly be a doubt, first, that there was one more slab sculptured with three Muses, and, second, that the slab with Apollo must have occupied a central position. The presence of six Muses lends probability to the conclusion that at the time when these reliefs were made the Muses as accompanying Apollo had been already fixed at the number of nine. I must, however, leave this point for discussion hereafter. Assuming, then, that there were four slabs in all, and that the slab with Apollo occupied the central place, the next questions are whether of the two extant slabs with Muses the one containing the seated Muse is to be placed to right or left of the Apollo slab, and whether the remaining slab is to be placed at the extreme left or right. Mr. H. D. Hale, while a student at the American School at Athens, made the restorations[5] of the group and the base reproduced in Plate XV. Apart from all other considerations of composition which have led me to place the slabs as they are here given, i. e., the seated Muse immediately beside Apollo and the remaining slab to the left hand of this, there is one, apparently minute, but very interesting fact which finally confirmed me in this arrangement. Of the Muses there are four heads comparatively well preserved. Among these that of the seated Muse and the one immediately beside her are in full-face, while the two others are turned in different directions. The head of the Muse with the pipes is turned to our right in three-quarter view, that of the central figure in the other slab to our left. Now, there is a marked difference in the workmanship of these two heads; the inner side of the face of the Muse with the pipes is carefully finished, while the inner side

---

[5] I need hardly say that the statues are imaginary. The Apollo would probably not have been represented without any drapery. But I think Mr. Hale has been successful in giving a certain fourth-century character to his composition.

of the other head is comparatively unfinished, and the contrast is here the greater as the outer side of this head is beautifully worked. It is evident, from this fact, that the inner side of the face of the Muse with the pipes was designed to be prominently visible to the spectator looking at the group of three statues on the base; while the inner side of the other head was not meant to be carefully examined. Placing the slabs as they are here given, and imagining the spectator to stand opposite the centre of the base, the Muse with the pipes presents herself in three-quarter view, the inner side of the face becoming well visible, while the central Muse of the other slab exhibits her head in profile, the profile being exquisitely finished, while the unfinished inner side of the face does not show. Further, the Muse with the papyrus is the only one who has a larger bare space at her back, which gives a proper finish to the composition. I therefore place this slab at the left end. Then follows the other extant slab with Muses, then the slab with Apollo and Marsyas, and on this side the composition was brought to a conclusion by another slab with three standing Muses similar in composition to the slab at the other end. In Mr. Hale's drawing (PL. XV) the end slab has been repeated on the other side to give some idea of the ensemble of the composition.

This I postulate is the composition decorating the front of the base of the three statues; and with this postulate we will proceed to consider the main features of the composition, first, from the point of view of the subject represented, and, second, from the constructive or tectonic side.

The first task an ancient sculptor at work upon a group consisting of several figures had to deal with, was the proper arrangement of the figures with regard to their relative importance to the scene depicted, and this arrangement must then be modified by the constructive destination of such grouping. It is unnecessary to say that the most important figure or figures must occupy the middle. Moreover, when there were separate slabs, it was desirable, as far as possible, to place the central group on one slab. This is done in the present case by placing Apollo, Marsyas and the Scythian on one slab. If there had been five slabs in our composition, the arrangement would have been a comparatively easy task; for thus this slab would have been placed in the middle with two slabs on either side. But then it would have been desirable to place Apollo in the centre of this slab, perhaps with the Scythian on one side and Marsyas on the other. But the difficulty is still further increased by the actual number of figures represented in the whole of this composition. When there is an uneven number of figures, due prominence can easily be given to one figure, by placing it in the middle with an equal number of figures on either side. This is done, for instance, in both the pediments of the Temple of Zeus at Olympia. But when there is an even number of figures, it is not possible, from the considerations of symmetrical composition, to give prominence of place to one figure. In the western pediment of the Parthenon, the centre was equally occupied by two figures of equal importance in the scene enacted; moreover the sacred olive-tree really occupies the centre of the pediment with Athena and Poseidon in diverging lines on either side. I have several times hitherto pointed out how the careful study of extant ancient compositions forces us to conclude that the ancients studied most minutely such questions of grouping, and I would refer the reader to what I have written on the arrangement of the central figures of the Parthenon Frieze,[6] where I have endeavored to show that the introduction of the central incident was due, in a great degree, to the desire of giving proper prominence to three figures, viz., Zeus, Hera and Athena. Brunn, Flasch, and Treu, also, have pointed with emphasis to the careful consideration of symmetrical balance in such compositions. Having an even number of figures, namely, twelve, our artist could not place Apollo in the centre. The physical centre in our composition therefore lies between Apollo and the seated Muse. The artist has furthermore emphasized this as the centre by placing two seated figures on either side of the central point. This corresponded probably also to the general arrangement of the statues on the base, in which Leto was probably seated in the middle, while Apollo and Artemis were standing on either side. The discovery at Lykosoura has shown us that the two central figures (Demeter and Despoina) were seated, while Anytos and Artemis were standing on either side. The points immediately on either side of the centre would thus be occupied by two seated figures. But, no doubt, the danger would arise that Apollo and the seated Muse would be made equally prominent. Yet there is one striking point of difference in the compositions where this arrange-

[6] *Essays on the Art of Pheidias*, pp. 244–253.

ment obtains. If it had been the intention of the artist to give similar importance to both of the two seated figures grouped on either side of the centre, he would have placed them either face to face or back to back. In the frieze of the Parthenon, Zeus heads the one side of the Assembly of Gods, turned from the centre, and Athena the other, facing in the opposite direction,—an arrangement, too, which is highly conducive to symmetry. In our case, however, the seated Muse is not turned toward the other Muses as if she were heading that side of the composition, but is turned toward Apollo, and, by this attitude, throws the symmetry somewhat out, leaving the preponderance of interest and line toward the other side where what there is of drama is enacted. This is the only element of asymmetry in what is otherwise composed in almost extreme severity of balance. To realize how far this balance goes, I merely point to the fact that, while we have two seated figures in the centre, each with a stringed instrument, we have beside these respectively the only two figures that are approximately in full face. The lines of the arms of these two figures are what might be called rhythmically symmetrical: the arms of the Muse and of the Scythian that are toward the centre are both extended downward in a flattish curve, diverging from the centre; the arms away from the centre are drawn upward in a sharp curve toward the centre. The figures outside of these again, Marsyas and the slim Muse at the end of the slab, both have pipes which they hold toward the centre. I will not confuse the reader by pointing out further the system of balance and symmetry in the grouping of every single slab. I am most concerned with the demonstration of the continuity and completeness of this grouping, consisting of four slabs placed side by side.

The figure at the extreme left end, then, being turned squarely toward the centre, shows the general direction of line, and the seated Muse nearest the centre, being turned toward Apollo, again draws the eye away from the physical centre toward the adjoining slab, where Apollo and Marsyas form the chief group. Thus, in the difficult task of filling one slab with three figures enacting the scene, and of placing six Muses on the one side of Apollo and only three Muses on the other side of Marsyas, while yet maintaining a symmetrical arrangement with regard to the centre on the base, the artist has succeeded well in conciliating the opposed conditions of his problem.

It is most interesting to note, furthermore, how the sculptor has used the constructive suggestions of his work of decoration to emphasize the importance of the chief figure and scene. In the case of pedimental groups, and even of a continuous architectural frieze, greater importance can be given to a figure or to a group of figures by varying the outlines of the whole composition, so that the more important figures are taller or stand higher, and there is thus a natural climax of line corresponding to the rise in interest. This pyramidal form is the ordinary canon for composition. But such a rise of line on the pedestal of a statue or group, where the chief structural aim is that of stability for the figures which it holds, would be painfully unconstructive. It would suggest in line not only that the central statue was unstable, but that the statues on either side would be in danger of falling off. Our artist has thus adopted another device. He has felt that importance is given by variation of line; but, instead of making the lines rise as they approach the centre of importance, he has produced an abrupt depression of line in the centre which, in an equally effective manner, attracts the eye to the most important figure in the whole relief, though that figure does not occupy the actual centre. Five of the Muses on the left stand erect with the line of their heads horizontal, and then there is a sudden fall of line as we near the centre in the seated Muse, which becomes still more marked when we reach Apollo, who with his large lyre immediately attracts the eye, and, by his attitude, directs us toward Marsyas. Marsyas again, by his striking action, fixes our attention and holds it; for he is the only figure who, in bold contrast to the repose of all the others, is in violent action. While his action thus readily attracts the eye to that side of the centre, the general treatment of outline-composition in the reliefs as a whole properly draws our eye to Apollo. If, as I have done, we place the three slabs together with the arrangement proposed, and a drawing of equal dimensions containing three figures, similar in attitude and grouping to those of the left end, is placed on the extreme right, and if then we stand at some distance from the relief in the actual central line between the two seated figures, first, there will be no sense of want of symmetry in the composition as a whole; secondly, our eye will be at once attracted to Apollo as the most important figure, and from him it will naturally pass on to Marsyas.

Thus the composition in itself confirms the view, suggested to us by the evidence of similar known monuments, that these three slabs, with another that is missing, formed part of a continuous scene which would properly decorate the base of a group of statues, and that the base of the Mantineian statues was, according to all the evidence we have of dimensions, such as would require a frieze of the size of the one consisting of four such slabs.

If now we consider the date of these reliefs as it is manifested in the treatment of the subject and in the style of the work, I can see hardly any ground for assigning it to the late Hellenistic or the Roman period.

To begin with the moulding which finishes off the relief on the top: it is of so simple a character that I should defy an archæologist to adduce reliefs of the later periods that manifest a treatment so simple. But in these matters I would not trust my own judgment, and I am happy to adduce the opinion of Mr. Schultz of the British School at Athens, who has made a careful study of Greek mouldings, and according to whom this moulding points to the fourth, and would not be out of place even in the fifth, century B. C.

As regards the composition again, it appears to me that there is a simplicity bordering almost on severity in the arrangement of the figures side by side, an absence of that restless fulness of line approaching redundancy which characterizes the relief-work of the Hellenistic and of the Roman periods. It is true that there are occasional instances of Hellenistic sarcophagi ornamented by single figures placed without any connection with one another round the four sides, as one I have recently seen which Hamdy Bey discovered at Sidon; but these are so exceptional that they seem to me derivatives from such Hellenic works as that we are discussing. Moreover, such Hellenistic reliefs generally manifest some intrusion of an architectural nature in the relief itself, and the single figures are usually separated from one another by pillars or suggestions of niches. But, generally, where such reliefs of the later periods are not already full of lines in the violent action of the figures, trees or shrubs or other objects of landscape are introduced. For the arrangement as a whole I find the closest analogy in the relief of the pyrrhic dancers referred to above, which, as has already been stated, is a work of the fourth century B. C. It may moreover be observed that this fourth-century relief, which has a similarly simple moulding, has its figures subdivided into groups of three and four with intervening spaces, though there is no natural subdivision owing to a union of separate slabs.

If, furthermore, we take the general treatment of the subject represented, I should say that it is directly opposed to Hellenistic or Roman treatment. The flaying of Marsyas is a very favorite subject in these periods, and is commonly represented with dramatic vividness in the moment immediately preceding the barbarous punishment inflicted by Apollo upon his presumptuous rival.[7] Marsyas is suspended by the arms, and the barbarous Scythian, of whom the famous Aretino in Florence is the type, is in the act of whetting his knife to inflict the punishment. The attendant figures, moreover, all display some intense interest in the action. In our representation, on the other hand, extreme moderation is used even at the cost of a dramatic rendering of the story. The only figure shown in action is Marsyas himself, and for him the fourth century had a prototype which belonged to the archaic period, more than a century earlier than the age of Praxiteles, namely, the Marsyas of Myron. Everywhere, in the types of the figures as well as in their general arrangement and attitudes, the idea of beauty, one might almost say comeliness, seems to have been predominant, and to have prevailed over the desire of rendering the dramatic side of the story.

The Muses moreover in their conception are, as far as we know, of the character which would best correspond to their representation in the fourth century.[8]

As is the case with all the Greek mythological types, those of the Muses were not at once fixed in the form in which we know them; nor were they ever rigidly stereotyped in the conception of one period.

At first, in the earliest times, both in literature and in art, the personalities of the Muses were not distinct and they do not differ essentially from Nymphs, Horai, Charites, etc. Nor, in traditions differing from that of the Hesiodic poems, was their number fixed to that of nine. There is evidence that the number of three was the more common number even down to the middle of the fifth century B. C. Nor were the names attributed to them, under which we know them, definitely assigned to each till a comparatively late time. Even down to the Alexandrine period, there appears to have existed con-

---

[7] *Vide* two sarcophagi published by TRENDELENBURG, *Annali dell' Inst.*, 1871, tav. d'*Agg*. D from Villa Pacca, Rome; the other from the Villa Medici, *Annali*, tav. d'*Agg*. E; also one published by WIESELER (who mentions others in footnote, p. 122), *Annali*, 1861, a sarcophagus in cathedral of Palermo. See, also, the complete list of representations of the *Musikalischer Wettstreit des Marsyas* in OVERBECK, *Griechische Kunstmythologie*, Leipzig, 1889, III. pp. 420-82.

[8] Dr. OSCAR BIE has summarized what is known concerning the treatment of Muses in ancient art: *Die Musen in der Antiken Kunst*, Berlin, 1887.

siderable fluctuation in the form and attribution of such names, as well as in the assignment to the different Muses of their provinces, functions, and attributes.

At first the Muses are merely the musical companions of the gods who rejoice their hearts with song (*Iliad*, I. 603), and afterward the followers of Apollo, when, in the transformation of the personality of this deity at Delphi, the sterner python-slayer becomes the gentler leader of song and music. Song, music and the dance are their chief pursuits.

With Aristotle the subdivision and classification of the arts and sciences are first developed, and are fixed and thoroughly differentiated by his followers at Alexandria, until the departments become stereotyped. Corresponding to this process, the Muses become classified and every one of them is, as far as possible, made the personified mythical type for some branch of art or learning. This of course leads to the multiplication and specification of attributes. In the fourth century B. C. this development has not yet taken place. We find only the musical instruments, attitudes of dancing, the papyrus or scroll, and the diptych corresponding to a book. The mask for the comic muse, and the globe for Urania have not yet been introduced. The latter attribute is distinctly late.

The earliest extant work of art representing the Muses is the so-called François vase[9] by Klitias. This vase is certainly as early as the sixth century B. C. and is thoroughly archaic in character. The Muses here accompany the gods in the procession in celebration of the marriage of Peleus and Thetis. They are nine in number, are led by Kalliope and have the well-known[10] names given in the Theogony of Hesiod. But in later vases the numbers vary—in fact we hardly ever find nine Muses. Four and six seem to be the predominant numbers. Dr. Bie thinks that these vases tend to show that in the periods which they mark the Muses were still fluctuating in number.

As I have on several previous occasions maintained, the purely decorative and tectonic considerations of vase-compositions were paramount to the vase-painter and influenced and modified even his treat-

[9] *Arch. Zeit.*, 1873, p. 24 seq.
[10] Ταῦτ᾽ ἄρα Μοῦσαι ἄειδον Ὀλύμπια δώματ᾽ ἔχουσαι,
ἐννέα θυγατέρες μεγάλου Διὸς ἐκγεγαυῖαι,
Κλειώ τ᾽ Εὐτέρπη τε, Θάλειά τε Μελπομένη τε,
Τερψιχόρη τ᾽ Ἐρατώ τε, Πολύμνιά τ᾽ Οὐρανίη τε,
Καλλιόπη θ᾽ ἣ δὲ προφερεστάτη ἐστὶν ἁπασέων.
ἡ γὰρ καὶ βασιλεῦσιν ἄμ᾽ αἰδοίοισιν ὀπηδεῖ (*Theogonia*, 75 seq.).

ment of mythological scenes and types; we may therefore go wrong if we attach too much importance to representations on vases for the detailed interpretation of mythical scenes. So in the case of the Muses, the number of figures introduced by the vase-painter was entirely determined by the number of figures his composition demanded. Among the vases I would single out for comparison several red-figured ones[11] which correspond in spirit to the Mantineian reliefs and are themselves not later than the fourth century B. C. Among these, moreover, none of the later attributes, such as the mask or the globe, occur. They have the different forms of lyre, barbiton, syrinx, etc., flutes, and scroll. More florid ones of a later period have more figures and fuller lines.[12]

The earliest historical artistic representations mentioned in ancient authors are the chest of Kypselos,[13] and the altar of Hyakinthos at Amyklai.[14] The sculptors who made statues of Muses in the beginning of the fifth century[15] were Ageladas, Kanachos and Aristokles. These Muses had the lyre, barbiton and syrinx, the χέλυς, and flutes. A Muse of Lesbothemis[16] has the sambyke (a stringed instrument, probably the same as the trigonon). Toward the middle of the fifth century we hear of the famous group of Apollo with Leto and Artemis and the Muses[17] decorating the eastern pediment of the Temple of Apollo at Delphi. This was by Praxias, the pupil of Kalamis. Dr. Bie thinks that there were probably only three Muses in this pediment. I see no reason for believing this; on the contrary, from the nature of such pedimental compositions it appears more likely that there were nine.

It is however quite certain that the group of Muses in the Helikonian sanctuary of the Muses, by Kephisodotos[18] the elder, the father of Praxiteles, consisted of nine figures, and from this time on, though

---

[11] Among these a very fine Volcentian kalpis with Apollo and seven Muses, GERHARD, *Trinkschalen und Gefässe*, II. 17. It was bought from the collection of Lucien Bonaparte in 1841, and is now at Berlin. Plate 18 gives a krater (so-called oxybaphon) now at Berlin with Apollo, Terpsichore and Kleio. A fine vase with Muses and a poet (Mousaios) is published in WELCKER, *Alte Denkmäler*, III. pl. 31. This vase, also from Vulci, is now in London. A fine one with Marsyas, a Panathenaic amphora, is published in LENORMANT and DE WITTE, *Élite Céramogr.*, II. pl. 75; another, II. 79.

[12] *Élite Céramogr.*, II. pls. 70–73. Quite a florid one in Naples, vide *Arch. Zeit.*, 1869, taf. 17.

[13] PAUS., V. 18. 4.   [14] PAUS., III. 19. 5.

[15] *Anthol. Gr.*, II. 15. 35; OVERBECK, *Schriftquellen*, No. 395.

[16] ATHEN., IV. 182; OVERBECK, *S. Q.*, 2083.

[17] PAUSANIAS, X. 19. 4; OVERBECK, *S. Q.*, 857.

[18] PAUSAN., IX. 30. 1; OVERBECK, *S. Q.*, 878. Three were the work of Kephisodotos, three were by Strongylion, three by Olympiosthenes.

single Muses were frequently represented in statues, the number of nine must certainly have been fixed as the recognized number of their full chorus. It is likely, too, that many of the later Roman statues are reproductions of the types established by Kephisodotos and his colleagues. In the case of Praxiteles, we have instances of the manner in which father and son worked on the same traditions, the Hermes with the infant Dionysos being the continuation of a type of figures introduced by Kephisodotos. It thus appears highly probable that the Mantineian relief reproduces in a modified form the Muses of Helikon. And this becomes the more likely, when we remember that these Muses on the relief have struck archæologists as being reproductions of single statues.

I will not touch here upon the Muses of Ambrakia which Dr. Bie[19] has treated with great thoroughness. Of extant reliefs I would point to the circular base of a statue from Halikarnassos published by Dr. Trendelenburg.[20] This relief is supposed to be of the third century B. C. and at latest of the Hellenistic, not of the Roman, period. In this there is as yet no distinction between the tragic and the comic Muse, the globe does not occur, and the style is not of the late redundant form. But from the introduction of the trees and the general character of composition and execution of single figures, the work is certainly considerably later than is our Mantineian relief.

A much later work, manifesting fully the treatment as influenced by Alexandrine learning and art, is the *tabula Archelai*,[21] the apotheosis of Homer by Archelaos of Priene which is fixed by the palæographic character of the inscription as of the first century B. C. Here we have all the names and all the late attributes. This representation differs in character from the Mantineian reliefs almost as much as do the Roman sarcophagi referred to above.

Now, the fact that we have two standing Muses without attributes in the centre of each of the two Muse-slabs makes it almost necessary that the non-extant slab should have had a similar figure in the centre. The globe and mask could not have been massed into this one slab. A possible restoration suggests itself with one erect figure in the centre, at the extreme right end a Muse holding something like the diptychon, and at the other end a Muse with a musical instrument.

[19] *Die Musen*, pp. 24 seq.   [20] *Winckelmann-Programm*, Berlin, 1876.
[21] OVERBECK, *Kunstarch. Vorl.*, p. 214; KORTEGARN, *De tabula Archelai*, Bonn, 1862.

At all events, from the mythological treatment of the Muses on the Mantineian relief, when viewed in the series of such representations, it appears conclusive, that, as regards the rendering of these types, they cannot be later than the fourth century and are probably of the immediate period of Praxiteles. Finally, to consider the single figures: that of Apollo, seated in dignified repose, would not only point to the fourth century but might even go back to a prototype of the fifth. It is probable that the artist exercised some restraint in this figure, which partook of a religious character. The relation of the Marsyas to the Myronian statue has already been pointed out. Moreover other instances of the adaptation of Myronian types in Praxitelean art have been dwelt on by Kekulé.[22] As regards the Scythian, I have already maintained that in the treatment of this figure there is nothing pointing to the later periods. On the contrary we should contrast him with the Aretino, which typifies the treatment of a barbarian in what is probably Pergamene art. If Overbeck sees something uncommon and late in his headdress and general drapery, I would ask for instances of the treatment of such figures in the fourth century and earlier periods. The examples present to my mind are those of the Archer, probably Paris, in the eastern pediment of the Temple of Athena at Aigina, a work of the early fifth century B. C., in which this foreign warrior wears the Phrygian cap, and has the close-fitting sleeves and trousers; second, as far as we can make them out, the foreign warriors on the frieze of the Temple of Nike Apteros; third, some of the Amazons of the frieze of the Mausoleum of Halikarnassos, and for the lower part of the body the colossal horseman from Halikarnassos. If this headdress is commonly worn in later times by Paris, Amazons, Artemis, Adonis and Attis, it means that these later representations have been taken from such earlier types as the Scythian here represented. The same applies still more to the figures of Muses. If the seated Muse reminds us of some of the most graceful Tanagrean terracottas, it shows us whence the makers of these terracottas got their prototypes; for we have never assumed that the works of these minor artists were always original inspirations. Vague general analogies in the wearing of the drapery may also be found between some of these Muses and Roman draped female figures. But as I have had occasion to set forth once before,[23]

[22] *Der Kopf des Praxitelischen Hermes*, 1881.
[23] *Journal of Hellenic Studies*, VII (1886), p. 247.

the general arrangement of the drapery of some of these statues of the Roman period was borrowed from earlier prototypes, especially of the fourth century B. C. And if we can point out analogies in the treatment of drapery and in attitudes between the Mantineian Muses and figures that are undoubtedly of the fourth century, we must, taking into account the sober and distinctly Hellenic technic of the relief-work of these slabs, assign them also to the fourth century B. C. I have little doubt in my mind, that the fact that these Muses have superficial likeness in the arrangement of drapery to some works of the Hellenistic period existing in the Italian museums, has been the efficient cause which has led some archaeologists to assign them to the later date. Now I merely ask the student to compare these Muses as regards the arrangement of drapery: first, with the colossal figure of Mausolos and of Artemisia from Halikarnassos,[24] undoubtedly made about the year 350 B. C. These statues appear to be the prototypes to many draped figures of the Hellenistic period. Secondly, I would compare them with the draped female figure on the drum of the column from the Temple of Artemis at Ephesos,[25] also a work of about the same period in the fourth century. I would further adduce the statue of the Lateran Sophokles,[26] probably going back to the same time. Then let us compare the drapery of the second and third Muses to our left with the drapery of the standing female figure on a beautiful large sepulchral slab in the National Museum at Athens, here published for the first time, and without doubt a work of the fourth century (PL. XVI, left). It will be noticed how in the arrangement of himation and chiton, how in the folding and even in such details as the cross-band of folds about the waist, and the small knot or end of drapery pulled under the end of this cross-band, the arrangement is essentially the same. Another fourth-century sepulchral relief in the same museum hitherto unpublished (PL. XVI, right) bears the closest analogy, in the treatment of the figure and of the drapery, to the slim Muse with the pipes. Finally if we compare this figure of the third Muse with the two central female figures on the base of the pyrrhic dancers previously referred to, not only must we be struck with the close analogy, but we should certainly be led to the opinion that these two female figures are in the treatment of the drapery and the heads slightly later modifications of the types as shown in the two Muses to which they bear analogy. But

[24] Mrs. MITCHELL, p. 470, etc.; *Monumenti*, v. 18.
[25] RAYET, *Monuments Antiques*, II. pl. 50. [26] *Monumenti dell'Inst.*, IV. 27.

by the inscription on this base the work has been assigned to the second half of the fourth century B. C. It is thus beyond a doubt that the Muses, as here rendered, have their closest analogies in works of the age of Praxiteles, and if we add to this the general feeling in the attitude, with slight inclination of the head, of the Muse with the pipes, and consider the sentiment of all these figures, we cannot but appreciate that they are in all their characteristics expressive of Praxitelean art. By this we do not mean that these sculptures are necessarily by the hand of Praxiteles, but that they contain features which point to his influence as it has been manifested to us in the works we now assign to him.

To sum up: At Mantineia reliefs are found representing Muses grouped with Apollo and Marsyas with the pipes. These reliefs are better suited to decorate the front of the base of a large group of statues than to any other function we can think of. From what we know of the bases of such temple-statues the dimensions of four such slabs would just correspond in extent to appropriate ornament of this purpose. The technical and artistic treatment of the relief, the conception of the subject, the grouping of the figures, and the style and feeling of every single figure, correspond most with the art of the period of Praxiteles. We now read in Pausanias that the base of the temple-statues of Leto, Artemis and Apollo was ornamented with a representation of Marsyas with the pipes and a Muse. The conclusion seems evident. Is it probable that at Mantineia there existed another relief, not an architectural frieze, nor a balustrade, representing the same subject as that described by Pausanias, made without any relation to the same scene as represented by the great artist in the same place? It might be urged that the present reliefs are a later copy of the earlier sculptures that had been injured or destroyed. Well! a bad Roman copy it certainly is not; and we can see no reason for thus shirking the responsibility of assigning to Praxitelean art a work which we have the good fortune to possess. Such shirking reminds one of the pleasantry made by a maintainer of the personality of Homer: that the Homeric poems were not written by Homer but by another man of the same name.

CHARLES WALDSTEIN.

American School of Classical Studies at Athens.
January, 1890.

A GREEK FRAGMENT OF THE EDICT OF DIOCLETIAN FROM PLATAIA.

[PLATE XVIII.]

NOTE.—The inscription here published by Professor Mommsen was discovered at Plataia during the excavations of the American School of Classical Studies at Athens, in the month of March, 1890 (see REPORT, above, p. 255). While the Latin Preamble found in the previous year and published by Messrs. Tarbell and Rolfe (see above, pp. 233–244), came from the site of the Byzantine Church marked 1 in Messrs. Washington and Hale's map of Plataia (see above), this Greek fragment of the Edict of Diocletian was found in Church V at a considerable distance to the southwest of Church I. This slab together with another containing an inscription with female names and dedicated to some goddess (Artemis or Demeter), served as covering-stones to a Byzantine grave immured in the west wall of the church. The hypothesis expressed by me (*l. c.*) that the Latin Preamble may have preceded the Greek text of the edict containing the prices of which this inscription forms a part may lack sufficient foundation. There would, if this were not the case, have been a Greek as well as a Latin version of the edict at Plataia.

CHARLES WALDSTEIN.

The slab of white marble, of which we offer a facsimile [PL. XVIII] after the drawing of Mr. Lolling, is 1.10 m. high, where it is best preserved; 3.73 broad; and between 0.09 and 0.10 in thickness, as it is not worked smoothly on the back. The form of the crowning ornament is shown in the plate; the letters engraved there are of no importance, having been added afterward by some idler. The two sides are wrought so that other slabs could be joined to this and form with it a whole. The slab, in its present state, has lost the left corner and the lower part, so that of the three columns it contained when complete, the first 44 lines of the first column are reduced to a few letters and all three are defaced at the bottom. In its present state the first column numbers 76 lines, mostly incomplete, the second and third 68 lines each. As the part wanting between the second and third columns has been preserved in the other fragments of the Edict, corresponding to ch. 17, 18–50—*i. e.*, 33 lines of my edition,—the number of lines of the slab in its complete state must have amounted to about 100. This cannot be ascertained exactly, as the division of the lines is not at all regular.

For the arrangement of the Edict generally the Plataian fragment is very useful, though it only confirms the arrangement adopted in my edition conjecturally. It shows that what is there given as ch. 16, really preceded the following, and it allows a nearly complete restitution of these two important chapters.

I give the text as it has been copied, with his habitual accuracy, by Mr. Lolling, corrected in a few passages by the squeeze he sent me.* I have added the variations of the other texts, so far as they correspond with the new one; where the defects of the Plataian copy are filled up by another, the supplements have been put in brackets []. In general the reader is referred to my recent paper on the Edict in *Hermes* (vol. XXXV, pp. 17–35), where he will find indicated all the fragments discovered since my edition of the Edict in the *Corpus Insc. Lat.*, vol. III (1873), p. 801 *seq.* It is marvellous how much has been added to the old stock in the last few years, and it may well be admitted that this growth is due not so much to good fortune, as to the growing energy and intelligence of studious researches.

FIRST COLUMN.

16, 40   21 [ἰς χλαμύδα Μουτουνησίαν ὀ. α   ✱] ΚΕ
16, 41   22 [ἰς χλαμύδα Λαδικηνὴν Μουτουνησίαν ὀ. α ✱] ΚΕ
16, 42   23 [βαρβαρικαρίῳ διὰ χρυσοῦ ἐργαζομέν]ῳ
         24 [ὑπὲρ ἔργου πρωτείου   ✱] ΄Α
16, 43   25 [ἔργου δευτερείου   ✱] Ψ Ν
16, 44   26 [βαρβαρικαρίῳ ἰς ὁλοσηρικὸν ὑπὲρ ὀ. α] ✱ Φ
16, 45   27 [ἔργου δευτερείου ὑπὲρ ὀ. α   ] ✱ Υ
16, 46   28 [σηρικαρίῳ ἐργαζομένῳ εἰς σονψειρικὸν τρεφομένῳ] ✱ ΚΕ
16, 48   29 [εἰς ὁλοσηρικὸν σκουτλᾶτον   ] ✱ Ζ
16, 49   30 [γερδίᾳ τρεφομένῳ ὑπὲρ εἱματίου πεξοῦ τῶν ϲ]ἰς πα-

16, 42, ΙѠ Plat. 16, 47, ἰς ὁλοσιρικὸν ἄσημον τρεφομένῳ ἡμερήσια ✱ΚΕ *is wanting in* Plat. 16, 48, ✱Ζ thus Plat. and Karyst. ✱Μ Theb.

*These corrections were mostly entered by Dr. Lolling in the facsimile, but the two texts still disagree in some minor points.   A. C. M.

	31 [ράδοσιν ήμερήσια]	✻ ΙΒ
16, 50	32 [ἐν εἱματίοις Μουτουνησίοις ἢ τοῖς] λοιποῖς	
	33 [τρεφομένῳ]	✻ ΙΒ
16, 51	34 [λ... αρ.... ζομένῳ Μουτουννήσι]α ἢ θα-	
	35 [λάσσια τρεφομένῳ λ.]α	✻ Μ
16, 52	36....... [τεινην ἢ Λαδ]ικηνὴν	
	37.......... λι. α.	✻ Λ
16, 53	38....... [δευτερείας ὑπὲρ] λι. α	✻ Κ
16, 54	39....... τριτείας ὑπὲρ] λι. α	✻ ΙΕ
16, 55	40..... [εἰς] ἔργον πρωτῖον	✻ Μ
16, 56	41 [εἰς ἔργο]ν δευτερίον τρε.	✻ Κ
	42 [περὶ φουλλ]ώνων	
16, 58	43 γναφεῖ ὑ]πὲρ χλανίδος τῶν εἰς παρά-	
	44 [στασι]ν καινῆς	✻ Ν
16, 58α	45 στί]χης τῶν εἰς παράδοσιν καιν.	✻ ΚΕ
16, 59	46 ἀσήμου ἐξ ἐρέας τραχυτέρας	✻ Κ
16, 60	47 ἐνδρομίδος ἤτοι ρακάνης καιν.	✻ Λ
16, 61	48 δαλματικ[ο]μαφόρτου τραχυτέρ.	✻ Ν
16, 62	49 δαλματικ[ο]μαφορ. καιν. πεξοῦ καθα.	✻ Ρ
16, 63	50 στρικτω[ρ. καινῆ]ς πεξῆς καθαρ.	✻ Ν
16, 64	51 δαλματικῆς καιν. συ[ψη]ρικ. ἀνδ.	✻ Ϲ
16, 65	52 στίχης καινῆς συψηρικοῦ	✻ ΡΟΕ
16, 67	53 δαλματικο[μαφόρτου] καιν[ο]ῦ συψ[η]ρ.	✻ Τ
16, 68	54 δαλματί[κῆς ὀλοσειρ]ικ. ἀνδ.	✻ Υ
16, 69	55 δαλματικ[ομαφόρτου καινοῦ] ὀλ[ο]σειρ.	✻ Χ
16, 70	56 στίχης [καινῆς ὀλοσει]ρικοῦ	✻ ϹΝ
16, 71	57 ἀσήμου [καινοῦ ὀλοσει]ρικοῦ	✻ Ϲ
16, 72	58 χλαμύδ[ος Μουτ]ουνησίας διπλ. και.	✻ Φ
16, 73	59 χλαμ[ύδος Μου]τουνη. ἁπλῆς	✻ ϹΝ
16, 74	60 φιβλατωρίου Μουτουνη. καινοῦ	✻ Ϲ
16, 75	61 φιβλατωρίου Λαδικηνοῦ καιν.	✻ Ϲ

50 33, ΙΒ Plat. ΙϚ Theb. Ι Karyst. 16, 55 40, πρωτεῖον ἡμερ. Karyst. 56 42, ΔѠΝѠΝ Plat. 16, 61, ... αψέρτου καινοῦ τραχυτέρου Theb. 16, 62, ... ιερτου καινοῦ πεαου καθα. Theb. 16, 64, ... ψιρικοῦ ἀνδρείας καινῆς Theb. 16, 65, ... ρικοῦ καινῆς Theb. 16, 66, [δελματικ]ῆς συψηρικοῦ ἀσήμου καινῆς ✻ ΡΚΕ Theb. is wanting in Plat. 16, 67, καινοῦ Theb. omits. 16, 68, καινῆς added in Theb. Karyst. 16, 71, καινοῦ Karyst.... ης Theb. 16, 72, χλανίδος καινῆς Μουτουνησίας Karyst. Theb. 16, 73, χλανίδος καινῆς Μ. ἁ Karyst. Theb. 16, 74, καινοῦ Μουτ. Karyst. Theb. 16, 75, καινοῦ Λαδ. Karyst. Theb.

16, 76	62 χλαμύδος Λαδικηνῆς καιν.		✳ Ϲ
16, 78	63 Βίρρου Λαδικηνοῦ καινοῦ		✳ ΡΟΕ
16, 77	64 Βίρρου Νερβικοῦ καινοῦ		✳ Χ
16, 79	65 Βίρρου ρειπησίου καὶ ταυρογαστρικοῦ		✳ Τ
16, 80	66 Βίρρου Νωρικοῦ καινοῦ		✳ Ϲ
16, 81	67 ὑπὲρ τῶν λοιπῶν Βίρρων		✳ Ρ
16, 82	68 Βίρρων Ἄφρων ἢ Ἀχαικῶν		✳ Ν
	69 περὶ τειμῆς τῶν σιρικ[ῶν]		
16, 83	70 σιρικοῦ λευκοῦ λι. [α		✳ Μ͞Β]
16, 84	71 τοῖς τὸ σιρικὸν λύουσι[ν . . . .]		
	72 σιν μετὰ τῆς [τροφῆς ὁ. α		✳ Ζ͞Δ]
	73 περὶ πορφύ[ρας]		
16, 85	74 μεταξαβ[λάττης λι. α		✳ Μ͞]
16, 86?	75 πορφ[ύρας		
16, 87?	76 πορφ[ύρας		

Here are wanting about 24 lines, of which the first half corresponds to ch. **16, 88–100** and continues the prices of purple; the latter contained the price of flax.

SECOND COLUMN.

1	φόρμης α	λι.	α	✳ ΑϹ
2	φόρμης β	λι.	α	✳ ΛΖ
3	φόρμης γ	λι.	α	✳ ΩΝ
4	Πάλιν ὅπερ μετὰ τὴν φόρμαν τη.			
5	τρίτην τὴν προειρημένην			
6	φόρμης πρ[ώ]της	λι.	α	✳ ΥΚ
7	φόρμης β	λι.	α	✳ Χ
8	φόρμης γ	λι.	α	✳ ΥΝ
9	Λίνου τραχυτέρου εἰς χρῆσιν τῶν ἰ-			
10	διωτίδων τε καὶ φαμιλ[ι]αρικῶν			
11	φόρμης α	λι.	α	✳ [Ν
12	φόρμης β	λι.	α	✳ ΡΚ[Ε]
13	φόρμης γ	λι.	α	✳ ΟΒ
14	Στίχων ἀσήμων φόρμης		α	

16, 76, χλανίδος καινῆς Λαδικηνῆς KARYST. . . . . . Λαδικηνῆς καινῆς THEB. **16, 78** and **77** are transposed in KARYST. **16, 79**, ἢ ταυρογ. καινοῦ KARYST. **16, 81**, ὑπὲρ wanting in KARYST. **16, 84**, λύουσιν μετὰ KARYST. **16, 86**, βλάττης λι. α KARYST. **16, 87**, ὑποβλάττης λι. α KARYST.

	15	Σκυτοπολειτανῶν	ἱστὸς α	✳ 'Z
	16	Ταρσικῶν	ἱστὸς α	✳ 'ς
	17	Βιβλίων	ἱστ. α	✳ 'Ε
	18	Λαδικηνῶν	ἱστ. α	✳ 'ΔΦ
	19	Ταρσικ.'Αλεξανδρεινῶν ἱστ. α		✳ 'Δ
	20	φώρμης δευτέρας		
	21	Σκυτοπολιτανῶν	ἱστ. α	✳ 'ς
	22	Ταρσικῶν	ἱστ. α	✳ 'Ε
	23	Βιβλίων	ἱστ. α	✳ 'Δ
	24	Λαδικηνῶν	ἱστ. α	✳ 'ΓΦ
	25	Ταρσικ. 'Αλεξανδρειν. ἱστ. α		✳ 'Γ
	26	φώρμης τρίτης		
	27	Σκυτοπολειτανῶν	ἱστ. α	✳ 'Ε
	28	Ταρσικῶν	ἱστ. α	✳ 'ΓΦ
	29	Βιβλίων	ἱστ. α	✳ 'Γ
	30	Λαδικηνῶν	ἱστ. α	✳ 'ΒΦ˙
	31	Ταρσικ.'Λλεξανδριν. ἱστ. α		✳ 'Β
	32	Στίχων στρατιωτικῶν φώρμ. α		✳ 'ΑΦ
	33	φώρμης β ✳ 'ΑΓΝ φώρ[μ]ης γ		✳ 'Α
	34	ἀπὸ λίνου τραχέως εἰς χρῆσιν τῶν ι-		
	35	διωτίδων ἤτοι φαμιλιαρικῶν		
	36	φώρμης α	ἱστ. α	✳ /
	37	φώρμης β	ἱστ. α	✳ /
	38	φώρμης γ	ἱστ. α	✳ /Φ
	39	Δαλματικῶν ἀσήμων γυναικίων		
	40	φώρμης πρώτης		
	41	Σκυτοπολειτανῶν	ἱστ. α	✳ ΜΑ
	42	Ταρσικῶν	ἱστ. α	✳ Μ̂
	43	Βιβλίων	ἱστ. α	✳ Θ
	44	Λαδικηνῶν	ἱστ. α	✳ 'Η
	45	Ταρσικ. 'Λλεξανδριν. ἱστ. α		✳ 'Ζ
	46	Δαλματικῶν ἀνδρίων ἤτοι κολοβι-		
	47	ων φώρμης α		
17, 1	48	Σκυτοπολειτανῶν	ἱστ. α	✳ Μ̂
17, 2	49	Ταρσικῶν	ἱστ. α	✳ 'Θ
17, 3	50	Βιβλίων	ἱστ. α	✳ 'Η
17, 4	51	Λαδικηνῶν	ἱστ. α	✳ 'ΖΦ
17, 5	52	Ταρσικ. 'Αλεξανδριν. ἱστ. α		✳ 'ςΦ

53 Δαλματικῶν γυναικίων φορμ. β

17, 6	54	Σκυτοπολειτανῶν	ἰστ.	α	✱'Θ
17, 7	55	Ταρσικῶν	ἰστ.	α	✱'Η
17, 8	56	Βιβλίων	ἰστ.	α	✱'Ζ
17, 9	57	Λαδικηνῶν	ἰστ.	α	✱'ς
17, 10	58	Ταρσικ. Ἀλεξανδριν.	ἰστ.	α	✱'ΔΦ

59 Δαλματικῶν ἀνδρίων ἤτοι κολο-
60 βίων φώρμης β

17, 11	61	Σκυτοπολειτανῶν	ἰστ.	α	✱'ΖΦ
17, 12	62	Ταρσικῶν	ἰστ.	α	✱'ςΦ
17, 13	63	Βιβλίων	ἰστ.	α	✱'ς
17, 14	64	Λαδικηνῶν	ἰστ.	α	✱'Ε
17, 15	65	Ταρσικ. Ἀλεξανδρ.	ἰστ.	α	[✱'Δ]Φ

66 Δαλματικῶν γυναικί[ων]

17, 16	67	Σκυτοπολειτ[ανῶν	ἰστ.	α	✱'Ζ] .
17, 17	68	Ταρσικῶ[ν	ἰστ.	α	✱'ς]

Here must follow **17, 18–50** of my edition.

THIRD COLUMN.

17, 51	1	Λαδικηνῶν	ἰστ.	α	✱'Γ
17, 52	2	Ταρσικ. Ἀλεξανδ.	ἰστ.	α	✱'[ΒΦ]

3 Ἅπερ ἀπὸ φώρμης γ´ ἥττονα
4 εἰσὶν ἀναβολέων

17, 53	5	φώρμης α	ἰστ.	α	[✱'ΒCΝ]
17, 54	6	φώρμης β	ἰστ.	α	✱'ΑΥΝ
17, 55	7	φώρμης γ	ἰστ.	α	✱'ΑCΝ

8 Ἀπὸ λίνου τραχαίος εἰς χρῆσιν τῶν
9 [ἰδιω]τῶν ἤτοι φαμιλιαρίων

17, 56	10	φώρμης α	ἰστ.	α	✱ω
17, 57	11	φώρμης β	ἰστ.	α	✱Χ
17, 58	12	φώρμης γ	ἰστ.	α	✱Φ

13 Φακιαλίων ἀσήμων φόρμ. α

17, 59	14	Σκυτοπολειταν.	ἰστ.	α	✱'ΓCΝ
17, 60	15	Ταρσικῶν	ἰστ.	α	✱'Γ
17, 61	16	Βιβλίων	ἰστ.	α	✱'ΒΦ

III, 4, ΕΥΕΝ Ger. III, 8, τραχαίος should be τραχέως. III, 9, "Perhaps the first I of ΙΔΙΩΤΙΔΩΝ II, 9. 10 served not only for the second column, but also for the third." Lolling. **17, 61**, Βυβλίων Ger. almost always.

17, 62	17	Λαδικηνῶν	ἰστ. α	✶ ΒϹΝ
17, 63	18	Ταρσικ. Ἀλεξαν.	ἰστ. α	✶ ʻΑΥΝ
	19	φώρμης β		
17, 64	20	Σκυτοπολειτ.	ἰστ. α	✶ ʻΒΦ
17, 65	21	Ταρσικῶν	ἰστ. α	✶ ʻΒϹΝ
17, 66	22	Βιβλίων	ἰστ. α	✶ ʻΒϹΝ
17, 67	23	Λαδικηνῶν	ἰστ. α	✶ ʻΒ
17, 68	24	Ταρσικ. Ἀλεξανδ	ἰστ. α	✶ ʻΑΦ
	25	φώρμης γ		
17, 69	26	Σκυτοπολειταν.	ἰστ. α	✶ ΒϹΝ
17, 70	27	Ταρσικῶν	ἰστ. α	✶ ʻΒ
17, 71	28	Βιβλίων	ἰστ. α	✶ ʻΑΥΝ
17, 72	29	Λαδικηνῶν	ἰστ. α	✶ ʻΑΦ
17, 73	30	Ταρσικ. Ἀλεξ.	ἰστ. α	✶ ʻΑϹΝ

31 ″Απερ ἀπὸ φώρμης τῆς προειρη-
32 μένης καταδεέστερα εἶεν
33 Φακιάλια

17, 74	34	φώρμης α	ἰστ. α	✶ Α
17, 75	35	φώρμης β	ἰστ. α	✶ ΥΝ
17, 76	36	φώρμης γ	ἰστ. α	✶ Φ

37 ἀπὸ λίνου τραχέος εἰς χρῆσιν τῶν
38 ἰδιωτῶν ἤτοι φαμιλιαρίων

17, 77	39	φώρμης α	ἰστὸ. α	✶ ΤΝ
17, 78	40	φώρμης β	ἰστ. α	✶ Ϲ[ΚΕ]
17, 79	41	φώρμης γ	ἰστ. α	✶ Ϲ
	42	Καρακάλλων φώρμης α		
17, 80	43	Σκυτοπολειταν.	ἰστ. α	✶ ʻΓΦ
17, 81	44	Ταρσικῶν	ἰστ. α	✶ ʻΓ
17, 82	45	Βιβλίων	ἰστ. α	✶ ʻΒΦ
17, 83	46	Λαδικηνῶν	ἰστ. α	✶ ʻΒϹΝ
17, 84	47	Ταρσικ. Ἀλεξανδ.	ἰστ. [α]	✶ ʻΑΥΝ
	48	φώρμης β		
17, 85	49	Σκυτοπολειταν.	ἰστ. α	✶ ʻΓ
17, 86	50	Ταρσικῶν	ἰστ. α	✶ ʻΒΦ
17, 87	51	Βιβλίων	ἰστ. α	✶ ʻΒϹΝ
17, 88	52	Λαδικηνῶν	ἰστ. α	✶ ʻΒ

17, 63, ʻΑΦΝ Ger.: error. 17, 68, ΑШ Ger.: error. III, 31, φώρμης] φόρ. γ Ger. 17, 75, ΥΝ]Ϋ Ger.: error. 17, 78, ϹΟ/ Plat. 17, 86, ʻΒΫ Ger.: error.

PLATAIAN FRAGMENT OF THE EDICT OF DIOCLETIAN. 309

17, 89	53	Ταρσικ. Ἀλεξαν.	ἰστ.	α	✶ ʹΑΦ
	54	φώρμης γ			
17, 90	55	Σκυτοπολειτανῶν	ἰστ.	α	✶ ʹΒΦ
17, 91	56	Ταρσικῶν	ἰστ.	α	✶ ʹΒΕΝ
17, 92	57	Βιβλίων	ἰστ.	α	✶ ʹΒ
17, 93	58	Λαδικηνῶν	ἰστ.	α	✶ ʹΑΥΝ
17, 94	59	Ταρσικ. Ἀλεξ.	ἰστ.	α	✶ ʹΑΕΝ
	60	Ἅπερ ἀπὸ φώρμης τῆς προειρημέ-			
	61	νης καταδεέστερα εἶεν καρακάλ.			
17, 95	62	φώρμης α	ἰστ.	α	✶ ʹΑ
17, 96	63	φώρμης β	ἰστ.	α	✶ ΥΝ
17, 97	64	φώρμης γ	ἰστ.	α	✶ Χ
17, 98	65	Ἀπὸ λίνου τραχέως εἰς χρῆσιν			
	66	[τῶν] ἰδιωτῶν γυναικῶν			
	67	[φώρμ]ης α			
	68	[φώρμης] β			

COMMENT.

I wish to add a few remarks on the new information derived from this discovery. The greater part of the Plataian text is already known from other sources, as will be indicated below; still some interesting facts now come to light for the first time.

Col. I, 1–20 are almost completely lost and cannot be restored, and the two other copies of this part, from Karystos (*C.I.L.*, III, p. 821) and from Megara (Dittenberger, *Inscriptiones Graecae Septentrionales* n. 23, printed, but not published) are so very defective that they give no help.

Col. I, 21–41, of which the Plataian copy has preserved some fragments, correspond to ch. 16, 40–56. They treat of the pay of silkworkers but, in their imperfect condition, offer nothing of importance.

Col. I, 42–68, have corresponding lines in three other copies, the two just quoted and the Theban (*C.I.L.*, III, p. 823); but especially the first lines (wanting in Karystos) are much better in the Plataian copy, and the portions hitherto wanting are now supplied, though still presenting many difficulties: one such occurs after the line εἰς ἔργον δευτερεῖον τρεφομένῳ ✶ Κ, which is more or less preserved at Plataia, Megara and Thebes (the Karystian copy has a gap here). The Theban,

17, 93, Ν omitted by GER. III, 60, φώρμης] φόρ. γ GER. 17, 98, τραχυτ. GER. III, 66 with ἰδιωτῶν GER. concludes.

which is not at all reliable, does not even indicate it, but evidently what follows NHCXN belongs to **16,** 58. The inscription is given thus:

Megara	Plataia
ΠΕΡΙΦΟΥΛΛΩΝ	/////////ΔΩΝΩΝ

It must have been περὶ Φουλλώνων, though the Δ in the Plataian is quite evident, and the formation of the word also is objectionable; at least we should expect φουλλωνίων or φουλλωνικῶν. But the Megarian copy is evidently right, and the fuller's work corresponds to the argument of the chapter. That it treats especially of wool-articles has been stated already in my paper (*Hermes*, xxxv, p. 22) and it is not much to be wondered at that the Greek workman stumbled in rendering a Latin word. The number of letters wanting before ΔΩΝΩΝ is about ten, so that eight fit in very well leaving some vacant space at the beginning as is usual in the prescripts.

The following matters in **16,** 58–66 of my edition are completed and bettered by the new copy, and deserve a special examination.

	Plataia	Megara	Thebes
16, 58	////// περ χλανίδος τῶν εἰς παρα-	περ χλανίδος τωι	νης ✱ N
	///// ν καινῆς ✱ N	καινῆς ✱ N	ιδος τῶμ εἰς παράστασιν καὶ
16, 58a	///// ης τῶν εἰς παράδοσιν καιν. ✱ KE	ιαδο	ἰς παράδοσιν καινῆς ✱ KE

The first short word, which is wanting, may have been γναφεῖ; at least I cannot find a better one. The E in the second number in the Plataian copy is very uncertain and wanting in Lolling's transcription; nevertheless, I believe a trace of it can be seen in the squeeze and the Theban copy has it. Whether in this the end of the first article was placed above the beginning by the artisan himself or by the copyist's blunder, is not to be made out. The sense is clear: the fuller's pay for the cloths prepared by him for the market (παράδοσιν and παράστασις seem to signify the same, and render the Latin *negotiatio*) is 40 *denarii* for the coat, 25 for the shirt.

16, 59 ἀσήμου ἐξ ἐρέας τραχυτέρας is filled up by the new copy: the Theban has only ... τραχυτέρων ✱ K. Probably there χλανίδος is to be understood, and the article to be referred to the coat of rougher wool, and not ornamented.

16, 60 is also completed now. The *endromis* is a woolen over-coat, as also *raxana*, the latter corresponding in ch. **7,** 60 to the *sagum*.

16, 61 and 62. The δελματικομάφορτος, composed of the *dalmatica*, a shirt without sleeves, and the *mafor*, a head-tippet, has already been yielded by the other copies (*C.I.L.*, III, p. 836, note).

16, 63. The *strictoria*, a shirt with sleeves, recurs in the Latin text 7, 56, 57, 58; 16, 24. In the first place it is rendered by the Greek στίχη.

16, 64 and 65. The substantives are supplied from the Plataian copy. The rest of the chapter offers no considerable variation, excepting that in 16, 69 the number, and in 16, 72 the word διπλῆς, are now added.

Col. I, 69–71 περὶ τειμῆς τῶν σιρικῶν is perfectly preserved in the Karystian copy and does not offer any remarkable reading; that, instead of λύουσιν, we here have λύουσι[ν ......]σιν is perhaps only an error of the artisan.

Col. I, 72–76 περὶ πορφύρας is very important, but better preserved in the Karystian copy, and part of it in that of Megara. At Plataia only the first lines remain. That the second and third kind of purple are here introduced by the word πορφύρας, omitted in the Karystian copy, may be compared with 16, 89 where Karystos reads απλιου λι. α, Megara πορφύρ. .... What is wanting of this chapter at Plataia and preserved in the Karystian copy, fills up, as is said, about half of the gap between the first column and the second; but as the purple chapter is not complete in the Karystian copy some more is to be added.

Col. II, 1–13 corresponds to a fragment dug up at Atalante, unedited, but copied for me some years ago by Mr. Lolling and mentioned in *Hermes*, XXXV, p. 19, n. 9. As the Atalante fragment is much damaged and the Plataian is in this part complete, I only mention the imperfection of the first, the place of which is now, for the first time, determined with certainty. The Plataian copy does not give the beginning of the linen chapter but does certainly give the second part of its first subdivision, since, as we have already shown, at the end of the first column at the utmost about ten lines remain for the linen. This important discovery shows that the linen tariff began with that of the flax, of which the prices are actually given after the weight. Here too as afterwards three different standards are established, the first probably without qualification, the second qualified as inferior to the first, the third as serving for home use by the women of the household (ἰδιωτίδες ἢ φαμιλιαρικαί). In each of these three standards three degrees are mentioned, so that a pound of first-rate flax amounts to 1200, that of the commonest sort to 72 *denarii*. The place whence the flax comes was not taken as a basis for its value; the places mentioned in the following chapter refer, as is well known, to the weaving.

Col. II, 14–38 is also new, the first lines recurring, as the preceding, in the Atalante fragment. This second subdivision of the linen ware treats of the simple shirts, στίχαι ἄσημοι. It has the same three standards of three degrees each, as all these chapters, but the second class here is represented by the soldier shirts, στίχαι στρατιωτικαί.

Col. II, 39–68 respond to ch. **17**, 1–17 taken from the Geronthraian copy; the beginning 39–47, wanting in this, is now supplied by the Plataian copy; the end defective in Plataia is supplied by the Geronthraian copy **17**, 18–37. This passage regulates the prices of another sort of shirt, the dalmatica, distinguishing between woman's shirts which precede, and the cheaper men's shirts. It offers nothing of considerable interest; the first part also, though new, could have been almost made out by mere analogy. Only it may be observed, that at the beginning the dalmatica treated here is described as ἄσημος, as it should be.

Col. III, 1–12 treats in the same way of the linen ἀναβολεύς, the cloak. The beginning is missing, but as we have the whole passage from Geronthrai, ch. **17**, 38–58, this is of no material importance.

Col. III, 13–41 follows the *faciale*. This passage too is only a second copy of **17**, 59–72.

Col. III, 42–68 treats of the *caracallus* and corresponds to **17**, 80–98. The Plataian copy has at the end a few more words than the Geronthrian, but they give nothing not otherwise known.

The last part of the third column and the slab joined to it, contained what we read on the first column of the Elateia copy, which treats of the *coxalia*, the *oraria* and certain γυναικεῖα, and after these, what in my edition is given, from another slab (of Geronthrai) as chapter **18**, treating of the κεραλοδέσμια, the σίνδονες, the τύλαι, all belonging to linen ware.

THEODOR MOMMSEN.

Berlin.

APPENDIX.

INSCRIPTIONS FROM IKARIA, Nos. 8 AND 9.

As this volume is about to go to press, the third part of Vol. IV. of the *Corpus Inscriptionum Atticarum* comes to hand, containing a republication of the inscriptions mentioned above. They are printed by the editor from a hand copy made by Dr. Lolling, without a squeeze to correct the common errors of a copyist. I possess more than one squeeze of each of these inscriptions, taken with the utmost care, and it is easy to decide from them in general between the printed copies. As the inscriptions appear above (pp. 93, 96), some errors occurring in the Journal have been corrected, and as they thus stand my squeezes confirm Mr. Buck's readings in almost every case. This would not need mention here, except for a reading of inscription No. 8, as given in the *Corpus*. In line 6 a division-mark is placed after the first I (ΠHI : KAPIO); and accordingly the reading KAPIO, instead of IKAPIO, is accepted throughout the inscription, though with great hesitation by the editor. He imagines that the money may have belonged to the Karian Zeus. He says: "Interpunctio illa, quam Lollingius notavit vs. 6, si revera exstat in lapide, non Icarii hae sunt pecuniae, sed Iovis illius Carii, quem cultum fuisse ab Isagorae gente tradit Herodotus, 5, 66, existimandae, cui fieri potuisse ut etiam aliis locis regionis Atticae sacra fuerint non est cur praefracte negemus. Utrum verum sit, mihi quidem, cui lapidem ipsi inspiciendi copia data non sit, in dubio relinquendum est necessario."

My squeezes, otherwise so faithful, exhibit no trace of the division-mark in line 6; neither do they in line 9, where even Dr. Lolling failed to find any. This shows that the reading of the *Corpus* is at least doubtful. Further, the entire absence of division-marks elsewhere in both these entries harmonizes with the later character of the entries, and diminishes greatly the probability of any occurrence of the division-marks in them.

But if it be granted that they do exist on the stone, must the reading of the *Corpus* be accepted? It is a generally received dictum in epigraphy as in palaeography, that a text must be construed within the fairest limits of common sense and of the environment of the writer. But this reading does not accommodate itself in the least to such a fair interpretation of our knowledge of Ikaria. Indeed, it is totally irreconcilable with it; while IKAPIO is in complete accord with the traditions of the place, with everything that was discovered there, and above all with that unique and singularly pertinent expression of the Dionysiac inscription above, No. 1 (p. 71), "the *Ikarians* and the deme of the Ikarians." Here we are told as plainly as words can speak, that the figure which fills the Ikarian horizon, and, as I believe, was the object of the gentile worship, was Ikarios, and not a Karian Zeus, of whose worship in Attica we have no literary evidence except the passage of Herodotus in relation to the family of Isagoras. Because Isagoras of the Plain worshipped a Karian Zeus would be good reason for supposing that the Diakrians of the Ikarian district did not. Indeed, their affinities are with the Ionian Tetrapolis of Marathon, from which they obtained their Apollo Pythios. Hence we may justly hold that even if the division-mark exists on the stone where it is placed by Dr. Lolling's copy, it ought to be regarded as an error of the stone-cutter, and either expelled entirely, or treated as a case of misplacement, and read, ΓΗH : IKAPIO.

A. C. MERRIAM.

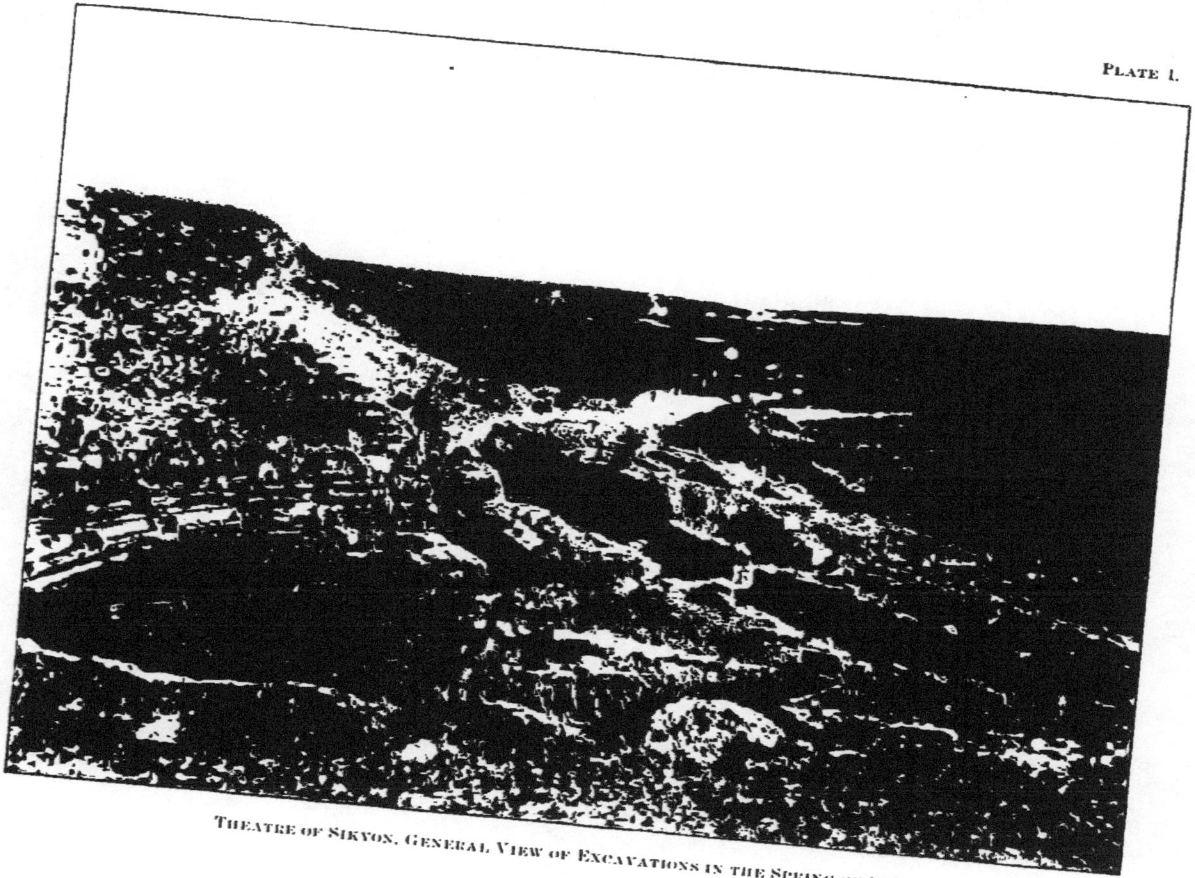

PLATE I.

THEATRE OF SIKYON. GENERAL VIEW OF EXCAVATIONS IN THE SPRING OF 1887.

PLATE II.

THEATRE OF SIKYON. SEATS AND SEMICIRCULAR CONDUIT.

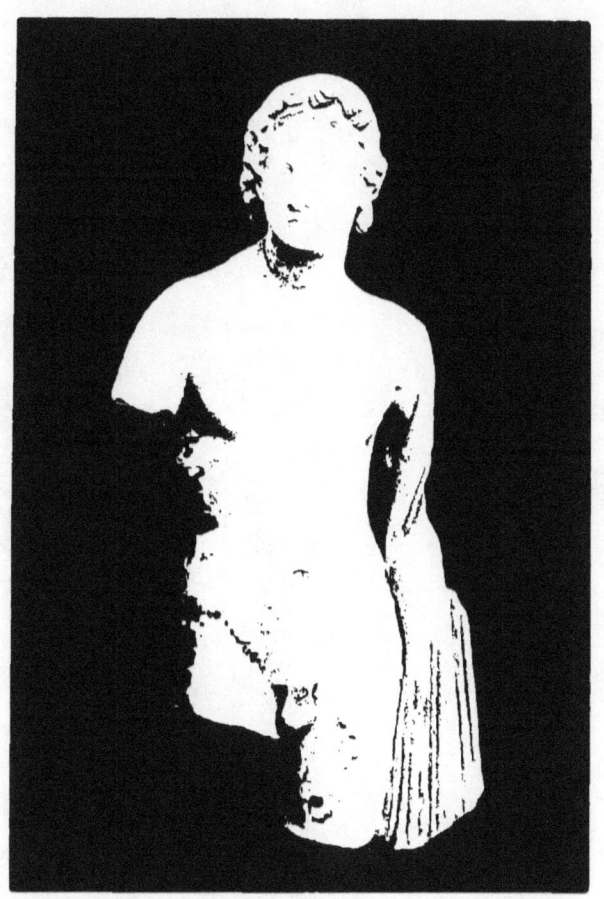

PLATE IV.

IKAIGA. SOUTH VIEW OF CHURCH WITH CHOKAGE MONUMENT.

PLATE V.

IRASBA. VIEW EASTWARD OVER EXCAVATIONS AND CHORTEN MONUMENT.

IKARIA. SOUTH-EASTWARD OVER THE PYTHON TO PENTELIKON.

Plate VIII.

PLATE X.

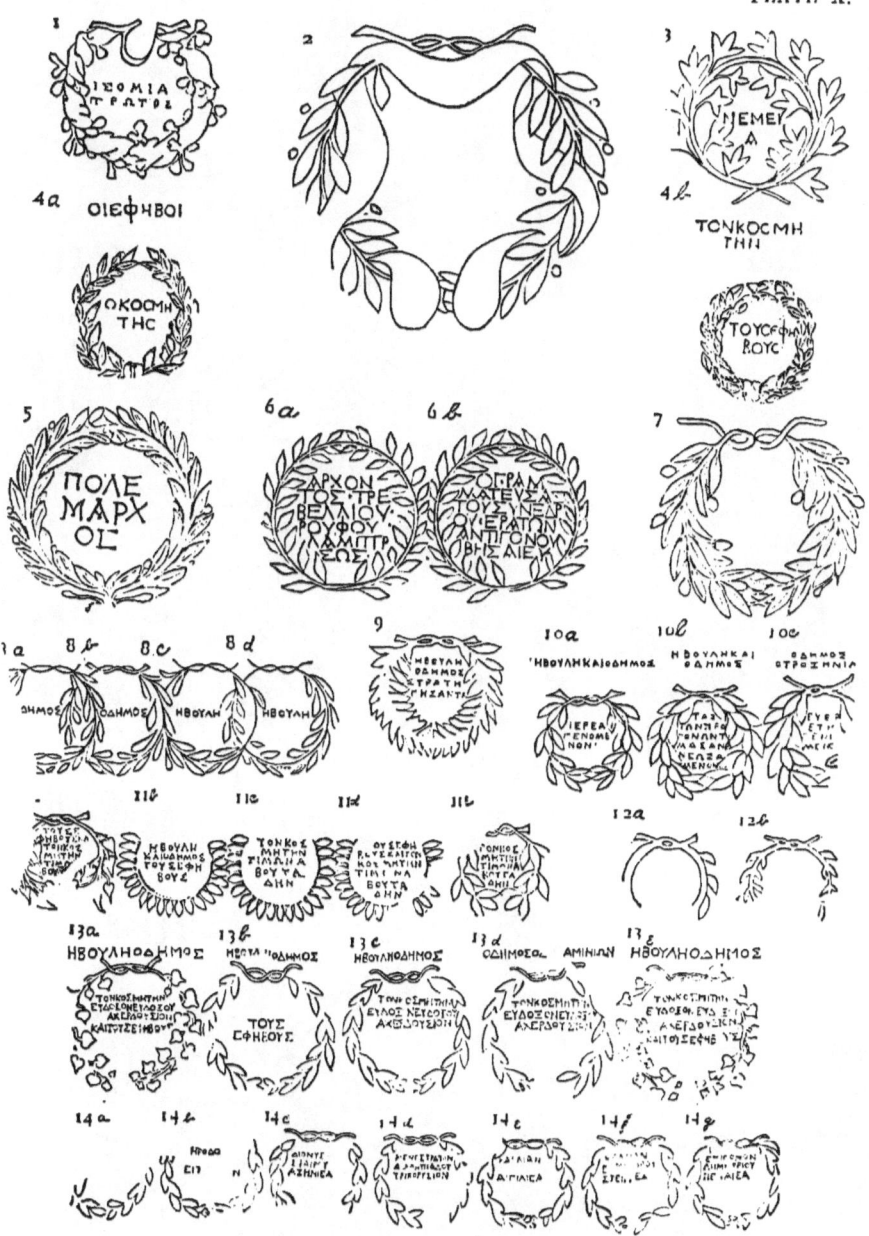

GREEK SCULPTURED CROWNS.

PLATE XI.

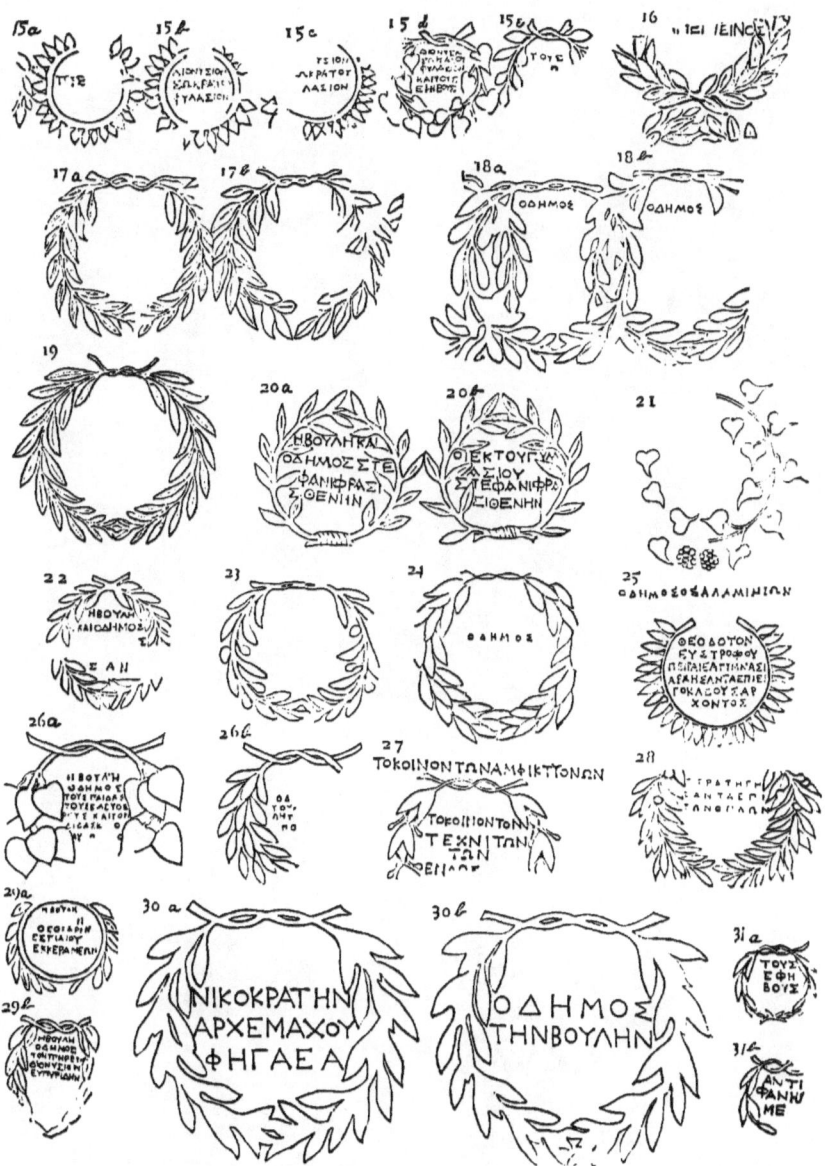

GREEK SCULPTURED CROWNS.

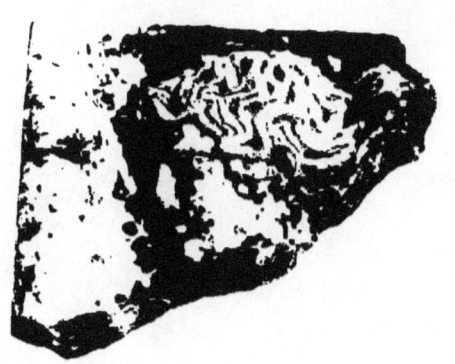

ANTHEDON. BRONZE IMPLEMENTS.

PLATE XV.

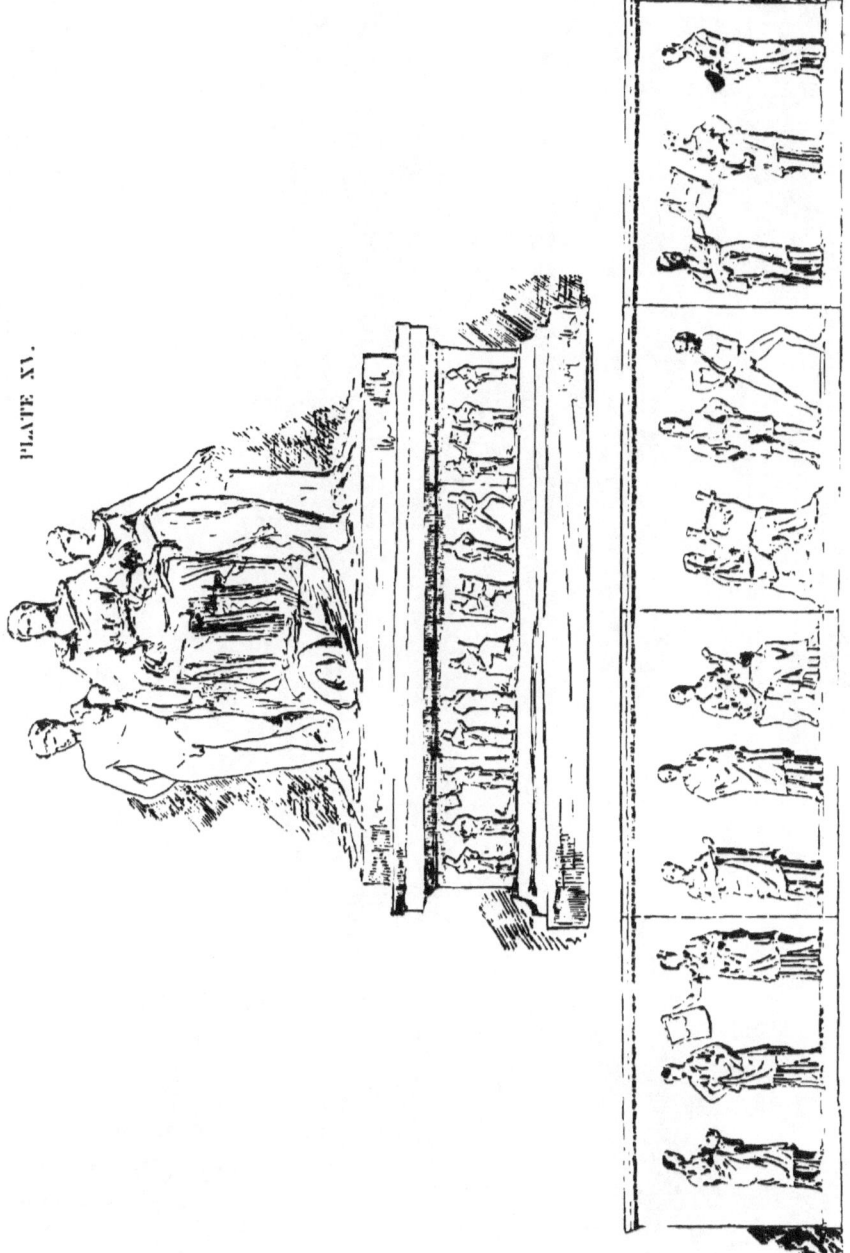

PLATE XVII.

PLATAIA. TOWER OF UPPER CROSS-WALL, FROM THE S.W.

PLATAIA. LOWER CROSS-WALL AND TOWER, FROM THE S.W.

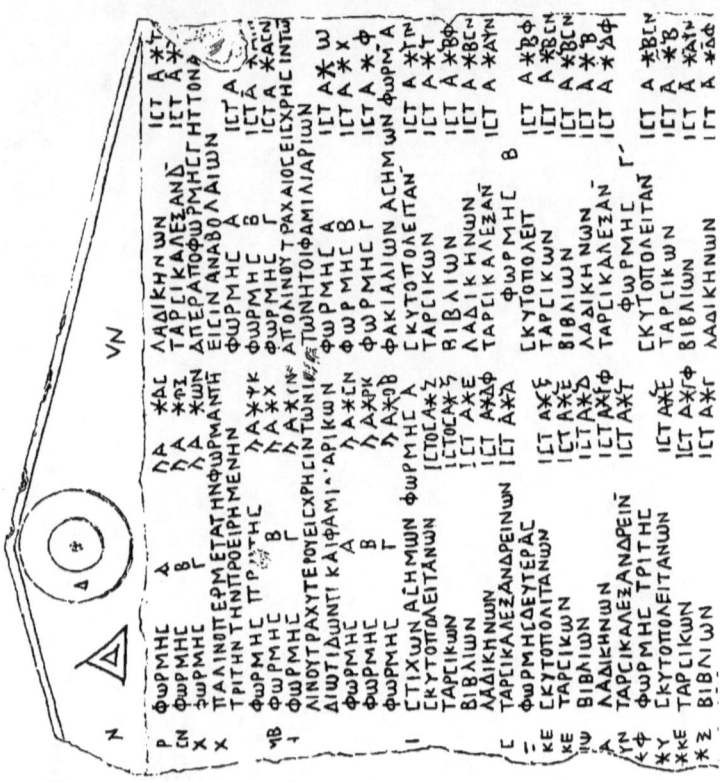

PLATE XVIII.

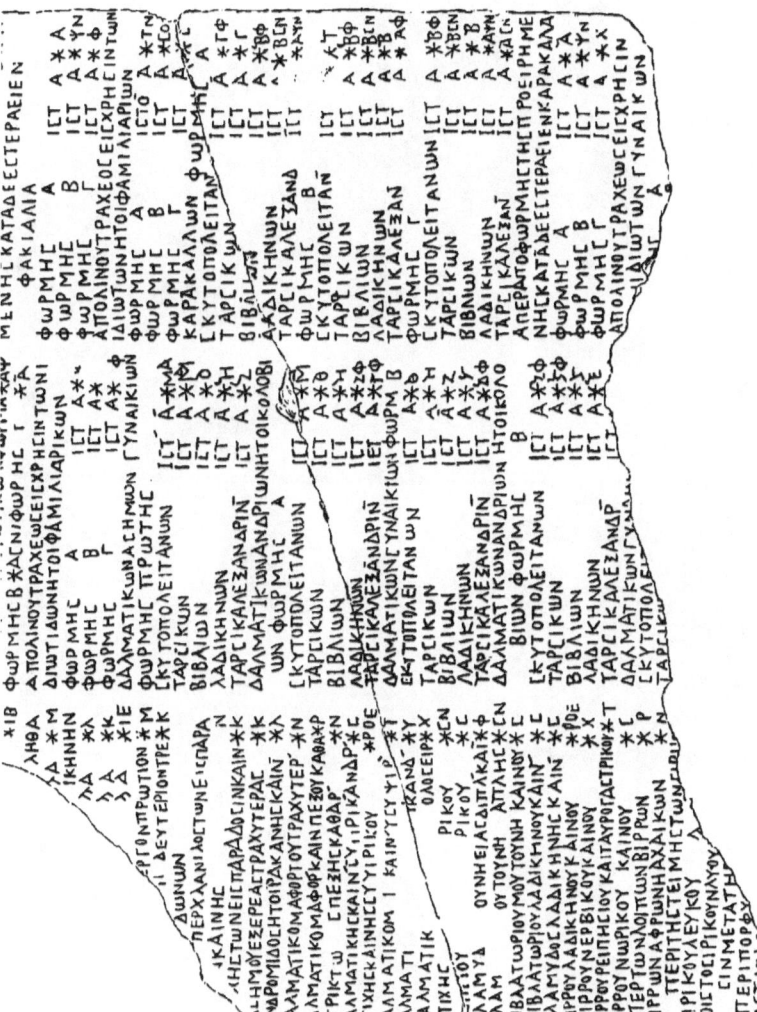

PLATAIAN FRAGMENT OF THE EDICT OF DIOCLETIAN.

Archæological Institute of America

AMERICAN SCHOOL OF CLASSICAL STUDIES AT ATHENS

February, 1892

AMERICAN SCHOOL OF CLASSICAL STUDIES AT ATHENS.

1890-1891.

A corporation was formed in March, 1886, under the statutes of the Commonwealth of Massachusetts, with the name of "The Trustees of the American School of Classical Studies at Athens," to hold the title to the land and building in Athens belonging to the School, and to hold and invest all permanent funds which may be received for its maintenance.

The Board consists of the following gentlemen: —

JAMES RUSSELL LOWELL,* Cambridge, *President.*
EDWARD J. LOWELL, Cambridge, *Treasurer.*
WILLIAM W. GOODWIN, Boston, *Secretary.*
MARTIN BRIMMER, Boston.
HENRY DRISLER, New York.
BASIL M. GILDERSLEEVE, Baltimore.
HENRY G. MARQUAND, New York.
CHARLES ELIOT NORTON, Cambridge.
FREDERIC J. DE PEYSTER, New York.
HENRY C. POTTER, New York.
WILLIAM M. SLOANE, Princeton.
JOHN WILLIAMS WHITE, Cambridge.

Executive Committee of the Trustees.

JAMES RUSSELL LOWELL.*
WILLIAM W. GOODWIN.
CHARLES ELIOT NORTON.

* Died August 12, 1891.

Managing-Committee.

THOMAS D. SEYMOUR (*Chairman*), Yale University, New Haven, Conn.
H. M. BAIRD, University of the City of New York, New York City.
I. T. BECKWITH, Trinity College, Hartford, Conn.
FRANCIS BROWN, Union Theological Seminary, 1200 Park Ave., New York City.
MISS A. C. CHAPIN, Wellesley College, Wellesley, Mass.
MARTIN L. D'OOGE, University of Michigan, Ann Arbor, Mich.
HENRY DRISLER, Columbia College, 48 West 46th St., New York City.
O. M. FERNALD, Williams College, Williamstown, Mass.
HENRY GIBBONS, Amherst College, Amherst, Mass.
BASIL L. GILDERSLEEVE, Johns Hopkins University, Baltimore, Md.
WILLIAM W. GOODWIN, Harvard University, Cambridge, Mass.
WILLIAM G. HALE, Cornell University, Ithaca, N. Y.
ALBERT HARKNESS, Brown University, Providence, R. I.
WILLIAM A. LAMBERTON, University of Pennsylvania, Philadelphia, Pa.
MISS ABBY LEACH, Vassar College, Poughkeepsie, N. Y.
SETH LOW (*ex officio:* President of the Archæological Institute of America), Columbia College, New York City.
THOMAS W. LUDLOW (*Secretary*), Cottage Lawn, Yonkers, N. Y.
AUGUSTUS C. MERRIAM (*Chairman of Committee on Publications*), Columbia College, 640 Madison Ave., New York City.
CHARLES ELIOT NORTON, Harvard University, Cambridge, Mass.
BERNADOTTE PERRIN, Adelbert College of Western Reserve University, Cleveland, Ohio.
FREDERIC J. DE PEYSTER (*Treasurer*), 7 East 42d St., New York City.
RUFUS B. RICHARDSON (*ex officio:* Annual Director of the School), Dartmouth College, Hanover, N. H.
WILLIAM M. SLOANE, College of New Jersey, Princeton, N. J.
FITZ GERALD TISDALL, College of the City of New York, New York City.

JAMES C. VAN BENSCHOTEN, Wesleyan University, Middletown, Conn.
CHARLES WALDSTEIN (*ex officio :* Director of the School), Cambridge, England.
WILLIAM R. WARE, School of Mines, Columbia College, New York City.
JOHN WILLIAMS WHITE, Harvard University, Cambridge, Mass.

Executive Committee.

THOMAS D. SEYMOUR (*Chairman*).
WILLIAM W. GOODWIN.
THOMAS W. LUDLOW (*Secretary*).
CHARLES ELIOT NORTON.
FREDERIC J. DE PEYSTER (*Treasurer*).
WILLIAM R. WARE.

Co-operating Colleges.

ADELBERT COLLEGE OF WESTERN RESERVE UNIVERSITY.
AMHERST COLLEGE.
BROWN UNIVERSITY.
COLLEGE OF THE CITY OF NEW YORK.
COLLEGE OF NEW JERSEY.
COLUMBIA COLLEGE.
CORNELL UNIVERSITY.
DARTMOUTH COLLEGE.
HARVARD UNIVERSITY.
JOHNS HOPKINS UNIVERSITY.
TRINITY COLLEGE.
UNIVERSITY OF THE CITY OF NEW YORK.
UNIVERSITY OF MICHIGAN.
UNIVERSITY OF MISSOURI.
UNIVERSITY OF PENNSYLVANIA.
VASSAR COLLEGE.
WESLEYAN UNIVERSITY.
WELLESLEY COLLEGE.
WILLIAMS COLLEGE.
YALE UNIVERSITY.

Direction of the School.

1882-1883.
Director: WILLIAM WATSON GOODWIN, Ph. D., LL. D., D. C. L., Eliot Professor of Greek Literature in Harvard University.

1883-1884.
Director: LEWIS R. PACKARD, Ph. D., Hillhouse Professor of Greek in Yale University.
Secretary: J. R. SITLINGTON STERRETT, Ph. D., Professor of Greek in the University of Texas.

1884-1885.
Director: JAMES COOKE VAN BENSCHOTEN, LL. D., Seney Professor of the Greek Language and Literature in Wesleyan University.

1885-1886.
Director: FREDERIC DE FOREST ALLEN, Ph. D., Professor of Classical Philology in Harvard University.

1886-1887.
Director: MARTIN L. D'OOGE, Ph. D., LL. D., Professor of Greek in the University of Michigan.

1887-1888.
Director: AUGUSTUS C. MERRIAM, Ph. D., Professor of Greek Archæology and Epigraphy in Columbia College.

1888-1889.
Director: CHARLES WALDSTEIN, Ph. D., Litt. D., L. H. D., Reader in Archæology at the University of Cambridge, England.
Annual Director: FRANK BIGELOW TARBELL, Ph. D., Instructor in Harvard University.

1889-1890.
Director: CHARLES WALDSTEIN, Ph. D., Litt. D., L. H. D.
Annual Director: S. STANHOPE ORRIS, Ph. D., L. H. D., Ewing Professor of the Greek Language and Literature in the College of New Jersey.

1890-1891.
Director: CHARLES WALDSTEIN, Ph. D., Litt. D., L. H. D.
Annual Director: RUFUS BYRAM RICHARDSON, Ph. D., Professor of Greek in Dartmouth College.

Students.*

LOUIS BEVIER (1882-83),†
  Associate Professor in Rutgers College, New Brunswick, N. J.
WALTER RAY BRIDGMAN (1883-84),
  Professor in Lake Forest University, Lake Forest, Ill.
CARLETON LEWIS BROWNSON (1890-).
CARL DARLING BUCK (1887-89),
  Student in the University of Leipzig.
N. E. CROSBY (1886-87),
  Instructor in the College of New Jersey, Princeton, N. J.
JOHN M. CROW (1882-83),
  Professor in Iowa College, Grinnell, Iowa. Died Sept. 28, 1890.
WILLIAM LEE CUSHING (1885-87),
  Head Master of the Westminster School, Dobbs Ferry, N. Y.
MORTIMER LAMSON EARLE (1887-88),
  Instructor in Barnard College, New York City.
THOMAS H. ECKFELDT (1884-85),
  Principal of the Friends' School, New Bedford, Mass.
A. F. FLEET (1887-88),
  Superintendent of the Missouri Military Academy, Mexico, Mo.
ANDREW FOSSUM (1890-91),
  Instructor in the Drisler School, New York City.
HAROLD NORTH FOWLER (1882-83),
  Professor in Phillips Academy, Exeter, N. H.
JOHN WESLEY GILBERT (1890-91).
HENRY T. HILDRETH (1885-86),
  Professor in Wooster University, Wooster, Ohio.
W. IRVING HUNT (1889-90),
  Tutor in Greek, Yale University, New Haven, Conn.
GEORGE BENJAMIN HUSSEY (1887-88),†
  Instructor in the University of Nebraska, Lincoln, Neb.
FRANCIS DEMETRIUS KALOPOTHAKES (1888-89),
  Student in the University of Berlin.
JOSEPH McKEEN LEWIS (1885-87).
  Died April 29, 1887.
GONZALEZ LODGE (1888-89),†
  Associate Professor in Bryn Mawr College, Bryn Mawr, Pa.

* The year of residence at the School is placed in a parenthesis after the name. Italics indicate students of the year 1890-91
† Not present during the entire year.

WALTER MILLER (1885-86),
 Professor in the University of Missouri, Columbia, Mo.

WILLIAM J. McMURTRY (1886-87),
 Professor in Yankton College, Yankton, South Dakota.

Miss EMILY NORCROSS, (1888-89),
 Instructor in Smith College, Northampton, Mass.

Miss ANNIE S. PECK (1885-86),
 865 North Main Street, Providence, R. I.

JOHN PICKARD (1890-91),
 Student in the University of Munich.

DANIEL QUINN (1887-89),
 Professor in the Catholic University of America, Washington, D. C.

JOHN CAREW ROLFE (1888-89),
 Assistant Professor in the University of Michigan, Ann Arbor, Mich

WILLIAM J. SEELYE (1886-87),
 Professor in Wooster University, Wooster, Ohio.

JOHN P. SHELLEY (1889-90),
 Professor in Grove College, Grove City, Pa.

PAUL SHOREY (1882-83),
 Associate Professor in Bryn Mawr College, Bryn Mawr, Pa.

Miss EMILY E. SLATER (1888-89).
 Instructor at Science Hill, Shelbyville, Kentucky.

J. R. SITLINGTON STERRETT (1882-83),
 Professor in the University of Texas, Austin, Texas.

FRANKLIN H. TAYLOR (1882-83),
 Instructor in St. Paul's School, Concord, N. H.

OLIVER JOS. THATCHER (1887-88),
 Professor in Alleghany Theological Seminary, Alleghany, Pa.

S. B. P. TROWBRIDGE (1886-88),
 Architect, New York City.

HENRY STEPHENS WASHINGTON (1888-91).†

JAMES R. WHEELER (1882-83),
 Professor in the University of Vermont, Burlington, Vt.

ALEXANDER M. WILCOX (1883-84),
 Professor in the University of Kansas, Lawrence, Kan.

FRANK E. WOODRUFF (1882-83),†
 Professor in Bowdoin College, Brunswick, Me.

THEODORE L. WRIGHT (1886-87),
 Professor in Beloit College, Beloit, Wisconsin.

THE AMERICAN SCHOOL OF CLASSICAL STUDIES AT ATHENS.

OCTOBER, 1891.

THE American School of Classical Studies at Athens, founded by the Archæological Institute of America, and organized under the auspices of some of the leading American Colleges, was opened October 2, 1882. During the first five years of its existence it occupied a hired house on the Ὀδὸς Ἀμαλίας in Athens, near the ruins of the Olympieion. A large and convenient building has now been erected for the School on a piece of land, granted by the generous liberality of the Government of Greece, on the southeastern slope of Mount Lycabettus, adjoining the ground already occupied by the English School. This permanent home of the School, built by the subscriptions of its friends in the United States, was ready for occupation early in 1888.

The new building contains the apartments to be occupied by the Director and his family, and a large room which will be used as a library and also as a general reading-room and place of meeting for the whole School. A few rooms in the house are intended for the use of students. These will be assigned by the Director, under such regulations as he may establish, to as many members of the School as they will accommodate. Every student admitted to the privilege of a room in the house will be expected to undertake the performance of some service to the School, to be determined by the Director ; such, for example, as keeping the accounts of the School, taking charge of the delivery of books from the Library and their return, and keeping up the catalogue of the Library.

The Library now contains more than 1,600 volumes, exclusive of sets of periodicals. It includes a complete set of the Greek classics and the most necessary books of reference for philological, archæological, and architectural study in Greece.

The advantages of the School are offered free of expense for tuition to graduates of the Colleges co-operating in its support, and to other

American students who are deemed by the Committee of sufficient promise to warrant the extension to them of the privilege of membership. It is hoped that the Archæological Institute may in time be supplied with the means of establishing scholarships, which will aid some members in defraying their expenses at the School. In the mean time students must rely upon their own resources, or upon scholarships which may be granted them by the Colleges to which they belong. The amount needed for the expenses of an eight months' residence in Athens differs little from that required in other European capitals, and depends chiefly on the economy of the individual.

A peculiar feature of the temporary organization of the School during its first six years, which distinguished it from the older German and French Schools at Athens, was the yearly change of Director. This arrangement, by which a new Director was sent out every year by one of the co-operating Colleges, was never looked upon as permanent. The School will henceforth be under the control of a permanent Director, who by a continuous residence at Athens will accumulate that body of local and special knowledge without which the highest purpose of such a school cannot be fulfilled, while an Annual Director also will be sent out annually by one of the Colleges to assist in the conduct of the School. The School was able, even under its temporary organization, to meet a most pressing want, and to be of service to classical scholarship in America. It sought at first, and it must continue to seek for the present, rather to arouse a lively interest in classical archæology in American Colleges than to accomplish distinguished achievements. The lack of this interest has heretofore been conspicuous; but without it the School at Athens, however well endowed, can never accomplish the best results. A decided improvement in this respect is already apparent; and it is beyond question that the presence in many American Colleges of professors who have been resident a year at Athens under favorable circumstances, as annual directors or as students of the School, has done much, and will do still more, to stimulate intelligent interest in classic antiquity.

The address of the Chairman of the Managing-Committee is THOMAS D. SEYMOUR, New Haven, Conn.; that of the Secretary, THOMAS W. LUDLOW, Yonkers, N. Y.

PUBLICATIONS OF THE AMERICAN SCHOOL OF CLASSICAL STUDIES AT ATHENS.

1882–1890.

The Annual Reports of the Committee may be had gratis on application to the Secretary of the Managing-Committee. The other publications are for sale by Messrs. Damrell, Upham & Co., 283 Washington Street, Boston, Mass., and by Harrassowitz, Leipzig, Germany.

First, Second, and Third Annual Reports of the Managing-Committee, 1881–84. pp. 30.
Fourth Annual Report of the Committee, 1884–85. pp. 30.
Fifth and Sixth Annual Reports of the Committee, 1885–87. pp. 56.
Seventh Annual Report of the Committee. 1887–88, with the Report of Professor D'Ooge (Director in 1886–87) and that of Professor Merriam (Director in 1887–88). pp. 115.
Eighth Annual Report of the Committee, 1888–89, with the Reports of the Director, Dr. Waldstein, and of the Annual Director, Dr. Tarbell. pp. 53.
Ninth Annual Report of the Committee, 1889–90, with the Reports of the Director, Dr. Waldstein, and of the Annual Director, Professor Orris. pp. 49.
Bulletin I. Report of Professor William W. Goodwin, Director of the School in 1882–83. pp. 33. Price 25 cents.
Bulletin II. Memoir of Professor Lewis R. Packard, Director of the School in 1883–84, with Resolutions of the Committee and the Report for 1883–84. pp. 34. Price 25 cents.
Preliminary Report of an Archæological Journey made in Asia Minor during the Summer of 1884. By Dr. J. R. S. Sterrett. pp. 45. Price 25 cents.

PAPERS OF THE SCHOOL.

Volume I. 1882–83. Published in 1885. 8vo. pp. viii and 262. Illustrated. Price $2.00.

CONTENTS: —
1. Inscriptions of Assos, edited by J. R. S. Sterrett.
2. Inscriptions of Tralleis, edited by J. R. S. Sterrett.
3. The Theatre of Dionysus, by James R. Wheeler.
4. The Olympieion at Athens, by Louis Bevier.
5. The Erechtheion at Athens, by Harold N. Fowler.
6. The Battle of Salamis, by William W. Goodwin.

Volume II., 1883–84, containing Dr. J. R. S. Sterrett's Report of his Journey in Asia Minor in 1884, with Inscriptions, and two new Maps by Professor H. Kiepert. Published in 1888. 8vo, pp. 344. Price $2.25.

Volume III., 1884–85, containing Dr. Sterrett's Report of the Wolfe Expedition to Asia Minor in 1885, with Inscriptions, mostly hitherto unpublished, and two new Maps by Professor Kiepert. Published in 1888. 8vo, pp. 448. Price $2.50.

Volume IV. 1885–86. Published in 1888. 8vo, pp. 277. Illustrated. Price $2.00.

CONTENTS: —
1. The Theatre of Thoricus, Preliminary Report, by Walter Miller.
2. The Theatre of Thoricus, Supplementary Report, by William L. Cushing.
3. On Greek Versification in Inscriptions, by Frederic D. Allen.
4. The Athenian Pnyx, by John M. Crow; with a Survey of the Pnyx and Notes, by Joseph Thacher Clarke.
5. Notes on Attic Vocalism, by J. McKeen Lewis.

Reports of the work, and particularly of the excavations, of the School are published, as the work progresses, in the AMERICAN JOURNAL OF ARCHÆOLOGY.

www.ingramcontent.com/pod-product-compliance
Lightning Source LLC
Chambersburg PA
CBHW032018220426
43664CB00006B/285